Novel
History

Historians

and

Novelists

Confront

America's Past

(and Each Other)

✑

MARK C. CARNES,
Editor

Simon & Schuster

New York London
Toronto Sydney Singapore

SIMON & SCHUSTER
Rockefeller Center
1230 Avenue of the Americas
New York, NY 10020

Designed by Chris Welch
Manufactured in the United States of America

1   3   5   7   9   10   8   6   4   2

Library of Congress Cataloging-in-Publication Data
Novel history : historians and novelists confront America's past (and each
other) / Mark C. Carnes, editor.
   p. cm.
  Includes bibliographical references.
  1. Historical fiction, American—History and criticism.   2. Literature and
history—United States.   3. Historiography—United States.   4. United
States—Historiography.   I. Carnes, Mark C. (Mark Christopher), 1950-
PS374.H5 N68 2001
813'.08109—dc21   00-066176

ISBN 0-684-85765-0

To my father, Jack C. Carnes,
for helping me with this book—and with everything else

Contents

⟡

Part IV   Religion, American Culture

Part V   War

Novel
History

Introduction

cy/P

A few years ago I was reading a novel with my ten-year-old daughter, Stephanie. It was entitled *My Name Is Not Angelica*, by Scott O'Dell, about a slave rebellion in 1733 on the island of Saint John. In the final chapter the slaves are trapped by a French army. Rather than risk capture and a return to captivity, the slaves toss down their weapons and leap from a cliff to their death.

"Did that really happen?" Stephanie asked.

"I don't know," I replied. "But if it's a good story, does it have to be true?"

She didn't answer.

"I mean," I asked, "does it really matter *to you* whether the story was true?"

She remained silent for a time and then fixed me with a stare: "Dad, is this some sort of psychology question?"

Only a professor could ask a question of such ponderous silliness. Of course we want stories to be true. We want to identify with real heroes and heroines. Youngsters and perhaps the downtrodden of all ages may prefer fantasies of transcendent potency—of Jack slaying the giant, of Superman bounding buildings, of child-wizards zapping evildoers—but most of us want to learn from real people who have endured what we fear and done what we dream, whose experiences offer guidance as we seek to understand our place on the planet as it spins through the cosmos.

We like stories because they tell us about our world and enable us to learn from the experiences of others, an imaginative capacity that is one of the principal endowments of our species. The *Iliad*, the Bible, the Mahabharata, and countless stories about the past disseminate and explain the cultural traditions that shape our lives. Stories, too, counsel us on existential dilemmas of soul and psyche. In *The Call of Stories*, child psychiatrist Robert Coles notes that stories "not only keep us company, but admonish us, point us in new directions, or give us the courage to stay a given course. They can offer us kinsmen, kinswomen, comrades, advisers—offer us other eyes through which we might see, other ears with which we might make soundings."[1] Stories attract us by resonating with our anxieties; they allay our anxieties by conveying information or conferring wisdom.

If we rely on stories to guide us through life, we want the guide to be reliable and truthful, and to tell it like it really is; however, we also want the guide to be artful and witty, and to lead us along paths with which we are familiar. The historical novel has emerged to satisfy these conflicting desires. It is inescapably a contradiction in terms: a nonfictional fiction; a factual fantasy; a truthful deception.

In the *Poetics*, Aristotle contrasted the constricted world of actual events—history—with the boundless imaginative realm of the storyteller's art. History was circumscribed and particularistic: "the thing that has been," poetry was unconstrained and universal: "a kind of thing that might be." An artful story was thus "a higher thing" than history. Herein rests the justification for poetic license. If the merit of a story is derived from the moral or poetic "truths" it teaches and the artistry with which it is told, why fuss over whether the story actually happened as set forth by the storyteller?

Whatever the morality of the matter, however, people have persisted in demanding that stories be "true." Diodorus, writing several centuries after Aristotle, was disturbed that so many listeners were put off by the classics. Too often, he wrote, the Greeks set up "an unfair standard" and required of the ancient myths "the same exactness as in the events of our own time." This, he said, was wrong. "A man should by no means scrutinize the truth with so sharp an eye."[2] What he meant by "truth" here is unclear; presumably he defined the concept in aesthetic or psychological terms. This nebulous formulation, or one similar to it, has sustained storytellers for millennia.

The tension between good storytelling and "truthful" storytelling, between art and history, is similarly bound up with the evolution of the novel. Daniel Defoe, father of the English novel, steadfastly maintained that *Robinson Crusoe* (1719) was based on a real person. For the introduction to the sequel, Defoe even produced a "Crusoe" who obligingly insisted that the original tale was truthful and not a "romance." Defoe later chafed at the "envious and ill-disposed Part of the World" that challenged the book's authenticity: *Robinson Crusoe*, he insisted, was "all historical and true in Fact." Defoe's subsequent assertion that the novel was an allegorical representation of his own life did little to clarify what he meant by "historical," "truth," and "Fact."

Sir Walter Scott, generally identified as father of the historical novel, was more candid about the contradictory elements of the genre he did so much to advance. In the preface to *Ivanhoe* (1820), he explained that while a novel should be faithful to history, it must also "translate" the past into "the manners, as well as the language, of the age we live in." The past was distant and shrouded in impenetrable shadows, but somehow the artist would illumine its real features and make them recognizable to contemporary readers. How this was to be done, he did not say; and, in fact, his novels did not reconcile the opposing elements of the historical novel so much as make readers unmindful of them.

For the past two centuries, novelists and critics have wrestled with the problem, with literary fashion oscillating between "realism" and "romance," or some variant of these terms. But never before has the tension between "history" and "art" been more debated, or the boundary between fiction and nonfiction more porous. Television producers routinely enhance the news with reenactments and "docudramas" and they invent fantasy islands where accountants and hairdressers pretend to be survivors of shipwrecks. (Are these latter-day Crusoes more or less "real" than the original?) We discuss "virtual reality" in all seriousness and communicate with Internet "buddies" in on-line "chat rooms" with people whose identities are fictitious. We "reenact" Civil War battles that are "authentic" to the tiniest detail, save the bullets, while actual soldiers push buttons to fight simulated battles (and an occasional real one) in war rooms that resemble video arcades. Novelists write fictional accounts with accurate footnotes, while historians write biographies with fictional characters and imaginary footnotes.

And then there's Hollywood, whose watery notion of reality has seeped deep into the bedrock of American culture. Ever since D. W. Griffith blended history with racist romance in *Birth of a Nation*, the movie industry has pointed its cameras at sets resembling the past and steadfastly depicted the sensibilities of the present. Filmmakers now routinely blur fact and fiction, as when Oliver Stone slyly spliced documentary footage of the JFK assassination into his own grainy shots in *JFK*, or James Cameron showed fish gliding silently through the actual wreckage of the *Titanic*, or the directors of *The Blair Witch Project* nurtured rumors that their film had indeed been recovered from missing teens.

This subject was considered in *Past Imperfect: History According to the Movies* (1995), a collection of essays I edited that bears some resemblance to the present volume. While working on that book, however, I was struck by an awkward asymmetry in the way historians and filmmakers went about their business: filmmakers worked with images and thought chiefly in visual terms; historians worked mostly with words—historical documents and texts—and relied on verbal expression. In a good film, the pictures *replace* words: a wordy movie script is almost by definition a poor one. But the historian's art is all about words. (Some in the profession judge a history book by the distance between its covers.) Filmmakers' emphasis on the *appearance* of films and historians' preoccupation with the *scripts* often resulted in a fundamental disjunction in purposes. I concluded that *Past Imperfect* had only begun to explore the tangled conceptual realm that lies somewhere between art and history and yet encompasses both.

ഇ

THIS BOOK WAS conceived as a more thoughtful expedition into this difficult terrain. The focus is on novels because many novelists have thought hard about the past and made it an object of concerted study, and novelists use words, and often use them better than anyone else. Here, there is no incompatibility of medium. Because there is no single "historical" or "novelistic" perspective, I recruited twenty important historians and nearly as many important novelists to give their views on the subject.

Each historian's essay on a novel is followed, wherever possible, by a response from the author of that novel. (An exception is Thomas Fleming, who here is allowed to display his professional schizophrenia as both historian and novelist.) I have grouped the essays into five topics: "biography," the West, slavery, religion and culture, and war.

This book is about the historical imagination; it does not pose as literary criticism. The novels included here were chosen, sometimes in consultation with the novelist, sometimes not, because they illustrated important issues related to the novelists' conception of the past. John Updike's *Memories of the Ford Administration* and William Kennedy's *Quinn's Book* may not be their most representative literary works, but these novels best convey their thoughts on history and fiction.

Some of the novels included here are fairly traditional in narrative structure: Gore Vidal's *Burr*, Russell Banks's *Cloudsplitter*, Larry McMurtry's *Lonesome Dove*, Charles Frazier's *Cold Mountain*, Tom Fleming's *Time and Tide*, and Annie Dillard's *The Living*. But because the volume seeks to examine the historical imagination rather than a literary genre, it includes experimental approaches to the past such as Wallace Stegner's *Angle of Repose*, T. Coraghessan Boyle's *World's End*, Don Delillo's *Libra*, and Tim O'Brien's *In the Lake of the Woods*. Several other novels, such as F. Scott Fitzgerald's *The Great Gatsby*, Jane Smiley's *A Thousand Acres*, and Barbara Kingsolver's *The Poisonwood Bible*, concern history more obliquely.

The volume includes essays on some traditional classics, such as Nathaniel Hawthorne's *The Scarlet Letter* and Harriet Beecher Stowe's *Uncle Tom's Cabin*, but to promote a dialogue between historians and novelists, the book is heavily weighted toward contemporary fiction. The geographical framework of the book is America, though it has been defined expansively so as to include Gary Jennings's *Aztec* and Madison Smartt Bell's *All Souls' Rising* (about Toussaint Louverture and the slave rebellion in Haiti).

I regret the absence of some important contemporary historical novels. A few novelists declined or failed to respond to my invitation to participate. But the great majority of the novelists were supportive of the enterprise if understandably wary. "It is neither the novelist's business nor right to explicate his own fictions," T. C. Boyle explained in his response. Jane Smiley professed to be weary of *A Thousand Acres*, her most famous novel but the one least "congenial" to her sensibility. Larry McMurtry reported that *Lonesome Dove* was now as remote to him as the Arthuriad. Annie Dillard despaired of explaining how she devised the compelling stories in *The Living*. "It began with a solitary figure in the distance," she told me. Then her voice trailed off. But most novelists were intrigued, even bedeviled by the relation of the past to their fictional imagination, and nearly all agreed to participate in the discussion.

In a few instances, a novelist agreed to write a response, but the historian I commissioned failed to write an essay worthy of inclusion. I apologize to those novelists who were thus denied, through no fault of their own, the opportunity to contribute.

The book contains some sharp criticisms, and the historians did spot some mistakes. The cattle drive from Texas to Montana in McMurtry's *Lonesome Dove* fails to cross any of the transcontinental railroads: McMurtry explains that in plotting the novel, he planned to have the crossing occur during a windstorm and even left a note to himself to this point, but subsequently forgot it. Madison Bell, author of *All Souls' Rising*, learned to his horror that Toussaint Louverture was himself free and a slave-owner at the outset of the rebellion, an awkward fact that Louverture sedulously concealed from other rebels and posterity. The loggers in Annie Dillard's *The Living* unwisely located in remote mountains, when they could have more sensibly camped along rivers upon which they could have floated trees to market. In *Burr*, Gore Vidal underestimated eighteenth-century sensitivity to questions of honor, which prompted him to assume, perhaps wrongly, that only a charge of incest with his daughter could have been sufficiently heinous to provoke Burr to demand satisfaction from Hamilton.

But "mistakes" such as these do not reveal much about novel history. Historians make mistakes, too. Indeed, Gore Vidal bids that the historian-critic of *Burr* pay for hers by mounting the scaffold. In any case, novel research is not inherently inferior to that of the historian; more-over, the novelists' mistakes are counterbalanced by numerous instances where their inspired intuitions proved more accurate than the historians' research. For example, Gary Jennings maintained that the warring Aztecs and Tarascans persisted in trade relations, though the surviving docu-ments suggested otherwise. Only after Jennings's *Aztec* was published did archaeologists find evidence of Tarascan trading objects in Aztec sites dating from this period. In *A Thousand Acres*, published in 1991, Jane Smiley hypothesized that the circumstances of midwestern farm life in the 1970s left women especially vulnerable to spousal abuse. Subsequent interviews and historical studies have confirmed this judgment. William Kennedy's *Quinn's Book*, published in 1985, recounted all manner of irra-tional religious and sexual excitations in antebellum America, a theme de-veloped by social and cultural historians during the past decade. And if Vidal misunderstood eighteenth-century notions of honor, as historian Joanne Freeman asserts, then his delineation of the foibles of the Found-ing Fathers, including Jefferson's affair with Sally Hemings, has been amply confirmed in recent years. Novel history is neither slipshod nor in-accurate.

✺

A BOOK CONTAINING so many diverse and strong opinions is not in-tended to generate consensus. However, I was struck by the novelists' re-peated and uncritical acceptance of poetic license. "I assume," Russell Banks writes, "that when a reader opens my novel, he or she will do so knowing that I have not written it as a biographer or historian." Gary Jen-nings's response to requests for footnotes was yet more emphatic. "Shit," he wrote to me, "I was writing a novel, not a Ph.D. thesis." A novel, being a species of fiction, was entitled to be fictional.

The argument is incontrovertible, but none of the novelists regarded it as sufficient. Most professed a preference for historical facts and confessed to a reluctance to modify them. Charles Frazier explained that he initially lamented the lack of information on Inman, his great-great grandfather's brother, the protagonist in *Cold Mountain*. (The surviving facts about

Inman, Frazier writes, could be scrawled on the back of an envelope.) This paucity of information, rather than a claim to poetic license, provided Frazier with the moral justification to "make it all up." Madison Smartt Bell had the opposite problem, given the richly documented record of the Haitian revolution: "I found myself extremely unwilling to invent actions or speeches for Toussaint that I could not document in some way, or at least reason to be probable." He believed that this historical literalism resulted in some degree of "aesthetic failure." Wallace Stegner's desire for authenticity in *Angle of Repose* prompted him to incorporate—verbatim—large chunks of the actual correspondence of Arthur and Mary Hallock Foote, on whom the characters of Oliver and Susan Ward were largely based. The borrowings were so extensive that the owners of the Foote letters accused Stegner of committing a kind of plagiarism. Good novelists, in short, not only endorse historical accuracy in principle, but also pour much of the actual historical record into their work.

When novelists have altered or added to history, moreover, many have felt obliged to enumerate and justify their actions. In an afterword to *Burr*, Vidal begins by asserting the novelist's "right not only to rearrange events but, most important, to attribute motive." He confesses that "in three instances, I have moved people about" and then justifies his manipulations. The historical facts matter enough to be set straight.

The novelists' pursuit of the real past is reflected in their extensive research. When describing their labors in the archives, moreover, they *sound* like historians. They write of their preference for old letters and original documents, and they say that they prefer the researching to the writing. "It was pleasant," Updike wrote, "and, the mind ever accumulating rust, salutary for me to feel how one's ignorance widens along with one's researches, wherein book would lead to book *ad infinitum*." Nearly all historians can relate to this statement.

The novelists' identification with the historian was often literal. In fully one third of the novels in this volume, the story is told through an "historian": Updike's Alf Landon Clayton presents his researches on Buchanan, as well as his addled ruminations on his own confused life, to his colleagues in the Northern New England Association of American Historians. Vidal's Charles Schuyler compiles, for political purposes, a partisan history of Aaron Burr. Wallace Stegner assumes the persona of an historian who seeks to gain perspective on his own marriage by refracting it through the parallel experiences of his grandparents. Thomas Fleming's *Time and Tide* is told as the reminiscence of a sailor-turned-historian, rather like Fleming himself. T. C. Boyle's *World's End* is filled with historians: some litter the countryside with historical markers, and others sift through the archives as local or amateur historians. William Kennedy entitles his first-person novel *Quinn's Book* so as to allow it to be the story of a memoirist. Tim O'Brien's novel on the remembering (and forgetting) of the Vietnam War introduces a shifty narrator who produces footnotes and scours the actual historical record.

But unlike historians, who are not supposed to change facts or exclude those that contradict their theses, nearly all of the novelists were obliged to make some changes in the historical record. These they justified, after Aristotle, on the grounds that their art cast light on the human condition rather than on any particular historical episode. Walter Scott maintained that the passions are "generally the same in all ranks and conditions, all countries and ages." "Emotions," novelist Russell Banks similarly writes, "do not grow old":

> This, to me, is the true voice of history in fiction, the voice that insists on our enduring humanity and deliberates it. We are the species that over and over has to learn what it is to be itself.

Jane Smiley alludes to this enduring humanity to justify her use of Shakespeare's *King Lear* as the framework for a novel about an American farm family: "It is because the Lear material is so basic and so ancient that we can link it to the behavior patterns of wolves, horses, chimps, gorillas, farmers, corporate executives, movie stars."

Don DeLillo's *Libra*, about Lee Harvey Oswald, illustrates how a novelist's fictions transcend any particular person or moment. DeLillo's Oswald is a paradigmatic loser. Thus, DeLillo assumes that Oswald's third shot at President Kennedy in Dallas missed, a matter of consternation to historian David Courtwright, who points out that this detail contradicts DeLillo's overall conclusion about the assassination and the Warren report. To DeLillo, these historical particulars, weighed against the larger meaning and purposes of the novel, are irrelevant:

> I thought Oswald would fire prematurely and he does this in the novel. . . . Oswald in my mind had to act impatiently. He could not get things right. This is why he misses the third shot. Not because the ballistics evidence is so deeply shaded by endless conflicts of interpretation and ideology that one might justify any number of deductions concerning gunshot patterns or types of wounds. And certainly not because I felt it would be otherwise awkward to account for the curbside bullet mark found in Dealey Plaza. He misses because he is Oswald.

Novelists aspire to universal truths, and assert that people are basically the same in all places and all times, and yet novelists ultimately look within themselves to find their words and ideas. The "inner voice" of a novel, Russell Banks observes, is "as individual, as personal, as downright physical as the voice of a lover, a child, or a parent."

The quest for universal truths—for art—is thus bound up with the subjectivity of the individual novelist. Indeed, novelists search the past (as do historians) in order to learn who they are. T. C. Boyle explains that in *World's End* he conceived of Colonial Peekskill, New York, "as a point of departure for a meditation on what my life has been, where I came from, what my antecedents and the antecedents of the region I grew up in were." Boyle puts words down on paper, he explains, to "chase the meaning I need to build my own life." Tim O'Brien's novels on Vietnam are similarly part of an anguished journey of self-discovery. In the final footnote (!) to *In the Lake of the Woods*, O'Brien (as novelist, or as a character in this "historical" novel?) surrenders to the subjectivity of the enterprise: "Nothing is fixed, nothing is solved. The facts, such as they are, finally spin off into the void of things missing, the inconclusiveness of conclusion. Mystery finally claims us. Who are we? Where do we go?"

As novelists listen to the voice within, straining to hear larger truths that reverberate into the future as art, they cannot filter out the steady din generated by their own culture. Which meanings genuinely come from the soul, and which from parents, or teachers, or lovers, or popular songs, or books? Insofar as their novels appeal to a mass audience, moreover, novelists must possess a special affinity to their own culture. How, then, can they find meanings that transcend it? *The Scarlet Letter* is a timeless consideration of the corrosive effects of hypocrisy. Yet, as historian David Reynolds points out, Hawthorne's classic was derived from an extensive body of antebellum fiction on adulterous ministers. Joan Hedrick similarly observes that *Uncle Tom's Cabin* ingeniously reworked existing middle-class notions of women as crusading reformers, and drew a powerful parallel, in an age of religious ferment, between Uncle Tom and Christ. Both classics were *products* of the antebellum era. Great art rises far above the world from which it issues, but never floats entirely free of it.

✑

HISTORIANS AND HISTORICAL novelists do many of the same things and in much the same way. They research old documents and materials; they work with words, both as objects of study and implements of their trade; they seek perspective on the human experience by examining it from a chronological remove; they endeavor to speak to a contemporary audience; they aspire to represent the past truthfully and yet know that their representations cannot be "truthful," "objective," or "accurate" because logical clarity is incompatible with human affairs.

But the differences between novelists and historians are profound. If they scour much the same sources, they look for different things. Updike explains that when he undertook research he sought "the kind of fact which a fiction-writer depends upon, the witnessed and experienced particular"—the sensory or revelatory detail that subtly conveys an image or sensation that inflects an entire paragraph, or chapter, or book. Charles Frazier similarly finds that he was drawn less to the historical record than the evocations of nature. "Walking a few miles of remnant dirt road that once linked two now-vanished villages," Frazier recalls, "often proved more useful than a stack of Mathew Brady photographs in shaping my sense of the past." Historian John Lukacs observes that often the novelists' chief contribution to historical understanding is their ability to discern the elusive "style"—the feel, the sensation, the aesthetics—of an historical moment.

Novelists explore the subjective realm of the self that, though molded by the social and cultural pressures of their own place and time, acquires suppleness through immersion in a deep literary tradition. When novelists fail to communicate their personal revelations, even revelations steeped in historical context, they cease to be novelists.

Historians are unalterably enslaved by facts, the essence of their discipline. Some historians may reach far into regions devoid of documents and proof; some may abandon or modify the rhetorical conventions of the profession so as to ponder the human condition. But few historians are constitutionally capable of cutting their imaginations free from the facts and from a particular historical context. When their ideas wander too far from a verifiable source, most historians become uneasy, and their colleagues reach out to pull them back. And there are always posses of volunteers, deputized by the professional journals, who patrol the frontiers of the discipline to lasso renegades and outlaws. This is perhaps as it should be. The facts do matter. Tim O'Brien reminds us that real people died in Vietnam. This reality grows indistinct over time, blurred by distance and rendered hazy by the imaginative fictions we superimpose upon memory, but real bones decompose in the dirt. When historians alter facts or suppress those that bear awkwardly on a point at hand, or when they retreat from a commitment to the particularities and peculiarities of the historical moment, they cease to be historians.

The past exists only in our remembrance of it. Historians and novelists remember in different ways; either is incomplete. The historians' preoccupation with facts and confirmatory evidence renders them less sensitive to the imaginative and emotional aspects of life, while the novelists' craving for personal meaning and contemporary relevance may inhibit their ability to perceive the ways in which people in the past differ from us.

Historians need the novelist's guidance on the workings of the emotions and imagination. Novelists need the historian's discipline to anchor the imagination to fact. The joining of these perspectives is not accomplished in the oxymoronic historical novel, in which fiction has been infused with historical detail. In novel history, however, the fragmentary and fossilized facts of the historical record are reanimated with imaginative meaning and aesthetic truth. Novel history, like alchemy, is an inaccessible science and elusive art, but to readers who seek understanding of themselves and the world, its riches are real.

Notes

1. Robert Coles, *The Call of Stories: Teaching and the Moral Imagination* (Boston: Houghton Mifflin, 1989), 159–60.

2. Cited in Paul Veyne, *Did the Greeks Believe in Their Myths?*, trans. Paula Wissing (Chicago: University of Chicago Press, 1983), 47–48.

PART I

Biography

History As Told
by the Devil Incarnate:
Gore Vidal's *Burr*

Joanne B. Freeman

Aaron Burr: Gore Vidal could hardly have chosen a historical figure better suited for fiction. Fallen grandson of the famed Reverend Jonathan Edwards; slayer of Alexander Hamilton in America's most famous duel; would-be emperor of the American West; enemy to the loftiest inhabitants of America's political pantheon—Burr has long been the *enfant terrible* of the founding period, an errant soul snaking his way through America's creation myth. In the morality-tale version of America's founding, the idealistic Jefferson and the pragmatic Hamilton struggle for the soul of the republic under George Washington's solemn and watchful eye. Aaron Burr—when included at all—is a morality tale in and of himself, a fallen angel whose unbridled passions and ambitions brought him crashing to ruin.

But the truth is obviously more complex, as the young Charles Schuyler, the narrator of Gore Vidal's *Burr*, learns from the founder himself. Encouraged to write about Burr for the *New York Evening Post*, Burr's law clerk Schuyler ends up transcribing the aged Burr's memoirs as dictated directly by the grand old man. Peering at Burr through the dusk in Trinity Church graveyard, standing near Hamilton's final resting place, Schuyler initially envisions Burr as the devil incarnate, but he grows to see things differently over time. Exposed to Burr's iconoclastic worldview day after day, and lectured about Burr's wickedness by moralistic contemporaries, Schuyler learns that history is largely a matter of perspective. "My side of the story is not, necessarily, the accurate one," Burr readily admits as he overturns idols, one by one (p. 26).

In bursting the bubble of historical myth, the fictional Burr reveals a fundamental truth about the politics of his younger days. Well aware that they were fated to be "Founders" if they played their cards right, Burr's contemporaries were extraordinarily self-conscious, shaping their legend long before their demise. As Burr suggests in his sessions with Schuyler, America's founders were constantly watchful of their reputations; however sincere their desire to serve the public good, they were equally eager to earn immortal fame, a quest that unavoidably brought a certain degree of posturing in its wake. This desperate desire for acclaim—this deliberate forging of a founding myth—is at the core of Burr. Through the eyes of the most renowned outcast of the founding pantheon, we learn that our historical demigods were only human after all.

Of course, Burr goes much farther than this, depicting the founders as seen from Burr's acid perspective. Betrayed and traduced throughout his public career, he viewed his contemporaries with a sharp edge, in life as in fiction. Thomas Jefferson looms large among this legion of enemies. To Burr, Jefferson was the foulest foe of all, seducing Burr into his inner circle to capitalize on the New Yorker's political savvy, dangling before him the lure of high office, and then casting him aside upon ascending to power, condemning him as a villain in the process. And so Jefferson appears on the pages of Burr, a seductively charming malevolent force. Vidal captures the keen political acumen behind Jefferson's dreamy detachment, particularly in the novel's re-created conversations between Jefferson and Burr, taken almost verbatim from the historical Jefferson's notes.

In real life, the power and pain of Jefferson's accusations ultimately drove Burr to commence his memoirs. Reading Jefferson's private memoranda in 1830, published after the Virginian's death in 1826, Burr was horrified to see decades of Jeffersonian abuse seemingly cast in stone. In Jefferson's closely scribbled notes (carefully prepared for publication by their author in his old age), Burr is a toady, a liar, and a cheat. Outraged by this final thrust from the grave, Burr goaded his political lieutenant

Matthew Davis to refute Jefferson's charges by recording the "truth." The result was Davis's two-volume *Memoirs of Aaron Burr*, a source that Vidal mines to good effect.

Indeed, a good look at Davis's *Memoirs* reveals Vidal's close attention to the historical Burr's manner and character; there is a reason that the fictional Burr seems to leap from the page. For example, Vidal captures Burr's vision of his public career, as memorialized by Davis. Rather than recounting Burr's political accomplishments, Davis's *Memoirs* centers on a trio of enemies—Washington, Hamilton, and Jefferson—the focus of the fictional Burr's memoirs as well. To a man as uninterested in political theorizing as Burr, this clashing of power-hungry titans was the heart of the period's politics. It was Burr's unlucky fate to lock horns with three masters of self-defense who destroyed Burr's reputation by protecting their own.

Davis's *Memoirs* also captures something of Burr's conflicted relationship with Hamilton, and Vidal echoes this perfectly on the pages of *Burr* exploring the mutual recognition of two like-minded men of enormous charm and ambition. Rather than reducing Hamilton to an evil antagonist, Vidal reveals Hamilton's virtues as well as his vices, suggesting that his intense rivalry with Burr stemmed in part from his very nature, not from a simple clash of ambitions. As depicted by Vidal, Hamilton had a tragic inability to suppress his impulses, literary or otherwise. Hamilton's "tragedy was also his gift," Burr explains to his young protégé Schuyler. "Unable to remain silent on any subject that excited him he, literally, dug his own grave with words" (p. 212). As Burr quips on another occasion, Hamilton's "tombstone should have been carved in the shape of a pen" (p. 290).

Burr's real-life memoirs are not Vidal's only source of insight into the historical Burr's character. Vidal also makes good use of James Parton's *The Life and Times of Aaron Burr* (1857). Parton, one of America's first self-styled "biographers," interviewed Burr's surviving intimates for anecdotes and insights into the enigmatic founder. Wonderfully, some of *Burr*'s most memorable scenes are based in reality, most remarkably Burr's return to the heights of Weehawken in his old age. Accommodating the curiosity of a young friend, Burr did indeed return to the site of his 1804 duel with Hamilton, positioning his companion where Hamilton stood, and reenacting this shattering moment of his past. Parton offers a gripping retelling of this tale, as well as many other episodes in Burr's eventful life, leading some reviewers to condemn his biography as too sympathetic—a tribute to the enduring power of America's moralistic founding legend. To at least some readers, there was no way that Burr could be anything other than wicked, and his fellows anything other than virtuous.

Parton's critics offer some insight into the challenges of wrestling with Burr's reputation, for like his fictional incarnation, Burr was a most unfounderlike Founder, and those who force him into the traditional "Founder" mold deny his very essence. For, in many ways, Burr was not like his peers. His letters reveal a man with an unapologetically libidinous appetite and an unusually wry sense of humor about himself and his ambitions; like Vidal's Burr, the historical Burr maintained a quizzical detachment from the passions of political war. Uninterested in probing the depths of political theory, Burr was a campaign manager with an eye for detail and an exuberant love of the political game (admitting, with a candor rare for his time, that politics was "fun"). As contemporaries put it, Burr had no "pernicious theories, but is a mere matter-of-fact man," an invaluable ally during electoral contests to be held at arm's length with the closing of the polls. As Burr's peers well realized, with no anchoring ideology—feigned as it might be—there was no telling where the winds would blow Aaron Burr. Rather than a conventionally virtuous man much maligned, Burr was a man of unique virtues.

How can one dispassionately depict this anomalous founder, particularly given his open contempt for the highest-ranked gods of America's political pantheon? Even during Burr's lifetime, this proved problematic. Defending Burr would unavoidably malign his attackers—national idols all. Fearing the repercussions, Burr's memoirist Matthew Davis almost refused to take on the task. The occasional outrage at Vidal's *Burr* should thus come as no surprise. When *Burr* was published in 1973, some reviewers criticized it for its savage treatment of Burr's famous contemporaries, and there is no denying the sting of Burr's pen portraits. A dim, huge-buttocked Washington waddles his way through *Burr*'s memoirs; Hamilton is a malicious, strategically charming little man with a secret passion for women's novels; a sly and humorless Jefferson of shifty gaze and purring voice grasps at power through deception, unleashing his pent-up fury by savagely beating his horses; and Andrew Jackson has an unfortunate drooling problem. As one reviewer noted, "Burr-Vidal" obsessively drags the founders down to his level. But is this not precisely what Burr would have done (and to some extent did) in his memoirs? Self-assured and even arrogant in the knowledge of his talents, he intended his memoirs to set the record straight, or at least to pierce the veil of historical myth. In fiction, as in life, this mission provoked a howl of protest.

Thus, despite the grumbling of some critics, *Burr*'s fictional musings on past men and events are entirely in character, and even imaginatively grounded in fact. The solemn and stately Washington could seem dull in comparison with the sparkling intellects that surrounded him (and, as his contemporaries would have put it concerning his horsemanship, he did indeed have an "impressive seat"); Jefferson was a masterly politician who scored victories through indirection; and Hamilton was undeniably mercurial, charming, and self-destructive. Which is not to say that *Burr* offers an objective, dispassionate view of early American politics and politicians. Rather, it presents a strikingly convincing Burr's-eye view of that world, and in so doing, captures something of the essence of Aaron Burr.

It is this emotional truth that lends the novel its sparkle and power. What better way to goad us into reevaluating our founding myth than by charming us into it? In fact as in fiction, Burr pushed the envelope of propriety through sheer charm, seducing people into sharing his confidences, mocking not only his lofty contemporaries but himself as well, and enjoying himself immensely in the process. The historical Burr scored political victories with this formula, winning friends and allies with his "fascinating" manners, bemused irreverence, and *joie de vivre*. As one of his converts attested after an evening's entertainment, Burr was "a mighty winning fellow." Just listen to the way that he challenged the period's poses and conventions. Commenting on the saying "Never put off till tomorrow what you can do today," Burr declared it "a maxim for sluggards," and proposed instead: "Never do to-day what you can as well do to-morrow; because something may occur to make you regret your premature action." On another occasion, Burr chided Hamilton for missing his chance to overturn the government for something better; as inspector general of the United States Army from 1798 to 1800, Hamilton had the means within his grasp. When Hamilton declared that this "could not have been done without guilt," Burr replied, " 'Les grandes âmes se soucient peu de petits morceaux' " ("Great souls care little about small things"). Burr's comment stunned Hamilton (though Burr was probably twitting him rather than declaring revolution; someone less compulsively suspicious of Burr would have gotten the joke). In life, as in art, Burr's natural magnetism and sense of humor enabled him to get away with much—though he didn't entirely get away with murder.

This personal perspective is particularly well suited to the politics of Burr's times, for in the absence of organized political parties, early national politics revolved around character, reputation, and personal alliances. "Character assassination" set the tone of political debate; to destroy a man's character was to destroy his reputation, and to destroy his reputation was to crush the very foundations of his public career. Such was Burr's fate. As his fictional persona confesses, his worst mistake "was supposing that one could not be hurt by a lie" (p. 181). Secure in his reputation and focused on the adventure of the moment, Burr did not fend off vicious rumors and accusations, and so toppled into infamy. As Davis explains in Burr's real-life memoirs, this failing dashed Burr "from the proud eminence he once enjoyed to a condition more mortifying and more prostrate than any distinguished man has ever experienced in the United States."

As profound as Burr's failure was Jefferson's success, and *Burr* reveals why, offering insight into the Virginian's political methods. In a culture that rejected political parties as reprehensible knots of self-interested schemers, the most successful politician was the one who seemed least political of all. Thus Jefferson's political ascendance. As suggested in *Burr,* Jefferson was a master of dinner table politicking, converting fence-sitters into allies with his eloquence, charm, fine wines, and broad interests—a technique that one Federalist dubbed Jefferson's "epicurean . . . artifices." *Burr* reveals Jefferson's method in action, a wiser and older Burr reflecting on the power of Jefferson's hushed, purring eloquence and philosophical reveries. Viewed in this light, Jefferson's notorious 1791 botanical expedition takes on new significance. Traveling north with James Madison ostensibly to study the flora and fauna, Jefferson spent some time in New York, Hamilton's home base. Although some scholars insist that the trip was a purely scientific venture, it was undoubtedly political, as Vidal's *Burr* well recognizes (p. 200). Over a series of dinners with Hamilton's powerful enemies to the north, Jefferson and Madison won invaluable allies.

Burr's emotional realism thus reveals much about the small-scale, personal world of early national politics. It also hints at something of the spirit of the time in the new republic, the sense of limitless possibilities— for good or evil. As Burr explains to Schuyler, "We were living in a time when for the adventurous and imaginative man anything was possible" (p. 399). There were frontiers to conquer, armies to lead, constitutions to draft, and nations to build. There could hardly be a more powerful fuel for the hopes and ambitions of a generation. But with so much unsettled, disaster seemed ever to loom on the horizon. One corrupt and ambitious man of talents, one modern Catiline who could ride a wave of demagogy to tyrannical power, and the entire political experiment could come crashing to ruin. Burr epitomized both sides of this republican equation. Perhaps more than any of his equals, he openly and unabashedly vied for power and glory, reveling in the opportunities of the moment. But without any apparent ideological restraints, he seemed to be the very embodiment of ambition unleashed. Thus the rampant distrust of Aaron Burr.

As Burr could well attest, political experimentation was a risky business. With the nascent republic still struggling to define itself, more than personal reputations were at stake. To national leaders, given the unsettled state of the times, the slightest mistake, the most trivial of decisions, could have enormous political consequences. In *Burr*, this inflated self-consciousness is Burr's primary target. For example, mocking Washington's somber consideration of his reputation in all circumstances, Burr recounts an "audience with His Mightiness" that ended with a half-hour examination of "tableware, trying to find a truly republican balance between too plain democratic ware and too rich royal plate" (p. 193). Remarkably, this anecdote is true to fact: Washington consulted with several people concerning properly republican tableware. Burr attributes this to Washington's obsessive interest in "the trifles and show of wealth and position," and, indeed, in the republic's heady formative years, the wise politican did well to avoid looking too aristocratic, in the interest of his reputation and political career. Yet there was a vital political dimension to such seemingly trivial concerns. America's national leaders believed that their actions and decisions would determine national character, and thereby decide the fate of the republic. The common folk would naturally emulate their betters—so the argument went—so aristocratic dishes or lace or carriages at the national capital could prove fatal to the general good, corrupting the republic beyond repair.

Burr's emotional realism brings such improbable concepts to life. Hard as it might be to identify with the denizens of an alien past, human emotion often bridges the gap; in the ever-shifting eddies of historical change, human hungers and passions are reliably constant. This makes *Burr* enormously useful in the classroom, for (hedged in with cautions about objectivity) the novel brings something of the period's political ethos to life. But this personal approach to history does have its short-comings. As much as we might identify with the feelings of *Burr*'s charac-ters, feelings alone cannot always explain historical fact, a failing that is most apparent concerning that most alien of rituals, the duel.

While *Burr* explores how the forces of this small, intense political world drew Burr and Hamilton to the field of honor, it offers little insight into the logic behind Burr's challenge. Vidal's explanation of Hamilton's unpardonable insult—too horrible for the urbane Burr even to men-tion—has more to do with twentieth-century sensibilities than eigh-teenth-century conventions. It *is* sensationally hard to resist. "What did Hamilton say of the Colonel?," Schuyler asks one of Burr's friends toward the book's close. "Why, he said that Aaron Burr was the lover of his own daughter, Theodosia" (p. 356)—a shocking accusation by modern stan-dards, as it would have been in Burr's time as well, but one with little con-nection to historical fact. As Vidal himself explained to psychobiographer Arnold Rogow, "The incest motif is my invention. I couldn't think of any-thing of a 'despicable' nature that would drive A[aron] B[urr] to so drastic an action."[1]

Vidal's statement is enormously revealing. Not because he admits to inventing the "incest motif"—he has admitted this before. Rather, he confesses that he could not imagine a charge serious enough to merit Burr's challenge. By twentieth-century standards, only an unimaginably severe insult would drive Burr to such drastic measures, and incest is as severe an insult as any. However, by eighteenth-century standards, any number of charges could demand a challenge. Particularly for politicians, whose public careers relied on their reputations, any attack on one's character deserved careful consideration. Seemingly innocuous insults such as "puppy" and "rascal" thus had a peculiar power two centuries back; denying one's manhood and personal integrity, they virtually invited a duel. For example, in 1797, when James Monroe called Hamilton a "Scoundrel" during a charged conversation, both men instantly recognized the severity of the insult. "I will meet you like a Gentleman," Hamilton blurted. "I am ready, get your pistols," Monroe responded, at which point friends separated the two men and defused the situation. (Burr ultimately helped settle this near-duel—one of many quirks of fate in the entangled lives of Hamilton and Burr.)

Nor was initiating a duel so unimaginably drastic. Most of Burr's friends engaged in at least one affair of honor; several dueled. The thin-skinned Hamilton negotiated his way out of a duel at least nine times. Burr himself fought two duels and considered others. Rather than a drastic measure requiring the severest of insults, dueling was a method of self-defense—extreme, but possessing a logic that must be recognized before we can hope to understand the Burr-Hamilton duel.[2]

Other such misconceptions about dueling are similarly misleading. "You are perfectly innocent of any crime since the bastard Hamilton was under no obligation to meet you," Matthew Davis tells the fictional Burr in a note (p. 362). Objectively speaking, this might be true of some would-be duelists, but in the specific context of the Burr-Hamilton encounter, it is not. Confronted by Burr's initial letter of complaint about Hamilton's insult, Hamilton returned an ambivalent and conflicted response. Hoping to avoid a duel, he attempted to placate Burr with an elaborate discussion of the "infinite shades" of meaning of the word "despicable"—a grammar lesson that Burr found evasive, manipulative, and offensive. To salvage his honor and self-respect, Hamilton then pronounced Burr's vague inquiry "inadmissable," declaring himself willing to "abide the consequences" should Burr persist in his present course—a display of bravado that Burr found insufferably arrogant. Burr responded by insinuating that Hamilton was behaving like no gentleman, a charge that no gentleman could abide. As Hamilton put it, it was impossible to ignore something so "positively offensive." Thus began the downward spiral to the field of honor, each man unable to avoid a duel without sacrificing his honor.

Burr contains other inaccuracies that invite the sharp intake of breath so instinctive to the scholarly expert, though they do little to detract from the book's power and purpose. The political world was not divided into Federalists and Republicans in 1791; Jefferson did not dress like a dandy after leaving French shores; Abigail Adams had no maternal fondness for Alexander Hamilton (she would shudder at the very idea); and Hamilton had some qualms about the Sedition Act. But such factual slips ultimately mean little in the book's larger scheme. Indeed, their relative unimportance testifies to Vidal's success at the task he set himself—to re-create Burr's distinctive vision. Seeming errors, misconceptions, and omissions are entirely understandable when attributed to Burr's peculiar worldview. Was Hamilton a British agent? Did Burr single-handedly open Senate proceedings to public view? Are Tories and Federalists one and the same? Did political principles have so minimal a role in America's founding? Historically speaking, no, but to Aaron Burr? One never can tell.

For the reader, as for Schuyler, *Burr* thus accomplishes Vidal's purpose, charming us into reconsidering the past. Such issues of fact and fiction are at the heart of the writing of history, joining the historical novelist and the historian in shared effort. No matter how careful the research, no matter how seamless the logic, historians can do little more than proffer their version of history in the hope of crafting an argument more persuasive than those that came before; thus, trends of scholarship shift and change over time. There is good history and bad history, deep research and careless generalizations, contextualized hunches and blind stabs in the dark. But in the end, the good historian, like the good historical novelist, has produced one of many plausible versions of the past, as different as their purposes, audiences, and evidence might be. As Burr reminds Schuyler—and us—throughout Vidal's narrative, history is largely a matter of perspective. And as Schuyler learns by the book's end, in tracing historical pathways, we learn much about ourselves.

Notes

1. Private communication, as quoted in Arnold A. Rogow, *A Fatal Friendship: Alexander Hamilton and Aaron Burr* (New York: Hill and Wang, 1998), 240.

2. On the significance of honor culture to early national politics, see Joanne B. Freeman, "Dueling as Politics: Reinterpreting the Burr-Hamilton Duel," *William and Mary Quarterly* (April 1996): 289–318, and her forthcoming book, *Affairs of Honor: Politics before Party in the Early Republic* (New Haven: Yale University Press, 2001). On American honor culture in general, see Edward L. Ayers, *Vengeance and Justice: Crime and Punishment in the Nineteenth-Century American South* (New York: Oxford University Press, 1984); Dickson D. Bruce, Jr., *Violence and Culture in the Antebellum South* (Austin, Texas: University of Texas Press, 1979); Kenneth S. Greenberg, *Masters and Statesmen: The Political Culture of American Slavery* (Baltimore: Johns Hopkins University Press, 1985); Steven M. Stowe, *Intimacy and Power in the Old South: Ritual in the Lives of the Planters* (Baltimore: Johns Hopkins University Press, 1987), and, especially, Bertram Wyatt-Brown, *Southern Honor: Ethics and Behavior in the Old South* (Baton Rouge: Louisiana State University Press, 1982).

ॐ

Burr: The Historical Novel

Gore Vidal

Unlike the academic historian who gets his doctorate in, say, "God as Metaphor in the Federalist Papers," and keeps all his notes and lectures until they—or he—fall apart, I have accumulated seven theses in the course of writing what I call "narratives of empire." That is, seven novels from *Burr* to *The Golden Age*; from 1776 to 2000. But once I am done with a period, I move on to the next. During one of those rare intervals that I am on amiable terms with our chief court historian, Arthur Schlesinger, I asked him about a detail in one of his books on Franklin Roosevelt. He drew a blank: said something to the effect that he marveled at how much he had once known, put in a book, and then forgot. We agreed that any well-researched book is itself the ultimate sole repository for all the facts so painstakingly assembled, because if memory was required to hold all the beads that a writer has strung over time in time about time, the brain would burst. Even the historical novel . . . no, let's not use that phrase. One cannot generalize usefully about a form that varies so dramatically from one writer to another.

But I shall try to generalize about the novel set in history that may contain, in foreground or background, various figures that the turf-conscious academic historian may regard as his property and *not* to be illuminated by creative writing. Although I sympathize with him, I have, of course, been mowing his turf for a long time now; in fact, I am deeply in his debt, since I read history more attentively, I should think, than anyone outside an institution. So let me now seize by the throat, as it were, the great question: Why a novel and not a history or that increasingly lively sub-genre biography? History has obvious attractions for an inventive novelist and his reader. He can speculate, up to a point, on motives. He would be unwise, in my view, to enter the mind of Abraham Lincoln, say, simply as a matter of tact, not to mention caution. There are too many ways of getting it wrong. But he is . . . well, I felt I was perfectly able to enter the mind of Lincoln's second secretary, John Hay, and thus observe the president at close hand, based on the diaries and letters of that bright young man (finally being published in a full edition).

With Aaron Burr, there are his letters, diaries of the time, and his own distinctive tone of voice so well described by Joanne Freeman (yes, I'm coming to her). But before I do a few sharp intakes of breath upon the page, let me introduce you to a word that you should know but, most likely, don't, thanks to our educational system and its many prejudices (the historical novel is neither fish nor fowl). The world is *Einfühlen*. A neologism invented by the German philosopher Johann Gottfried von Herder (1744–1803). The word is often translated as "empathy," but Herder's use of it has far more reverberations than simply being able to put yourself in someone else's shoes. For one thing, the shoes in question are often in the past and the past is a different country with different air and full of people not like us but like themselves, and though we share, perhaps, the same DNA, the worlds back of them and before them are simply not our quotidian world and so it takes a certain kind of imagination and modesty to walk about in those shoes in a physical and moral landscape so entirely different from ours.

Herder's insight and practice have had a great influence on the writing of history from the eighteenth century on. Among Herder's essential works is one with the ironic title *Yet Another Philosophy of History.* He could immerse himself in the "climate" of other eras as well as in those exotic civilizations dismissed by his Eurocentric contemporaries. Herder's mind? He loathed Voltaire; Goethe got on his nerves—that tells us a lot. In our time Herder's chief apostle was the late Isaiah Berlin, who wrote of him:

> He has his preferences: he prefers the Greeks, the Germans, and the Hebrews to the Romans, the ancient Egyptians or the Frenchmen of his own time or of the previous century. But at least in theory, he is prepared to defend them all; he wishes and thinks he is able to penetrate—"feel himself" (*Einfühlen* is his invention . . .)—into their essence, grasp what it must be like to live, contemplate goals, act and react, think, imagine, in the unique ways dictated by their circumstances, and so grasp the patterns of life in terms of which alone such groups are to be defined.

Where the novel set in history often goes wrong is when the author can't visualize any time but his own and so imposes his own present on a different place. Also, such a novelist, as well as a clear majority of historians, arrives on the scene with a series of unquestioned prejudices and so is unable to begin to empathize with those of a different political persuasion, not to mention country, the past into which one must feel one's way.

Years ago George Steiner, in a review of my novel *Julian*, wrote that it was a book that would delight my friend (he, too, read the popular press) John F. Kennedy, as if I were making—because I could not help it?—a political 1964 statement that would please Ian Fleming's greatest fan. But I was writing of another world and of a fascinating figure who has no relevance at all to any American politician. Readers of my essays are often surprised how often figures for whom I have a certain visceral dislike— Woodrow Wilson, Harry Truman—are treated as sympathetically as they are in the novels *Hollywood* and *The Golden Age*. The answer is *Einfühlen*. I do enter, as well as I can, the climate of another time and place in order to understand why someone does as he does. Shakespeare is the obvious master of this kind of . . . no, not impersonation. Personation? No. Too

clumsy a word. In any case, you have the knack or you don't. Mary Re-
nault had it. Madame Yourcenar lacked it entirely. She worked entirely in
front of a mirror which she mistook for a window and what she took to be
Hadrian looking back at her was a French *bas-bleu*, not a Roman emperor
but her own vain, somewhat preposterous self. (Yes, my *Einfühlen* can put
me inside this great lady with suspicious ease!)

Now Joanne Freeman. You will climb these six steps to the scaffold,
holding in your hand a scarf. Kneel at the top. Place your neck on the
block and, when ready, drop the scarf and . . . But I am not in decapitat-
ing mood. Freeman is a good writer, something not often found in history departments, even at Yale. She has almost made me want to reread
Burr. Almost but not quite. In fact, on the evidence here, I suspect that
she, too, possesses *Einfühlen.* She immediately grasps how "extraordinarily self-conscious" the founders of our republic were, as they tried to look
back through the mirror at us in the future looking at them. They *knew*
they were historic. They were making what would be, in two centuries,
alas, Statesperson Albright's "one indispensable"—if not indisposable—
nation. In a sectarian world only recently rescued from canting religion
by the Enlightenment, Freeman notes that Burr alone did not moralize
about anything, unlike Jefferson, but rather like his enemy and other self,
in my view, Hamilton. Burr saw himself as a wise, worldly Lord Chester-
field, writing good sense to his beloved daughter, Theodosia, along with
details of his sex life as if she were a son and chip off the old block.

The duel. What could have made the unflappable Burr so angry that
he would call out Hamilton? According to my intuition, only a charge of
incest, par for the course for someone like Hamilton. Certainly, Theodosia was the only human being, as far as I could tell when I shared
his climate, that he ever loved. Arnold A. Rogow wrote to ask me where I
had come across this true or untrue fact, as Jefferson would say. After a
long immersion in the Burr-Hamilton world, I *felt* that this was the "despicable" business that Hamilton had alluded to. Later, I read in a newspaper interview—with Mr. Rogow?—that he had come round to my view.
Others have, too. I am told that Freeman has lately done admirable work
on the code *duello.* I have not read her on the subject. I do know that dueling was pretty much out of fashion by 1804. Proof? Dueling was illegal

in New York; hence, the boat ride to Weehawken, New Jersey, and dismal glory. Hence, Burr's subsequent indictment for murder.

My factual errors don't seem to me to be much in the way of breath-intaking errors. I'll quickly answer them and then charge Freeman with a very big error. Mind that top step, please. (1) She tells us that the political world was not divided into Federalists and Republicans in 1791. I've forgotten what I wrote but surely those who were styled "friends of the government"—that is, of the Washington-Adams administrations—were the Federalists-to-be. Certainly, by 1795, their faction had changed to something very like a party, while those in opposition, led by Jefferson, were already organizing a party as early as 1791. The labels aren't important here any more than they are today. (2) Surely, I have a scene of Jefferson wandering about the great barn of the White House in shabby slippers and dressing gown. (3) Of course Abigail loathed Hamilton, who gleefully wrecked her husband's administration, with a lot of help from His Rotundity, the irascible Adams. On the other hand, if I wrote that she had had a brief maternal feeling (she the least maternal of mothers to her own children), it would have had to be based on research (my *Einfühlen* rests upon a lot of note-taking). It sounds as if this was during the period when the government was at New York and Hamilton was very much the entrancing glamour boy of that city, his only competition Burr himself, often referred to as the "first gentleman of the United States."

One must never underestimate, by the way, the dramatic class difference between what a friend of Oliver Wendell Holmes's father called that "little West Indian bastard Hamilton" and the elegant heir of the Edwardses, et al. (4) I've forgotten what stand Hamilton took on the Alien and Sedition Acts, and don't plan to look it up. (5) Hamilton was indeed a British agent and Burr was an agent for the French Directoire. There is a good deal of literature on the subject. It was not particularly dishonorable in the case of two New York lawyers like Burr and Hamilton. Rather like lobbyists today: Kissinger and China. But the fact that the commanding general of the U.S. Army, James Wilkinson, was a Spanish agent meant that he, not Burr, should have been put on trial for treason.

Freeman errs when she writes that Burr wanted to be emperor of the American West. Had there been any hard evidence for this, don't think that Jefferson, busy suborning witnesses in the White House, wouldn't have produced it. After the duel and resignation as vice president, Burr went West with no settled plan. The West was distinctly unhappy with the Union in general and Jefferson in particular. Burr was a hero to the western separatists, among them his friends Andrew Jackson and Henry Clay. But Burr opted for Mexico, not secession. He would go down the Mississippi with as many men as he could muster, move on to Mexico, where, with the aid of Wilkinson, he would replace the Spanish government of Mexico with a Burrite utopia. Mad as a hatter? Well, this was the age of the astonishing Bonaparte, so why not? Burr was also not the only five-foot-four would-be emperor of Mexico. Until Weehawken, Hamilton was dreaming the same dream; and making tentative plans. When Jefferson got wind of all this, he wildly accused Burr of treason, and arrested him. Clay defended him at a first trial; then Chief Justice Marshall. . . . Oh, read the book. Or read that superb scholar Mary-Jo Kline, who vetted the manuscript of *Burr* so long ago.

Notes of a Disillusioned Lover: John Updike's *Memories of the Ford Administration*

Paul Boyer

Three quick observations. First, *Memories of the Ford Administration* has very little to do with the Ford administration. Second, John Updike is the best thing that has happened to James Buchanan since 1856. Third, the history profession lost a gifted recruit when Updike opted to major in English rather than history at Harvard, and then in 1954 when he sold that first story to the *New Yorker*. Historians' loss, of course, has been twentieth-century American literature's tremendous gain.

But what is it with Updike and Buchanan? Born in Pennsylvania, Buchanan's home state, Updike has long been fascinated by our fifteenth president—that Rodney Dangerfield of chief executives, stuck near the bottom of all presidential rankings, living out his ghostly posthumous existence in the shadow of his sainted successor. Buchanan didn't even have the good luck to be assassinated, the fate that assured Lincoln's deification and even gives a boost to the reputation of such a dim figure as James A. Garfield.

Having written a play about Buchanan in 1974, Updike now devotes a large chunk of this 1992 novel to him. All this ink spilled on poor old Buchanan simply because the novelist and the president share a common birth state! Had Updike been born in upstate New York, would he be lav-

ishing his talents on Millard Fillmore? In fairness, however, I must confess that Updike's fascination with Buchanan because of geographic proximity is entirely comprehensible to me: my earliest political hero was that
pompous, isolationist, antilabor, three-piece-suit-wearing senator from
Ohio Robert Alphonso Taft—for no better reason than that Taft hailed
from Cincinnati, near my own hometown of Dayton. Gloom spread
across southwestern Ohio, including the Boyer household, on that dark
day in 1953 when "Mr. Republican" passed on at sixty-three. So, one for-
gives Updike his Buchanan obsession, and asks what *Memories of the Ford
Administration* has to say to historians. The short answer is: quite a lot.

⁊∫⁊

THE NOVEL'S INTRICATE structure interweaves two widely disparate
eras, the long span of Buchanan's life (1791–1868) and Gerald Ford's
short presidency (1974–1977), both periods viewed from an early-1990s
perspective. The protagonist, a forty-something Vermont native named
Alf Landon Clayton (obviously fated by his very name to be a historian),
earned his Ph.D. in American history in 1962 and got a job at Wayward
Junior College, a women's school on New Hampshire's meandering
Wayward River, where he remains. For years he has been writing a biography of Buchanan, a project he is gradually abandoning.

The entire novel consists of Alf's long, Tristram-Shandy-like letter to
the Northern New England Association of American Historians
(NNEAAH), as his contribution to a projected volume to be entitled
*Memories and Impressions of the Presidential Administration of Gerald R.
Ford.* Within this capacious format, Alf unloads large chunks of his work-
in-progress on Buchanan, interwoven with extended accounts of his own
rocky progression through the Ford years. As the rambling memoir proceeds, Buchanan disappears for long stretches, but he always returns,
often in striking counterpoint to Alf's own recollections.

Updike, in composing his fictional historian's scholarly opus, has researched Buchanan's life carefully, and he writes about it, albeit somewhat
episodically, in illuminating detail. Alf's draft manuscript becomes
sketchier as Buchanan leaves his law practice in Lancaster, Pennsylvania,
and enters the public arena; indeed, Alf apologizes to his NNEAAH col-

leagues for its "fragmentary, unsatisfactory" nature. In fact, Alf's memories of his love life in the 1970s engage him more than the ins and outs of Buchanan's ascent from Lancaster lawyer to Democratic congressman, minister to Russia and England, U.S. senator, Polk's secretary of state, and eventually—the dubious grand prize—election as president and four years in the White House.

Updike is clearly having fun with the scope this novelistic conceit gives his satirical gifts, as he skewers, among many other targets, the furtive intrigues of academia and the plummy rhetorical flights of historical popularizers, whom Alf periodically imitates but whom, in other moods, he waspishly ridicules. Of Allan Nevins's purple prose, he sniffs: "This is history? This is word painting."

But Updike has larger concerns. Historians clearly loom large among the intended audience of *Memories of the Ford Administration*, as Updike offers extended reflections on their discipline, toward which he conveys a certain admiration and indulgent affection, tempered by amusement at its self-satisfaction and overweening assumptions. This is not, thankfully, a "historical novel" in the conventional sense of the term, but rather a novel of manners set in the 1970s, in which Updike again does what he does best: create a believable community of fictional characters and plunge them into the swirl of contemporary or near-contemporary American life. At the same time, however, through the voice of his protagonist Alf, he offers an extended treatment of Buchanan and his age, as well as more casually presented but still interesting commentary on the public events, mass culture, and social trends of the 1970s.

Updike has always been noteworthy for his attentiveness to historical detail. The four "Rabbit" novels, from *Rabbit, Run* (1960) to *Rabbit at Rest* (1990), tracing the life of the small-town Pennsylvanian Harry "Rabbit" Angstrom from high-school basketball star to retired car dealer with a bad heart, memorably evoked the social currents and cultural *Zeitgeist* of America from the 1950s through the 1980s. The same keen sense of history characterized Updike's novels of the 1990s, not only *Memories of the Ford Administration* but also *In the Beauty of the Lilies* (1996)—a religiocultural epic of twentieth-century America told through a multigenerational saga extending from a New Jersey Presbyterian minister who loses his faith to a descendant who joins a Branch-Davidian-like cult.

This concern with historical specificity is in the tradition of William Dean Howells, whose novels so vividly evoked Gilded Age America. *The Rise of Silas Lapham* (1885) may not explicitly allude to the national events of the day or the specific happenings and public figures of 1880s Boston, but it is as solidly rooted as any of Updike's novels in an unmistakable time and place: a post–Civil War America of crass, money-driven politics and ruthless self-made men like Philip Armour, Charles Yerkes, and Jay Gould, and a Boston where solid citizens (including Howells himself) were building elegant town houses in the recently drained Back Bay, and where the Brahmin elite and newly minted capitalist tycoons like the eponymous paint king Lapham were uneasily eyeing each other.

Admittedly, *Memories of the Ford Administration* did not rouse cries of protest among historians as did William Styron's *Confessions of Nat Turner* (1967), Gore Vidal's *Burr* (1973); Oliver Stone's Kennedy and Nixon films; or, for that matter, Edmund Morris's 1999 "memoir" of Ronald Reagan, *Dutch*. These fictioneers deliberately chose celebrated, controversial figures and reimagined their lives in deliberately provocative ways. Styron, in particular, offended historians and outraged African-American intellectuals with his psychosexual explanation of Turner's murderous uprising. Neither Buchanan nor Ford are historical figures of comparable magnitude, and Updike's treatment of Buchanan, at least in broad outline, as well as his allusions to the Ford era, generally follow the known historical record, and were hardly calculated to incite controversy. Updike further deflected criticism from the historical establishment with such phrases (so familiar to historians!) as "it is not impossible to imagine," and by attributing his invented dialogue and speculations about Buchanan to his somewhat flaky and self-indulgent fictional creation Alf Clayton. All the same, *Memories of the Ford Administration* is, in some respects, more slyly subversive of the received wisdom of academic historians than the literary and cinematic provocations mentioned above.

❧

UPDIKE'S FOREMOST AIM in writing *Memories of the Ford Administration*, one assumes, was simply to accomplish once again what he had accomplished many times before: create a readable fiction exploring a particular cultural moment in a specific setting that he knew well. Beyond this, however, he also pursued his long-standing personal interest in Buchanan while offering reflections on the larger historical enterprise. For historians, Updike's comments and reflections on the Buchanan era and the 1970s, and even more his broader ruminations on history-writing, repay close attention. Updike has combed the primary sources relating to Buchanan, and immersed himself, at least selectively, in the scholarly literature. One finds allusions to Eric McKitrick, Samuel Eliot Morison, Henry Steele Commager, Roy Nichols, Philip Shriver Klein (author of a 1962 Buchanan biography), Kenneth M. Stampp, Allan Nevins, Avery Craven, Bruce Catton, Wilbur J. Cash, Jonathan Spence, Ferdinand Braudel, Christopher Lasch, and others. Still, one must say that after Alf received his Ph.D. in 1962, he did not keep up very well with the scholarly literature. Of the works he cites, nearly all date from his college or graduate-school years. Stuck at Wayward with a heavy teaching load and time-consuming extracurricular activities, he seems to have neglected many recent historical monographs and journal articles relevant to his topic. He knows about the new social history and the new political history in a general way, but his comments about these trends are fairly dismissive. For a professional historian, he relies pretty heavily, although with reservations, on the old-time narrative histories, popularizers like Catton and Nevins, narrowly focused antiquarians, and monographs current a generation ago.

In fact, Alf is less interested in the great public issues and socioeconomic changes of antebellum America than in Buchanan's personal life, particularly the great crisis of Buchanan's young manhood: the broken engagement with Ann Coleman, daughter of Lancaster's richest man. Ann and James pledge their love in the summer of 1819, but she soon breaks the engagement after Buchanan, returning to Lancaster after a day in Philadelphia, spends an evening socializing at another household rather than immediately stopping to see Ann. A few weeks later, Ann falls ill and dies under unclear circumstances. Her father, stern Judge Cameron, returns unopened Buchanan's letter asking permission to view her corpse. In a long set piece, Alf imagines Ann's final hours, suggesting that she may have semideliberately taken an overdose of laudanum.

Alf has a good grasp of antebellum politics and diplomacy (less so of

social history), but these matters interest him primarily as they shed light
on his beloved Buchanan. For example, a second major set piece in his
manuscript (as he shoehorns it into his NNEAAH memoir) deals with an
1838 Senate speech by Buchanan urging conciliation of the slaveholding
South. In a breathtaking conjectural flight, Alf interprets this speech as a
sublimated "love song . . . , sung in the intimate old Senate chamber," to
Alabama senator (and future vice president) William R. King, with whom
Buchanan shared a Washington boardinghouse room from 1836 to 1844.
This speculation leads Alf to extended ruminations on the ambiguity of
nineteenth-century gender roles and homoerotic relationships. Apart
from such lovingly crafted set pieces (others include a Moscow ball scene
and a long evening of conversation between Buchanan and Nathaniel
Hawthorne, U.S. consul in Liverpool during Buchanan's ambassadorship
in London), Alf's manuscript remains, as he himself concedes, fairly
pedestrian and schematic.

Alf's difficulties in finishing his book, while reflecting his growing self-
doubts as a historian and his inability convincingly to link his psychobi-
ography of Buchanan to the larger political and social realities of the day,
relate also to crises in his personal life. Updike readers will be unsurprised
to learn that the 1970s sexual revolution looms large in *Memories of the
Ford Administration*. As the novel begins, Alf has left his wife, Norma, and
their children to pursue an affair with the lovely Genevieve Mueller, wife
of Brent Mueller, a deconstructionist in the English Department. Amidst
this grand passion, he also enjoys one-night stands with Wendy Wad-
leigh, wife of the Music Department chairman; Ann Arthrop, the mother
of a student; and an unnamed "slim blond woman, a guest speaker on
transactional analysis," who briefly visits Wayward. Learning of the
Arthrop dalliance, Genevieve dumps Alf to follow her husband to Yale.
By the novel's end, Alf is back with Norma and the kids, but still brooding
over Genevieve's departure and the realization that his Buchanan book is
going nowhere.

As for the promised "memories of the Ford Administration," don't
hold your breath. The public events of the Ford years are mentioned only
in passing, as background to Alf's bed-hopping and Buchananizing. From
headlines, newscasts, and cocktail-party chatter, he learns of Nixon's resignation, the *Mayagüez* crisis, the panicky exodus from Saigon, Mao Tse-

tung's death, the Helsinki Accords, and other events beyond the campus, but they make little impression. In his own life, as in his scholarship, Alf has trouble relating the personal and the public. Indeed, Updike deliberately underscores the disconnect between the two. One is reminded of Ang Lee's 1997 film, *The Ice Storm*, also set in the seventies, in which a teenage girl engaged in a fumbling sexual encounter with a neighbor boy impulsively puts on a Nixon mask, and public and private suddenly intersect, with jarring effect.

✒

LIKE ALL OF Updike's work, at least from this fan's perspective, *Memories of the Ford Administration* is a great read. But historians especially should find stimulating Updike's sympathetic but critical reflections on their discipline, and his perspective on some basic questions they at least occasionally confront—or should confront. Viewed as a book about history, the novel is concerned less with Ford, or even with Buchanan, than with the nature of memory; the process of writing history; and indeed whether "the past" can be recovered at all in any authentic sense, by professional historians or anyone else.

One of Updike's central themes is the self-delusion of historians in thinking that they can re-create a past time period, or even an individual life, through the crude methods and limited, semiopaque sources available to them. The more Updike's earnest, conscientious historian tries to understand Buchanan's life, the more baffling and elusive it becomes. Why, really, did Ann Coleman break the engagement? Was she a suicide? Does this trauma explain Buchanan's lifelong suspicion of emotion (including the raw emotionalism of the antislavery crusade)? And how did that distant 1819 event affect the course of history? In a fascinating exercise in counterfactual history, Alf imagines a happily married Buchanan settling down with Ann (and her inherited fortune) to practice law in Lancaster, so that the 1856 Democratic nomination goes to Stephen A. Douglas, who, being a more skilled politician than Buchanan, calms the sectional crisis and avoids the Civil War. Alf endlessly ponders such questions but never satisfactorily answers them, largely because the surviving sources are so sketchy and contradictory. The more he seeks to understand Buchanan and his era, the more frustrated he becomes.

Similarly, as Alf struggles to describe his own tortuous course through the Ford years, he seems figuratively to be wandering in the dark, waving a defective flashlight that blinks on and off, fleetingly illuminating small patches of a dense thicket. One is reminded of the aging Walt Whitman's comment on the Civil War: "The real war will never get in the books"— or Tolstoy's evocation in *War and Peace* of the confusion, chaos, countless trivial actions, and forgotten small tragedies that somehow added up to "Napoleon's retreat from Moscow"—an "event" treated with such brisk confidence by historians.

Alf's near-exclusive focus on his own subjectivity in this alleged memoir of "the Ford administration" underscores a larger point. The essence of lived experience, Updike suggests, is the intimate and personal—the inner emotional life and passing sensory impression—yet this is precisely what remains almost wholly inaccessible to historians. Alf's most vivid memories of the Ford years, apart from his epistemological crisis and his love life, are a jumble of movies, TV programs, popular songs, and Broadway shows. He recalls what people wore (the "resplendent . . . purple muu-muu" of Wayward's president at a party); the furniture (canvas-sling butterfly chairs, foam couches, flimsy paper lampshades from Taiwan); and the popular fabric tints—especially "salmon and washed-out lime green." "[D]ecor is part of life, woven inextricably into our memories and impressions . . . ," Alf insists defensively; "these inanimate things conspiring to reconstruct the past, to dam the flow of time with their fragile, obstinate shapes."

By contrast, the public events that dominate the textbook verson of the 1970s remain a blur, passingly mentioned in widely scattered paragraphs. Alf's sharpest recollection of a seventies public event is the night of October 21, 1975, when Carlton Fisk won the sixth game of the World Series for the Red Sox against the Cincinnati Reds—and what he recalls is the shouting and horn-blowing on the street outside the bedroom where he and Genevieve have just made love. Nixon's resignation is similarly embedded within a personal memory: Alf is back home for an evening, babysitting the kids while Norma goes on a date, and they watch Nixon's speech on TV.

Alf continually insists on the fundamental irretrivability of this most intimate level of past experience: "Our heaving spirits displace little matter; the past, insofar as it consists of human feelings, mostly vanishes, less enduring than recycled nitrogen." Or, again, epigrammatically: "History buries most men, and then exaggerates the height of those left standing." Interestingly, in a brief bibliography of historical works Alf includes at the end of his memoir, the only relatively recent title is Peter Gay's *Education of the Senses* (1984), a work that does try to recover the inner life of the nineteenth-century bourgeoisie.

But Updike's historical agnosticism runs deeper still. Alf endlessly reflects on the impossibility of retrieving not only the emotional component of past experience, but also the past itself.

> The texts [upon which historians rely] are like pieces of a puzzle that only roughly fit. There are little irregular spaces between them, and through these cracks, one feels, truth slips. History, unlike fiction and physics, never quite jells; it is an armature of rather randomly preserved verbal and physical remains upon which historians slap wads of supposition in hopes of the lumpy statue's coming to life.
>
> As in physics, the more minutely we approach them, the stranger facts become, with leaps and contradictions of indecipherable quanta. All we have are documents, which do not agree.

In another such passage, Alf reflects that the bits and pieces that do remain for historians to paw over are simply the random survivors of a "holocaust of documents that still rages—documents shredded, pulped, compacted, abandoned to the cleaning crew, bulldozed deep in green plastic bags, mercilessly churned in the incessant cosmic forgetting." The intellectual enterprise that Alf has doggedly pursued for years, he reluctantly concludes, is fundamentally pointless and futile: "Composing history is like packing a suitcase with objects that persist in overflowing or underfilling the space." "You know how it is, fellow historians—you look for a little patch not trod too hard by other footsteps, where maybe you can grow a few sweetpeas"; but "research [leads] to more research, and even more research [leads] back to forgetfulness and definitive awareness that historical truth is forever elusive."

Updike's portrayal of Alf's efforts to finish his book amid the wreckage of his personal life underscores his view not only of the ultimate futility of the history-writing process, but also of its utter subjectivity and contingency. Alf's Buchanan biography emerges from a complex interaction of his own guesswork and intuitions, the fragmentary evidence he has managed to accumulate, and his personal circumstances at the time of the research and writing. What Alf finds significant in Buchanan's history seems increasingly determined by his own preoccupations. Stumbling through a decade when all the rules appeared to have been suspended, for example, Alf revels in the early-nineteenth-century social conventions and courtship rituals illuminated by Buchanan's doomed relationship with Ann Coleman. For all his scholarly pretensions, he admits, his practice of history is "superstitious as well as unsystematic."

Alf's epistemological skepticism has ruined him as a historian, guaranteeing that his "precious nagging hopeless book" will remain unfinished. He had once hoped that from the clutter of "photocopies and scribbled index cards and overdue library books" he might extract "a clean narrative thread that would some day gleam in the sun like a taut fishing line"—but this dream fades with his loss of faith in his discipline's foundational assumptions. The collapse of his intellectual world matches that of his personal world. Alf's final judgment on his long effort to "pearl-dive into the past" and "unlock the mystery of James Buchanan" is devastating:

> [H]aving imagined an eagle's eye view that would make of his life a single fatal moment, [I] found myself merely writing more history, and without the pre-postmodernist confidence of Nevins and Nichols and Catton, yarn-spinners of the old narrative school. My opus ground to a halt of its own growing weight, all that comparing of subtly disparate secondary versions of the facts, and seeking out of old newspapers and primary documents, and sinking deeper and deeper into an exfoliating quiddity that offers no deliverance from itself, only a final vibrant indeterminacy. . . .

As Alf's memoir ends (and with it Updike's novel), he recalls an early-seventies ski trip, before all the affairs, before he had abandoned his book. Random sense impressions flood back: streaking down the slope shouting the Beatles' song "Yesterday" at full volume, excitedly rejoining a welcoming circle of faculty friends and their children decked out in a rainbow of winter gear. But he can't remember which mountain they were on, the precise year, or what was happening in the world at the time. This leads directly to the novel's final sentence: "The more I think about the Ford Administration, the more it seems I remember nothing." (In Alain Resnais's 1959 film *Hiroshima, Mon Amour,* when the visiting French actress describes the photographs and artifacts in Hiroshima's atomic-bomb museum, her Japanese lover repeatedly tells her, "You have seen nothing.")

✑

ONE SENSES THE relief with which Updike doffs the historian's hat and dons the novelist's hat, transmuting the Buchanan narrative, and Alf's muddled effort to write it, into a capacious fictional omnium-gatherum. The novel's interwoven narratives have a satisfying structure and symmetry missing from the fragmentary historical manuscript embedded within it, as Updike skillfully develops a series of parallels: Nixon is driven from the White House in disgrace just as Alf guiltily leaves his own family and household. Ann Coleman's behavior in crisis situations is influenced by her reading of Lord Byron; Alf's by his memories of suave movie heroes. Buchanan discreetly flirts with the well-upholstered czarina of Russia just as Alf has his lubricious night with the voluptuous Mrs. Arthrop. Genevieve brusquely ends her affair with Alf just as Buchanan realizes that William King has spurned his subtle gesture of love. Alf rejoins Norma and his family at the point in his Buchanan narrative where the ex-president returns to Wheatland, his home in Lancaster. As Buchanan's public career fades, Alf reflects of himself, "My life had at some unnoticed point peaked and passed into decline."

Further, the freedom of fiction allows Updike, through loquacious, opinionated Alf, to comment on the culture and politics of the 1970s with an abandon impermissible to historians constrained by the conventions of their guild:

On the academic life: "Norma and I are fairly content. College people acquire a certain grim yet jaunty expertise at aging, at growing grayer with each year's fresh installment of ever-young, ever-ignorant students. We roll with the annual punch."

On deconstruction: "Brent Mueller, ... with the clammy white skin of the library bound, ... explained to me that all history consists simply of texts, ... and texts are inevitably indefinite, self-contradictory, and doomed to a final aporia. ... [Mueller's] anti-canon deconstructionist chic ... flattened everything eloquent, beautiful, and awesome to propaganda baled for the trashman. ... [Fortunately, the deconstructionists'] anti-life con(tra)ceptions were ... becoming at last passé and universally der(r)ided."

On the 1970s sexual revolution: "Gerald Ford ... presided over a multitude—dare we say millions?—of so-called one-night stands. ... The paradise of the flesh was at hand. ... Bodily fluids had no deadly viral dimension in the dear old Ford days; one dabbled and frolicked in them without trying to picture the microscopic galaxies within. ... What had been unthinkable under Eisenhower and racy under Kennedy had become, under Ford, almost compulsory. ... [I]n those far-off Ford days it was assumed that any man and woman alone in a room with a lock on the door were duty-bound to fuck."

On Jimmy Carter: "However much Carter wanted to be liked, we could not quite like him: the South couldn't quite like him because he was a liberal and an engineer, the Northeast liberals couldn't because he was a Southerner and a born-again Christian, the Christians were put off because he had told *Playboy* he had *looked upon a lot of women with lust*, and the common masses because his lips were too fat and he talked like a squirrel nibbling an acorn."

On Yankee reticence: "I don't feel closed up to myself—just to other people."

ঞৎ

BOTTOM LINE? *Memories of the Ford Administration* should be read by all historians. It would be a great novel to assign to undergraduate majors or even in a graduate historiography seminar. Fascinated by and attracted to history-writing, Updike also has a novelist's keen sense of its limitations. His novel reminds historians of a useful home truth: a Ph.D., an academic appointment, a CV full of scholarly articles and conference papers, and an elaborate flourish of footnotes are not essential to the exercise of historical imagination, and may actively impede it. Indeed, critical reflection on the nature and limits of the historiographical enterprise itself may be more boldly and fruitfully addressed from outside the discipline than within. For all our hand-wringing, *Memories of the Ford Administration* suggests that historical interest is far from moribund in America, and, for that, historians owe John Updike a debt of thanks.

сЛ

Reply

John Updike

P aul Boyer's lively, friendly appraisal of *Memories of the Ford Adminis-tration* does not mention what I considered the pivotal intersection of Alf Clayton's Buchanan saga with his real, as remembered, life: his swooning into the arms of a student's mother, Mrs. Arthrop, upon hearing that her name, like that of Buchanan's lifelong love object, was Ann. "Oh. Ah. 'Ann,' I repeated. That tore it." This particular, history-inspired infidelity, discovered by Alf's own love object, Genevieve Mueller, tears their romance and sets Alf's life back, with a jolt, on track.

Nor does Professor Boyer identify by name my previous work on Buchanan, the long play *Buchanan Dying*, published in 1974 and per-formed in cut versions in 1976, twice—in Lancaster, Pennsylvania, and in San Diego, California. Though my publishing firm of Alfred A. Knopf, Inc., made a handsome volume of it—perhaps the handsomest, in design and typesetting, of any of my books—I remained unsatisfied with this packaging of the Buchanan matter, and tried again nearly twenty years later. The reasons for my dissatisfaction were, basically, the unwieldiness of an actual life, especially a long political one lived in the public eye from 1814 to 1868, and the embarrassments, forcefully described by Henry James in a memorable letter to Sarah Orne Jewett, of writing what he called " 'historic' fiction"—"The real thing," he warned, "is almost impossible to do and in its essence the whole effect is as nought." Some of my novel's scenes, such as Buck's fatal (for his fiancée) encounter with the charming Hubley sisters, and my dramatization of his notorious encounter as a young congressman with Senator Andrew Jackson, are taken pretty much from the play; some others, such as the conversation with Hawthorne and the Senate speech delivered in the presence of fellow senator and longtime roommate W. R. D. King, were invented for the novel. The novel, I think, delivers better than the play what I have to say about Buchanan because it wears its aesthetic discomfort, as it were, on its sleeve, in the person of the discomfited, all-confessing narrator, a teacher of history.

I do not want to repeat here what is spelled out in the long afterword to *Buchanan Dying*, and in a number of paragraphs on Buchanan to be found in two most recent collections, *Odd Jobs* (1991) and *More Matter* (1999). Buchanan was a Pennsylvanian, and one of the history books' losers: these were my incentives to love him enough to risk research. It was pleasant and, the mind ever accumulating rust, salutary for me to delve into the history of antebellum America, and to feel how one's ignorance widens along with one's researches, wherein book would lead to book ad infinitum. When I thought I knew enough, I began; of course more could be known, but the kind of fact which a fiction writer depends upon, the witnessed and experienced particular, does not come swimming out of memory where memory, however saturated with texts, has never been. The fearful effort of constructing a simulacrum of, say, Ann Coleman's suicide—itself far from historically certain—produces a glaze, a sweat on the surface of it quite absent, one hopes, from the freely recalled details of the eastern United States in the mid-seventies. And yet, just as I am chastised by Professor Boyer for not knowing enough of the "social history" (whatever that is—isn't all history social?) of Buchanan's lifetime, a young reviewer called David Lipsky chastised me for getting wrong many details of the Ford administration years (1974–1977). Apple computers did not exist, he wrote me, and futons were not yet fashionable; video games were not evolved beyond the rudimentary, nonchirping Pong; boom boxes did not exist; and Pachelbel's Canon in C, the theme song of Genevieve and Alf's romance, did not become popular until 1980, when it made the sound track of the film *Ordinary People*!

I could swear that my informant is wrong on some of these details, but where he is not, he bears out Alf's conclusion that he remembers nothing. We remember, certainly, less than we think, and the engines of distortion begin to work long before events pass into the distances of history. Journalists simplify what they learned an hour ago, eyewitnesses hallucinate, stenographers misspell, and each consciousness plays Hamlet in its own botched, truncated version of the drama. And there are nuances and elusive flavors in the living present, even the somewhat abstracted present of political events, that, like jellyfish, are too delicate to be lifted from the support of their vast momentary context; what will historians make of the Clinton/Monica/Starr/Hillary constellation, and contrive to know how the second presidential impeachment in the United States' long career was both very serious and, in its workings and significance to the public, not serious at all—a watery farce of personality tics transposed to the expensive national stage? The worst-case scenario, history may forget, would have given us President Al Gore, a less than earthshaking eventuality.

My own life story has the quirk that, for almost the entire period of the Ford administration, my concerns were so exclusively personal that I subscribed to no newspaper and learned of national events (which luckily were in a minor key) quite by the way. A quirk of Buchanan's administration is that between Lincoln's election in early November 1860 and the incumbent's surrender of the presidency in March 1861, an almost unprecedentedly hectic atmosphere generated conferences of which a remarkably full record, in the form of memoirs and documents and letters, exists. The cabinet meetings in my novel are taken from the record. The drama of a legalistic, compromise-minded president elected by southern interests being brought, crisis by crisis, to a minimum sticking point in defense of the Union, and the drama, furthermore, of a man early traumatized in life being led, through a long lifetime of cautious and evasive dealing, into the center of the supreme national trauma—such drama is there, in Buchanan's story, whether or not I had the wit to bring it out.

Some fakery is present in any fiction; among my own novels I count one set in the African Sahel, where I have never been, and one set in a Brazil I never experienced, and most recently an excursion into medieval Denmark. They are all as real as I can make them, while aware, on the reader's behalf, that their reality is in some large proportion fantastic. The act of writing and the format of fiction in themselves aerate the most mundane reconstruction with the fizz of the unreal. We shorten, we skirt, we skim, all to deliver back to the reader his own reality. Of the two worlds in *Memories of the Ford Administration*, my own pleasure and recognition attach more readily to the contemporary one, as, for example, in the scenes concerning Alf's involvement with Ann Arthrop. I am charmed by the little illuminations they generate as they unfold: "Ann answered my knock instantly, as if poised by the door; she was already in a bathrobe, in a room where but one dim bedside lamp, its parchment shade decorated with a pointing Labrador, added its beige glow to the moonlight pressing on the drawn curtains." A glimmer ricocheting off the surface of known things: this is where the fiction writer finds his poetry and his raison d'être. He rotates the contemporary details his mind has unwittingly stored. Yet I could not have written the episodes of the Ford era without the frame of the NNEAAH, of *Retrospect*, of my impudent assumption of the historian's robes.

I do not, may I add, consider Allan Nevins's prose purple, or anything but a regal shade of that color; I emerged from my own travails in mauve ink awed by the ability of narrative historians like Nevins and Roy Nichols and Philip Klein to take all their vast musty reading and give it the momentum and particularity of fiction. Insofar as history lives in the telling, and persuades us we are there, it is a species of fiction.

Russell Banks's Fictional
Portrait of John Brown

James M. McPherson

C loudsplitter" is the English word for the Indian name of Mount Tahawus, in the Adirondacks, 120 miles north of Albany and near the rural community of North Elba, where the abolitionist John Brown established a home in 1849. But the real cloudsplitter in this novel is John Brown himself, who launched lightning strikes against proslavery settlers in Kansas and whose thunderbolt descent on Harpers Ferry, in 1859, lit flames of civil war that were not fully quenched even at Appomattox, six years later. Russell Banks has constructed this complex narrative on two levels. The first is the story of John Brown and his large family from the 1830s to the moment of his defeat at Harpers Ferry. The second and more profound level consists of a prolonged meditation on the interrelationships of blacks and whites and fathers and sons.

The first-person narrator is a fictionalized Owen Brown, John Brown's third son and his principal lieutenant in the Kansas wars. The story takes the form of autobiographical notes compiled by Owen in 1899 for Katherine Mayo, the research assistant of Oswald Garrison Villard, who published in 1910 what still stands as the fullest biography of John Brown. The knowledgeable reader will recognize how Banks has employed novelistic license to describe events that never happened, to place Owen at scenes where in reality he was not present, and to date his composition of these notes eight years after the real Owen died. But of course this is a work of fiction, not history, and these contrivances enable Banks to construct a version of "truth" beyond that of literal history.

John Brown was an Old Testament warrior-prophet transplanted into the nineteenth century. He believed in a God of wrath and justice. He also considered himself God's instrument to free the slaves and punish their owners for the sin of holding human beings in bondage. One of his favorite biblical passages was from Hebrews 9:22: "Without the shedding of blood there is no remission of sins." Brown possessed a powerful personality that enabled him to dominate his seven grown sons, most of whom became soldiers in his war against slavery and three of whom were killed in that war. Brown's strange charisma also won other allies, both black and white, who followed him to death and martyrdom at Harpers Ferry or provided him with financial support for his armed crusade against the proslavery power that dominated Congress, courts, the presidency, and the army in the 1850s.

Many people then and later believed that John Brown was insane. This novel, however, conveys the message that Brown was insane only if slavery and white supremacy were sane. As Owen expresses it, his father had a capacity singular among white men to see the world from the black man's point of view. From that perspective, the insane became sane, and vice versa. "Something deep within [John Brown's] soul, regardless of his own skin color . . . went out to the souls of American Negroes," Owen writes,

> so that he was able to ally himself with them in their struggle against slavery and American racialism, not merely because he believed they were in the right, but because he believed that somehow he himself was one of them. . . . Father's progression from activist to martyr, his slow march to willed disaster, can be viewed, not as a descent into madness, but as a reasonable progression—especially if one consider the political strength of those who in those days meant to keep chattel slavery the law of the land . . . due to our obsession, we were, as it were, insane. Which to the Negroes, to Lyman, made us perfectly comprehensible and trustworthy—sane.

The Lyman in this quotation is Lyman Epps, a free black farmer and a neighbor of the Browns' at North Elba, where the wealthy abolitionist Gerrit Smith had granted land to blacks and to John Brown to establish a kind of exemplary interracial rural community. From North Elba, Epps and the Browns carry escaping slaves to Canada on the Underground Railroad from 1850 to 1855, when most of the Browns go to the Kansas territory. Epps was an actual person, but in this novel he looms larger than he did in real life. He plays a pivotal role in Owen Brown's self-awakening, which even more than John Brown's progression to martyrdom is the central theme of the novel.

Owen wishes to transcend his whiteness and, like his father, enter into the soul of blackness. But in the presence of blacks, he cannot forget his color, which "angered me in a way that left me secretly ashamed." Owen and Lyman, portrayed here as being about the same age, become close friends. But Owen realizes, in a sort of shameful epiphany, that he has fallen in love with Lyman's wife, Susan—an emotion that, as he will come to realize, is really a displacement of his love for Lyman. Consumed by guilt, he flails himself and experiences a surge of hatred for Lyman, which produces another round of racial guilt that is purged only when, in a climactic scene, Lyman accidentally shoots and kills himself in circumstances that Owen could have prevented if he had acted in time.

Owen thus convinces himself that he is a murderer and can atone for this atrocious act only by becoming the cold-blooded killer of slave-owners and destroyer of slavery that he believes his father wants him to become. "I was the man," Owen writes,

> who had never been able to forget that Lyman, while he lived, was black. Thus, until this moment, I had never truly loved him. He was a dead man now—finally, a man of no race. And as surely as if I had pulled the trigger myself, I was the man, the white man, who, because of Lyman's color and mine, had killed him. It was as if there had been no other way for me to love him.
>
> There was nothing for love, now, but all-out war against the slavers. . . . Father would be my North Star. . . . I had become outwardly a hard man, a

grim, silent warrior in my father's army, soon to be a killer more feared by
the slavers for his cold, avenging spirit than any Free-Soil man in all of
Kansas. More feared even than Father.

This passage suggests another dimension of Owen's self-awakening—his
contrapuntal dependent-independent relationship with his father. Here
Banks hints at an Oedipal interpretation, but he never develops it. Owen's
mother died when he was eight, a devastating experience, and Owen resented his father's marrying again even as he experienced overwhelming
love for his father, who forgave his youthful sins: "It was as if his words
had cleansed me, for at once I felt uplifted and strong again. Whatever
Father wished me now to do, I would do without argument, without hes-
itancy, without fear."

Instead of Oedipus, the Old Testament stories of Job and of Abraham
and Isaac become the models for this father-son relationship. God tested
Job's faith by letting Satan take everything from him—his wealth, his ser-
vants, his family, his health. Yet Job refused to curse God, and the Lord
rewarded him by restoring health, wealth, and family.

> The figure of Job was, of course, like no one so much as Father himself. As
> Job stood to God, Father did also. My terrible understanding was that I,
> too, was like no one so much as Job. Not, however, in my relation to God;
> but in my relation to Father.

Owen tries repeatedly to break free of his father's domination, to become
his own man, like his older brothers, Jason and John, Jr., but he cannot.
Like Isaac, he is compelled to obey his father, even if his father is commanded by the Lord to slay him as a sacrifice.

The death of Lyman Epps, by compelling Owen to become a killer of
slave-owners to atone for his sin, seems for a while to have reversed the
relationship of father and son. When the time comes for revenge against
proslavery depredations in Kansas, it is Owen who ruthlessly instigates
the cold-blooded murder of five settlers in the infamous Pottawatomie
massacre. John Brown was beset with indecision, so "I reached forward
and banged roughly on the door" of the first victim's cabin; "I kicked it
and swiftly put my shoulder into it"; "I remember raising the blade of my

sword . . . and then I brought it down and buried it in the skull," and so on for two pages. "And Father? Where was Father? All the while, he stood away from us, and he alone did not use his sword. He watched."

Shortly before Lyman Epps shoots himself, he tells Owen that Owen isn't half the man his father is. But after Pottawatomie, "I now found myself twice the man my father was." Yet, in another ironic twist, Pottawatomie galvanizes John Brown into becoming a fearsome guerrilla warrior, "so that before long it was no longer required of me to goad or brace him in the least, and in fact I found myself barely able to keep pace with him."

The final eighty pages of the novel, culminating in the Harpers Ferry raid, are something of an anticlimax, in contrast to the raid's climactic status in the history of the real John Brown. This anticlimax is important mainly for Owen's "betrayal" of his father and those brothers who died or were captured at Harpers Ferry. Left behind at the farm where the raiders holed up while they prepared for the assault, Owen is to take charge of arming the slaves who his father expects will flock to the banner of insurrection. When the assault collapses in disastrous failure and no slaves appear, Owen alone among the Browns escapes and survives to tell the tale. When he fails to join his father and brothers in Harpers Ferry, becoming instead an Isaac making his escape while "my father, Father Abraham [, was] making his terrible, final sacrifice to his God," it was "as if, after a lifetime bound to my father's fierce will and companionship by heavy steel manacles and chains, I had watched them come suddenly unlocked, and I had simply, almost casually, pitched them aside."

Of course, it did not actually happen that way. Owen could have done nothing to save his father and brothers. And many other crucial events in the novel did not occur as portrayed, or never occurred at all. Lyman Epps did not shoot himself; indeed, he sang John Brown's favorite hymns at Brown's funeral, in North Elba. For me as a historian to point this out is not to criticize Russell Banks as a novelist. In an "Author's Note," Banks states clearly that he has "altered and rearranged" historical events and characters "to suit the strict purposes of storytelling. . . . Accordingly, the book should be read solely as a work of fiction, not as a version or interpretation of history." Fair enough. Unlike some of my literal-minded colleagues, who grind their teeth in exasperation at every departure from fact in a historical novel, I am quite willing to recognize—and to learn from—the novelist's license to reconstruct the past in the interests of a reality deeper than literal fact.

But I do confess annoyance at the numerous minor historical errors in *Cloudsplitter* that have no bearing whatsoever on the development of the author's story and would harm nothing if they were corrected. Such errors seem to indicate a certain indifference to the careful research that should underlie historical fiction. One or two or even half a dozen mistakes of this sort would be negligible, but the large number herein become a vexation. To mention but a few: the number of slaves in 1859 was four million, not three; Martin Van Buren did not establish the National Bank but helped to destroy it; John Brown was executed on December 2, 1859, not December 12; William Lloyd Garrison was not a Quaker; Franklin Sanborn could not have been an editor of the *Atlantic Monthly* in 1850 or 1851, because the magazine was founded in 1857; none of the federal troops in Kansas in 1856 were conscripts; Sharps rifles were manufactured by a private firm in Hartford, not by the government in Harpers Ferry; and Lewis Washington, one of the hostages captured by the Harpers Ferry raiders, was a collateral rather than a direct descendant of George Washington. Finally, Owen repeatedly refers to Oswald Garrison Villard, for whom this "Secret History" of John Brown is intended, as "Professor Villard" of Columbia University. Villard was a journalist, and a proprietor and an editor of *The Nation* and the *New York Evening Post*, but never a professor at Columbia or any other university.

For most readers, however, such petty errors will not detract from the powerful passages and profound insights in this novel. It humanizes John Brown, a figure all too often demonized or idolized in history as well as in fiction. Our understanding of this tragic era in the American experience will never be quite the same again.

⟋⟍

In Response to James McPherson's Reading of *Cloudsplitter*

Russell Banks

I'm reluctant to respond to this occasion, to react in print to Professor McPherson's generous, but hedged, review of my novel, *Cloudsplitter*, because I am grateful for his generosity, after all, and because I have nothing but admiration for Professor McPherson's historical writings. Also, I'm reluctant to appear to be defending my novel. A novel must be its own best (or worst) defense. Nothing I say, therefore, to explain its inner workings or explicate its deeper meanings or to describe my own intentions and desires for the book will amplify what must already be there in the pages of the book itself, for better or worse.

Nonetheless, it might be to the point if I bring to the discussion between me and Professor McPherson my notion of the radically divergent uses made of "fact," whether historical or biographical (or journalistic or autobiographical, for it makes no difference where the "fact" comes from), by historians and biographers on the one hand and fiction writers on the other. And as this has been a subject of some recent controversy in the literary and academic and even the popular press, I will try to speak of my novel only inasmuch as its nature addresses the controversy, less than to answer Professor McPherson's specific criticisms.

The cover of *Cloudsplitter*, the title page, the copyright notice, every public description of the book, says that it is a novel, a work of fiction. And what is that? Cynthia Ozick, in a recent review of *Ravelstein*, Saul Bellow's *roman à clef* (a form of fiction whose relation to "fact" is not unlike that of historical fiction), says succinctly and accurately that a novel is a "persuasion toward dramatic interiority. A word-hoard that permits its inventor to stand undefined, unprescribed, liberated from direction or coercion." This liberation, this freedom, she continues, "makes sovereignty; it is only when the writer is unfettered by external expectations that clarity of character . . . can be imagined into being" (*New Republic*, May 22, 2000, p. 31). I assume, therefore, that when a reader opens my novel, he or she will do so knowing that I have not written it as a biographer or historian, as one who—in order to discover and reveal to himself and others the meaning of the life and times of the actual human being named John Brown—relies solely on his interpretation of data, fact, testimony, documentation, and primary and secondary sources. No, the word "novel" declares, as if it were a contract between me and my reader, that I have written this book solely under the restrictions, obligations, and responsibilities, and with all the freedoms, that control and liberate a fiction writer, more properly a *storyteller*. Which means that any investigation I might conduct into the contents of my imagination, where, in terms of my personal interests, the life and times of John Brown happen to have been residing since my childhood, will be conducted by means of imagery obtained by listening to language. Not data, fact, testimony, documentation, and so on. Language.

In an attempt to distinguish clearly between a historian's use of John Brown and mine, I pointedly placed at the front of *Cloudsplitter* an "Author's Note": *This is a work of the imagination. While some of the characters and incidents portrayed here can be found in accounts of the life and times of John Brown, the famous abolitionist, they have been altered and rearranged by the author to suit the strict purposes of story-telling. These characters and incidents, despite their resemblance to actual persons and known events, are therefore the products of the author's imagination. Accordingly, the book should be read as a work of fiction, not as a version or interpretation of history.*

I wrote this note in the hope that it would dissuade readers like Professor McPherson from seriously misreading my novel, from looking in it for history or biography, instead of for story. I wrote it because a story, like a poem, is not "about" anything: it is an object that may be someone else's subject, a critic's or even a historian's or biographer's, but does not have a subject itself. "Fiction is subterranean, not terrestrial," Ozick writes. "Or it is like Tao: say what it is, and that is what it is not" (*New Republic*, May 22, 2000, p. 27). It is strictly its own self, a cluster of images obtained solely from words structured and organized in such a way as to produce a clarifying dramatized vision of the truly human. At least, that is the fiction writer's hope. For while histories and biographies must have subjects and are unreadable if they don't, a story or novel has no subject outside itself. If it does it is likely to be a badly written story or novel. This is true of even a so-called historical novel, one that uses for its purposes the material that surrounds recorded events and a known historical figure, a person who actually lived, whose life was chronicled, someone whose name is known to every schoolchild in America—John Brown, say. Even a novel like that is not about anything. It is simply *told*, and having been told, if it is vivid enough and plausible enough and if its imagery has evoked powerful feelings from deep, previously unplumbed zones of our inner selves, then the story has a chance to be absorbed into our imaginative lives sufficiently, one hopes, to change our actual lives. Consider how the great stories have worked to do precisely that—even though, of course, they sometimes inadvertently do more. We do not find ourselves changed by *The Adventures of Huckleberry Finn* or *Moby Dick* or *The Sound and the Fury* because of what they are "about." Or because of their faithfulness to historical, biographical, journalistic, or autobiographical "fact" (though there is plenty of that in all three novels). To read any one of them as history or biography or autobiography (and critics frequently do this) would be grossly to misread it, would be to miss the point altogether, would be to deprive oneself of the chance to change one's actual life.

If there is history in a historical novel, if there is history in any novel, then it can only exist in the voice that we hear when we read the story. Let me seem to digress here for a few moments, to try to clarify what I mean by voice generally and historical voice in particular, so that we can come to a clearer understanding of the figure of John Brown as he figures in the novelist's, this novelist's, imagination. Eudora Welty put her finger on its origins, I believe, in a passage from her sweetly intelligent memoir, *One Writer's Beginnings*. "Ever since I was first read to, then started reading to myself, there has never been a line read that I didn't *hear*. As my eyes followed the sentence, a voice was saying it silently to me. It isn't my mother's voice, or the voice of any person I can identify, certainly not my own. It is human, but inward, and it is inwardly that I listen to it. It is to me the voice of the story or the poem itself. The cadence, whatever it is that asks you to believe, the feeling that resides in the printed word, reaches me through the reader-voice. I have supposed, but never found out, that this is the case with all readers—to read as listeners—and with all writers, *to write as listeners* [my italics]. It may be part of the desire to write. . . . I have always trusted this voice."

For Miss Welty, as for any storyteller, the voice in which her story gets told originates not on the page, but in her own ears, as if her ears were tuning forks or pitch pipes, and is heard back, more or less accurately, more or less in tune, when she writes; and if less accurately or if out of tune, *then* is when she acts, as she says, to make her changes, to adjust her receiver to the signal, as it were, to revise, eliminating the static and interference, so that the voice heard finally in her written sentences is true to the voice she heard when she was a child, when her parents first read to her, the voice she still hears today, in her late eighties, when she sits down and begins to read and write. Its origins, then, are in the profoundly personal, are in her earliest auditory experiences of the word, not strictly in the written word itself or even the heard word, but in that misty long-forgotten zone of awareness where the two overlap, where all that remains available to her ears, like a signal coming from an uncharted source in outermost space or light from a distant, long-dead star, is the dim, half-invented memory of a mother or a father reading stories to the child from the Bible, from Dickens, from Robert Louis Stevenson.

By the same token, there are certain qualities of voice, certain distinct qualities of emotion, that are *not* heard in her fiction—the erotic, for instance, or rage, or the pain of a profound psychological wound or spiritual terror. Compare Faulkner, for instance, or Flannery O'Connor, just to stay with southerners. But we could compare any first-rate fiction to hers, and in a single sentence we would hear the difference at once: the strong writer's voice on the page is as individual, as personal, as downright physical as the voice of a lover, a child, or a parent. Even if they say the same words or tell what appears to be the same story, we do not confuse the one speaker with another.

But what about the voice of *history* in fiction? It's one thing to assert the inescapable presence of the personal, as Miss Welty does, and as I'm doing here, but quite another to argue for the presence there of the historical as well. Fine to expect the voice of the author himself or herself, but isn't it too much to ask of fiction that it speak with the voice of *history* as well? It may be a contradiction, anyhow—impossible, perhaps, for the two to exist together in the same work of fiction.

How, then, did history, how did the life and times of John Brown, enter my story and become a crucial aspect of its voice? Let me try to track its route. I suppose I had been imagining and reflecting on Old Brown at least since my college days, when he kept turning up in my readings of Thoreau and Emerson and the New England Transcendentalists as a figure whose only modern (by which I mean 1960s) equivalent was Che Guevara. Brown was for me a powerful, resonant figure where many significant lines of force crossed or converged—race, certainly, and political violence, terrorism, religion, natural law, and so on. The life of John Brown and his death (as conscious a martyrdom as the death of Jim Jones or David Koresh) raised questions that were important to me personally. I was, like many of my contemporaries, a political activist in the 1960s, a founder of the SDS chapter at my university, an antiwar and civil rights protester. Thus, certain questions raised by the figure of John Brown— such as: When does an obsession with a cause, no matter how just, become fanaticism? and When, if ever, is a violent course of action against a democratically elected government justified?—were questions whose answers, or lack of answers, impinged upon my own life. I took them personally. They weren't merely theoretical. They weren't academic. The questions mattered to *me*, to the meaning of my life so far, and they continued to matter and grow increasingly difficult to answer as the years passed, even as I gained distance on those turbulent years and so few of the bright and shining promises of the 1960s were realized and I grew sadder and, presumably, wiser. Should we have been more violent or less? Should we have been more committed to our causes or less? Was our idealism tainted at the source by our naïveté, or by our hedonism? Or was it all hopeless from the start? Nearly 150 years after his death, the question of whether I could truthfully imagine John Brown as a heroic visionary or as a well-intended fanatic, or both, had meaning for me personally.

Before I could begin my novel and try to answer a few of these questions, I had to decide how to tell it. The material (the life and times of John Brown) was at hand in great dismaying abundance, of course, but I had to make a few decisions about form before I could make any fictional use of it, before I could transform it into story. Crucially, I had to decide from what, or whose, point of view my story would get told. One cannot write a sentence until one knows who is speaking it, who authorizes it, who is responsible for the information and opinions contained therein. The implications are vast. They are aesthetic, of course, but they are also inescapably moral.

The prevailing conventions of historical fiction suggested an omniscient point of view, an anonymous narrator/chronicler who was my and my reader's contemporary, not John Brown's. Thus, the voice of history, if I followed that line, would come, not from the past, but from the present, which was where the personal voice came from, too. Presumably he, my anonymous narrator, would already know the answers to the several questions I mentioned above, or he'd at least have a pretty good idea of where his interrogatory would lead. More of an idea, certainly, than the author had. This author, anyhow.

There is a wonderful but intimidating authority, an extraordinarily high degree of entitlement, informing that omniscient point of view, and I have never felt comfortable assuming it. I'll do almost anything to avoid taking on its mantle. Thus, for most of a year, I took that old writer's dodge—research, research, research—and in that way managed to avoid starting the novel for a good long while. In the course of my research, however, I was led eventually, by a long, circuitous route, to the Rare Book Room at the Columbia University library and the notes and drafts for Oswald Garrison Villard's 1909 magisterial biography of Brown. I discovered there a half-dozen cardboard boxes of tattered notes, photographs, transcripts, and typescripts, most of which had been compiled by Villard's young research assistant, Katherine Mayo, a remarkable woman who later became a well-known journalist.

Oswald Garrison Villard was a distinguished editor of the *Atlantic Monthly*, a historian and journalist, as Professor McPherson rightly notes—and as I was well aware when I decided to make him a professor instead, for the purposes of storytelling, just as I put roads where there were none, invented journeys not taken, let Brown attend Emerson's lecture on heroism in Boston that Emerson probably never gave. Anyhow, Villard's biography on Brown was intended to be definitive, as all are, I suppose, and to be published on the fiftieth anniversary of the 1859 raid on Harpers Ferry. His and Miss Mayo's research in the years 1903 to 1908 was greatly enhanced by the fact that several of John Brown's children were still living, an elderly man and two women out in Oregon, and Miss Mayo, I discovered one winter afternoon up there at Columbia, had actually interviewed them in person.

Her handwriting was clear, precise, unusually legible, and, as I recall it now, she had left her questions out of the transcripts of her interviews, so there were only the subject's answers on the sheets of yellowing old notepaper, as if each were a soliloquy delivered to an unknown, mute listener and not an interview at all. As I began to read, I became that mute listener. It was like hearing a ghost. Here was the voice of an old man, Salmon Brown, who as a mere boy had fought alongside his father, Captain John Brown, in the guerrilla wars of Bloody Kansas, who had ridden at Osawatomie, who had participated in the Pottawotamie Massacre, and who had refused to follow his father into certain death at Harpers Ferry, and who had brooded on these terrible events afterward for nearly half a century. Here were descriptions of John Brown at home on his farm in the Adirondacks, or at table in their home in Springfield, Massachusetts, or raising his blooded Merino sheep in Akron, Ohio. Here was the Old Man seen in private, recalled for us by his favorite daughter.

When interviewed by Miss Mayo, they were elderly people. They were not well-educated but were by our standards today extremely literate. They were the age then that Eudora Welty is now, which means that in a sense we are only two long generations away from the living memory of Harpers Ferry, and they spoke to a young twentieth-century listener, but were in fact mid-nineteenth-century American working people, farmers, who happened to have been political activists, and over time they became terrorists and were nearly killed for it. In these interviews, or soliloquies, the children of John Brown spoke with a voice that we simply do not hear anymore, but which seems to have been heard widely, if not commonly, in mid-nineteenth-century America. You may remember hearing it in the letters and diaries written by ordinary soldiers and civilians and read aloud by modern actors in Ken Burns's history of the Civil War produced for television. You can hear it in the memoirs of Ulysses S. Grant. You can hear it in many of the ex-slave narratives.

We hear in all these voices a simplicity and directness, a precision and eloquence, that Americans seem no longer able to speak or write to one another. With little formal education, but possessing great familiarity with the Bible, certainly, and the Book of Common Prayer, the *New England Primer*, and perhaps a half-dozen other examples of written English, men and women were able to say to one another exactly what they meant, thought, felt, and had personally experienced, and to say it without irony, without defensiveness, without groping for words, even. It's as if they shared with their fellow ordinary (by which I mean nonliterary and middle-class) Americans several crucial articles of faith regarding language that we no longer share. First, they believed that they had something important to say. Second, they believed that their native version of the English language was capable of articulating what they had to say. And, third, they believed that they would be understood by their listener or reader. This triangulation, between speaker, medium, and audience, is very powerful. It establishes a social contract, of sorts, concerning the use and powers of language, and it implies a trust in, and a respect for, self, language, and neighbor, which as a society we seem no longer to possess. It let those nineteenth-century Americans tell one another the truth. And it let them hear it.

Not surprisingly, by the end of my first hour of reading Miss Mayo's transcripts, I had found my narrator. I had located my point of view. I was hearing my voice of history. The personal voice would take care of itself, or not; there was probably nothing I could do about that, except, like Miss Welty, tune my receiver when I lost the signal. As Zola said, "Art is life seen through a temperament," and I was more or less stuck with mine. My narrator, the teller of my tale, would not be Salmon Brown, I decided, but his older brother, Owen, the third son of John Brown, a man who gave no interviews and wrote no memoirs but who, born in 1824, had been present as an adult at all the crucial battles and most of the crucial scenes in his father's life, who had participated in the awful Pottawatomie Massacre and the victories in Kansas that had thrilled the northern abolitionists and terrified slaveholding Southerners, who had been at Harpers Ferry and, miraculously, had escaped. The historical Owen Brown disappeared afterward into the abolitionists' equivalent of the Weather Underground and reappeared after the Civil War as a sheepherder living on a mountaintop in Altadena, California, where he lived mostly alone until

1889, when he died. So that his voice and story would not seem too antique to be taken personally by a man writing in the late twentieth century, a man troubled by certain questions of morality regarding race,
violence, and religion, I gave Owen Brown by authorial fiat an extra
eleven years and allowed him to live long enough to be interviewed by
Miss Mayo just as the twentieth century began. My novel would become
his chance to tell his story. And I would become, in a sense, merely his
mouthpiece, so that, for a reader, Owen Brown's would be the voice of
history in my work of fiction. His language, from my ear to the page,
would be its language. And in the writing of my novel, that is all I would
be true to. Thus, any reader who, like Professor McPherson, went there
for anything other than that voice and the story it told would be either
disappointed or seriously misled, and misled, might criticize my novel for
failing to be true to the "facts."

It was Faulkner who said that "the past is never dead; it's not even
past." We can't get away from it. Personally and collectively, the past, our
history, is alive today, and it emerges and is heard everywhere every time
we speak. It's in our language. In our mouths and ears. The voices we hear
in fiction are autobiographical, to be sure, and they are biographical as
well. They are both personal and anonymously impersonal. And if, in his
or her imagination, an author is a representative figure, as some of us, despite our overpublicized vanities and eccentricities, surely are, then we
will hear from him or her the voice of a representative man or woman of
his age. His will be the voice, like Miss Welty's, of his own lived and
mostly forgotten past and present speaking through his imagined past
and present. But if his narrator, like Ishmael aboard a whaling ship or
Huck Finn aboard a raft, or perhaps even Owen Brown escaping through
the bushes from Harpers Ferry, if he, instead of the author, is the truth-
telling representative figure of his age, that is, a character who is perfectly
poised, by virtue of his relation to the rest of society, to tell us the truth of
his times, then we will hear from him the voice of the concrete past speaking through and to our imagined present. That is the voice of history in
fiction.

Forms of fiction, artifice and genre, conventions and modes of storytelling, come and go. They are constantly being forgotten, rediscovered,
renovated, and refurbished, and after a while rejected and forgotten

again, until the new forms which displaced them have grown soft with use once more, and writers start groping around in the dark for something new. The very language we speak and write changes, too; it shrinks, swells, changes shape, color, and tone in a matter of mere generations; it is as much in transit and flux and as subject to influence from outside or inside as we. And languages, as we well know, can die or come to exist only in translation.

Yet even in that extreme a situation, the voice of history continues to be heard in fiction, for, as Miss Welty wrote, "Emotions do not grow old." Read the Bible if you disagree, or Homer. Fiction tends always toward the preservation and dramatization of that one truth. *Emotions do not grow old.* This, to me, then, is the true voice of history in fiction, the voice that insists on our enduring humanity and celebrates it. We are the species that over and over has to learn what it is to be itself. Against death, against our inhumanity, our stupidity and greed, the voice of history, whether in fiction or poetry or drama, may in the end be all that we have to sustain us.

Why Oswald Missed: Don DeLillo's *Libra*

David T. Courtwright

T his is a work of imagination," Don DeLillo writes at the end of *Libra*. "Any novel about a major unresolved event would aspire to fill some of the blank spaces in the known record. To do this, I've altered and embellished reality, extended real people into imagined space and time, invented incidents, dialogues, and characters." The latter include minor intelligence operatives who conspire with or, more accurately, use Lee Harvey Oswald in a successful plot to murder JFK. Anticipating the charge (leveled by conservatives anyway) that the book is "one more gloom in a chronicle of unknowing," DeLillo invites the reader to take refuge in *Libra* as a work of fiction, "a way of thinking about the assassination without being constrained by half-facts or overwhelmed by possibilities, by the tide of speculation that widens with the years."

The disclaimer seems at first unexceptionable, redundant. *Libra* evokes Oswald's world using stream of consciousness, invented dialogue, premonitions, and other transparently fictional techniques. It flashes back and forward, shifting constantly in time and place. Oswald and narrative discontinuity, the perfect marriage of subject and form. He constantly changes allegiances, aliases, jobs, residences. "The point of our century is people move," Marguerite Oswald observes. *Libra* moves with Oswald and the book's 124 other characters, tracks them, gets inside their heads, weaves their lives through the plot that breaks the back of the American century. It's plainly a work of imagination, and one cast on a Tolstoyan scale.

Yet a certain kind of reader will find DeLillo's disclaimer overly modest. Those who are familiar with the assassination literature cannot help but see in *Libra* something more than a polished work of fiction. They immediately recognize DeLillo as a fellow traveler in the assassination labyrinth. Though he is not a member of the research community—the intensely committed, faction-ridden network of amateur and professional students of the assassination—he is nevertheless a close reader and critic of the Warren Report. He doubts the official truth as well as the more conspiratorial improvisations on it. *Libra*'s wrappings of fiction barely conceal a sophisticated historical attempt, guided and constrained by ballistic, photographic, and documentary evidence, to recreate the crime of the century in a convincing way. The fiction here is disciplined, interstitial, aimed at evoking, if not the truth—who can ever know the full truth of the assassination?—then at least a closer approximation to it. "I purposely chose the most obvious theory," DeLillo explained to one interviewer, "because I wanted to do justice to historical likelihood." He "felt a very strong responsibility to fact *where we knew it*," he told another. "I really didn't take liberty with fact so much as I invented fresh fact, if you can call it that."[1] Novel though it may be—and *Libra* is a great novel, as technically accomplished as anything in late-twentieth-century fiction—I have chosen to explore it as a dissenting historical report and, beyond that, a meditation on the nature of history itself.

What Happened in Dealey Plaza?

Historians ask the same basic questions of the past that journalists ask of the present: who, what, when, where, how, and why. As a practical matter, historians of modern America seldom spend much time on the first four of these. They are most concerned with explaining the hows and whys of large events, like the Great Depression or the Vietnam War, whose factual outlines are generally agreed upon and widely known. The Kennedy assassination is the great exception. Only the what, when, and where are undisputed. President Kennedy was mortally wounded while riding in an open motorcade through Dealey Plaza in Dallas, Texas, at 12:30 P.M. on November 22, 1963. He was pronounced dead at nearby Parkland Hospital half an hour later. Who shot him, how, and why are widely disputed, and will remain so long after the last witness has died.

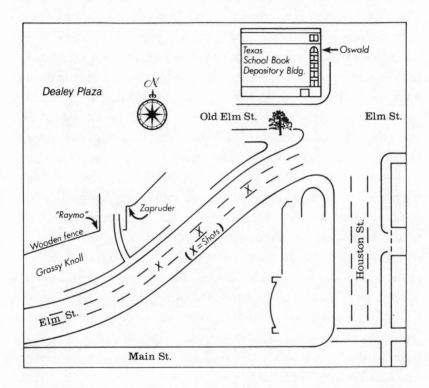

Oswald fired three shots at Kennedy after his motorcade turned left from Houston Street and proceeded west down Elm Street. The *X*s show the approximate location of the presidential limousine as each shot was fired. The Warren Commission decided that one of Oswald's three shots missed, one passed through Kennedy's and Governor Connally's bodies, and one hit Kennedy's head. DeLillo has Oswald's first shot hitting Kennedy's body, his second hitting Connally's, and his third missing everything—"Maggie's drawers." The fatal head shot is fired by Raymo, a fictional but ballistically plausible sniper lurking behind a wooden fence atop the Grassy Knoll. *Diagram adapted with permission from Michael Kurtz,* Crime of the Century, *2nd ed. (Knoxville: University of Tennessee Press, 1993), 223.*

The Warren Commission and its defenders, the best known of whom is Gerald Posner, contend that Lee Harvey Oswald, acting alone, shot President Kennedy. Crouched by a window on the sixth floor of the Texas School Book Depository (see diagram), he fired three shots from a scope-mounted, bolt-action Mannlicher-Carcano rifle as the limousine drove slowly past on Elm Street. One shot—the commission did not specify which one, Posner argues that it was his first—missed and hit a distant curb, wounding a bystander named James Tague with a bit of concrete. The second hit Kennedy near the base of his neck and exited his throat. It then hit Governor John Connally, sitting in front of Kennedy in the limousine. It traversed downward through Connally's chest, shattered a rib, passed through his wrist, breaking the radius bone, and embedded itself in his thigh. Oswald's third and final shot entered the back of Kennedy's head and exploded out the top, killing him.

Oswald hurriedly hid the rifle. He left the building, went to his rooming house, picked up his .38 revolver, and walked out. Ten minutes later, he encountered a police officer named J. D. Tippit and shot him four times. He fled to a nearby movie theater, where he was apprehended. Initially held as a suspect in the Tippit murder, Oswald quickly became the prime suspect in the Kennedy shooting. He denied killing anybody and never came to trial for either crime. Jack Ruby, the proprietor of a strip club, shot Oswald on the morning of November 24 as police were transferring him from the Dallas jail. He was rushed to Parkland Hospital, where he died a little after 1:00 P.M. Ruby had acted alone, the commission decided. Just like Oswald.[2]

The death of the prime suspect while in police custody during the investigation of a high-profile murder invites skeptical inquiry. What made the Warren Commission's findings lastingly controversial, however, was its reconstruction of Kennedy's murder. The motion of Kennedy's head, captured in Abraham Zapruder's famous home movie of the assassination, suggests—these words are DeLillo's—"that the lethal bullet was fired from the front."[3] Oswald was above and to the rear. The commission's single-bullet theory was even more widely disputed. Critics attacked it on the grounds of angle of fire and the (mis)alignment of Kennedy's and Connally's bodies. They said it was inconsistent with Connally's own testimony, the bullet holes in Kennedy's clothing, the autopsy findings, and the Zapruder film, which shows Kennedy reacting to the shot well before Connally appears to be hit. They ridiculed the notion that a relatively undamaged bullet, found on a stretcher at Parkland Hospital, could be responsible for two broken bones and seven wounds, four of entrance and three of exit. A minimum of four shots (Kennedy's back, Connally's back, Kennedy's head, and one miss) were needed to account for the forensic and film evidence. But Oswald did not have time for four shots and, in any case, left behind only three spent shells. Reduced to an equation, four shots equal two shooters. Two shooters equal a conspiracy—unless there happened to be two independent assassins operating in Dealey Plaza that balmy November day.[4]

DeLillo, who is fascinated by coincidences and makes them an important element of *Libra*'s plot, isn't buying that one. "The reason so many people think Oswald was not the lone gunman," he said in 1988, when the book was published, "is that the physical evidence, as we know it, argues against it in many respects." DeLillo did not begin with a conviction of conspiracy. His starting point was his long-standing interest in the chief suspect, rekindled when he wrote an essay on Oswald and other American assassins for *Rolling Stone* in 1983.[5] Oswald is the ultimate contrarian, a natural subject for a novelist attracted to misfits and outsiders. He's a Marxist and a Marine. A nonsmoker in a cigarette-mad society. A nondriver in freeway heaven. A dyslexic who learns Russian. A defector who redefects. *Libra* is, above all else, an attempt to figure out what made Oswald go, what combination of circumstances could produce such a strange character and give him the opportunity to switch history's train down another track. But in researching his anti-hero's life, using the twenty-six volumes of the Warren Report as his *Encyclopedia Oswaldiana*, DeLillo arrived at the conclusion that Oswald probably had not acted alone. His plot would have to feature more than one assassin.

Conspiracy Within a Conspiracy

Conspiracies require a motive. This one can be summarized in two words: Castro's overthrow. The Kennedy administration's failed and half-hearted attempt to achieve it, the 1961 Bay of Pigs invasion, caused bitter resentment in the exile community. Where was the promised air cover? It was, remembered one participant, like being abandoned by your big brother during the fight of your life. The settlement of the 1962 Cuban missile crisis made matters worse. Kennedy struck a deal with Khrushchev. No more invasions. "Kennedy had the chance to get rid of Castro and he ends up guaranteeing the man's job," a character named Laurence Parmenter complains. "The administration went from passionate and total dedication to an attitude of complete aloofness and indifference and they did it in goddam record time."

Parmenter, a DeLillo invention, is one of a group of CIA diehards who continue to meet after the Bay of Pigs, exploring unauthorized operations against Castro. The Agency learns of their meetings, puts their careers on ice. Walter "Win" Everett, Jr., is exiled to Texas Woman's University. He reads the *Daily Lass-O*, teaches his classes, plays the family man. But he secretly misses the action, obsesses about Cuba, cultivates his rage. He conceives a new plot, lets a select few in on it. We need an electrifying event, Everett says, something to provoke another invasion. An assassination attempt on the president, with a trail of evidence leading back to the Cuban Intelligence Directorate. It's to be Pearl Harbor, minus the *Arizona*. "We don't hit the President," Everett cautions. "We miss him. We want a spectacular miss."

One of Everett's fellow conspirators, T-Jay Mackey, has other plans. Charged with carrying out the attempt, he recruits two anti-Castro exiles, Ramón "Raymo" Benítez and Frank Vásquez, and a soldier of fortune named Wayne Elko. He neglects to tell them, however, that they are supposed to miss the president. Mackey wants Castro to take the blame, but he also wants vengeance. Someone has to pay for Cuba, and Kennedy is it. "Plots carry their own logic," DeLillo writes in an often-quoted line. "There is a tendency of plots to move toward death."

Everett intends to devise a patsy out of pocket litter, to invent a paper trail leading back to Havana. But he and the other conspirators learn, via George de Mohrenschildt and Guy Banister ("real" characters), about this oddball ex-Marine. He's lived in the Soviet Union. He's married to a Russian woman. He admires Castro, distributes "Hands Off Cuba" leaflets. He's purchased a mail-order rifle under an assumed name. He's used it to take a shot at Edwin Walker, a retired major general and big-oted superpatriot who has it in for Castro. Oswald is perfect, straight out of central casting. Even after Mackey quietly betrays Everett, switching the plot from miss to hit, he keeps Oswald in the picture: "He was one element of the original plan that still made sense."

Oswald's place of employment, the Texas School Book Depository, is another piece of fortune. "We didn't arrange your job in that building or set up the motorcade route," David Ferrie admits to Oswald. "We don't have that kind of reach or power. There's something else that's generating this event. A pattern outside experience." The book's astrological title, *Libra*, evokes these outside forces. Libra's sign, a pair of scales, symbolizes Oswald's contradictions, his ability to tilt either way. Will this left-winger play the assassin for right-wingers who want to kill the president? He agrees, expecting that they will help him escape to Cuba. There he will be acclaimed a hero, the David who slew the *yanqui* Goliath.

To Mackey, Oswald is just a patsy whose leftist background points in the right direction. As an assassin he's strictly backup, a doubtful marksman with a crummy rifle. Raymo, stationed behind a fence at the top of the Grassy Knoll, is the man with the firepower, a scope-mounted Weatherby Mark V loaded with soft-point bullets. Oswald, firing metal-jacketed rounds, misses Kennedy's head with his first shot. He hits lower down, near the base of his neck, wounding him but not fatally. He fires a second time. Connally doubles up. Wrong man. He sights on Kennedy again. A split second before his last shot, another miss, Oswald sees the president's head explode in his scope. He knows in that instant that there's a second sniper—it's Raymo, atop the Grassy Knoll—and suspects he's been set up. But he has no choice other than to head to the rendezvous point for his escape, the Texas Theater.

Escape is not what Oswald's coconspirators have in mind. Should he be found dead, the authorities will surmise that Castro's agents recruited him, used him, and then killed him. Alive, he might say he was recruited and used by the other side. Wayne Elko lurks in the theater, a silenced pistol at the ready. But he doesn't know that the police are after Oswald for the Tippit shooting. He waits a moment too long. The cops swarm over Oswald before Elko can get off his shot.

Enter Jack Ruby. Enraged that this nothing, this zero in a T-shirt—

serious men dressed in 1963—could shoot his beloved president and besmirch his adopted town, Ruby decides a little Texas vigilantism is in order. He's egged on by Jack Karlinsky, a Syndicate fixer who's been in touch with Carmine Latta, a Louisiana crime boss. Latta, who has his own reasons for wanting Kennedy dead, has been secretly funding Mackey's operation via David Ferrie and Guy Banister. Ruby is a familiar figure at police headquarters. He has access. He also has debts. He's in deep with the IRS. Karlinsky assures Ruby his financial problems will disappear should Oswald be taken off the calendar. The next day Ruby does just that.

The Logic of KISS

Readers unfamiliar with the assassination literature may find this synopsis suspiciously complex. Rogue agents betrayed by renegade agents, mobsters and their go-betweens . . . what's with all these exotic characters? Compared with other scenarios, however, *Libra* is a model of circumspection. Assassination theories fall along a continuum. One end is anchored by the Warren/Posner Oswald and the other by Oliver Stone's *JFK*, a movie DeLillo dismisses as "Disneyland for paranoids." (Plans to turn *Libra* into a movie, with a script by Alexandra Seros, are still in the works.)[6] Between the lone malcontent of the Warren Report and Stone's Grand Unified Theory lies a range of possibilities, everything from lowercase conspiracies to complicated uppercase varieties. The champions of Conspiracy would have us believe that several assassins killed Kennedy in a crossfire, that high government officials were involved in both the murder and the cover-up, and that they ordered the doctoring of evidence, including the Zapruder film, to frame Oswald.

DeLillo's take is anti-Conspiracy. "I don't think there was any orchestrated attempt by established offices in any intelligence agency," he says flatly. "I purposely chose the most obvious possibility—that the assassination was engineered by anti-Castro elements—simply as a way of being faithful to what we know of history."[7] DeLillo also nods toward historical likelihood by having his conspirators operate in accordance with KISS, that most fundamental of military maxims. Keep It Simple, Stupid. Complex plans fall apart in action. "I respect your methods," Banister says to T-Jay. "You want a unit that's small, tight and mobile. . . . Two or three men to do serious things." T-Jay not only changes the objective of Everett's and Parmenter's plot, he simplifies its tactics, cuts people out, reduces the chances of screwup and betrayal. If *Libra* is Warren Report revisionism in a fictional guise, it is nonetheless minimalist revisionism constrained by the author's respect for evidence and plausibility.

As someone who is skeptical of both the single-bullet theory and the Conspiracy schools, I found DeLillo's approach deeply satisfying. Conspiracies involving high government officials—Teapot Dome, Watergate, Iran-Contra—have a way of getting out. A top-down Conspiracy, with squads of shooters and underlings altering the president's bullet-riddled corpse, faking evidence, and rubbing out inconvenient witnesses, would not have survived scrutiny. Too many players, as the plotters would surely have recognized. But DeLillo serves up a modest little conspiracy, "a rambling affair that succeeded in the short term due mainly to chance." *Libra*'s plot, in the double sense of the word, makes it easy to suspend disbelief. It also meshes perfectly with the book's ambience and hyperrealistic style. DeLillo's dialogue, honed by his reading of Warren Commission transcripts, and his just-right details—Oswald's humiliating daily routine in the Marine brig, the contents of Ruby's slum of a car—slip us into the American underbelly, a world of pill-poppers and strippers and sad cases living out their precarious lives in rented rooms. A realistic, lowlife milieu demands a realistic, low-key conspiracy. Injecting Conspiracy into such a setting would have been, to put it mildly, dissonant.

One detail nags. Why would someone who had hewed so closely to the Warren Report have Oswald miss his last shot? Both the Warren Commission and the subsequent House Select Committee on Assassinations (1977–1979) concluded that the fatal shot entered the rear of Kennedy's head and blasted out the top right. Autopsy photographs (almost universally dismissed as fake by Conspiracy theorists)[8] show what appears to be an entry wound in the scalp, near Kennedy's cowlick. DeLillo does not account for it. Having Oswald miss necessarily raises the specter of a manipulated autopsy and doctored photographs. Yet, DeLillo doesn't think the famous and equally controversial backyard photograph of Oswald, Mannlicher-Carcano in hand, is fake. He even asked Viking to put it on *Libra*'s cover.[9]

Had Oswald hit the back of Kennedy's head with his third shot, the problem would not have presented itself. In fact, some crossfire theorists have argued that the motion of Kennedy's head in the Zapruder film shows a near-simultaneous front-and-back hit. Raymo and Oswald, one-two, finis JFK. DeLillo would still have had the curb ricochet to account for, but that might have been caused by all or part of Oswald's bullet deflecting through Kennedy's blasted-open skull. It's simpler, anyway, than leaving the question of the medical evidence dangling.

The Pattern in Things

DeLillo has never claimed that *Libra* is an argument for what really happened, only an exploration of one plausible variation.[10] There's no point getting too preoccupied with "the endless fact-rubble of the investigation," as the CIA historian Nicholas Branch, another DeLillo invention, puts it. Still, I found myself thinking hard about the significance of Oswald's last miss. It compels reflection, and not simply because of the forensic puzzle. I now believe that, whatever DeLillo lost in historical credibility by having Oswald miss, he gained in thematic coherence. The third shot, in its own way, exemplifies the art-actuality tension at the heart of historical fiction.

When historians answer the how and why questions of human behavior, their explanations generally fall into one of two camps. We call these, if you'll excuse a bit of philosophical jargon, the nomothetic and idiographic. Nomothetic writers explain things in lawlike terms, identifying the forces that govern human affairs and incorporating them into their explanation sketches. A student of revolution, for example, might appeal to the axiom that, when the price of bread rises, discontent rises with it. Nomothetic historians subordinate the individual to powerful physical, biological, economic, social, and psychological forces that they believe are the keys to understanding the human past.

Idiographic historians try to understand unique and nonrecurring events by focusing on particular historical actors and empathically reconstructing the choices confronting them at a given moment in time. Their subjects operate under various constraints and pressures. But they—some of them, anyway—are able to use reason to evaluate possible responses and will to carry through. It is these free individual decisions, some good and some bad, that propel history. The slaves were freed, not because Northern industrialism was destined to triumph over Southern slavery through some abstract dialectical process, but because Lincoln understood their emancipation to be both morally correct and strategically advantageous. Idiographic history permits, though it does not require, heroic actions. Nomothetic history, being deterministic, precludes them.

As it is with historians, so it is with artists. Among filmmakers, for example, Steven Spielberg and George Lucas clearly fall into the idiographic camp. Films like *Schindler's List* or *Star Wars* exude heroism. Luke uses the force, it doesn't use him. Orson Welles's *Citizen Kane* and Roman Polanski's *Chinatown*, in which individuals are mastered by inner and outer forces, are at the opposite, nomothetic pole of cinematic metaphysics. American literature arrays itself in like fashion, from Ben Franklin's determinedly cheerful and ultrarationalist *Autobiography* to the varieties of naturalism on display in the works of Frank Norris, Jack London, and Theodore Dreiser. It is even possible to name writers who switched sides during their careers. Mark Twain's *Adventures of Tom Sawyer* (1876), a historical novel set in an idyllic antebellum past, is full of individual initiative and heroic rescues. Yet *Pudd'nhead Wilson* (1894), published eighteen years later, is one of the most grimly deterministic historical novels in American fiction.

DeLillo is a writer who began with a nomothetic (or, perhaps, considering the occult flavoring, pseudo-nomothetic) approach. He stuck to it, refining it in his breakthrough work of the 1980s, and kept it prominently on display in *Mao II* (1991) and *Underworld* (1997). His characters are caught, not in the linear, cause-and-effect determinism of classical naturalism, but a looping pattern of interconnected systems.[11] They try, not always successfully, to name those systems, understand them, escape them, or just survive them from day to day. Jack Gladney, the historian-everyman of *White Noise* (1985), wakes up in the small hours, paralyzed by his own racking fears, lacking even the will and strength to get out of bed. Eventually, he has to cope with a real nightmare, an "airborne toxic event" packing a dozen poisons, moving across the land "like some death ship in a Norse legend." In *Mao II* and *Underworld*, the characters continually voice their anxieties, their sense of subjection to something that is big, sinister, Out There. "The future belongs to crowds," we're told in *Mao II*, a novel in which the archindividualist winds up dead. "What do we know?" a character asks in *Underworld*. "That everything's connected," answers another. DeLillo's prose sometimes takes on an overtly sociological character. "Capital burns off the nuance in a culture," he observes in the epilogue to *Underworld*. That's a sentence Max Weber might have written on a good day.

In *Libra*, Oswald becomes Lee Oswald, loser, through an unhappy combination of inborn traits and social circumstances. Like almost everyone who has studied him, DeLillo was struck by the disparity between Oswald's taped debates on Cuba—articulate performances by someone of obvious intelligence—and his childlike writing and difficulty in reading.[12] Dyslexia frustrates Oswald, holds him back from scholastic accomplishment and upward movement into a middle-class career. A successful paper-pusher would not have shot at the president. The boy is poor and fatherless in the bargain. His natural father died before his birth. In 1945 Marguerite married an older man, an engineer named Edwin Ekdahl, but they divorced acrimoniously in 1948. From that point on, the "basic Oswald memory" was sharing a series of cramped spaces with his mother.

Oswald fantasizes a way out of his miserable, claustrophobic existence. He will become a revolutionary like Lenin or Trotsky, fellow down-and-outers who managed to merge their lives with history, clambering aboard the locomotive of Progress. He will join a Communist cell, carrying out daring missions that require intelligence and stealth. He fails as badly in the secret world as in the conventional. He defects to the Soviet Union, imagining that he is carrying valuable information about the U-2 spy plane. Alek Kirilenko, the KGB officer in charge of his case, can't decide whether he's dealing with a false defector or a garden-variety shitbird. The test results are in, he muses, and only Oswald's urine got a passing grade.

Disillusioned, Oswald leaves the Soviet Union with his wife, Marina, and their infant daughter. Back in the States, it's more hand-to-mouth and cheap rooms. Marina, pregnant again, is tantalized by the *Amerikanski* consumers' paradise. Oswald's needs are deeper, psychological. He longs for a clear sense of role, a chance to make a move one time and not be disappointed. He's disappointed anyway. He takes a shot at Walker, about one hundred feet away in a brightly lit room, and misses, the bullet deflected by the window frame.

Oswald becomes Lee Harvey Oswald—fame and infamy being equally likely to earn a middle name in American-history textbooks—by a fluke. Oswald's sole value, Ferrie tells him, is that he matches a cardboard cutout the conspirators have been shaping all along. "You're a quirk of history. You're a coincidence. They devise a plan, you fit it perfectly. They lose you, here you are. There's a pattern in things." And this, precisely, is the role Oswald plays in the assassination. He does *not* kill the president. Foul-up to the end, he misses the fatal shot official history assigns to him. "Maggie's drawers," Oswald thinks as he moves back from the window. It's the derisive nickname for the red flag waved from the pit when a shooter misses the target completely. Had Oswald hit Kennedy's head, he might at least have had the satisfaction of knowing that he, too, had mortally wounded the president. DeLillo won't allow him that. He cannot be Oswald the giant-killer, at least not in this relentlessly antiheroic book. The notoriety of assumed guilt is all he has in the last hours of his life. He remains a pawn, sacrificed in a game someone else is playing.

Ruby, the book's other would-be hero, is in a similar situation. The Syndicate doesn't need him, they need someone *like* him, an excitable character with a gun and access. He doesn't so much decide to kill Oswald as get talked into it by Karlinsky, who exploits both his emotions and his debts. Ruby's in thrall like everyone else. Another zero in the system. He just happens to get too close to miss.

What then does kill Kennedy? In the end, it's a defect in the espionage system itself, its catastrophic lack of a braking mechanism. DeLillo describes, at length, the layered nature of the CIA's anti-Castro operations. There are four separate groups to insure security and maintain plausible deniability. Wouldn't want the president to know what the wet boys are doing. Everett's miniplot mirrors, as a matter of professional habit, this compartmentalization. He and Parmenter remain distant from Mackey's operations team. But separation diminishes their control. Everett has his suspicions, but he can't be certain of Mackey's intentions or whereabouts. He can't detect the betrayal, can't intervene, can't stop the tendency—a good nomothetic word—of the plot to move toward death. Raymo sights through his scope, fires. He does not miss.

Notes

1. Unless otherwise indicated, page references are to Don DeLillo, *Libra* (New York: Viking, 1988). Herbert Mitgang, "Reanimating Oswald, Ruby et al. in a Novel on the Assassination," *New York Times*, July 19, 1988, C20; William Goldstein, "Don DeLillo," *Publishers Weekly* 234 (August 19, 1988): 56, emphasis in original.

2. *Report of the Warren Commission on the Assassination of President Kennedy* (New York: McGraw Hill, 1964); Gerald Posner, *Case Closed: Lee Harvey Oswald and the Assassination of JFK* (New York: Random House, 1993).

3. Interview with Adam Begley, "Don DeLillo: The Art of Fiction CXXXV," *Paris Review* 35 (Fall 1993): 301.

4. A listing of all the works critical of the Warren Report is not possible here. Readers who wish to pursue the matter might begin with Stewart Galanor's *Cover-Up* (New York: Kestrel Books, 1998). This overview, while it reaches conclusions opposite those of *Case Closed*, shares two of its virtues: clear, nontechnical language and excellent illustrations. I want to thank my brother, Chris Courtwright, for calling this and other sources to my attention.

5. Don DeLillo, "American Blood," *Rolling Stone* December 8, 1983, pp. 21–28, 74. The quotation is from Goldstein, 20. Lack of preconceptions or conviction of conspiracy when beginning research: Elizabeth Mehren, "DeLillo's Novel Look at Oswald: Rescuing History from Confusion," *Los Angeles Times*, August 12, 1998, part 5, p. 2. DeLillo reiterates his suspicion that the fatal shot came from the front through the words of a character viewing the Zapruder film in *Underworld:* "And oh shit, oh god it came from the front, didn't it?" (part 3, chap. 5).

6. Brigitte Desalm interview, *http://baas.berkeley.edu/~gardner/desalm_interview.html,* accessed February 11, 1999 ("Disneyland"); personal communication from Seros, May 11, 1999. Stone, I might add, is a hero in the assassination research community. Researchers, who tend to share Stone's iconoclastic politics, credit *JFK* with forcing a reluctant government to release classified assassination records. DeLillo inspires more ambivalence, everything from qualified admiration to irritation.

7. Kim Heron, "Haunted by His Book," *New York Times Book Review*, July 24, 1988, p. 23.

8. Numerous eyewitnesses, including the Parkland doctors who went through the motions of trying to save Kennedy's life, described a very large *exit* wound in the back of his head, consistent with a shot from the front. The Bethesda autopsists originally described an entry wound, but located it much lower down, closer to the base of the skull. Something is therefore wrong either with the testimony or the photographs. Conspiracists: believe the testimony. Warren defenders: the testimony was mistaken.

9. Anthony DeCurtis, "An Outsider in This Society: An Interview with Don DeLillo," in *Introducing Don DeLillo*, Frank Lentricchia, ed. (Durham: Duke University Press, 1991), 56. Interestingly, Posner chose the identical shot for the spine of his magnum opus. In both cases, the photograph serves as an anti-Conspiracy flag.

10. DeCurtis, 57.

11. Paul Civello, *American Literary Naturalism and Its Twentieth-Century Transformations: Frank Norris, Ernest Hemingway, Don DeLillo* (Athens: University of Georgia Press, 1994), 143.

12. Ibid., 53.

ঞ

The Fictional Man

Don DeLillo

Lee Oswald was a man who fell out of history and into fiction. There he is, just turned twenty-four, living in a shabby rooming house apart from his wife and children, stuck in another dead-end job, being watched by the FBI, his desperate plans to go to Cuba, return to Russia, do something purposeful, be someone real—all reduced to drifting mist.

Things change one day.

His dreams and fantasies, the sway of his routine run-on thoughts, the mazes of consciousness, the secret messages he detects in movies on TV—these are the novelist's own drifting mist, the hidden life he finds in his character. But the power of coincidence is not so hidden. One day, Oswald learns that the president is coming to Dallas, his city, and will ride in a motorcade past the School Book Depository, the building where he works. The president's limousine will pass the building at precisely the time he is most likely to be alone on the sixth floor.

This was fiction and he was in it. So was I. But I wanted to find the real Oswald, not create some higher visionary myth. And I thought it was important to allow the enormous documentation of the case to seep into the texture of the novel. The dialogue is flat, the prose pretty simple, and there are times when biographical material is rendered directly. Because the Warren Report is crucial to most meditations on the case, it becomes the book's background radiation, the echo of central events.

But there are times when small inconsistencies and obscure motivations drive a character's actions. This is not normally accounted for in documentary material. I thought Oswald would fire prematurely and he does this in the novel, shooting through leaf cover, even though a shot at this point, interestingly, tends to challenge the Warren Report and at the same time corroborate the official finding of a lone gunman. Maybe I have out-Warrened Warren here. This is simply because the Oswald in my mind had to act impatiently. He could not get things right. This is why he misses the third shot. Not because the ballistics evidence is so deeply shaded by endless conflicts of interpretation and ideology that one might justify any number of deductions concerning gunshot patterns or types of wounds. And certainly not because I felt it would be otherwise awkward to account for the curbside bullet mark found in Dealey Plaza.

He misses because he is Oswald. As Professor Courtwright points out in his clear-eyed and knowledgeable essay, the antihero can't even be a hero to himself. Oswald has to know he has not killed the president. Another failure. It is the overwhelming theme of his life.

In a way, *Libra* not only uses elements of history, but also becomes a novel about the opposing flow of these forces in our lives. Think of Oswald the defector, the political activist, the earnest student of history. I think in the end he became a fictional character in his own life. He slipped out of history's skin. Long before a writer would imagine him as a figure in a novel, Oswald began to suspend reality and to pursue the dream release that fiction represents—a chance to collapse history and shape another kind of truth.

In the seven months between the night he took an errant shot at General Walker and the moment he fired three times at President Kennedy, his life had unraveled to the point where he moved in a kind of third-person delirium, watching himself stand at the window with a rifle in his hands.

In the past, he'd acted out of political conviction, determined to be part of the struggles that remake the world. There was no such conviction he might apply to the figure of the president. He seemed to admire Kennedy.

Oswald would not have walked two blocks to shoot at the president. But the president came to him.

PART II

The West

The Aztec World of
Gary Jennings

Michael E. Smith

T he contradictions of Aztec culture both puzzle and fascinate
modern readers. The Aztecs practiced a religion based upon
warfare, human sacrifice, and other violent and bloody rituals, but they also created exquisite works of art and beautiful lyric poetry
that still speaks to us today. These contrasts have led to a wide variety of
interpretations of Aztec culture. In the late 1970s, two anthropologists
claimed that cannibalism due to dietary protein deficiency was the engine
that drove the expansion of the Aztec empire. Aztec armies supposedly
conquered distant peoples in order to procure increasing numbers of victims for the sacrificial altar. Once their hearts were torn out in ritual sacrifice, the bodies were distributed to the hungry masses to satisfy their
need for protein. This theory received considerable play in the media before scholars disproved it by showing that the Aztec diet was perfectly ad-
equate in protein without the need for human flesh. In the late 1990s,
New Age aficionados created a very different depiction of Aztec culture.
The Aztecs were peaceful sun worshipers who spent their time in intellectual and artistic pursuits, particularly rituals that used crystals and
musical instruments. Human sacrifice—according to the New Age
view—was a myth invented by the invading Spaniards to justify their conquest and destruction of Aztec culture.

The Aztec reality, of course, is somewhere between cannibalistic warriors and New Age crystal-gazers. The juxtaposition of violent and aesthetic elements in Aztec culture provides fertile ground for fiction. The
novelist writing about the Aztecs has far greater creative latitude than
novelists writing about more recent and more familiar settings. For one
thing, the available documents on Aztec culture are quite limited in quan-
tity and quality. Hernando Cortés and a few members of his army of 1519
wrote descriptions of the conquest of Mexico; Spanish friars and the descendants of Aztec nobles recorded a number of detailed accounts of particular customs and institutions; Spanish legal proceedings provide some
useful observations; and the picture-writing of the Aztecs themselves illuminates certain aspects of religion and society. Archaeological fieldwork
is only beginning to furnish information about Aztec life and customs. In
short, we know considerably less about central Mexico on the eve of the
Spanish conquest than we know about the United States at any stage of
our past. Since most modern readers have little knowledge of Aztec culture or history, there is great opportunity for invention and fantasy in fiction concerning their society. A novelist can make up all sorts of
nonsense, and most readers will not know the difference. Furthermore,
scholars will have difficulty proving the novelist wrong.

There is certainly ample room for invention in Gary Jennings's monumental 1980 novel, *Aztec*. With over one thousand pages, this sprawling
account follows an Aztec scribe named Mixtli as he travels over much of
what is now Mexico and Guatemala, virtually the entire known world of
the Aztecs. The novel is told in Mixtli's voice. The son of a quarryman
from Xaltocan, a town in the Valley of Mexico, Mixtli shows great promise in school. He is given the opportunity for further education in the
court of King Nezahualpilli of Texcoco, the intellectual and artistic center and one of the two capitals of the Aztec empire. Mixtli becomes a pro-
ficient scribe, gains the goodwill of Nezahualpilli, and undertakes
military duty in the Texcoco army. He later moves across the lake to serve
in the imperial court of Tenochtitlan, the political and military capital of
the empire and the largest pre-Spanish city of the New World.

Mixtli next becomes a merchant, one of the renowned *pochteca*. These
guild-organized professional traders regularly went out on long expedi-
tions, and Mixtli journeys throughout the Aztec empire and beyond its

borders into the unconquered tropical jungles of the Maya peoples. His trading is astute, and he ends up a wealthy man. Later in life, Mixtli serves as a diplomat for the emperor, which brings him to the court of the enemy Tarascan empire of western Mexico. Mixtli also sets out on several voyages of solitary wandering in which he explores northern and western Mexico, even finding Aztlan, the perhaps mythical northern homeland of the Aztec peoples (scholars have searched for Aztlan without success for decades). Mixtli then participates in the major events of the Spanish conquest. His ability with languages, gained in his many travels, enables him to be the first Aztec to learn Spanish. He later dictates his life story to Bishop Zummáraga, who had been instructed by the emperor Carlos V to interview a typical Aztec about his life story. The texts of these interviews form the narrative of the novel. Zummáraga then has Mixtli burned at the stake as a heretic. His fiery death is a fitting end to a novel full of violence, blood and gore, and frequent sex.

How accurate is this portrayal of Aztec culture? I first tried to read *Aztec* in graduate school, soon after it was published. I was impressed by Jennings's knowledge of the major historical sources on Aztec society, although he refrains from mentioning or citing any sources. He builds a foundation upon known facts, and then adds plausible details of his own to flesh out what the sources don't tell us. Before I had delved halfway through the novel, I had begun to confuse the two types of information. I was lecturing to a class of undergraduates about Aztec religion and was about to state that commoners were afraid of priests, when I realized I didn't know whether that idea was from the historical sources or whether it was Jennings's invention. To avoid confusing myself further, I stopped reading the book.

Jennings's treatment of Aztec priests is a good example of his methods. We know from early Spanish descriptions that Aztec priests were always bloody, dirty, and smelly—they pierced their ears and other body parts for ritual bleeding, and they never bathed. The sources say that their hair was matted with blood, and one way to recognize a priest in Aztec pictorial books is by the red bloody marks below their ears. Jennings puts it like this: "He was surrounded by a horde of priests who, with their filthy black garments, their dirt-encrusted black faces, and their blood-matted long hair, made a somber contrast to [king] Axayacatl's sartorial flamboy-

ance" (p. 62). We also know that priests sometimes chose local commoners—both adults and infants—for sacrificial victims, but the sources do
not provide much information on just how they selected the victims. It
makes perfect sense that people would have feared and avoided priests,
but that interpretation has little support in the sources.

Another example of this method concerns the death of the Aztec emperor Motecuhzoma. We know the following facts. Cortés was holding
Motecuhzoma captive in a palace, and many Aztecs were angry with their
king for cooperating with the Spaniards. A dangerous mob threatened to
overrun the building, and Cortés brought the emperor out on a balcony
to try and quiet the crowd. People threw stones at Motecuhzoma, and
shortly after that he was found dead. Scholars do not know whether he
was killed by his own people or by the Spaniards. In *Aztec*, Motecuhzoma
is knocked unconscious by a rock, and Cortés instructs Mixtli (who is at
the heart of the action, as usual) to take the king inside and put him at
ease. The protagonist sets Motecuhzoma down and kills him with a knife.
Again, Jennings has given a plausible interpretation to an event whose details will never be known for sure.

Twenty years later, after publishing four books and numerous scholarly articles on the Aztecs, I felt secure enough in my knowledge of the
sources to read the whole novel, and I enjoyed it thoroughly. My more extensive and confident knowledge of the historical descriptions of Aztec
society allowed me to appreciate the extent to which Jennings's Aztec
world is based upon a solid empirical foundation. As one of my students
put it, he manages to incorporate almost every interesting tidbit of
knowledge from the sources into the story. Jennings even includes one of
my favorite pieces of Aztec trivia. "My mother shifted her grip so that one
of her hands was free, and with it she flung into the fire a number of dried
red chilis. When they were crackling and sending up a dense yellow
smoke, my Tene [mother] took me again by the ankles and suspended me
head down in those acrid fumes. I leave the next little while to your imagination, but I think I nearly perished" (p. 28). This punishment for mis-
behaving children appears in a painting in the Codex Mendoza[1] with the
accompanying text: "They punished the eleven-year-old boy or girl who
disregarded verbal correction by making them inhale chili smoke, which
was a serious and even cruel torment." Jennings, however, makes the

punishment vivid with his first-person account. Examples like this, taken from the documentary sources, are scattered throughout *Aztec*.

Gary Jennings's depiction of Aztec society through Mixtli's eyes is reasonably accurate. The sharp gulf between nobles and commoners in the novel reflects our knowledge from the sources. Nobles owned most of the land and controlled the government. Commoners owed the nobility labor service and tribute in goods. Membership in the nobility was strictly hereditary, and most commoners could never hope to become a noble, or even to spend time in the presence of nobles. There were two routes of social advancement, however—commerce and the military— and Mixtli was able to follow them both. Merchants, although nominally commoners, could become wealthier than many nobles, although they had to hide their wealth lest the nobles take offense and confiscate their property and possessions. All Aztec men had to perform military service, and success on the battlefield brought social advancement. Early in the Aztec empire, a category of honorary noble was created to reward the most successful and talented commoners. Mixtli reached this level, and thus his successes—as a scribe, a merchant, and a soldier—gave him access to the highest circles of the Aztec nobility. Jennings is thereby able to give the reader access to all levels of society, from slaves and prostitutes to nobles and kings, through the eyes of a single protagonist. The only difficulty here is that the honorary noble rank was abolished by Motecuhzoma, a development not mentioned in the novel.

As in any historical novel, Jennings makes a number of minor errors. For example, his Aztec priests use Spanish, Christian-style incense burners that swing from ropes instead of the long-handled "frying-pan style" actually used (p. 64; a good drawing of an Aztec priest with such a censer is shown in the Codex Mendoza); Aztec priests used chert knives, not obsidian knives, to cut open the chests of sacrificial victims (p. 64); the Tarascans did develop the technology to produce bronze, but they did not use it for weapons as suggested in the novel (p. 527); and his description of the famed *chinampa* agricultural fields is incorrect in several ways (p. 119).

Most of the errors are of minor importance. It is almost impossible to avoid such glitches when presenting complex material to a general audience, and I must admit to perpetuating some errors of this kind myself.

An article on my excavations of Aztec villages in the magazine *Scientific American*[2] was illustrated with attractive paintings that reconstructed scenes of a market, a household, and an agricultural field, done by an artist on the magazine's staff. The editing and production were done under a tight deadline while I was in Mexico doing fieldwork, and I was only able to give brief comments on the first version of the paintings. I thought that the resulting art was very good, with only a few small errors. Nevertheless, some of my colleagues took great glee in compiling a long list of problems with the paintings.

The most significant errors or distortions in *Aztec* are Jennings's treatment of writing and sex. The Aztec writing system was one of five different scripts known from ancient Mesoamerica. Unlike Maya writing, which was a complete script capable of recording any sentence that could be spoken in the Maya language, Aztec writing was a much more limited, special-purpose collection of glyphs. Only a few kinds of information were recorded in Aztec pictorial books, including histories of ruling dynasties, place names, tribute payments, and esoteric religious knowledge of the calendar, rituals, and gods. In Jennings's Aztec world, scribes write long messages to one another, a practice that just wasn't possible with Aztec writing. I suspect that the author knew better, yet deliberately portrayed writing in this way to help advance the plot.

A similar motivation must account for the treatment of sex in the novel, which is frequent, explicit, inventive, and almost certainly out of line with actual Aztec practices. When I asked a colleague (not an Aztec specialist) if she had read *Aztec*, she said, "I think the novel circulated among our field crew in the Peruvian Andes years ago—isn't that the book where there is a sex scene every thirty pages?" We actually know a fair amount about the Aztecs' views of sex and morality, thanks to the efforts of the Spanish friars to convert people to Christianity. Most Aztecs were far more circumspect about sex than the characters in the book, and moderation in sex and other affairs was an important and fundamental Aztec virtue.[3] Much of the sexual behavior in the novel, however, is bizarre. There is a Mexica princess who kills a series of adulterous lovers, boils their bodies to free the bones, and then has artists use the skeletons as frameworks for life-size ceramic models of her lovers. In Tarascan territory, Mixtli participates in a strange practice in which a group of specially trained small children come into his bed to give him sexual pleasure. Descriptions of incest in the novel are tame in comparison.

The treatment of sex in Jennings's sequel, *Aztec Autumn*, suggests that he realized the extent to which he distorted sexual attitudes and behavior in the earlier novel. Sex scenes are far less frequent in the sequel, and at one point the protagonist of that book, Tenamixtli, even says, "But my Azteca people, and the Mexica, and most others, always had been almost as prudish as Christians in regard to sex" (p. 154). One further error—my pet peeve—should be mentioned. Jennings employs an idiosyncratic spelling scheme for names and words in Nahuatl (the Aztec language), with abundant use of accents incorrectly applied. Current conventions for spelling Nahuatl terms produce words that look sufficiently exotic in English, and I found the orthography distracting and just plain wrong.

∂ℓ℘

ONE ATTRACTION OF fiction as a way to present the historical past is that authors need not limit themselves to the available sources. This does not mean that authors of historical fiction are free to make up anything they please, but rather that they can go beyond the empirical historical record both to flesh out the past and to suggest new ideas and interpretations that might not occur to the cautious, data-bound scholar. Scholars must also go beyond the empirical record of their sources to supply context and meaning for the facts of history. When historians stick too closely to their sources, they may produce incomplete, biased, or even erroneous accounts of the past.

The privileges and obligations of the Aztec nobility furnish a good example. The standard Spanish-language sources all agree that nobles did not pay tribute before the Spanish conquest, and most modern textbooks echo this, saying something to the effect that a major difference between commoners and nobles was that the former paid tribute, and the latter did not (*Aztec* agrees with the textbooks, but Jennings does not belabor this point). But this notion, based on self-serving lies by surviving Aztec nobles in the early Spanish period, is simply wrong. In setting up their own system of tribute and labor obligations, the Spaniards used Aztec practices as a model. When they asked Aztec nobles about their prior tribute practices, the nobles replied that only commoners had paid tribute. One can just see these colonial-period Aztec nobles winking and grinning at each other as the Spaniards went along with their lie and exempted them from tribute requirements. But, in recent years, scholars studying local administrative records written in Nahuatl have found clear evidence that all nobles, except for the emperor Motecuhzoma, paid tribute to their local king, to the emperor, or to both.[4] The Spanish administrators may or may not have been gullible—they needed the cooperation of the Aztec nobility to govern their new imperial provinces and could easily have overlooked this deception—but modern scholars were certainly gullible in accepting an interpretation that didn't make sense even though it was described in the colonial documents.

This refusal to be limited by the available sources led Gary Jennings to propose an economic practice that scholars didn't find evidence for until after publication of the novel in 1980. The Aztec economy was the most highly commercialized economy of any ancient culture in the New World. Scores of *pochteca* and other merchants traveled throughout Mexico and Guatemala, many of them making significant personal fortunes (just as Mixtli does in *Aztec*). Marketplaces thrived in every town and city, and several forms of currency were in common use. These features are described accurately and vividly in the novel. Although the documentary record is full of references to markets, merchants, and money within the Aztec empire, these features are not mentioned when the sources talk about relations between the Aztecs and the Tarascans. The Tarascan king ruled a powerful empire just to the west of the Aztecs, and the two empires fought to a standstill in the 1480s. The border was then sealed off by a series of fortresses on each side, and the historical sources focus on the continuous animosity and battles between these two polities.

From the documentary sources, one would not think that the Aztecs and Tarascans traded with one another. Yet, in *Aztec*, there is active commercial exchange between these hostile kingdoms. At one point, Mixtli is sent by the Aztec emperor on a mission to the Tarascan court. He notes that the Tarascans, although enemies of the Aztecs, "allow our travelers and merchants unhindered passage across their country. They engage freely in trade with us" (p. 527). This is a reasonable idea given the importance of commerce in both Aztec and Tarascan society, but scholars, limiting themselves to the available sources, perhaps did not pay sufficient attention to the heavily biased and sometimes incorrect Aztec portrayal of their relations with the Tarascans.

Confirmation of Jennings's notion of Aztec-Tarascan trade came from archaeological fieldwork in the 1980s and 1990s. By applying sophisticated methods of chemical analysis to artifacts, archaeologists identified two Tarascan products present in significant quantities at Aztec sites. The commoners at these communities owned tools of obsidian (volcanic glass that produces an extremely sharp edge when flaked) from many different regions, including Tarascan territory. They also had sewing needles and other objects made of bronze, whose copper can be traced to Tarascan mines.[5] Jennings's account of Aztec-Tarascan trade in 1980 was prescient. Although the interpretations of a novelist are no substitute for empirical evidence, he deserves credit for showing that this idea was reasonable when most scholars had not even entertained it. For scholars, the lesson is that it is dangerous to limit one's consideration to a single kind of evidence, whether that be Spanish-language documents at the expense of Nahuatl-language documents, or written sources at the expense of archaeology.

We have already seen two of the contributions that historical fiction can make to advance the study of the past. Authors of novels can flesh out the details of people's behavior and daily life by building upon a foundation of historical facts, and they can suggest plausible ideas (such as Aztec-Tarascan trade) that might not occur to scholars who are too bound to their sources. But perhaps the biggest contribution of good historical fiction to the study of the past is its role in communicating the facts and processes of history to a wide audience. The Aztec world constructed by Gary Jennings is remarkably accurate and true to what we know, and his biggest distortions are easily recognizable as novelistic devices. Jennings's book has reached millions of readers; the books that my scholarly colleagues and I have written have not.

The ability of fiction to communicate historical information is not limited to historical novels and films. I have employed this device in my textbook, *The Aztecs*,[6] in a key chapter, and I have noted a growing popularity of fictional vignettes in books by archaeologists written for students or a general audience. To me, some of the most fascinating features of

Aztec society are the cities, which ranged from the huge cosmopolitan metropolis of Tenochtitlan (now buried under Mexico City) to small regional capitals. When I started writing *The Aztecs*, I was eager to write about Aztec cities for a more general audience, since I had done fieldwork and historical research on the subject. I wrote descriptions of two cities—Tenochtitlan and a smaller city—and was disappointed to find that these passages were boring. I needed to make them more vivid, to portray the cities as they would have appeared to Aztec people. My first revision was terrible prose—highly artificial and awkward descriptions of the form "if the reader could have visited an Aztec city, he/she would have seen such-and-such."

At that point, I took the plunge and invented fictional visitors to the two cities. My descriptions took the form of their reactions to the sights and activity around them as they entered the cities. I gave these visitors some individuality and personality (a merchant leading an expedition visits the smaller city, and a young provincial noble visits Tenochtitlan for the first time), and my descriptions improved remarkably. Nevertheless, I was worried and insecure about using fiction in a scholarly, nonfiction account. Would my colleagues think that I had sold out? Would readers find it awkward or confusing to have two small fictional vignettes in the middle of a fairly straightforward historical/archaeological account? I had a group of undergraduates read drafts of my chapters for feedback, and they took the fictional passages in stride, suggesting that my characters needed names. The transitions between scholarly narrative and fictionalized descriptions do not seem to trouble students at all. I can't decide whether this reflects positively or negatively on today's undergraduates.

I survived my brush with fiction with my scientific and scholarly credentials intact, gaining a greater appreciation for the power of fiction to communicate the past to a wider audience. I must admit that I got excited while working on those passages and entertained brief delusions of writing a novel about the Aztecs. But then we already have *Aztec*. I am disappointed that Jennings did not include a section on his use of sources and the origin of some of his information. As a scholar I always look for that information in historical novels, and I think it helps the general reader as well. I recently received an e-mail message from someone who had just finished reading *Aztec* and wanted to know whether it was accurate or not

(I assured him that the book is quite accurate about most things). Maybe Gary Jennings didn't care whether readers think his Aztec world is true to life or not; maybe he was only interested in telling a good story. But I for one would like readers to know how accurate the book is, and I suspect that he would have liked them to know as well.

Notes

1. Frances F. Berdan and Patricia R. Anawalt, eds., *The Codex Mendoza*, 4 vols. (Berkeley: University of California Press, 1992) f. 59v.

2. Michael E. Smith, "Life in the Provinces of the Aztec Empire," *Scientific American* 277(3): 56–63.

3. Louise Burkhart, *The Slippery Earth: Nahua-Christian Moral Dialogue in Sixteenth-Century Mexico* (Tucson: University of Arizona Press, 1989).

4. James Lockhart, *The Nahuas After the Conquest: A Social and Cultural History of the Indians of Central Mexico, Sixteenth Through Eighteenth Centuries* (Stanford: Stanford University Press, 1992), 106.

5. Michael E. Smith, *The Aztecs* (Oxford: Blackwell, 1996), 96–98.

6. See Note 5.

ᘓᔕ

My Indignant Response

Gary Jennings

Gary Jennings died in 1999, before Michael Smith's piece had been completed. What follows is Jennings's initial letter to the editor of *Novel History*. The editor had sent Jennings a copy of *Past Imperfect: History According to the Movies* (1995), which served as something of a model for *Novel History*. Jennings's response is published here because it reflects his thoughts on historical writing and "accuracy" in his *Aztec*. "It may sound to you," he wrote, "as if I'm already compiling my indignant response." So be it. The letter appears nearly in its entirety.—Editor

[From Gary Jennings to Mark C. Carnes]

12 July 1997

Dear Mark—

Many thanks for the gift book. I had already purchased one, but now I have one to lend to other film buffs. I enjoyed it immensely. If I had any niggling criticism, it would have been of the book's oh-so-academic *earnestness.* I was many times inclined to murmur, "C'mon, guys, lighten up a little. We're dealing with *movies.*"

You can certainly count on my unstinting cooperation—bar any unexpected deluge of work—in the making of your *Novel History.* And in this book I would fully *expect* (not be put off by) the most earnest and painstaking dissection of the works under consideration. However, I have a few tentative caveats to impart. Mind you, these are inspired only by my own experiences at novelization with the aid of and/or versus the professional historians.

Unless the historians whom you hope to corral are of the calibre of Herodotus, Caesar, al-Idrisi, Josephus, Gibbon, et al.—that is to say, men who've actually trodden the grounds of whatever area or era they're "experts" on—I fear you'll wind up with a coterie of graybeards looking down their noses from atop the ivory towers they've built up from a foundation of sources secondary, tertiary, etc.

Well, hell, a lot of historical novelists likewise rely on those same "received wisdoms." I know one guy who has written a novel apiece on the pre-Columbian Aztecs, the Maya and the Inca, without ever once setting foot outside the college campus he inhabits in New Hampshire (or Vermont, I forget). Other historical novelists (notably Michener) depend on battalions of legmen, not necessarily reliable, to do their on-the-scene research for them.

I speak only from my own experience, and here I will comment only on my *Aztec.* Among the reams of fan mail have occasionally cropped up letters from academicians, and they all fall into one of three categories:

A) The wonderingly praiseful. "Where in the world did you dig up that fact X on page xxx? It confirms a theory I have long held, but until now have had not the least evidence for backup."

B) The peevishly critical. "How *dare* you assert so-and-so on page xxx?

Nowhere in all the literature on the subject have I encountered any mention of same!"

C) The willing-to-be-convinced. "Why the hell didn't you append a bibliography of sources?"

Shit, I was writing a novel, not a Ph.D. thesis, and novels don't generally include bibliographies. If mine had, it would have been indeed quaint, e.g.:

p. x, note x—Oral history. This told to me by a certain tribe's ancient Rememberer of History, and has purportedly been handed down from generation to generation.

p. x, note xii—Watched this particular cure effected by a Chiapas jungle witch-doctor.

I'll admit that I did a helluva lot of bookwork as well as legwork. But I relied most heavily on those historians and memoirists like Bernal Diaz and Sahagun who'd actually "been there and done that"—and very little, if at all, on later historians like Bancroft, who merely cribbed from their predecessors. I also took the trouble to learn the Nahuatl ("Aztec") language, hence was able to make some assertions based on linguistic analysis. For example, ask nineteen different professional Mexicologists where the name "Mexico" came from, and you'll get nineteen different answers; but I believe the derivation I unearthed comes closest to the truth.

I'll admit, too, that I did considerable extrapolation, but only from irrefutable starting points. One academic critic chided me for giving my Aztecs the burning-glass lens, "let alone the complex monocle that your hero uses to correct his myopia" because "nothing of the sort exists in any archaeological museum or is mentioned in any known monograph." It happens that I had *seen* the so-called Sun Stone, dating from Aztec times, owned by a remote village—it contained four separate burning-glasses, each employed in turn to kindle sacred fires at certain seasons. I felt safe in assuming that if those "primitives" could grind a double-convex lens, they could as easily grind a plano-concave "monocle."

It may sound to you, Mark, as if I'm already compiling my indignant response to whatever historian may eventually do the critical review of *Aztec*. Actually, I'm only trying to particularize toward a generalization: *viz*, that you be as selective in choosing which (non-ivory-tower) historians review the novels as you are in choosing the novels themselves.

Anyhow, yes, count on me to participate, in any way I can. And the remuneration is of no consequence. Strike it out entirely.

All best,

Gary

A Review of
Annie Dillard's *The Living*

Richard White

Historical novels like Annie Dillard's *The Living* face a double jeopardy. By claiming to be both fiction and, in some sense, history, they are judged as both. There are two trials and two different standards of evidence. In one case, historians sat as historians seeing if the novelist's imaginative re-creation of the past matched their own scholarly re-creation, at least in broad outlines. In the other, they sat as readers trying to follow the logic of a story set in a fictional world of the past. I used to think that one case was immaterial to the other, even if historians sat as jurors in both, but after reading *The Living*, I no longer think so.

Although the two readings of historical fiction are connected, I still recognize the real differences between history and fiction. History is one way of presenting the past, but it is not the only way. It operates according to a set of rules that is not necessarily applicable to a novel. Novels, like memory and myth, make claims on the past and represent it without being historical. At the simplest level, novelists are allowed to invent things, to take things out of order, to rearrange the facts. Historians can't do any of these things. Both historians and novelists are storytellers, but historians are storytellers operating under rather severe constraints.

Because *The Living* was about the past without being a history, when I read it as a historian, I accepted that Annie Dillard would sometimes get facts wrong and engage in convenient invention. "Historical novel" is an oxymoronic combination that can't be taken literally. A book can be a great novel or a riveting history, but how can it be both? Since historians aren't allowed to make things up or invent people, or even put things out of order, what could possibly be historical about a novel? But "historical novel" is common usage. What unites the two terms is an attempt to summon up a sense of the past, as people alive then understood it. Engaging in invention in pursuit of a larger truth—in this case, a truth about the past—is what fiction is supposedly all about. And if she could make things up, I could hardly complain if she rearranged other things that actually had happened. And so, in reading the book as a historian, I decided to accept a set of ground rules, a kind of formalism, for judging the relation of *The Living* to the past. I would not get upset about factual mistakes and inventions; I would judge the book by whether it created fictionally a place that I could recognize as compatible with a time and place that I knew historically. History and fiction were both acts of imaginative re-creation. I would compare the results and see if they roughly coincided. The larger issue here, the basis for my verdict, would be the big picture: Annie Dillard's success in evoking the strangeness of the past.

At the same time, of course, I read *The Living* as a novel. Annie Dillard is a wonderful writer and so I could hardly do otherwise. I became caught up in the story; I tried to understand the motives and actions of the characters. In this, of course, the details mattered because a skilled novelist communicates by insinuations and suggestions that can only take place through details. And here, very often, precisely because I am a historian, the details that were supposed to suggest and insinuate only confused me.

My problems were not, admittedly, the problems of most readers and reviewers. Mixing history and fiction creates very tricky intellectual terrain, but you would never know that from the reviews of *The Living*. This relationship between history and fiction is a difficult one, and Annie Dillard's admirers certainly do her no favors by making it seem that writing one is pretty much the same as writing the other. Reading *The Living* six years after it was published means confronting little chunks of newspaper and magazine prose labeled "Praise for *The Living*" on the back cover and the opening sheet of the paperback edition. Newspaper prose doesn't age well, and encountering these excerpts is like stepping in things soft and smelly on your way to the door. The *Los Angeles Times* thought *The Living* "an impressive piece of fiction and a riveting chunk of history." The *Washington Post* said it revealed "the precarious, wondrous, solitary, terrifying, utterly common condition of human life." The *Hartford Courant* declared, "Dillard's accomplishment in rendering the bone-cutting, heart-searing experience of these men and women of the frontier is breath-taking." Sort through this and it appears that history and fiction, the utterly common human condition and the particular heart-searing frontier experience, all have amalgamated in one gooey, adjectival mass.

The confused gushing about *The Living* indicates the odd results that historical fiction produces. Historians like to think that the past is another country, not merely a collection of poster children for the universal human condition. There is, of course, something common in being human, but history emphasizes the contingent, strange, and particular ways that humans deal with their condition. The art of history is to make the strange familiar, not to dress up the familiar in some exotic costume and drop it in a strange place. An author is not necessarily responsible for the confusion of her reviewers, but their readiness to pair opposites without any sense of contradiction is a sign of the murkiness of the genre.

The Living is the story of a set of linked families living along and near Bellingham Bay in Washington Territory during the mid- and late-nineteenth century. It would be a growing-up-with-the-country novel, except so few of the characters manage to grow up. There were plenty of ways to die in nineteenth-century Washington, and Annie Dillard pretty much covers them all. She even finds or invents some that I have never encountered.

The novel is about death, and the human problem of living in the midst of it, as much as it is about Washington Territory. Much like Tinker Creek, the setting of her earlier book, nineteenth-century Washington Territory gives Annie Dillard fecund life and ubiquitous death. Emotionally, at least, it is her home country. There are times when you think that Tinker Creek rather than the Skagit or the Nooksack runs through the heart of Annie Dillard's Washington Territory.

Annie Dillard follows families over time, and the families thin out alarmingly. People drown, die in wells, burn up in houses, fall off horses, get murdered (usually inventively), and die of diseases that no one has a clue how to cure. Annie Dillard gives death a horrible beauty and dignity. The characters' dying, or their preparing to die, or people meditating on their deaths, takes up a good proportion of the text. The prose is striking and often moving.

Those people who survive are, by and large, a busy lot. The whites make farms and boost towns and hope for the railroad to come and make them all rich. The Indians die or make their accommodation with whites, fishing, logging, and working on farms.

The Indians are one of the triumphs of the book. Indians in most historical novels these days are usually pretty noble, but they still stand for the passing order. They have a limited range. They have no place in the modern world. If Indians are particular Indians in historical novels, they are particular only in their ethnological markers: they have a specific combination of feathers, ceremonies, and traditions that identify them as Nooksack or Lummi. To Annie Dillard's great credit, there aren't really "Indians" in *The Living*; there aren't even Lummis, Nooksacks, and Haidas and Skagits. There are characters who happen to be Lummi or Skagit. There is Jim, for example, or Queen of the May. Indians in the book live in the midst of death as much as whites do, and they, too, are forced to find their particular nineteenth-century ways toward their own deaths.

Annie Dillard exaggerates the camaraderie between settlers and Lummis, but she does so to combat cultural clichés of inevitable conflict that capture far less of the complexity of nineteenth-century Washington. The relations she details between settlers and Lummis are evocative of a particular past, no matter how exceptional, and they are described subtly, almost offhandedly. She writes that the Samish the whites call Plug Ugly came for cane syrup everyday and told Ada "his troubles, which were many, and she told him hers, which were many." It is almost an aside, but it captures a combination of difference, disdain, and a common humanity in a sentence. In dealing with the Indians, Dillard has imaginatively re-created something that she had discovered in accounts of the past, but in dealing with the details of settlement, she is far more apt to go along with cultural conventions about pioneers. Her settlers are nineteenth-century settlers, but they often could just as well be in the woods of Wisconsin or Michigan. When they see a tree, they start chopping. When actual settlers—as distinct from loggers—saw cedar, hemlock, and Douglas fir, it gave them pause. Early settlers liked to look for places without trees.

The novel opens with the arrival of Ada and Rooney Fishburn and their five-year-old-son, Clare, and baby son, Glee, on Bellingham Bay. Their middle son, Charley, is already dead, run over by a wagon. They work their claim, meet their neighbors, and get along well with the surrounding Lummis. Except for the neighbors' funerals, things go smoothly enough for the Fishburns until Rooney dies digging a well in 1872.

That is the year John Ireland Sharp goes up the Skagit River with his grandfather, who has married a Skagit after his first wife died. They are looking for a possible railroad route, and on the journey, they find a young Skagit Indian who has met a gruesome death at the hand of Thompson River Indians. The Northern Pacific Railroad's decision to go to Tacoma busts the new settlement of Whatcom. Ada and Clare Fishburn move up to Goshen, and the Sharp family goes to the San Juans. There all the Sharps drown except for John Ireland, who ends up living with the Obenchains and their son Beal. Beal is big. Beal is strange. Beal is mean. Beal is best avoided.

While living in Goshen, Ada and Clare meet Eustace Honer and his wife, Minta, who is the daughter of a Maryland senator. Eustace is not long for this world, but he is productive. He establishes a successful hop farm and has three children, of whom the oldest is Hugh. (Don't worry, the younger two are not worth keeping track of; they are not long for the book or the world.) Eustace dies before his son's eyes clearing a logjam on the river. When the senator and the rest of Minta's family come West to console her, her house burns down, killing the two youngest children. Her sister, June, will eventually return to marry Clare. Senator Randall thinks his new son-in-law is something of a dolt.

Deaths are a handy way to dispatch characters so that the denouement in Whatcom doesn't get too crowded. The survivors, except for Minta and Hugh, who remain close friends with Jim and Queen of the May, gather in Whatcom, which is booming in the 1880s. John Ireland Sharp teaches school and has a beautiful wife, Pearl, who shoplifts. Clare invests

June's money in the Bellingham Bay Improvement Company and becomes a major town booster. Even Beal Obenchain ends up in the Whatcom of the 1880s. It takes Ada a little longer to get there. She has
remarried, but her new husband soon dies.

Beal Obenchain has by now gotten murderously strange. He's been
reading too much Nietzsche, and he doesn't bathe. He reads, murders a
Chinese immigrant, and decides to conduct a psychological experiment
on Clare. He tells him that he will murder him, and then stands back to
watch his man deteriorate. By now it is 1891 and the psychological
writhing, financial ups and downs, and eventual peace of Clare Fishburn
take up the last half of the book. Clare "has to learn how to die," and poor
John Ireland Sharp has to learn how to live, or rather to buy his way out
of the life he has created and despises. Both Clare and John learn how to
do what they have to do, leaving Clare alive and happy in Whatcom and
John Ireland Sharp a contented recluse on the San Juans. Pearl gets to
buy a bunch of stuff. Whatcom goes bust once again.

Beal Obenchain, the truculent, unpleasant, smelly angel of everyone's
destiny (in ways too complicated to relate here), gets killed by Johnny
Lee, who is avenging his dead brother. With Beal gone, the novel drifts to
a close.

This is, all in all, a more dangerous West than I am familiar with, but
there is such a thing as pure bad luck, and my historian's ground rules
allow Annie Dillard a lot of freedom with details. I was after the big picture.

But as a reader, I realized the details were bothering me. The discordant details began to swarm like mosquitoes on a mountain lake. Enough
of them and you forget about any larger view.

The trouble, I began to realize, was that the novelist couldn't be cava-
lier with the details even if she succeeded in getting the big picture right
precisely because the historical novel is a novel. If I, as a historian, am
going to grant her the freedom to make things up and move things
around, she should do so in the service of the larger project of creating a
reasonable replica of nineteenth-century Whatcom. In a novel, the details supposedly are there for a purpose, and the details that are made up
should be a relatively seamless fit with the details borrowed from history.

It is the details, for example, that convince the reader that Beal Oben-chain is strange.

An occasional mistake on the details didn't bother me as a reader, but repeated mistakes forced me out of the story. I had to keep mentally editing it: "She doesn't really mean this," I would say to myself. After a while, I couldn't always decide whether an outlandish detail in the story was a clue or simply a mistake. Reading *The Living*, I began to think that to enjoy a historical novel, to get the best of what it offers, it is best not to take history too seriously. It may be best not to know anything about the setting in which the author has placed her characters. A historian may very well be the worst possible reader, not so much because historians can't suspend belief and enter fully into the fictional world, but rather because, once in the fictional world, they become either terminally confused or begin editing information in ways that detract from the fiction.

We are barely into the book (p. 10), for example, when Dillard makes two small historical mistakes. Rooney files on a beachfront claim of 320 acres, and the "U.S. Army and the Nisqually and Yakima tribes east of the mountains were heating up for a war." The Nisqually are west of the mountains and live near Puget Sound, and maybe this mistake tells us something about Rooney; he is new and maybe he is confused. The 320 acres tells me that Rooney took a Donation Claim, but since he came after 1850, he could not get 320 acres by himself. He could file on 160 acres, but his wife, Ada, had to file for an additional 160 if the family was to have 320. That Ada did not file is Dillard's mistake; in a book full of assertive women and fully developed female characters, this is not a minor mistake in terms of the possibilities it leaves unopened, but it doesn't confuse me. The Donation Land Act is complicated; mistakes are easy to make.

What does confuse me is where Dillard locates those 320 acres. Dillard makes it clear that Rooney and Ada purposefully took 320 acres of forest. A glance at Donation Claim maps shows that what the claimants wanted was clear land. They didn't take forest unless they were planning to build a city like the settlers of Seattle. Usually, they took prairies or they dispossessed Indians from their potato lands or tried to take land from the Hudson's Bay Company. What were Ada and Rooney thinking?

When Mark Twain hilariously took on Fenimore Cooper, his point was that Cooper's fictional Indians were not credible; they were not convincing inventions. Twain's evidence was the details. The details too often subvert Annie Dillard's characters as convincing inventions. Just as Cooper's Indians were supposed to be masters of woodlore but behaved like dolts, so the actions of Dillard's settlers make them less rational and discerning than she intends them to be. Their actions make no sense given the time and place they are supposed to inhabit.

The opposite is also true. When she tries to demonstrate how wrongheaded they were, a historian can find the example confusing. To show how ignorant the settlers initially were of their surroundings, Dillard has one haul a Douglas fir, the most common tree of northwestern forests, all the way from the East. But there were no Douglas fir in the East at that time, so I am left wondering less about the poor fool's ignorance than his resourcefulness. Where did he get that tree?

But then people do go out of their way in *The Living*. In 1859 Rooney thinks about building a schooner and going to Alaska for halibut. What has got into the man? The Strait of Juan de Fuca and the nearby coast were swarming with halibut in 1859. And then there are the Finns. Putting a whole lumber camp of Finns on the Skagit River in the 1860s gets this immigration well ahead of itself, but if she wants Finns, I'll let her have Finns. What, however, are they doing in the mountains? Logging camps historically stayed as close to tidewater as they could until the railroads came because, if they didn't, they could not move their logs. Are these guys logging as a hobby? Beal Obenchain is hardly the only one behaving strangely.

As with the Finns, Annie Dillard sometimes just can't wait for the nineteenth century to develop. When she wants to use something, she just uses it. Sometimes these are significant juxtapositions. Characters with progressive attitudes typical to the late nineteenth century or early twentieth century appear in the 1860s and 1870s. Cholera kills Indians at a time when smallpox and influenza and syphilis were killing them, and then smallpox shows up later when it was no longer such a great danger. Sometimes, they are just chronological mistakes: Bryan and McKinley jump the gun and are on everybody's lips in 1893. It is as if Annie Dillard had issued a cast call for Western history and the whole nineteenth century showed up. She just inserts people and things any place she chooses, and it gets distracting. A novel about a particular time and place drifts out of focus. Similitude gives way to mere labeling. Whatcom, 1880, might as well be a sign posted on the way into town. Wherever you post the sign, there is Whatcom in whatever year you claim.

The chronological promiscuity of the novel, however, is countered by particularities of place. Annie Dillard certainly did research in writing *The Living*. I have no idea what her method was, but the result is like an early-twentieth-century Braque or Picasso that incorporates shreds of old newspapers and other found objects. Ezra Meeker, the Puyallup hop farmer who sympathized with Indians, knew them intimately, and wrote a long nostalgic memoir of his pioneer days in Washington, is moved up to Whatcom. He gets a sex and personality change, and becomes Minta. Local vignettes like deaths in wells are lifted from the newspapers and reinscribed in the novel. Invented characters cohabit with characters borrowed from local history.

I'm confident that Annie Dillard recognizes that her sources might be partial and self-serving. Ezra Meeker was not your common settler in Washington Territory, and his sometimes halcyon descriptions of old-time relations between Indians and the first settlers fall apart when you look closely at other sources on the period. But Annie Dillard goes ahead and populates Whatcom with variations on Ezra Meeker. And for a novel's purpose, that is fine. I'm much happier that she erred on the side of a hesitant common life rather than vanishing or uniformly hostile Indians. It is a touch that counteracts the sometimes generic frontier markers and makes Whatcom a particular place.

Reading page after page and having the discordant details swarm around me, I began to have sympathy for Beal Obenchain. Too much reading can upset a man, even make him crazy. Too much reading could make a man mean.

I couldn't ignore the details as a reader, but I did try to stick to my original historian's criteria. I did look for the big picture of a recognizable nineteenth-century place full of people who thought and acted like nineteenth-century people. And although it might seem that a book where so many details seemed distracting and out of place couldn't ever create a semblance of the past, I had to admit how much was right about the book.

It might be Annie Dillard's sensibility. It might be dumb luck; it might be deep skill; it might be happy coincidence, but in making the characters of this novel preoccupied with death and uplift and progress, Annie Dillard displays a sometimes near perfect nineteenth-century pitch. These were nineteenth-century American concerns.

For all the signs that Annie Dillard doesn't know all that much about nineteenth-century Washington, she creates characters whose thinking reeks of the mid- and late-nineteenth-century United States. They try to greet death of loved ones impassively but long to send bodies back home for burial. They work hard for little return and dream of speculative riches. Ada as an old woman remembering her trip across the plains wonderfully combines a grim meditation on death and the transience of human ambition and achievement with a seemingly contradictory but very nineteenth-century sense of progress.

Bad historical fiction resembles a James Michener novel: the setting is exotic, and maybe even correct down to the last detail, but the people inhabiting it might as well live next door. The characters are just your neighbor Bob dressed up as a cowboy and his wife, Cheryl, playing a plucky homesteader. Ada, Clare, and even Minta in her less uplifting moments are not people you know.

The Living, by this criterion of grasping the strangeness of the past, is not bad historical fiction. It is very good historical fiction. The characters in *The Living* are colored by the strangeness of the past, and Dillard, through the characters she creates, makes the past familiar and its own logic comprehensible.

This is a considerable triumph, one far more difficult than getting the facts right, and yet, to my surprise, the factual mistakes mattered for the book as a novel. The novelist surrenders some control in trying to portray the past. Invention is constrained by the demands of the period. Details subvert her intentions in complicated ways. Struggling for one effect, she sometimes achieves another. *The Living* is a work of wonderful imagination, but it succeeds mostly on a grand scale. It is best not to look too closely.

On the Trail with Gus and Call: *Lonesome Dove* and the Western Myth

Elliott West

When Larry McMurtry's *Lonesome Dove* was published in 1985, virtually every review included the term "epic." "Deeply affecting" was a close second in the flow of praise for what one critic called "the Great Cowboy Novel." Its critical success was capped with the Pulitzer Prize and its mass popularity with a television miniseries graced by a rare combination of fine acting and high ratings. By then, *Lonesome Dove* was being called a Western classic. And it is, although not for reasons that would gladden every fan of Louis L'Amour and Zane Gray.

Lonesome Dove is perhaps most impressive as a literary balancing act. Its characters are comfortably familiar sorts who suddenly do the unexpected—and who always speak with the most wonderfully original blather. The story moves languidly for long stretches, then suddenly ignites in gun battles, stampedes, and gut-cuttings to satisfy the most demanding action fan. Above all, for history students, McMurtry keeps *Lonesome Dove* centered between myth and antimyth.

The story begins in the late 1870s in Lonesome Dove, a sunbaked speck of a town on the Texas-Mexico border. The turmoil during and immediately after the Civil War has subsided, and with it the need for aging former Texas Ranger captains like the book's two primary figures,

Woodrow Call and Augustus McCrae. With Pea Eye, Deets, Lippy, and others in the Hat Creek Cattle Company, they pass time in and around the town's one saloon, the Dry Bean, where the prostitute Lorena conducts her business. Enter the handsome Jake Spoon, another ex-Ranger, who persuades the restless Call to drive a herd of three thousand cattle northward twelve hundred miles to the grassy valley of Montana's Yellowstone River, nearly to the Canadian border. The equivalent would be pushing a herd of balky and highly independent animals from Madrid to Helsinki, from Atlanta to beyond Ottawa, or (with a long swim) from Tunis to Moscow. Lorena, infatuated with Jake and looking for someplace cool, comes along, as does the seventeen-year-old Newt, who we learn is Call's illegitimate son.

The long drive and its adventures consume most of *Lonesome Dove*, with several subplots woven in. Except for a few terrifying freelancers like Blue Duck, the Indians by now are defeated and their means of independent living going or gone. The plains have been swept nearly clean of bison, leaving only "roads of bones." There are vague references to Custer's recent difficulty and to the Sioux and Cheyennes' confinement to Dakota reservations. The action unfolds on the march north: Lorena is kidnapped by Blue Duck and rescued by Gus; Jake falls in with rustlers and is caught and hanged; the men pause with Gus's old flame Clara, now a ranchwoman. The outfit has barely reached Montana when Gus is wounded in an Indian skirmish. When he dies rather than have his leg amputated, Call packs his corpse in charcoal and hauls it back to Texas. The story ends where it starts, back on the border.

For readers after historical authenticity, *Lonesome Dove* is mostly accurate, at least in the term's narrowest sense. There are a few anachronisms and startling omissions. The Indians who send Gus to his deathbed with a rotting leg are presumably Blackfeet, who in fact were mostly in Canada by this time or starving on what remains today one of America's bleakest reservations. It's hard to imagine that the Hat Creek outfit sees no farmers; in western Kansas alone, sixteen counties were created during the 1870s, with more land broken to the plow than would have fit into Connecticut and Delaware combined. And where are the railroads? Every historical development in the novel's background—cattle trailing and ranching, buffalo hunting, and the Indian wars—was either spun off directly or facilitated by the first transcontinentals built during the previous decade. Montana-bound drovers would have crossed three major lines. Various characters in the novel pass time in Dodge City, Ogallala, and Miles City, towns that were creatures respectively of the Atchison, Topeka and Santa Fe, the Union Pacific, and the Northern Pacific. Except for some Mexicans and Irish, there is not much in *Lonesome Dove* to suggest that the plains West was quite an immigrant stew. The percentage of foreign-born persons in the Montana McMurtry describes was twice that of New York.

Still, given the story he chooses to tell, McMurtry is faithful in both broad strokes and detail. He catches beautifully the feel of the plains at the moment, just after the national centennial, when power tipped finally and quickly from Indians to whites. Very few have taken us more authentically into the grimy ordeal of traveling this country. River crossings and stampedes are standard stuff, but not the stunted sprawl of mesquite trees bristling with some of the nastiest thorns on the planet, or the yawning openness beyond that, an agoraphobic's nightmare, and over it all the hammering of an erratic, sometimes murderous climate. This might have been cheapened into a hyperrealism, but McMurtry balances the plains' austerity with a true loveliness equally hard for outlanders to picture, the broad rolls of low hills and "a plain of grass so huge it was hard to imagine a world beyond it" (p. 620).

The novel gives us as well a true feel for cowboying. Besides his own experience, McMurtry seems to have drawn heavily from two classics, Teddy Blue Abbott's memoir, *We Pointed Them North* (1939), and an early instance of what would later be called a nonfiction novel, Andy Adams's *The Log of a Cowboy* (1903), both accounts of similarly long cattle drives. McMurtry borrows some material directly from the historical record. Call's moving epitaph to Deets after his friend is killed trying to return an Indian child is an almost exact transcription of the tribute by the Texas rancher Charles Goodnight to Bose Ikard, a former slave who was Goodnight's most trusted hand. The psychopath Blue Duck has elements of Charlie Bent, the mixed-blood son of the Cheyenne Owl Woman and the prominent trader William Bent, who preyed mercilessly on Colorado whites after the Sand Creek massacre, and perhaps of the Kiowa warrior Satanta (White Bear). Blue Duck's death, "flying" out the third-floor courthouse window just before he is to be hanged, is a mimic of Satanta's suicide by diving headfirst from the second floor of the Texas state prison hospital in 1878.

McMurtry chose the cowboy's West for his setting partly because that place and story are his and his family's. Late in the nineteenth century, his grandparents took up ranching near the north Texas town of Archer City, where McMurtry lived and worked until leaving for Rice University. He heard the stories and absorbed, but didn't share, his father's longing to have worked the country at the time of the cattle drives. McMurtry has commented that he was moved to write *Lonesome Dove* partly by the "thrill of the vernacular," the desire to re-create the speech and the dailiness of life among plainsmen of his grandfather's time.

Clearly, however, he is up to much more than that. Embedded in this novel is McMurtry's vision of pioneering, of what those of his grandparents' time found, or hoped to find, and how they and their world changed each other. This makes *Lonesome Dove* a Western in both meanings of the term. It is a wonderfully entertaining set piece from the legendary terrain of the cattleman's plains. It also wrestles with the meanings, truths, and deceptions in what amounts to our national creation myth.

Like most such myths, the Western is a deceptively simple story told by people with a common identity (many Americans in this case) to explain who they are and how they've come to be. It runs something like this: Long ago, with the first European settlement on the Atlantic Coast, people from an old world came into a new one. The old world was crowded and set in its ways. Its individuals lived within narrow possibilities. The new world was open and full of promise and essentially a social void, without cultural form or shape. It was a wilderness, full of unforeseen dangers and undreamt-of challenges.

The people came brimming with hope and ideals and set out with a great determination to build new lives for themselves and to plant in the new land the first civilized order—schools, churches, government, civility broadly defined. But the wild land fought them hard. Its weather battered them; its native inhabitants (human and animal seemed often interchangeable) lashed out ferociously; its distances swallowed them. Many of the people were lost, and all suffered, but in the end they endured and the wilderness was brought under their dominion.

The heart of the story, however, is not the conquest of the land but the transformation of the conquerors. The people who tamed the wilderness learned new ways, found in themselves unexpected potential, and fashioned new beliefs. As they earned a place in the country, they also grew away from the world that had first shaped them and their ancestors. It wasn't so much that they forged a new identity. Rather, it was forged for them out of the heat and the grinding struggle. Our western myth, then, tells of a dual metamorphosis, a violent sort of blood wedding of the people and the land, and at the end it's not always easy to say who and what is victorious. The wild country was subdued, but it absorbed and shaped the people, too; the people mastered the land but were reborn into a life inseparable from the country that was now their home.

What this abstract thumbnail sketch cannot suggest is, first, the remarkable range of forms the myth has taken in American culture, high and low. Saturday-afternoon serials, the political appeals of Andrew Jackson, Abraham Lincoln, Theodore Roosevelt, and John Kennedy, countless potboilers and pulp paperbacks, rodeos, music from Antonín Dvořák, Gene Autry, Aaron Copland, and Johnny Paycheck, F. Scott Fitzgerald's fresh green breast of the new world, national parks, accountants from Akron wearing cowboy boots and hats of great gallonage, dozens of television series and hundreds of movies, Cather and Steinbeck and L'Amour and so much more. Nor does it hint at the myth's astonishing global appeal, once again across the intellectual spectrum. James Fenimore Cooper, who became the first American to make a living as a novelist by giving the myth its first literary expression in the Leatherstocking saga, was wildly popular from London to Jerusalem. Dumas and Tolstoy stole his plots; Conrad called him his favorite author; Goethe was so smitten he seriously considered writing a Western. One of Germany's best-selling authors of the twentieth century was Karl May, whose stories of Old Shatterhand's exploits in the Far West were the boyhood favorites of Albert Schweitzer and Adolf Hitler.

The rest of the world loves the Western because of its dramatic settings, hairbreadth action, and colorful characters. But like all cultural creation myths—the Book of Exodus, for instance, or the Navajos' perilous journey out of the earth and into what we call Arizona—it speaks to its

own with an intimacy nobody else feels. *Lonesome Dove* resonates with
that myth, but it is anything but a straightforward retelling of it. The
book's poignant appeal, and its interest to cultural historians, lies in its
ambivalence toward what that creation story tries to teach us.

Recently, McMurtry commented that while writing *Lonesome Dove*, he
thought he was "demythicizing" the West. This seems odd on the face.
The novel is a virtually full roster of the Western's most familiar characters: cowboys and Indians, Texas Rangers, nasty renegades, bumbling
deputies, rustlers, a likable and beautiful whore, a strong ranchwoman, a
trapper turned buffalo hunter turned bone picker, a colorful cook, and an
alcoholic doctor, just to name the most obvious. Its skeletal narrative, the
cattle drive, is one of the Western's three essential story lines (the wagon
train and the Indian war being the others). Like all Westerns, it is about
men; women have no roles except as motivators and commentators. Its
subplots and bits of business are the usual fare: Newt's coming of age
through tutelage of older men, for instance, and the bantering tension
between two vastly different friends sealed inseparably by the passage of
years.

The Western's great army of fans know these characters and situations
as well as or better than they know their families. The people and plots
have been grooved into their brains. These readers don't want to be surprised, except in details of the familiar plot. They expect to respond to
such a story mythically—that is, as a reiteration of patterns that feed
something inside them that badly needs to be fed. The minor miracle of
Lonesome Dove is that McMurtry stays squarely within the Western's
form, yet with a novelist's magic he forces his readers to break loose from
what they expect. What are normally clichés of genre fiction—the camp-
fire gab and saloon scenes and encounters with rustlers—become the setting for a genuinely new story. We're not sure where the story is heading
because Gus and Call and most of the others are originals. McMurtry
gives them humanity and inherent interest, and so it matters to us what
happens to them and how the story turns out.

Here, then, is one way *Lonesome Dove* demythicizes the West, simply
by giving a fresh and true voice to figures long ago kidnapped from history and held hostage to the demands of legend. That McMurtry chose
the West's most clichéd setting to pull this off is truly impressive. I don't

know whether it is culturally appropriate to apply "chutzpah" to a Scots-Irish Texan, but if it is, McMurtry has earned the term.

Just as surely, he means to go farther than that. Implied in his fiction and more explicit in his essays is a commentary on the western character as it truly was. As original as Call and Gus are, they are also walking and riding demonstrations of what McMurtry thinks that life on the actual frontier did to those who were drawn to it. In this, of course, he moves toward the center of the western myth, the junction of history and the spirit it supposedly produced.

In the classic western myth, the frontier experience was grandly ennobling. The pioneers' trials cultivated in them a long list of virtues: self-reliance, strength, inventiveness, toleration, independence, and respect for the individual. As their characters were being transformed, westering Americans were also transplanting the best of their past. Families, schools, law and government (the pure local variety), and churches all took hold in the virgin soil of the West. As the frontier passed and communities were set in place, the finest qualities of the former were woven into the new social fabric (although Westerns never address in any detail how this was done). A purified America was born, a blend of pioneer virtue and values tested over the centuries. The transition from frontier to a civilized order was apparently smooth, free of bumps and contradictions.

In *Lonesome Dove*, McMurtry tells another side of this story. The frontier may have left its people strong in some ways, he says, but it took quite a toll as well. The hunger for land brought out a passion among pioneers, not simply to improve their lot, but to accomplish something truly grand, to give life to whatever dream they found inside themselves. But this passion became its own force. Soon pioneers were not drawn but driven, caught up in an unappeasable restlessness. That, more than anything, seems to define Woodrow Call. Soon after I first read *Lonesome Dove*, I loaned it to a graduate student, a fellow Texan from the ranching town of Big Spring. He returned it with a note: "This is the perfect western novel. Everyone is in continual movement, and to no apparent purpose." Gus makes the same point about Call when they arrive in Montana. "Now that we're here, do you plan to stop," he asks his partner, "or will we just keep going north until we get into the polar bears?"

Feverish movement toward some vague goal had seemed to many to be the essense of the frontier from the time pioneers began spilling over the Appalachians. Moses Austin, a miner, land speculator, and would-be colonizer of Texas, asked the crowds he met in 1795 what they thought was waiting for them in Kentucky: "the Answer [they gave] is Land. have you any. No, but I expect I can git it . . . did you Ever see the Country. No, but Every Body says its good land . . . here is hundreds Traveling hundreds of Miles, they Know not for what Nor Whither, except its to Kentuckey." Ten years later, the explorer Zebulon Pike, after crossing the treeless wind-scoured southern plains, hoped that this country would force the relentless pioneer movers, "so prone to rambling and extending themselves on the frontiers . . . , to limit their extent on the west to the borders of the Missouri and the Mississippi." The plains, that is, might require Americans at last to settle down and tend to business. It was a naive notion, as thousands testified by flooding into the Texas colony founded by Moses Austin's son Stephen in the 1820s.

McMurtry's grandparents came to Archer County in the last stage of this push onto the plains frontier. For his father, who stayed in place, the pioneer's unscratchable itch seemed translated into a relentless drive to master the country. His few spare moments away from ranch work were spent in a hopeless campaign to push back the mesquite thickets with an ax, a spade, and a can of kerosene. An urban equivalent would be marching with a flyswatter into the city dump.

In McMurtry's West the open promise of the land becomes something like a gravity field that distorts some virtues and crushes others. Men like Gus become ramblin' boys, fond of daytime whiskey and whorehouse pokes, likable and garrulous but irresponsible and hopeless as material for decent society. For others, an honest day's work becomes a life exhausted by the pursuit of what can't be had or even defined. A comically surreal variation in *Lonesome Dove* is Aus Frank collecting bison bones, literally night and day, and piling them into gigantic pyramids, not to sell them but apparently just to do it. Honor becomes an excuse to continue what would otherwise be pointless or destructive. When Call sets off to carry Gus's body back to Texas, we know he's found one more occasion just to keep moving, even though his son, Newt, badly needs his attention. "A promise is a promise," Call tells Clara when she upbraids him, but she throws his true duty back in his face: "A promise is words—a son is a life."

McMurtry is hinting here of other costs hidden within the idealized myth. The almost unimaginable load of work of settlement left little time or room for anything else. The basics of human community suffered, starting with simple talk. "This is the longest conversation I've had in ten years. Goodbye," the rancher Charles Goodnight tells Call, using the last 11 of the 187 words he takes time to speak. The western myth might celebrate the planting of the family, but McMurtry's frontier wore them down and ripped them apart. Except for Clara's household, where her husband lies in a permanent coma, there is not one nuclear family in *Lonesome Dove*, but rather a spraying of solitaires, runaways, castoffs, orphans, bastards, and parents who take the modern term "dysfunctional" into an entirely new dimension. This familial abrasion survived in the cattle country of McMurtry's own youth. The emptiness, loneliness, and grind, he writes elsewhere, took the heaviest toll on the women. Although his paternal grandmother lived with him until she died, in his eighth year, he cannot recall her speaking a single word to him.

And despite the army of schoolmarms in hundreds of popular Westerns, the legacy he remembers valued reading and literature about as much as modern dance and ice sculpture. By his own account McMurtry grew up intellectually starved, gobbling what few books he found at home and in the drugstore's rack of paperbacks, before leaving for college and reading his way eastward toward the cultural life of the Atlantic Coast and Europe. In *Lonesome Dove*, it's important to notice what is *not* there. Its characters would be flabbergasted to hear that anything they chose to do had the slightest civilizing purpose, with the possible exception of killing Indians. This frontier is a place of almost total cultural atrophy. Perhaps this is the joke behind the motto Gus adds to the sign for the Hat Creek Cattle Company: "Uva uvam vivendo varia fit." It's faux Latin gibberish, a mockery of cultural pretense.

So there is lots here to demythicize the West: a near-neurotic obsessiveness, a cultural erosion, a hardening of character and dimming of sensibility, a flight from true responsibility that hides in the guise of manly purpose. Others have made the same points. A. B. Guthrie, Jr.'s *The Big Sky* is to mountain men what *Lonesome Dove* is to cowboys and rangers. Its protagonist, Boone Caudill, is drawn to the roaming life of the trapper but ends up killing his best friend and smothering his own humanity.

Why, then, are we drawn so powerfully to the Caudills and Gus McCraes and Woodrow Calls? *Lonesome Dove*, to McMurtry's surprise, has become "an American Arthuriad." What is it that its readers find heroic? What do they see to connect these characters' destructive, dead-end lives to some grander vision of the West and America?

To start with, these men are free and they are brave, at least in facing physical dangers that would turn most of our bowels to jelly. McMurtry's West was a testing ground for courage, and it was the last time in our history when, for the cost of a ticket or a long hike down the road, you could break into country twice the size of Europe and move virtually unfettered and act without concern for any but the most immediate risks. At this irreducible core, he is saying, the mythic and the real West were the same. More to the point, the West was free as a realm of perceived possibilities, a seductive sense of limitless options that inspired an extraordinary determination, energy, and imagination among those pulled into it.

To McMurtry, this imaginative passion must always be given a respect equal to the frustration, the destructive self-deception, and the spiritual gnarling. Look far enough behind the apparent lunacies—chopping mesquite, moving cattle from one end of the country to the other, building pyramids of bones—and you'll find the great dream. The dream itself was largely illusion, but as an inner reality it was undeniable. At the heart of the Western is that vision of cutting loose from the settled to the wild, of shaping new country to the individual will. Whether we should be ashamed or proud of that emotional force is another question. The point here is that the dream was truly there, and because as Americans we instinctively recognize it, it continues to give Westerns an undeniable power.

And that in turn makes Westerns ultimately tragic. Whatever reality the dream held, the end was bound to come. The transition from frontier to full settlement was not smooth and unrumpled; it was a painful jolt. In the cattleman's West, the end came quickly. Longhorns were first driven to Kansas the year before Grant was elected. By the time he left office, ranching was shifting to the northern plains and the Indians were defeated. In another decade, barbed wire had mostly closed the open range and ranching had become a corporate enterprise. Twenty-five years, tops, and whatever true freedom had ever been there was fenced and mort-gaged.

Lonesome Dove holds us with such a grip because we feel the dream in Call and Gus, and so we also feel the awful sadness as we watch it all slip-ping away. If a myth is a story we tell to say who we are, there is something in that telescoping of time, and in the longing for what is given and then snatched back, that speaks from the heart of the American experience. The variations run through our national library: Fitzgerald's receding green light, Leatherstocking sent in exile from his beloved forest, and Steinbeck's Okies taking the road to the golden land and getting their heads cracked in its orchards. McMurtry adds to this literature the long trek to Montana and Call's return in an evening's gathering dark to Lone-some Dove, where his house is full of rats and the Dry Bean has burned down.

As with the historical details of his view of the plains, we can peck at McMurtry's portrayal of men forced to watch the dream pulled out of their reach. Plainsmen frequently did all they could to hustle in the set-tled world of towns and fences. Christopher Columbus Slaughter used money made driving longhorns to Kansas to start a cattle empire west of the McMurtry ranch. After squeezing out smaller competitors, he moved to Dallas, bankrolled the First Baptist Church (today the largest congre-gation in the country), built houses for himself and his sons on fashion-able Cole Avenue, and spent his last years spying on his children through binoculars. No free-roaming, live-and-let-live ranger here. Even the buf-falo hunters were just as likely to become businessmen and county com-missioners as the flyblown misfits McMurtry describes in *Anything for Billy*, "old tired bears whose coats had worn shabby." Bill Tilighman, who killed more bison in a season than anyone else, went on to serve as a law-man and delegate to the 1904 Democratic National Convention, make early movies, and raise racehorses. One of his favorites, Chance, won the 1892 Kentucky Derby.

And always, of course, it is crucial to keep in mind that chasing one dream usually involves shutting down another. Women, who McMurtry knows were blighted by the ranching life, often had little or no say in the choice to take it up. The plains West, furthermore, was not an unpeopled cultural void when pioneers showed up. The newcomers' expanding possibilities came at the expense of the rapidly contracting worlds of Comanches, Cheyennes, Sioux, Arapahos, Kiowas, and other tribes. Every historian must throw their disaster into the balance when weighing the myth and its role in our continental story.

But McMurtry is a novelist, not an historian, and so he is freer to choose where his emphasis will be. His choice is for the dreaming—its beauty and its terrible costs and the tension between the two. It's a theme that runs strongly through American fiction, although the West sometimes seems its special home. *Lonesome Dove*, whatever its limits as a narrative of fact, manages something doubly remarkable as a novel within that mythic vein. In a tradition we've come to know as clichéd and austere, it charms us with a story with flesh and humor. Doing that, it causes us to see all the clearer the yearning, loss, and illusion that sit at the heart of our spiritual history.

જી&

On *Lonesome Dove*

Larry McMurtry

Writers, singers, prolific artists of many stamps have sometimes found, to their bafflement, that they have been more or less trapped by the unexpected and unrelenting popularity of a work to which they themselves had initially attached little importance. Henry James was pestered all his life by fans of what was, to his mind, a slight story, *Daisy Miller.* Bing Crosby grew very, very tired of having to sing, over and over again, a little ditty called "White Christmas."

In my case the culprit is *Lonesome Dove*, a book which now seems as remote from me as the Arthuriad, or the Matter of Troy, but which blooms eternally—a living myth-flower—to its readers (or watchers).

Like the corpus of stories about King Arthur and his knights, or those about the fall of Troy, *Lonesome Dove* long ago burst past single authorship into a ubiquity of forms. A subdivision I pass on my way to Dallas is called Dove Estates. The dog that won the Westminster Dog Show a few years ago was named Lonesome Dove. A honky-tonk not thirty miles from where I write is now the "Lonesome Dove." A TV series featuring several characters I had myself killed off was filmed in Canada; it flourished for three seasons on the Fox network. A few of the characters may even have been killed twice, having succumbed not only in my pages but also in a spurious (but legal) sequel called *Return to Lonesome Dove*. In television, death just doesn't have much of a sting.

What I suspect this means is that it's hard to go wrong if one writes at length about the Old West. I thought I had written about a harsh time and some pretty harsh people, but, to the public at large, I had produced something nearer to an idealization; instead of a poor man's *Inferno*, filled with violence, faithlessness, and betrayal, I had actually delivered a kind of *Gone With the Wind* of the West, a turnabout I'll be mulling over for a long, long time.

I have the greatest difficulty thinking about my books once I have finished them—and a like difficulty reading anything about them, whether good, bad, dumb, smart, friendly, hostile. I thought Professor West's piece was smart and good-natured, but what else to say?

First, that *Lonesome Dove* was an unproduced screenplay for twelve years, done for John Wayne, James Stewart, Henry Fonda. Had the film been produced, I wouldn't have written the book.

Second, that I almost did not finish the book. I stopped and wrote two other books (*Cadillac Jack*, *Desert Rose*) and only resumed *Lonesome Dove* when I saw an old church bus sitting by a Texas road that said Lonesome Dove Baptist Church. Acquiring a good title provoked me to finish the tale.

Third, that a cattleman named Nelson Story drove a herd of cattle from Texas to Montana in 1866—and sold them at a profit. I thought of the drive in *Lonesome Dove* as occurring in the late 1860s or early 1870s. I made a note to myself in the first draft to put in the Union Pacific Railroad—I wanted them to cross it in the big sandstorm—but then I forgot my own note. A long novel often involves such sloppiness.

Last, that I think of the West as the phantom limb of the American psyche, not there, but not forgotten.

Real Lives and
Other Fictions: Reconsidering
Wallace Stegner's
Angle of Repose

John Demos

*I*t is the 1960s, in Wallace Stegner's novel Angle of Repose. An elderly
historian, recently retired from university teaching, has gathered a large
collection of papers and other memorabilia from the lives of his grandparents, as a way to create his own "frame of reference." He tells himself: "I am
everything I ever was . . . I am much of what my parents and especially my
grandparents were" (p. 11).[1]

Thus begins an elaborate process of imaginative reconstruction. The historian-
narrator's grandparents, here called Oliver and Susan (Burling) Ward, had
"gone west" following their marriage in 1873 (in New York). Oliver was then a
young engineer, bent on a career in mining, Susan an aspiring artist and writer.
The story of their subsequent struggles, personal and otherwise, ranged across
many years and a variety of colorful settings: New Almaden, California;
Leadville, Colorado; Michoacan, Mexico; Boise, Idaho. They raised two children;
a third died young, in a tragic accident. Oliver's career followed a ragged, mostly
unrewarding, track; promising "schemes" unraveled, one after another "boom"
passed him by. Susan's work went better. Her drawings and stories, closely based
on personal experience, were taken up by magazines and book publishers; eventually she gained a considerable reputation as a "Western writer." But for the most
part Susan felt herself to be an "exile" from the more cultured life of the East; and,
partly as a result, her relation to Oliver grew increasingly tense and difficult.

All this their grandson rediscovers—one painstaking piece after another. And he uses it in multiple ways: to take the measure of his own work as a historian, to ponder the meaning of history itself, to refract his rather jaundiced view of his current surroundings, and, finally, to confront some painful issues in his personal life. . . .

Skip now to the 1970s; another historian—actual, not fictional; young, not elderly—has been given a copy of Angle of Repose. *His mother has said, "It's a lot like the story of my parents," a remark that is sure to get his attention. He reads somewhat haltingly at first—he does not feel quite comfortable spending time on novels—but then with a gathering sense of involvement and inspiration. Yes, there are indeed parallels between the story of the Wards and the lives of his own grandparents (restless, "boomer" husband; genteel, "nesting" wife; years of wandering, hoping, failing, despairing).[2] But his interest quickly outruns these personal connections. He feels an almost literal sense of transport—to the scenes, the everyday ambience, the very pulse of the Old West; in short, he experiences "time travel" of a remarkably vivid sort.*

Moreover, Angle of Repose *seems aimed at the core of his particular expertise, the subfield known to scholars as "family history." He had been fortunate, from his first years as a graduate student, to find such a fresh and lively intellectual center. He was linked now to the so-called "new social historians," a group of (mostly younger) scholars pointed toward previously uncharted subject areas (ordinary people, everyday life) and armed with a brace of novel research techniques (quantification, social science theory). Within scarcely a decade, this burgeoning scholarly movement had brought large new vistas from the life of the past into sharp focus. For him, as for all his academic soul mates, it was a heady time of consciousness—and confidence—raising.*

However, Angle of Repose *would change his consciousness, and shake his confidence, enormously. When at last he finished the book, and put it down—in tears, in the small hours of a winter night—he knew that his historian's life would never again be quite the same.* Angle of Repose, *he thought, was a deeper, more powerful evocation of "family history" than anything done by scholars. Perhaps, too, the same could be said of its relation to western history. And yet: it was plainly identified as a* novel; *indeed, it had won the Pulitzer Prize for fiction. How, then, should he understand its bearing on his own work (and that of the "new social historians" at large)? What lessons could he learn from it? To what extent, and in what specific ways, might it suggest alterations in his (or any scholar's) modus operandi? What new light did it throw on the generally accepted boundary between works of history and of fiction? And where, in all this, did it leave the large, vexing, nebulous question of historical "truth"?*

✑

OF COURSE, THIS little scenario of the two historians includes, and is mediated by, a third party: the author of *Angle of Repose*, Wallace Stegner himself. And Stegner is hard to classify. Best known as a writer of fiction, and as a longtime professor of English at Stanford, Stegner nonetheless had powerful credentials as a historian. Certainly, he appreciated history, and felt the power of history (thus the historical project he puts at the center of *Angle of Repose*). Certainly, too, some of his writings would pass muster as history in a fairly straightforward sense. His account of the nineteenth-century Mormon migrations, entitled *The Gathering of Zion* (1964), involved much archival research and careful scholarly judgment. So, too, did his biographies of John Wesley Powell (*Beyond the Hundredth Meridian* [1954]) and Bernard De Voto (*The Uneasy Chair* [1974]). Yet these works also introduced, at particular points, the attitude and activity of a novelist. Thus, his own most recent biographer, Jackson Benson, is right to describe Stegner as a "writer whose fiction often crossed over into history, and whose histories often crossed over into the use of fictional techniques."[3]

With *Angle of Repose*, the situation is especially, perhaps uniquely, complicated. In fact, there is a deeply historical core to this work, for it was from its inception inspired and shaped by the course of an actual life. The character of Susan Ward is closely modeled on that of a woman named Mary Hallock Foote. Stegner had learned, years before, something of Foote's work, as a result of his interest in western writing. Then one of his graduate students had discovered a large cache of Foote letters, and begun a doctoral dissertation based on them. When that failed to ripen, Stegner had taken the material in hand for himself. After a period of further reflection, he decided to use both life and letters (and also Foote's autobiographical "Reminiscences") to "hatch" (as he put it) a novel.[4]

As it stands, *Angle of Repose* follows the line of Foote's life in many ways, large and small.[5] Much of her specific work in writing and illustration is attributed here to Susan Ward. The novel's geographical movement, and its leading venues, directly mirror Foote's experience. Certain of the secondary characters are closely matched to real people in her immediate surround. Furthermore, her actual letters are used here, almost verbatim, as if written by Susan Ward. According to Benson's count, roughly 10 percent of the novel's text involves this sort of semidirect quotation. The Foote "Reminiscences" appear throughout in a similar light. Hence the overall result is, at the very least, a strong correspondence between the fictional figures of Susan and Oliver Ward and the real Mary and Arthur Foote.

For all that, much else in *Angle of Repose* is pure invention. The historian-narrator, for one. (Mary Foote had no such grandchild.) The various additional modern-day characters, for another. The numerous, and crucial, passages of dialogue—in both the modern and the historical parts—for still another. Moreover, there are many particular details of landscape, and episode, and milieu, for which no factual basis exists. Finally, the underlying frame and meaning of the work—the whole complex theme of past shadowing present, and present refracting past—come straight from Stegner's imagination.

Stegner signaled his conflating of the real with the fictional, of Foote with Ward, in a short acknowledgment that followed the book's title page: "My thanks to J. M. and her sister for the loan of their ancestors." And he offered this explicit disclaimer: "Though I have used many details of their lives and characters, I have not hesitated to warp both personalities and events to fictional needs. This is a novel which utilizes selected facts from their real lives. It is in no sense a family history."[6]

The "J. M." of the acknowledgment was Mary Foote's granddaughter Janet Micoleau, one of the custodians of the original letters and Stegner's chief contact with the family as a whole. Unfortunately, however, there were to be serious misunderstandings between the author and (some of) the descendants. From the latter would come, after the book's publication, bitter charges of unethical "borrowing." Moreover, the Foote granddaughters found a scholar or two to take up their cause—and even to propound the strange argument that Mary Foote, not Wallace Stegner, should be seen as the real creator of *Angle of Repose*.[7] The critics' position boiled down to a pair of somewhat contradictory points. On the one hand, they alleged, Stegner had mirrored the reality of Foote's career so closely as to broach a kind of "plagiarism." On the other, he had significantly changed parts of that reality—by imagining, for example, an adulterous affair and certain dark currents of intrafamily tension. As a result, the work amounted finally to "slander."

Stegner would confess, in an interview given years later, to feeling "irritable" about all this—a word that probably understated his true feelings.[8] He had tried to inform the granddaughters as fully as possible about his intentions, and had followed their own wish in not acknowledging Mary Foote by name. The link to Foote's life and work had emerged in spite of his own best efforts, when the "Reminiscences" were published (independently and coincidentally) a year or two after the novel.[9] All things considered, he felt himself to have been misused. And clearly he took it hard that his greatest accomplishment as a writer should be crossed with such sharp public controversy.

The plagiarism-cum-slander charge would be hard to sort out without a detailed record of all the dealings between the author and family members. But perhaps it need not be a central issue here. The historian who was so deeply stirred upon reading *Angle of Repose* still struggles with the question it raised for him twenty-five years ago. The boundary between history and fiction is, if anything, a livelier issue now than it was then. And if one accepts that *Angle* remains fundamentally a novel, one must still ask how it achieves at the same time such extraordinary historical resonance.

The figure of the narrator is, for a start, highly persuasive *as historian;* working scholars will surely recognize themselves, and their experience, in much that is attributed to him. Thus he appears, by turns, evaluating specific bits of evidence, formulating new questions, inferring motives and results, and performing other mental acts common to everyday research. Moreover, Stegner uses him to show things that do not find their way onto most historians' pages but are nonetheless key parts of their process. At some points, the narrator virtually converses with his characters: for instance, "For God's sake, Grandmother, I feel like saying to her, what was the matter with him?" At others, he passes ironic judgment: "A terrible snob you were, Grandmother!" At still others, he teases: "A little Western boastfulness? *You,* Grandmother?" Sometimes, indeed, he teases himself: "When I catch grandmother thinking in this fashion, I shy away and draw the curtains lest I smile. It does not become a historian to smile." Such passages remind readers that scholarship can be personal, in a very immediate sense.[10]

The historical authenticity of *Angle of Repose* depends not only on the role assigned to its leading character, but also (and even more) on its portrayal of a specific past. Here, surely, lies the heart of our question. And, just as surely, the answer begins with a meticulous attention to the fine points of ordinary experience. The novelist Margaret Atwood has commented recently on this element in her own work. "Historical novels," she declares, must consistently evoke "the now-obscure details of daily life" in the past. While preparing to write her book *Alias Grace,* based on a nineteenth-century murder case, Atwood carried out extensive research into such matters as "how to clean a chamber pot, what footgear would have been worn in winter, the origins of quilt pattern names, and how to store parsnips."[11]

Likewise for Stegner, with *Angle of Repose;* he, too, has armed himself well in advance with innumerable bits of period detail. His deep knowledge of mining history, for example, enables him to carry off key scenes in the career of Oliver Ward. He writes confidently of "skips" and "tommy-knockers," of timbered shafts and glistening cables, of blast holes and draining ditches. He is equally well informed about nineteenth-century house-building, horsemanship, diet, drawing room furniture, clothing, climate—in short, all the material trappings of that particular time and culture. The tactile and tonal sharpness of all this is frequently dazzling. An elk's head, hung on a cabin wall as a trophy, is described thusly: "The varnished muzzle, coated with eighteen months of dust, shone as if wet in the light. A phantasmal fire glinted in the eyeballs. It might have bugled at any moment." At one point, two of the novel's main characters engage in a lengthy discussion of "the Sandwich Islanders" (the period name for Hawaii). At another, a group of young people play "the newly popular game of croquet." (And croquet was indeed "newly popular" in the 1870s and 1880s.)[12]

Even more important, perhaps, is Stegner's ability to evoke *place.* Building no doubt on his own long experience of western landscapes— and, too, on his love for those landscapes—he vividly re-creates their look

and feel and touch and timbre. He writes of "promontories blackened
with mussels and tide plants to high water mark, yellow from there to
their furzy tops." And of a mining town that "made its appearance as a
long gulch, littered with wreckage, shacks, and mine tailings . . . rutted
deep by ore wagons, scalped of its timber." And of mountain roads which
"passed through a scattering of alpine firs, runty and gnarled, and gave
way to brown grass that showed the faintest tint of green on the south-
ward slopes and disappeared under deep snowbanks on the northward
ones."[13]

Yet another piece of Stegner's achievement here involves diction—the
substance, the pitch, the pacing, of the novel's copious dialogue. In fact,
he exquisitely captures the *sound* of the late nineteenth century. (Or at
least what one imagines as its characteristic sound.) The speech of the
leading characters is marked throughout by a carefully measured, slightly
mannered quality. "I can consult no one but myself," declares Susan
Ward to her friend Augusta Drake upon deciding to marry Oliver. "I expect that was Mrs. Kendall," says Oliver in regard to a sudden arrival.
"You are not to be angry with me," says a certain Mrs. Elliott at a moment
when Susan is indeed annoyed. "I should think you'd hold a grudge
against Horace Tabor then," comments Susan in the midst of another
conversation with her husband.[14] "Consult," "expect," "are not to be,"
"should think"—these verbs, and their particular inflections, express a
distinct tone of formality. Yet formality does not mean rigidity, or con-
striction, or coldness. To the contrary, such speech forms stretch across a
remarkably wide emotional range.

Perhaps the unifying note in much of this is *irony*. And irony itself, in
Stegner's skillful hands, bends nicely in various different directions. Here
is irony as a form of affectionate teasing, when Susan questions her husband about their new home in a California mining camp. " 'You're no
fun,' she said. 'You won't let me gush. Tell me about our cabin in the
ditch. Is it really logs?' 'Really logs, [he replied]. A dollar a log.' 'Long
logs, how big is it?' 'Short logs. What do you expect for a dollar?' 'Has it
got a view?' 'The only way you could avoid a view up there is to go underground.' " And here is irony pressing toward tenderness, as Oliver
greets his little son after a separation of many months. " 'Here's a young
fellow I want to meet. Is your name Oliver Ward?' Not quite certain of

his ground—after all, his mother had kissed the other man first—Ollie said, 'Yes?' 'You know something? That's my name too. Do you suppose you're my little boy? I've got one somewhere. Ollie Ward. You suppose you're the one?' " And here, irony moving into reproach, as husband and wife wrangle over an opportunity to move to a remote mine in South America: " 'I'm *sorry* we're such a millstone around your neck.' " [15]

It is worth lingering over these fine points of dialogue because—perhaps more than anything else—they anchor the story in its own time and place. We will never be able to check them fully, since we cannot hear the nineteenth century "talk"; but they seem utterly plausible, and convincing, as the reconstruction they indubitably are. They comport nicely with what we know of nineteenth-century character (if one can speak in such terms). And they correspond as well to the written record from and about that time—including the personal writings of Mary Hallock Foote.

Yet another element in the novel's verisimilitude is its representation of period values and attitudes. In an early chapter, the narrator declares his liking for "the strenuousness, aspiration, and decorum of my grandmother's life, and the masculine steadiness of my grandfather's." Somewhat later, he adds this to his picture of Susan: "Work, progress, and the inviolability of contract, three of the American gospels, met and fused in her with the doctrines of gentility and the cult of the picturesque." It would be hard to imagine a sharper, more succinct summary of the core values of Victorian America's *haute bourgeoisie.* [16]

There are, at many points, pungent reflections of class difference. For example, Susan notes the way a group of miners' wives seemed impervious to the loneliness she felt, and wonders, "Was there something gnarly and tough about working-class people that kept them from feeling all that more delicately organized natures felt?" A bit later in the story, the narrator recounts an incident when company managers arranged to burn down the house of a recalcitrant miner—and adds this: "Which demonstrates our need of a sense of history; we need to know what real injustice looked like." Meanwhile, at the same moment, Susan herself, "standing outside of this casual revelation of how deep and violent were the divisions in the camp . . . felt as a woman running an orderly household might feel if she looked out the window and saw men fighting in the street." [17]

The novel offers a complex view of women's place and role in the late

nineteenth century—especially in its portrayal of Susan. "She came before the emancipation of women, and she herself was emancipated only
partly. . . . The impulse and the talent were there, without either inspiring models or full opportunity . . . [Still] there was an ambitious woman
under the Quaker modesty and the genteel conventions. The light foot
was for more than dancing, and the bright eye for more than flirtations,
the womanliness for more than mute submission to husband and
hearth."[18]

Through the voice of the narrator, Stegner is able to pronounce similarly shrewd judgments on all sorts of characteristic themes and tendencies. For example, this one about patriotism: "One of the charming things
about nineteenth-century America was its cultural patriotism—not jin-
goism, just patriotism, the feeling that no matter how colorful, exotic,
and cultivated other countries might be, there was no place so ultimately
right, so morally sound, so in tune with the hopeful future, as the U.S.A."
And this, about the process of western settlement: "So much that was
cherished and loved, women like her had to give up; and the more they
gave it up, the more they carried it helplessly with them. It was a process
like ionization: what was subtracted from one pole was added to the
other. For that sort of pioneer, the West was not a new country being created, but an old one being reproduced."[19]

In sum: From the details of diction and place, through the doings of its
central characters, to the broadest levels of historical and cultural generalization, *Angle of Repose* rings true—very true. As western history, as family history, as (part of) national history, it succeeds, it persuades, it
informs. So, what is the moral here, if any, for scholars—for those of us
who will never write fiction, but who (instead) will continue to follow a
more conventionally academic track? One point, perhaps, is an increased
willingness to re-create textures, as opposed to structures—and surfaces,
as opposed to underlying dynamics. Of course, there is always a balance
to strike in this regard; but it may be that modern scholarship (most of it
anyway) has overplayed the structural and the dynamic. Our question-
asking, hypothesis-testing, argument-framing mode, while enormously
fruitful in so many ways, has sometimes lost touch with ground-level realities in the life of the past. And where scholars have vacated this terri-

tory, others—including novelists and some nonacademic, nonfiction writers, too—have readily migrated in. Wallace Stegner is but one of a much larger group and trend. Margaret Atwood is another. Also the Canadian writer Brian Moore (whose novel *Black Robe,* closely based on historical sources, probes the relationship of missionaries and Indians in seventeenth-century New France), and the British novelist Barry Unsworth (whose *Sacred Hunger* offers an astonishing view of slavery and the slave trade).

Indeed, the list can be made quite long; "historical novels" seem to be reaching new levels of popularity and sophistication. Meanwhile, too, there are growing signs, from the side of academic history, of a convergent trend: of scholars attempting to practice in a more "novelistic" way. Robert Rosenstone's pioneering book *Mirror in the Shrine* (1988), Simon Schama's *Dead Certainties* (1991), Jonathan Spence's *The Question of Hu* (1988), and Stella Tillyard's *Aristocrats* (1994) can all be mentioned in this connection, along with two recent works, Donna Merwick's *Death of a Notary* (1999) and Linda Gordon's *The Great Arizona Orphan Abduction* (1999). All offer human detail and experiential textures not found in more conventional scholarly writing. All attend, in careful ways, to issues of plot and character. And all embrace some form of narrative sequencing. Moreover, the appearance of the present volume is itself testimony to new concerns among historians—and to an increased interest in reconnoitering the fact/fiction boundary. It should be said, if only in passing, that the choices posed here need not yield an either/or resolution. Analysis and interpretation will remain important goals even for those historians who aim to write in a more textural way. The trick is to make analysis congruent with, and embedded in, a narrative and descriptive treatment. As the old saw has it, this means more "showing" and less "telling."

With all this laid out, a final aspect of historical novels like *Angle of Repose* remains as yet unmentioned. What are such works finally *about?* Are they not something more than fictionalized evocations of past times and places? Do their creators have some further, and deeper, intentions—particularly, one supposes, around the matter of plotting? Listen to the narrator, in *Angle of Repose,* commenting on his project with his Ward grandparents, during a conversation with his son. " 'I'm not writing a book of Western history,' I tell him. . . . 'I'm writing about something else. A marriage, I guess.' " His reflections continue, but now in an interior way. "I have never formulated precisely what it is I have been doing, but the minute I say it I know I have said it right. What interests me in all these papers is not Susan Burling Ward the novelist and illustrator, and not Oliver Ward the engineer, and not the West they spent their lives in. What really interests me is how two such unlike particles clung together, and under what strains, rolling downhill into their future until they reached the angle of repose where I knew them. . . . That's where the meaning will be if I find any." [20]

Of course, this is Stegner himself talking—ventriloquizing, as it were, through the figure of the narrator. And what, exactly, is he saying? His subject is, in the first instance, "a marriage"—one particular marriage, molded by quite specific personalities and possibilities (including historical ones). But surely "a marriage" is also an instance of a larger *type* of marriage, where "unlike particles" are matched and roll in complicated ways toward their ultimate destinations. Moreover, from "type" there is a further progression, implied but supremely important, to marriage in general—or even to relationships in general. Which is to say that the fundamental "interest" of a novelist (any novelist?) is nothing less than generically significant experience.

Finally, then, what about history and historians? Are they also to be involved with the "generic"? Perhaps their concerns stop short of this crucial waterline. Perhaps a feeling for, and a focus on, particularities are what principally shape their enterprise. The generic, after all, seems by definition to transcend historically delimited time and place. Perhaps this is, for them, alien territory—best left to novelists (plus poets, philosophers, theologians, and others of their ilk).

But then again, perhaps not! Stegner's narrator is, after all, a fictional historian—which seems an important authorial choice. Those of us who operate as real-life historians might even feel emboldened by *Angle of Repose* to take a larger view of our own efforts. We do, and we always will, start from the particular. We go from there to the general—the type, the average, the trend, the tendency. But may we not hope, following the lead of the novelists, to proceed further still—to embrace the truly generic, to confront those parts of all lives (including our own) which can be lumped together as (how else to say it?) simply, and quintessentially, "human"?

꿈

SOME MONTHS, OR years, have passed. (We aren't told how many.) The narrator is at the end of a long process. (And the novel itself is ending.) Night falls; he sleeps; he dreams vividly—of past and present, of opportunities taken and missed, of hopes fulfilled and lost, of his own failed marriage and that of his grandparents. The various currents of his life cross, and recross, and come together—in a loudly resounding, deeply integrative way.

Upon waking, he reflects. The dream, he knows, was about forgiveness and fellow feeling, about the "intersection of lines"—and lives—and the "angle" needed to achieve at the end "some meeting." His grandparents, he thinks, "were vertical people, they lived by pride, and it is only by the ocular illusion of perspective that they can be said to have met." Still, their nearly simultaneous deaths (when very old) suggest "that at that absolute vanishing point they did intersect. Indeed, they had intersected for years, for more than he especially would ever admit."

But what, after all, is the "angle of repose"? Perhaps it is no more than "the angle at which two lives prop each other up, the leaning-together from the vertical which produces the false arch. For lack of a keystone the false arch may be as much as one can expect in this life. Only the very lucky discover the keystone." He is not among the lucky; he will never know the keystone. But he ends (and the book ends) not entirely without hope, "wondering if I am man enough to be bigger than my grandfather."[21]

Skip now to the late 1990s. The "real" (but no-longer-young) historian rereads these last lines. He experiences the same rush of emotion as formerly. And the same sense of recognition. And the same gratitude. He cannot entirely connect the dots that go from the narrator, and Susan, and Oliver, to himself. But he feels their presence and power, yet again. And feels, too, the way his own life is illuminated in the process.

He has made the journey through Angle of Repose *many times. He has recommended it to friends, discussed it with colleagues, taught it in his college*

courses. He is still unsure what to call it. Fiction? Of course. History? Why not.
And then he wonders: Does it really matter?

Notes

1. Wallace Stegner, *Angle of Repose* (first published by Doubleday & Co., Inc., New York, 1971: paperbound ed. by Fawcett Crest Books, New York, 1972). All page references in this essay are to the Fawcett Crest edition.

2. Alexander McMorran (1856–1924) and Julia May Putnam (1859–1943), married circa 1880. In the 1880s, the McMorrans homesteaded land near Newport, Washington. Subsequently, they lived in Spokane, Seattle, Bellingham, and Olympia. Alexander was involved in various prospecting schemes; he also worked for some periods as a pharmacist. Julia May was a homemaker.

3. Jackson J. Benson, *Wallace Stegner: His Life and Work* (New York: Viking, 1994), 108. Other biographical studies are Forrest G. Robinson and Margaret G. Robinson, *Wallace Stegner* (Boston: Twayne Publishers, 1977) and the essays in Charles E. Rankin, ed., *Wallace Stegner: Man and Writer* (Albuquerque, NM: University of New Mexico Press, 1966) and in Curt Meine, ed., *Wallace Stegner and the Continental Vision: Essays on Literature, History, and Landscape* (Washington, DC: Island Press, 1997). For comments by Stegner himself, see the very useful compilation in Wallace Stegner and Richard Etulain, eds., *Conversations with Wallace Stegner on Western History and Literature* (Salt Lake City: University of Utah Press, 1983).

4. For Stegner's own account of this sequence, see Stegner and Etulain, eds., *Conversations.*

5. On the life and work of Foote, see Lee Ann Johnson, *Mary Hallock Foote* (Boston: Twayne, 1980).

6. *Angle of Repose* (front matter).

7. The most emphatic of Stegner's scholarly accusers is Mary Ellen Williams Walsh; see her "*Angle of Repose* and the Writings of Mary Hallock Foote: A Source Study," in Anthony Arthur, ed., *Critical Essays on Wallace Stegner* (Boston: G. K. Hall & Co., 1982), 184–209. See also David Lavender, "The Tyranny of Facts," in Judy Nolte Lensink, ed., *Old Southwest/New Southwest: Essays on a Region and Its Literature* (Tucson, AZ: Tucson Public Library, 1987), 62–73.

8. Stegner and Etulain, eds., *Conversations*, 86.

9. Rodman W. Paul, ed., *A Victorian Gentlewoman in the Far West: The Reminiscences of Mary Hallock Foote* (San Marino, CA: The Huntington Library, 1972).

10. *Angle of Repose*, 57, 82, 116, 79.

11. Margaret Atwood, "In Search of *Alias Grace*: On Writing Canadian Historical Fiction," in *The American Historical Review* 103 (December 1998), 1514.

12. *Angle of Repose*, 248, 170, 165.

13. *Angle of Repose*, 150, 208.

14. *Angle of Repose*, 55, 128, 165–94.

15. *Angle of Repose*, 193, 254, 152.

16. *Angle of Repose*, 26, 110.

17. *Angle of Repose*, 96, 133, 132.

18. *Angle of Repose*, 283.

19. *Angle of Repose*, 284, 246.

20. *Angle of Repose*, 186.

21. *Angle of Repose*, 510–11.

The Historical Imagination
of *A Thousand Acres*

John Mack Faragher

I s Jane Smiley's *A Thousand Acres* (1991) a historical novel? A national best-seller that won the Pulitzer Prize and the National Book Critics Circle Award, the book has inspired a substantial critical literature. But that commentary focuses on what one writer calls the book's "enduring psychological truth" and another characterizes as its "timeless themes." I'm guessing most readers would agree. In fact, when I first suggested writing about the book for this collection, Smiley herself was skeptical. "Do you really consider *A Thousand Acres* a historical novel? I don't."[1]

I do. For me, the power of *A Thousand Acres* comes from Smiley's decision to root her story in American soil. True, the book is set in the recent not the distant past, its plot revolves around local not national events, and its characters are ordinary Americans, not important historic figures. Yet I am struck by the novel's historical resonance. It reconstructs and inhabits a specific past place and time—the midwestern farm crisis of the 1980s—and details the human relationships behind the headlines. It delves into the deep background of the tensions fueling the plot—the way modern farming can pollute the earth, capitalist land markets can fracture communities, and patriarchal families can wound women. Finally, it explores the ways the past and history itself can haunt the thoughts and actions of the characters. As a novelist, Smiley has the freedom to imagine a past that is in some ways truer than history. While it may not be a historical novel in the ordinary sense of the term, then, I believe that *A Thousand Acres* is an exemplar of what the historian and historical novelist Thomas Fleming calls a "novel of the historical imagination."[2]

❧

A THOUSAND ACRES is best known for Smiley's feminist retelling of Shakespeare's *King Lear.* The novel opens, as does the play, with an aging patriarch resolving to divide his kingdom among his three adult daughters. Sixty-six-year-old Larry Cook owns a thousand acres of rich Iowa prairie, making him the closest thing to a king in Zebulon County. Oldest and middle daughters Ginny and Rose, both in their mid-thirties, live with their husbands in homes of their own down the road, but cook, clean, and keep house for their father—their mother having died of cancer years before. The sons-in-law, Ty and Pete, help work the land, but Larry treats them little better than hired hands. Both couples welcome the old man's retirement and make plans to mortgage the farm to finance improvements. But little sister Caroline, a lawyer living in Des Moines, hesitates. She is Larry's favorite child and he has concocted this scheme to get her back on the farm. All she does is express a doubt—"I don't know"—but it cuts her father to the quick and he angrily signs the farm over to the others. Like Lear, Larry's a man accustomed to getting his way, and, like Lear, he "impulsively betrayed himself." Disaster follows. Larry plunges into dark depression, drinks too much, and behaves erratically. One stormy night he explodes and vows to get his land back. He reconciles with Caroline, who files suit against her sisters to reclaim the farm. The trial rips the family apart. The improvement project is blocked and the bank forecloses the mortgage. The farm kingdom is lost to the creditors. Larry dies of a broken heart.

Given the parallels with *King Lear,* it is no surprise that critics have given relatively little consideration to the book's treatment of history. Yet, from the opening pages, Smiley offers a detailed consideration of the historical setting. "Zebulon County" and the other local place-names Smiley employs are her own inventions, but her portrayal of the central Iowa countryside carries conviction. We first see it through the eyes of Ginny, who narrates the story. It is the spring of 1979 and the plowing has left the land exposed, black and fecund. Ginny stands atop a little rise north of the family farm and surveys the flat earth, the domed sky, the county roads running to the cardinal points along the section lines. A mile to the east stand the silos marking the Cooks' northeast corner, a mile to the south their cluster of barns and homes. It is an iconic midwestern landscape. There is "no sign of anything remotely scenic in the distance."

For many readers, the American countryside is terra incognita. They associate rural places with the distant past or even timelessness. Smiley will have none of this. Zebulon County is not some idealized rural world, but a little piece of 1970s America. The televisions are tuned to *Let's Make a Deal*, *Wheel of Fortune*, or *Phil Donahue*. Characters buy takeout at Kentucky Fried Chicken or heat up frozen "French bread pizza with pepperoni and extra cheese." Others are preoccupied with trendier food fads. The family's banker comes to breakfast carrying his own six-pack of Perrier and offering dietary proscriptions—"it's not what you eat, but the order you eat it in that counts." Jesse Clark, son of a neighboring farmer, has returned from Canada, where he fled to avoid the draft; a vegetarian and sometime Buddhist, he hopes to convert the family place into an organic farm. Zebulon County is awash in American culture.

Smiley not only creates a historical moment, she also carefully historicizes the landscape itself. In its natural state, the Cook farm had been a wetland, with water flowing over the surface to a depth of two feet, creating a maze of marshes and ponds. When Ginny's ancestors arrived in the 1890s, they found the land "a shimmering sheet punctuated by cattails and sweet flag." Immediately they set to work—digging cisterns, wells, and trenches, and laying drainage tile—redirecting the flow of water underground. Reclaiming the land required a quarter-century of hard labor but resulted in a warm, workable, and wonderfully fertile soil. Ginny knows that "however much these acres looked like a gift of nature, or of God, they were not." Her father speaks of farming with "reverence," but what he reveres is man's dominion over nature.

Larry Cook is an apostle of high-tech farming. His world has not been static and timeless at all, but dynamic and full of change. During his lifetime, an industrial revolution in agriculture has reinvented the practice of farming, and Larry was an early convert to the new faith. Ginny discovers an old issue of a farm newspaper featuring her father as the model progressive farmer. "There isn't any room for the old methods anymore," he is quoted. "Farmers who embrace the new methods will prosper, but those that don't are already stumbling around." During the postwar period, mechanization, genetic engineering, mineral fertilizers, and chemical pest control boosted agricultural productivity at a rate twice that of the manufacturing sector of the economy. By the 1970s, an hour of labor on the most advanced industrial farms produced four times more corn and five times more pork than a quarter-century before. Farming became a highly competitive enterprise. Larry's perspective is echoed in the reaction of Ginny's husband, Ty, to Jesse Clark's organic farming. "People don't realize there isn't any room any more for something that might not work out. . . . It's more complicated than people think, just reading books."

In the spring of 1979, the farmers of Zebulon County have reason to be optimistic. The decade was a time of unprecedented agricultural boom. In 1971, President Nixon "unpegged" the dollar, allowing its value to float relative to other currencies, making American products much less expensive in foreign markets. Simultaneously, poor weather conditions and low crop yields around the world created tremendous demand for American agricultural commodities. In 1972, the United States and the Soviet Union negotiated a multiyear contract for wheat and grain, and within two years the price of wheat doubled and corn tripled. Agriculture Secretary Earl Butz called on American farmers to plant "fencerow to fencerow" and challenged them to "get bigger, get better, or get out." As the value of farmland climbed apace with demand, many farmers negotiated loans to expand and modernize their operations. New steel storage structures sprouted all over the county, squat, black Slurrystores for hog waste, and Harvestores for livestock feed, "blue and efficient, with clean lines and round edges." New closed-cab, air-conditioned tractors worked the fields. Harold Clark proudly shows off his brand-new International Harvester, complete with onboard cassette player for listening to his tapes of Bob Wills and the Texas Playboys. The thing cost him $40,000, financed with a mortgage against the Clark farm.

"Shit, Ty," Harold's son Loren exclaims to Ginny's husband, "that lit-

tle debt nestled right into our net worth and got lost." The Cook place
has never been mortgaged, but the banker assesses it at $3,200 an acre, a
net worth of considerably more than $3,000,000, and Ty dreams aloud
about the improvements this makes possible. "Those Slurrystores are
great. They hold eighty thousand gallons of hog slurry. After it cools off,
you can put it right in the fields. I'd like one of those. And a hog confinement building. Air-conditioned. I want one of them too." Ty rolls over in
bed and smiles at Ginny, who is worried. "It makes me feel weird to toss
around all these high numbers. Anyway, who would buy at these prices?
And everybody's bitching about interest rates." Ty brushes her concerns
aside. "But interest rates are always up, and maybe prices will go higher."
Creating a world through the novelist's magic of description, dialogue,
and emplotment, Smiley incorporates the essential elements of the historical backdrop without belaboring them.

Equally implicit is Smiley's judgment of this history—horrified by the
culture as well as the practice of industrial agriculture. Despite lives spent
working the land, Larry Cook and other male characters in the novel harbor a fear and loathing of the natural world. "Daddy's not much for untamed nature," Ginny remarks. With the exception of a dump behind the
outbuildings—significantly, the place where Ginny and Jesse Clark share
secrets and consummate a sexual affair—Larry has converted virtually
every square foot of his land to production, even draining, filling, and
plowing over a small pond where his daughters loved to swim. He and his
friend Harold Clark ruthlessly destroy the small animals that invade their
fields, and Larry scorns the sentimentality of the people on a neighboring
farm who populate their barnyard with cows, goats, and sheep, chickens,
geese, and turkeys, simply "because they like them." There will be a price
to pay for this environmental hubris.

By the seventies farmers in the Corn Belt were applying millions of
pounds of fertilizers, pesticides, and herbicides to their corn and soybean
fields. Larry is one of the first farmers in his locality to have his fields
sprayed by crop dusters. Over many years, these chemical compounds
seep into the groundwater and accumulate to lethal levels. As readers, we
suspect, long before we're told, that these poisons are responsible for
Ginny's many miscarriages. Her sister Rose has two young daughters, but
the poisons are responsible for her cancer—which has already claimed a

breast and will eventually kill her—as well as the cancer that killed the girls' mother and the mother of the Clark boys. Ginny gradually becomes fully aware of "the loop of poison we drank from, the water running down through the soil, into the drainage wells, into the lightless mysterious underground chemical sea, then being drawn up, cold and appetizing, from the drinking well into Rose's faucet, my faucet." Farm chemicals are dangerous. Before the novel's end, Harold Clark will be blinded by an accidental spray of anhydrous ammonia.

Smiley's take on modern farming is uniformly negative, too one-sided for me. The novel offers no acknowledgment of the remarkable achievements of industrial agriculture, more than keeping up with population growth, with the result that Americans are generally better fed and healthier today than ever before. The virtual epidemic of cancer in the novel also strikes me as over the top, although there are good reasons to credit Smiley's pollution scenario. In laboratory tests the chemicals in agricultural runoff have been identified as carcinogens. Moreover, some of them are "endocrine disrupters"—compounds that when broken down by the body mimic human hormones such as estrogen, greatly increasing the risk of breast cancer in adult women. The epidemiological data are not yet sufficient to allow scientists to make firm connections between incidents of cancer and the agricultural pollution of groundwater. But according to a 1994 study released by the Environmental Protection Agency, many rural Corn Belt communities suffer with drinking water supplies heavily contaminated by chemical runoff and face cancer risks 10 to 116 times the federal benchmark of acceptability.[3]

Still, I am not yet willing to abandon faith in the power of technology to improve and society to regulate. In a recent study of agricultural industrialization, economist Emery N. Castle examines American views of modern farming. Many people take a "hands off" approach, arguing that despite undesirable effects such as chemical pollution, any tampering with the free market will lower productivity and raise the price of farm commodities. Smiley invests most of her male characters with some version of this attitude. At the other extreme are those who condemn "agribusiness" and argue for the complete restructuring of the system. Both these views, Castle argues, are wrong because they ignore history. All industrial systems, farming included, require monitoring and managing. This is the only realistic option, although it requires facing tough questions on a situation-by-situation basis. Castle finds that most farmers accept and support this position, but it is a view that is little represented in *A Thousand Acres*.[4]

I suspect that my difference with Smiley has less to do with the evidence than with the distinction between her art and mine. It would be ludicrous to argue that the novelist shares the historian's responsibility to account for complications, contradictions, and conundrums. First and foremost, novelists must tell a good story.

✑

ONE OF THE most important stories the novel tells is how the Cook family acquired their thousand contiguous acres. Ginny's grandfather and father "saved their money and kept their eyes open, and when their neighbors had no money, they had some, and bought what their neighbors couldn't keep." During the hard times of the Depression, they purchase several hundred acres from a family too down and out to pay their taxes. In the late 1950s Larry bought out a neighboring farm family who were not tough-minded enough to make a success of it. Ginny is virtually weaned on this "satisfying story" of progress, with its moral lessons of thrift and enterprise. But outside the family, neighbors grumble and gossip about Larry's success. Ginny wonders if those opportunities "had really landed in his lap, or if there were moments of planning, of manipulation and using a man's incompetence and poverty against him." What's bad for some farmers is good for others. "A land deal was a land deal, and few were neighborly," she concludes. "The seemingly stationary fields are always flowing toward one farmer and away from another." In *A Thousand Acres*, the shape of modern farming is determined by the logic of capitalism, not the logic of community.

The transition to market capitalism in American agriculture has been the focus of a good deal of historical attention. There is a consensus among historians that while nineteenth-century American farmers participated in the market economy, the force of community among them was strong. Local families were bound together by kinship, Christian communion, frontier community building. People relied on their neighbors, not only for company but for labor and resources. Barn-raisings and quilting bees are only the best-remembered of many mundane working connections. But let's be clear about this. The conflicting traditions of community and commerce—of sharing and acquiring—were always in tension, yet both remained vital forces into the twentieth century. It was the industrial revolution in agriculture that drastically tipped the scales away from sharing and in favor of acquiring. Anthropologist Kathryn Marie Dudley, who interviewed dozens of farm men and women for her wonderfully nuanced portrait of today's farming communities, finds that an "entrepreneurial ethos" has become the dominating force.[5]

Dudley's conclusion applies full well to Smiley's Zebulon County, where neighborliness has morphed into what Ginny calls *The Eye*—the always watching, always judging, always calculating gaze of neighbor on neighbor. She recalls childhood tours of the countryside in the family's big Buick, her parents supplying commentary on each passing farm. "Their tones of voice were unhurried and self-confident, complacent with the knowledge that the work at our place was farther along, the buildings at our place more imposing and better cared for." Her father knows "who owned what indistinguishable flat black acreage, how he had gotten it, what he had done and should have done with it, who got it after him and by what tricks or betrayals." Everyone watches, and everyone hides. "Don't tell your neighbors your business," Larry teaches his children, and his favorite remark about things in general is "Less said about *that*, the better." The essential thing is "keeping up appearances." When the Cooks wage civil war over the fate of the farm it matters all the more what *The Eye* sees. "Appearances are everything," insists the lawyer preparing to defend against Caroline's suit. Ginny is particularly good at it. "I was so remarkably comfortable with the discipline of making a good appearance! It was like going back to school or church after a long absence. It had ritual and measure." These are the rituals of a seriously dysfunctional society, what Dudley calls the "fragile community" of rural America.

The Cook family turmoil coincides with a particularly perilous time in the recent history of American agriculture. The case comes to court in

October of 1979, the same month American farmers took the first of a devastating one-two punch. In a move calculated to break the back of inflation—which had risen to an annual rate of more than 10 percent—the Federal Reserve reversed its former policy and began to increase interest rates. The strategy eventually succeeded, but not before the cost of borrowing had been driven well into double digits. Higher interest rates meant increased costs of production and a corresponding reduction in the earning capacity of farmland. Even as farmers were still reeling from the implications of this policy shift, they were knocked cold by an unexpected second blow—the grain boycott of the Soviet Union imposed by President Carter in January 1980 in response to the invasion of Afghanistan. The resulting steep decline in foreign demand was exacerbated by the rising value of the dollar, pumped up by interest rates. In anticipation of lower agricultural profits, the inflated value of farmland and machinery went into free fall. Suddenly, farmers who had taken on large debt found their net worth insufficient to secure their loans. Over the next few years, thousands of families lost their farms, hundreds of rural banks collapsed, and the nation's agricultural credit system teetered on the brink of bankruptcy.

In the novel, Caroline's suit is dismissed, but not before the Cooks are forced to hang out all their dirty laundry. The banker is watching carefully along with everyone else. "I can't hide from you I'm worried," he tells Ginny. "Everyone down at the bank is worried about this thing with your dad." With the changes in the economy, the Cook farm is worth much less, and because it is already encumbered with large debt, the bank eventually refuses to make loans for spring planting. "Those hog buildings killed me, that's what it was," Ty later reflects. He tries to raise capital by selling the small place he'd inherited from his own father—which he'd been renting out—"but property values weren't anything like they'd been, and what I got didn't cover much of the loan. . . . Just got behind. And then more behind." The land is eventually bought up by covetous neighbors. The special pain of farm loss, writes Dudley, "comes from a culture in which members of a community are authorized to ignore—and yes, profit from—the sufferings of their neighbor." In myriad ways, the Cook family crisis mirrors a larger social crisis of the modern farm community.[6]

JP

As DISASTER PILES upon disaster for the Cooks, Ginny thinks to herself, "Wouldn't it be a relief to have everything out in the open for once?"
But instantly she recognizes "that the one thing our family couldn't tolerate, that maybe no family could tolerate, was things coming into the
open." Ginny herself is afraid of confronting the truth. For most of her
adult life, she realizes, "I had stopped thinking about the past"—there
was much to forget. After the storm-tossed confrontation with their father, Ginny and Rose sit up talking late into the night. Rose grows impa-
tient with her sister's attempts to understand Larry's behavior. "Ginny,
you don't remember how he came after us, do you?" Indeed, Ginny
doesn't remember and she's stunned when Rose insists that their father
sexually abused them both when they were teenagers. "He was having sex
with you. . . . After he stopped going in to you, he started coming in to
me." Ginny angrily denies it. She has repressed all memory of the trauma.
But some days later, while wandering through the rooms of her father's
abandoned house, vivid images of being raped by her father come rushing
back to her. She wonders how much more there is to remember. Her past
she visualizes as "mysterious bulging items in a dark sack, unseen as yet,
but felt. I feared them. I feared how I would have to store them in my
brain, plastic explosives or radioactive wastes that would mutate or even
wipe out everything else in there. . . . Discussion would open that terrible
sack and shine a light into it." Ginny's coming to terms with her own
place in history is the core struggle of *A Thousand Acres*.

   She can't do it without the help of Rose, who unlike Ginny is clear
about what happened and why. Among the three daughters, Rose is the
one most like her father. "The hardest thing for me is not grabbing
things," she tells Ginny. "I *want* what was Daddy's," she admits. "I feel
like I've paid for it, don't you? You think a breast weighs a pound? That's
my pound of flesh." Rose's grabbing is not endearing. One of the things
she goes after is Jesse Clark—who cuts off his adulterous affair with
Ginny and begins another with Rose—driving her husband, Pete, to suicide. Ginny is overcome with jealously and loathing, and even plots her
sister's murder. But through it all, Rose's words resonate with the ring of
truth. "Say the words, Ginny!" she demands. "If he hadn't fucked us and

beat us we would think differently, right? . . . But he did fuck us and he did beat us." Ginny is soothed by "the simple truth" of what her sister says, "as if we'd finally found the basic atoms of things, hard as they were." Rose has thought it all through. "We were just his, to do with as he pleased, like the pond or the houses or the hogs or the crops." Early in the novel, talking about Caroline's impending marriage, she jokes that "according to Daddy, it's almost too late to breed her. Ask him. He'll tell you all about sows and heifers and things drying up and empty chambers. It's a whole theoretical system." A system called patriarchy.

Smiley's hard line on male domination echoes one of the positions in an ongoing debate among historians of rural America. Some have argued that the importance of women's labor on the farm mitigated gender inequality, overriding the political and economic factors otherwise subordinating women. Others—among whom I count myself—read the evidence quite differently. Yes, women's contribution has always been critical to the success of farming, but labor alone never has conferred power. Rural women have traditionally had little decision-making authority within the family. Their work kept them confined to the home place, and because American farms tend to be spread out over the countryside, rather than clustered in villages, most farm women lived terribly isolated lives.[7]

There is also accumulating evidence that these conditions fostered a culture of violence against women. Historian David Peterson del Mar finds it in late-nineteenth-century court records. One man, defending himself against the charge of wife-battering, explained to the judge that "a man should rule over his wife in everything except religion." Another argued that he had used only the violence "necessary and reasonable to enforce rightful obedience," and swore he'd hit his wife again "if she did not do to suit." A father, testifying on behalf of his daughter's petition for divorce, said that many times he'd seen evidence of her husband's abuse. "I saw her with a very black eye," he told the judge, and when he asked about it, she told him, "Pa, the world will never know what trouble I have seen." Records of this type emphasize the worse, of course, but other sources suggest that domestic violence was commonplace. Readers of Nebraska writer Mari Sandoz's biography of her homesteader father, *Old Jules* (1935), are shocked at his violent treatment of women. When

Sandoz's mother asks her husband to help her with the work around the farmyard, he rages—"You want me, an educated man, to work like a hired tramp!"—and throws her against a wall. When Sandoz was eight, her father brought a convicted child molester from the state penitentiary to work on their farm and live in their home. One night he came after Mari, and she had to defend herself with a gun. Sandoz makes it clear that these men were typical of many she knew growing up in Nebraska. A woman was something to exploit—for work, for sex, and for bearing children.[8]

Historian Deborah Fink, in an important project of the 1980s, interviewed dozens of rural Nebraska women about their personal histories. These conversations, she writes, "opened onto a sea of pain." Women told stories of young girls sexually molested, not only by hired hands, but fathers and brothers. One woman told Fink that when she reached puberty, her father forced her to have sex with him repeatedly. Another confronted her father-in-law with her suspicions that he was sexually abusing her daughter. He justified himself by saying that the sexual fondling of children on the farm was so common he was surprised she paid any attention to it. Fink finds evidence in such abundance she concludes that the sexual abuse of women was a basic underpinning of their subordinate status.[9]

Ginny's painful recognition that her father's abuse is part of a "system" throws up insuperable obstacles with her husband. Ty is one of the more complicated characters in the novel, and I can't shake the feeling that in not providing him with the opportunity to grow, Smiley wasn't fair with him. He is a good man, but there is no one to struggle with him the way Rose struggles with her sister. Instead, Ginny hides things from him: the knowledge of her recent miscarriages, her affair with Jesse Clark, her discoveries about her past. Ty is reduced to offering advice that seems painfully insensitive. "I've always thought the best way to deal with your father is to sort of hunker down and let it blow over . . . You don't always have to take issue. You ought to let a lot of things slide." Ty shares his basic assumptions with the other men in Ginny's life. A farm, Harold Clark tells her, is "more than one person is. One person don't break a farm up that lots of people have sweated and starved to put together. . . . Women don't understand that." Jesse Clark, despite his belief in organic farming, is no different. When Ginny wearily questions whether it's all worth it, Jesse responds—"A big farm and the chance to run it the way you want is a reward." "You're kidding," she says, but he's not. He has come home to claim the farm, and when that doesn't work out, he leaves. Ty's perspective is much the same. Running his own farm his own way—"That was my dream, and it was coming true. . . . I never thought it would be easy, but I thought I was making progress, and then you women just wrecked it." Ginny comes to think of Ty as "forthright and good and blind," and concludes that his "real loyalties lay with Daddy." They stop having sex and they stop communicating. By the time the court case ends, their alienation is complete and Ginny leaves him. "I gave my life to this place," Ty yells at her as she stumbles out of the house. "Now it's yours," she shouts back.

Ginny moves to St. Paul, Minnesota, where she supports herself by waitressing. She sees Ty one last time when he comes to ask for a divorce. He has decided to relocate to Texas, where he hopes to make a new life on the land. He has heard from Rose the story of what Larry did to his girls. The way he reports this makes it clear to Ginny that he doesn't believe it. "Maybe it happened. I don't say it didn't," he says. But "people should keep private things private." He sounds like Larry.

The two of them begin to argue. "I was on the side of the farm, that was all," Ty explains. "For years, it was right, and we prospered and we got along and we did the way we knew we should be doing, and sure there were little crosses to bear but it was right." He takes a deep breath and lowers his voice. "There was real history there!" Ginny responds after carefully choosing her words. "I can remember when I saw it all your way!" The history of the farm as a proud tale of progress—the gradual accumulation of land, the first tractor in the county, the record harvests.

"I can remember all of that like prayers or like being married. You know. It's good to remember and repeat. You feel good to be a part of that. But then I saw what my part really was. You see this grand history, but I see blows. I see taking what you want because you want it, then making something up that justifies what you did. I see getting others to pay the price, then covering up and forgetting what the price was. Do I think Daddy came up with beating and fucking us on his own? No, I think he had lessons, and those lessons were part of the package, along with the land and the lust to run things exactly the way he wanted to no matter what, poisoning the water and destroying the topsoil and buying bigger and bigger machinery, and then feeling certain that all of it was 'right,' as you say."

"I guess we see things differently," says Ty. "More differently than you imagine," Ginny concludes.

Ginny returns to Zebulon County only once more, for the bankruptcy sale of the farm and a reconciliation with Rose, who is dying of her cancer. She will raise Rose's two girls in the city. None of them will have anything more to do with farming. She is left battered and regretful, but not destroyed. Opening the dark sack of the past and examining its contents—coming to terms with her own history—has saved her from despair.

Notes

1. Reviews of *A Thousand Acres* in the *London Financial Times*, October 17, 1992, and *The Toronto Star*, March 7, 1992.

2. Thomas Fleming, "Before You Write Your Historical Novel," *Writer* 108 (February 1995):9–13.

3. Environmental Working Group, *Tap Water Blues* (Washington: Environmental Protection Agency, 1994), reported in *USA Today*, October 19, 1994.

4. Emery N. Castle, *Agricultural Industrialization in the American Countryside* (Arlington, VA: Henry A. Wallace Center for Agricultural and Environmental Policy, 1998).

5. Kathryn Marie Dudley, *Debt and Dispossession: Farm Loss in America's Heartland* (Chicago: University of Chicago Press, 2000), 156.

6. Dudley, *Debt and Dispossession*, 229.

7. John Mack Faragher, *Sugar Creek: Life on the Illinois Prairie* (New Haven: Yale University Press, 1986).

8. David Peterson del Mar, *What Trouble I Have Seen: A History of Violence Against Wives* (Cambridge, MA: Harvard University Press, 1996), 1, 24, 25, 31; Mari Sandoz, *Old Jules* (Boston: Little, Brown, 1935), quoted in Susan Armitage and Elizabeth Jameson, eds., *The Women's West* (Norman, OK: University of Oklahoma Press, 1987), 113.

9. Deborah Fink, *Agrarian Women: Wives and Mothers in Rural Nebraska, 1880–1940* (Chapel Hill: University of North Carolina Press, 1992), xviii, 86.

✑

Not a Pretty Picture

Jane Smiley

Reading Professor Faragher's essay on *A Thousand Acres* is not, for me, a happy reexperiencing of a novel-writing episode that I enjoyed or remember fondly. I have always felt somewhat removed from my most famous novel, always felt that the material was not my own and not congenial to my sensibility, either as an author or as a citizen. Nonetheless, I accept, as a reader and as an observer, that there is a rightness about how it all fits together. For me, this bolsters my long-standing opinion that a novel is an extended piece of logic, a narrative that in some sense "uses" an author to birth it, but owes as much to its own internal system as it does to the thought processes or the attitudes of the author.

The obvious internal system of *A Thousand Acres* is *King Lear*. The material of the play was already very ancient by the time Shakespeare got to it, which means that the patterns of human behavior that it recognizes and explores are deeply ingrained ones. You might say that the Lear material runs parallel to and comments upon the ongoing tensions within families of fathers and daughters as they express themselves at different points in history. These tensions would naturally be about power, sexuality, love, and isolation. In different cultures and eras, ideas about what a family is would be superimposed upon the basic father/daughter situation rather lightly, and considerable drama would come from the contrast and conflict between cultural norms of family life and what you might call the biological or mammalian urges that the dominant male has toward his offspring of the opposite sex. Issues of sexuality are no different from issues of the power hierarchy. The daughters mate and bring alien males into the group. The ownership of the territory comes into question. The question is worked out. It happens every day. It is because the Lear material is so basic and so ancient that we can link it to the behavior patterns of wolves, horses, chimps, gorillas, farmers, corporate executives, movie stars.

While I did not write *A Thousand Acres* as a historical novel, I knew that its appropriate historical moment was a specific one—a time when land values were so high that any farmer who might die and leave the farm to his children would risk their losing the farm, or part of it, to high inheritance taxes. That this moment was followed by the crash of the midwestern farm economy was understandable and even predictable—the history of farming in America, and of agriculture itself, has always been cyclical, because agriculture encourages the human species to be out of balance with the natural world. Being out of balance with the natural world, in fact, being in conflict with the natural world, is the *point* of farming, and, indeed, the point of culture, which farming allows. Agriculture wrests abundance from nature by making use of the way in which annual crops overreproduce themselves. If the seeds are saved rather than lost, and the annual production of green matter is divvied up between the soil and foraging animals, something seems to have been gotten for nothing, and civilizations result. But the very experience, for the human, of creating abundance and then hoarding it convinces him that the specter of scarcity is real, and as he then overreproduces himself, the possibility of scarcity becomes more and more real.

For the Cook family, the feeling that scarcity always haunts them is a strong motivating force. Everything is too scarce. If crop production is high, then prices will be low. When land is plentiful, time will be short. If the family owns more and more land, then labor will be costly or absent. If a great deal of money has been spent on equipment to save time and labor, then money will be short. If everyone is out in the fields working, or in the house working, then they will feel a deprivation of love and kinship, both within the family and within the community. Larry Cook, obviously, is the most powerful and isolated of all. He is irascible and unsociable and he has lost his wife. But he has an abundance of daughters. To turn toward them for a distorted sort of intimacy is a natural, though of course not a culturally condoned, thing to do. Feelings of scarcity al-

ways cause isolation and fear. For a man like Larry, for whom there is no
felt, countervailing force, like faith, to balance his fears of scarcity, there
is nothing in his world but the unspeakable. Every subject of conversation
leads too readily to terror, and so there is no conversation. Life looks like
stoicism or stolidity, but really it is a tissue of avoidance lightly masking
seething fear and its product, anger.

I lived in Iowa through the farm crisis and knew many farmers. My
views of farming and farm life were like those of most city folk. I thought
things were peaceful and bucolic out on the farm, though I regretted the
necessity farmers felt of using poisonous farm chemicals on the land
around me. I shared with most Americans the aesthetic appreciation of
what farms look like, the notion that a farm is first and foremost a beautiful, orderly thing. When I brought together the material from *King Lear*
and the structure of midwestern farming, I did not understand where the
conjunction would take me, but I did think it was an appropriate conjunction, if only because the *King Lear* material and farming are of similar age
and equally embedded in our culture. The structure of one was not the
structure of the other, but they were applicable to one another, I hoped.
The resulting novel, I thought, showed that my original instinct that
the two could illumine one another was correct. I suspected that the
structure could include incest, partly because in other parts of the world,
farmlike isolation has given rise to incest and child abuse and partly because some folklorists have linked the Lear material to other folk narratives of incest. Therefore, though I did not read any of the material cited
by Dr. Faragher in his article, I was not surprised to discover it. But just as
King Lear is not the story of every family, *A Thousand Acres* is not the story
of every farm, or of farming in general. *King Lear* is very specifically a
tragedy; that is, the author has chosen a literary form with its own conventions as a lens or a mold for his material, probably because he senses
that the material is congenial to that form. *A Thousand Acres* follows *King
Lear* in its form, and so is a tragedy, not an investigative report about
American farming. The very historical details that Dr. Faragher cites are
there to build the illusion that the novel is "reportlike," and to make the
tragic vision of the novel convincing as "Realism," a form that novels
may take. But tragedy is above all things like every other literary form, an
imposition of meaning and order upon otherwise meaningless details.

The writer and the reader use the form together to make a transitory meaning that enlightens them in passing about how the world works. In the end, though, every form is a compromise and every work is limited, and for both writer and reader, the limits of each work and form give rise to a yearning for something else.

PART III

Slavery

Commerce in Souls:
Uncle Tom's Cabin and the
State of the Nation

Joan D. Hedrick

Perhaps more than any other novel, *Uncle Tom's Cabin* is entwined with our national history. Harriet Beecher Stowe undertook the novel in response to the passage by Congress of the Fugitive Slave Law in 1850. This law required that all U.S. citizens assist in the capture of runaway slaves and mandated fines and imprisonment for those who dared to aid them in their flight. Northerners who may have preferred not to think about the South's "peculiar institution" now had to decide what they would do in the event that a runaway slave came knocking at their door. In *Uncle Tom's Cabin*, Stowe unabashedly urged them to civil disobedience.

In one of the crisscrossing plots of the novel, which appeared in weekly installments from June 5, 1851, until April 1, 1852, in the antislavery *National Era*, Eliza Harris flees with her five-year-old son, who is about to be sold to satisfy a debt. On her way to Canada, Eliza seeks refuge at the home of Senator and Mrs. Bird. Mrs. Bird, who, like Harriet Beecher Stowe, had recently lost a child, opens her heart and the bureau drawer which contains her little boy's clothes. The Birds clothe the refugees, feed and comfort them, and finally help them to escape. They do, Stowe suggests, what any human being would have done when confronted with their human distress. But this creates a dilemma for the "patriotic Senator, that had been all the week before spurring up the legislature of his native state to pass more stringent resolutions against escaping fugitives, their harborers and abettors!" Senator Bird had distinguished himself before his colleagues with his eloquence, and "scouted all sentimental weakness of those who would put the welfare of a few miserable fugitives before great state interests!"

> He was as bold as a lion about it, and "mightily convinced" not only himself, but everybody that heard him;—but then his idea of a fugitive was only an idea of the letters that spell the word,—or, at the most, the image of a little newspaper picture of a man with a stick and bundle, with "Ran away from the subscriber" under it. The magic of the real presence of distress,— the imploring human eye, the frail, trembling human hand, the despairing appeal of helpless agony,—these he had never tried. He had never thought that a fugitive might be a hapless mother, a defenceless child,—like that one now wearing his lost boy's little well-known cap; and so, as our poor senator was not stone or steel,—as he was a man, and a down-right noble-hearted one, too,—he was, as everybody must see, in a sad case for his patriotism.[1]

This can stand as an example of Stowe's method throughout *Uncle Tom's Cabin*. She takes the bare reality of "the letters that spell the word," the reality described in a newspaper ad for a fugitive slave, and then with her novelist's imagination gives flesh and personality and speech and familial ties to this "property." She also melded the plot of slave narratives to the genre of the historical novel, producing, in some sense, the romance of slavery. In particular, she showed slaves in heroic and martyred postures. Both of these, while controversial, embodied a new way of seeing African slaves.

It was an effective strategy. A traveler in the United States from England told of staying in a strange house, and being kept awake by the sounds of a man "alternately groaning and laughing." He "knocked upon the wall and said, 'Hallo there! What's the matter? Are you sick or reading 'Uncle Tom's Cabin?' " The man was reading Stowe's novel.[2] It sold 300,000 copies in the first year of publication, was translated into sixty-three languages, and generated an industry of Uncle Tom plates, spoons, candlesticks, games, wallpapers, songs, and stage spin-offs that ran continuously for the next ninety years.

From the time of its publication, *Uncle Tom's Cabin* has been held up to a standard of truth. To answer a wide array of questions and objections, Stowe wrote *A Key to Uncle Tom's Cabin*. Unlike William Styron, who when challenged about the character of Nat Turner took refuge in the license of the artist,[3] Stowe acknowledged that her novel was "*treated* as a reality,—sifted, tried and tested, as a reality; and therefore as a reality it may be proper that it should be defended" (p. 412) and she provided a multitude of sources for characters and incidents. Stowe's documentary response is characteristic of the nineteenth-century historical novel, where notes and appendices illustrating the evidentiary basis of the narrative were common ever since Sir Walter Scott copied the technique from Jane Porter, whose novel *The Scottish Chiefs* (1810) was Scott's inspiration.

Southerners, enraged by the sensation Stowe's novel enjoyed, argued that her portrait of slavery was highly colored. Stowe disarmed these critics by admitting that the book was "a very inadequate representation of slavery," for "in some of its workings, [slavery] is too dreadful for the purposes of art. A work which should represent it strictly as it is would be a work which could not be read. And all works which ever mean to give pleasure must draw a veil somewhere, or they cannot succeed" (p. 412). At least one contemporary reviewer noted her restraint, observing that "the usual antislavery novel was filled with lacerating descriptions of floggings and burnings to death," but that *Uncle Tom's Cabin* "contains no such dreadful details."[4] Stowe does not gratuitously serve up scenes of violence. While Tom's martyrdom is the climax of the story, she discreetly places his physical punishment between chapters. It was the genius of Stowe's polemic that she did not make it hinge on extreme cases but on the routine and the everyday. "Talk of the *abuses* of slavery!" exclaims Augustine St. Clare, the character whose views most closely reflect Stowe's. " 'Humbug! The *thing itself* is the essence of all abuse!' " (p. 242).

For Stowe, looking at "the thing itself" meant focusing on the domestic slave trade. With the exception of the final, dark triptych in which Tom is under the cruel Simon Legree, her sketches focus less on plantation labor than, as she entitles a chapter, "Select Incident[s] of Lawful Trade." This commerce in human flesh exposes the bare bones of slavery, that a human being was declared property under the law. *Uncle Tom's Cabin* opens with a portrait of a slave trader and proceeds to scenes of catching runaway "property," separating mothers from their children for the benefit of a more productive sale, and examining slaves in a slave warehouse as if they were a horse or a chair. The original subtitle of *Uncle Tom's Cabin* was *The Man Who Was a Thing*, and Stowe's insistent look at the commerce in human flesh underscores the contradiction that inheres in slavery as an institution: that it alienates a human being from himself or herself. This is the fundamental violence of slavery. This structural approach brings the reader up against the legal realities of the system and at the same time presents vividly realized scenes that dramatize the human suffering created by the slave trade, particularly the separation of families.

Necessary to this commerce is the slave trader. *Uncle Tom's Cabin* opens with a negotiation between "two gentlemen," a slave-owner, Mr. Shelby, and a slave-trader, Mr. Haley. Stowe's description of Haley is a good specimen of both her satirical voice and her precision as a sociological historian.

> For convenience sake, we have said, hitherto, two *gentlemen*. One of the parties, however, when critically examined, did not seem, strictly speaking, to come under the species. He was a short, thick-set man, with coarse commonplace features, and that swaggering air of pretension which marks a low man who is trying to elbow his way upward in the world. He was much over-dressed, in a gaudy vest of many colors, a blue neckerchief, bedropped gaily with yellow spots, and arranged with a flaunting tie, quite in keeping with the general air of the man. His hands, large and coarse, were plentifully bedecked with rings; and he wore a heavy gold watch-chain, with a bundle of seals of portentous size, and a great variety of colors, attached to it,—which, in the ardor of conversation, he was in the habit of flourishing and jingling with evident satisfaction. His conversation was in free and easy defiance of Murray's Grammar, and was garnished at convenient intervals with various profane expressions, which not even the desire to be graphic in our account shall induce us to transcribe. (P. 82)

Stowe develops page after page of brilliant satire of this "Man of Humanity" whose concern for the slaves he buys and sells extends only to what might "damage the article"—satire almost exclusively conveyed through Haley's own words. His language, as Ellen Moers has observed, "is shot through with money . . . even religion is money, for everything with Haley is a matter of trade. 'Some folks don't believe there is pious niggers . . . but *I do*. I had a fellow, now, in this yer last lot I took to Orleans—'t was as good as a meetin, now, really, to hear that critter pray; . . . He fetched me a good sum, too . . . I realized six hundred on him. Yes, I consider religion a valeyable thing in a nigger, when it's the genuine article, and no mistake.' "[5] As Haley incriminates himself, he puts before the reader the commercial realities of slavery, including the sexual degradation of "the fancy trade" and the routine separation of parents and children.

Haley's eye is drawn to a newspaper notice like many that routinely appeared:

Executor's Sale,—Negroes!—Agreeably to order of court, will be sold, on Tuesday, February 20, before the Court-house door, in the town of Washington, Kentucky, the following negroes: Hagar, aged 60; John, aged 30; Ben, aged 21; Saul, aged 25; Albert, aged 14. Sold for the benefit of the creditors and heirs of the estate of Jesse Blutchford, Esq.

> Samuel Morris,
> Thomas Flint,
> *Executors.*

There is nothing remarkable about this. It is an everyday announcement of a lawful trade. But Stowe imagines for the reader the human reality behind this terse ad. Hagar, aged sixty, and Albert, aged fourteen, are transformed into a mother and son.

She might have been sixty, but was older than that by hard work and disease, was partially blind, and somewhat crippled with rheumatism. By her side stood her only remaining son, Albert, a bright-looking little fellow of fourteen years. The boy was the only survivor of a large family, who had been successively sold away from her to a southern market. The mother held on to him with both her shaking hands, and eyed with intense trepidation everyone who walked up to examine him. (P. 166)

Haley pushes his way into the crowd and prepares for the auction by examining an old man for sale: he "pulled his mouth open and looked in, felt of his teeth, made him stand and straighten himself, bend his back, and perform various evolutions to show his muscles." Having satisfied himself by similar examinations that he will bid on "the youngerly ones and the boy," and that Hagar is "an old rack o' bones,—not worth her salt," coolly purchases the mother's only remaining child. When Hagar breaks into passionate sobbing, Haley is unmoved. " 'Come, take her off, can't some of ye?' said Haley, dryly; 'don't do no good for her to go on that ar way.' " Among Haley's other purchases is a young man. " 'I've got a wife,' spoke out the article enumerated as 'John, aged thirty,' and he laid his chained hand on Tom's knee, 'and she don't know a word about this, poor girl!' " "Poor John!" interposes Stowe's narrative voice. "It was rather natural; and the tears that fell, as he spoke, came as naturally as if he had been a white man" (p. 169).

Stowe's method is similar when she describes a slave warehouse in New Orleans. Dispelling the "horrible visions" the reader may have of such a place, she comments, "Human property is high in the market; and is, therefore, well fed, well cleaned, tended, and looked after, that it may come to sale sleek, and strong, and shining. A slave-warehouse in New Orleans is a house externally not much unlike many others, kept with neatness; and where every day you may see arranged, under a sort of shed along the outside, rows of men and women, who stand there as a sign of the property sold within." Stowe acknowledges the routineness of this commercial transaction: "Then you shall be courteously entreated to call and examine, and shall find an abundance of," as Stowe pointedly calls them, "husbands, wives, brothers, sisters, fathers, mothers, and young children, to be 'sold separately, or in lots to suit the convenience of the purchaser' " (p. 317). Unlike chairs, tables, and bales of hay, this human property has emotional, familial ties that are ruptured by sale.

The slave trade, as commerce, connects *Uncle Tom's Cabin* in a close way to the geography of the country. Stowe had lived for eighteen years in Cincinnati, which was the center of commerce in what was then called "the West," and knew the bustle of the Cincinnati landing, where all manner of goods and produce was received and shipped via the Ohio River to points east and via the Mississippi to points south. These rivers feature prominently in *Uncle Tom's Cabin.* The Ohio River, the ice-packed barrier that Eliza and her son must cross in their flight to Canada, is the boundary between the slave state of Kentucky and the free state of Ohio. The crisscrossing plots of the novel are themselves tied to the geography of slavery, for as the Harrises make their way to Canada and a new life, Tom is borne by the Mississippi River to Louisiana and death.

The geographic movements of her characters give Stowe a wide scope for describing the regional variety of the nation: the backwoods of Kentucky through which Eliza and Harry flee, the Quaker settlement in Ohio where they take refuge, the ornate New Orleans home of Augustine St. Clare, where Tom is taken, the decaying plantation on the Red River where Tom meets his end under Simon Legree. Stowe's ability to capture regional types was evident in the first story she published, in 1833, shortly after coming to Cincinnati from Connecticut. Called "Uncle Lot," it was a character sketch of her uncle Lot Benton, who, from her new vantage point in the West, she perceived to belong to the species "New England farmer," a Yankee to the core with regional speech and a farm in which his tools were always hanging on the proper hooks. In *Uncle Tom's Cabin,* Stowe brings New England into sharp focus through the character of St. Clare's sister Ophelia, who visits New Orleans from Vermont. Ophelia, determined to bring order to the lackadaisical domestic arrangements of her brother, meets her match in the passive resistance of Dinah, the cook, who is "studious of ease in all her arrangements." Dinah is engaged in preparing for dinner by "sitting on the kitchen floor, smoking a short, stumpy pipe, to which she was much addicted, and which she always kindled up, as a sort of censer, whenever she felt the need of an inspiration in her arrangements." Stowe continues,

> When Miss Ophelia entered the kitchen, Dinah did not rise, but smoked on in sublime tranquility, regarding her movements obliquely out of the corner of her eye, but apparently intent only on the operations around her.
>
> Miss Ophelia commenced opening a set of drawers.
>
> "What is this drawer for, Dinah?" she said.
>
> "It's handy for most anything, Missis," said Dinah. So it appeared to be. From the variety it contained, Miss Ophelia pulled out first a fine damask

table-cloth stained with blood, having evidently been used to envelop some
raw meat.

"What's this, Dinah? You don't wrap up meat in your mistress' best
table-cloths?"

"O Lor, Missis, no; the towels was all a missin',—so I jest did it. I laid out
to wash that ar,—that's why I put it thar."

"Shif'less!" said Miss Ophelia to herself, proceeding to tumble over the
drawer, where she found a nutmeg-grater and two or three nutmegs, a
Methodist hymn-book, a couple of soiled Madras handkerchiefs, some
yarn and knitting-work, a paper of tobacco and a pipe, a few crackers, one
or two gilded china-saucers with some pomade in them, one or two
thin old shoes, a piece of flannel carefully pinned up enclosing some small
white onions, several damask table-napkins, some coarse crash towels,
some twine and darning-needles, and several broken papers, from which
sundry sweet herbs were sifting into the drawer. (Pp. 231–32)

Stowe has been rightly credited for her descriptions of domestic life
and what was called "women's sphere." As the specificity of her inventory
of Dinah's drawer suggests, these are essential to the creation of a tex-
tured, realistic narrative. But what is just as striking in *Uncle Tom's Cabin* is
Stowe's sure grasp of the material reality of male culture: pistols, taverns,
horses, slave catchers "hot with brandy." Her tavern scenes are populated
by regional types such as "[g]reat, tall, raw-boned Kentuckians, attired in
hunting-shirts, and trailing their loose joints over a vast extent of territory, with the easy lounge peculiar to the race" (p. 155). Colloquial and
regional speech further etch the geography of the land into the narrative:
Haley calls for cigars and sugar and rum and announces to his cohorts in
the tavern, "We'll have a blow-out" (p. 127). St. Clare, negotiating with
Haley the purchase of Tom, asks "what's the damage, as they say in Kentucky; in short, what's to be paid out for this business?" (p. 188).

The originality of her book sprang from Stowe's grasp of the national-
ity of her material: an epic theme—republican ideals in conflict with a
feudal institution—was enshrined in a narrative bristling with regional
types. Writing about the issue that divided the nation, Stowe probed the
nature of the ideals on which the United States was founded. Like Lincoln in his Gettysburg Address, she asked whether a nation so constituted

could endure. Her theory of history was biblical; after going to some pains to enlist the reader against the vulgar and self-serving slave trader Haley, Stowe gathers up the reader's disdain and turns it back, with a vengeance:

> Are you educated and he ignorant, you high and he low, you refined and he coarse, you talented and he simple?
>
> In the day of a future Judgment, these very considerations may make it more tolerable for him than for you. (P. 177)

For a nation whose laws required the turning away of the fugitive stranger, Stowe warned of the fate of Sodom and Gomorrah. Instead of exalting the Anglo-Saxons as conquerors and beacons of light, Stowe's heroes are the Africans. In inverting the racial expectations of her white audience but employing a romantic genre in which they were heavily invested, Stowe effected a revolution in consciousness. *Uncle Tom's Cabin* hymns the desire that led to the nation forming—the desire for liberty— but now expressed by and embodied in a slave.

This desire is most directly and eloquently expressed by Eliza's husband, George Harris, whom Stowe modeled on Frederick Douglass. Without knowing that Eliza will soon flee to protect their son, George decides to make his way to Canada. A man of superior intelligence and enterprise, George has the misfortune to be owned by "a vulgar, narrow-minded, tyrannical master." Hired out by his master to a local bagging factory, George invents a machine for cleaning hemp. When his master learns of the invention of his "intelligent chattel" and is congratulated for owning "so valuable a slave," the master "began to feel an uneasy consciousness of inferiority. What business had his slave to be marching round the country, inventing machines, and holding up his head among gentlemen?" (p. 90). He brings him back and works him in the fields, going against his economic interest for the sake of maintaining his feeling of superiority. He further plans to break George by giving him the meanest tasks and by insisting that he take a new wife. Stowe's shrewd perception of the psychology of master-slave relations will be developed at greater length in the relationship between Legree and Tom in the final chapters of the book. George's conviction that he is more of a man than his master, his fierce desire to be his own person, drive him to flee. In his desire to escape a caste system, to rise as high as his individual talents will take him, George Harris replicates the desire that led many in straitened circumstances in Europe to flee to this country.

Stowe underscores these seemingly patriotic sentiments when George paraphrases Patrick Henry by declaring, " 'I'll be free, or I'll die!' " (p. 95). He makes good on that promise by his willingness to defend himself with a gun, in a dramatic escape in which he and his party have taken refuge among some rocks suspended over a thirty-foot chasm. George and his fellow fugitives are at this point passing through the state of Indiana, where the land has a preternatural flatness. Stowe knew this terrain, having visited her brother Henry in Indianapolis any number of times in the 1840s. But the geographical reality was not as salient as the heroism and romance of the moment, which demanded steep rocks "perpendicular as those of a castle" and a "breast-work" from which George and his party could peer around at the pursuing slave catchers. This is the work of an author who in her youth had competed with her brothers and sisters in remembering passages from Sir Walter Scott's novels and had called hills and glens of their neighborhood by names borrowed from his romances. As one critic has observed, "It seems likely that her rocks came not from Indiana where thirty-foot chasms are scarce, but from either Scott's *Rob Roy*, in which the most memorable scene pictures Helen Campbell MacGregor stopping the soldiers in a narrow defile, or Cooper's *Prairie*, in which Ishmael Bush and party take refuge atop a rock formation of equal topological improbability."[6]

From this dramatic height, George makes what Stowe calls his "declaration of independence," telling his pursuers that he is a "free man" and means to defend himself. Stowe pointedly comments:

> If it had been only a Hungarian youth, now bravely defending in some mountain fastness the retreat of fugitives escaping from Austria into America, this would have been sublime heroism; but as it was a youth of African descent, defending the retreat of fugitives through America into Canada, of course we are too well instructed and patriotic to see any heroism in it; and if any of our readers do, they must do it on their own private responsibility. (P. 224)

Of course, her readers did, and this was precisely the point. By portraying black people in heroic postures, Stowe encouraged her readers to identify with them. This knocked a crucial prop out from beneath proslavery thought: Haley, justifying the breakup of slave families, explains, "These critters an't like white folks, you know; they gets over things, only manage right" (p. 85). Stowe's character echoes the sentiments of James Henry Hammond of South Carolina, who, arguing with an English abolitionist, told him that in the matter of separation from their families "Negroes are themselves both perverse and comparatively indifferent."[7] Stowe did not attempt to argue back. She simply painted pictures. As she wrote to her editor, "There is no arguing with *pictures*, and everybody is impressed by them, whether they mean to be or not."[8]

Stowe's pictorial method is not, as we have seen, without psychological insight, but she refrains from going inside her characters' heads. Instead, she interprets their outward behavior, speech, hesitancies, and outbursts in psychological terms. This allows her to convey even the psychology of the family dog in the episode in which Eliza steals away in the night with her son.

> Old Bruno, a great Newfoundland, who slept at the end of porch, rose, with a low growl, as she came near. She gently spoke his name, and the animal, an old pet and playmate of hers, instantly, wagging his tail, prepared to follow her, though apparently revolving much, in his simple dog's head, what such an indiscreet midnight promenade might mean. Some dim ideas of imprudence or impropriety in the measure seemed to embarrass him considerably; for he often stopped, as Eliza glided forward, and looked wistfully, first at her and then at the house, and then, as if reässured by reflection, he pattered along after her again. (P. 108)

Such carefully observed homely details create a presumption of truth and contribute to the documentary feel of the narrative. They bring the reader into the scene and, as Alice Crozier has written, "include us imaginatively in its sights and sounds and drama." Like Scott, Stowe used verisimilitude both "to verify events and to stir the reader's poetic imagination."[9]

One of the most remembered passages in the book is Eliza's heroic es-

cape across the ice of the Ohio River. It was said that when the novel was
put on stage at the National Theater in New York, there was not one dry
eye when Eliza and her boy reached the other side of the river. Stowe
knew that if she could evoke that response on behalf of escaping slaves,
she had already made her case. As the man who helps Eliza out of the river
on the Ohio side exclaims, " 'You're a right brave gal. I like grit, wherever
I see it.' " In 1850–1851, as the newspapers carried stories of the enforcement of the Fugitive Slave Law, similar morals emerged to the resistance
of "property." In Pennsylvania, six white men burst in on a black family in
the middle of the night in an attempt to capture a fugitive. In the story
printed in the *Pennsylvania Freeman* and reprinted in the *New York Independent*, one of the deputy marshals reported "that the slaveholder was so
impressed by the heroism displayed by these brave colored people that he
remarked:—'Well, if this is a specimen of the pluck of the Pennsylvania
negroes I don't want my slaves back.' "

It is well known that for her plot Stowe drew on the narratives of escaped slaves, particularly those of Josiah Henson and Henry Bibb, both of
whose adventures took them to Cincinnati. The slave narrative—more
properly called the "freedom narrative," as Toni Cade Bambara has
pointed out—is a highly exciting genre focused on escape. That all of the
energies of this genre are focused on the point at which, to invoke one of
Stowe's chapter headings, "Property Gets into an Improper State of
Mind," highlights the agency of the teller of the tale. Property that has a
will of its own demonstrates self-ownership. The act of escape and the
life-imperiling risks that flight entailed impressed a populace that had
not, until the Fugitive Slave Law, given a lot of thought to the subjectivity of the oppressed, assuming in many cases that the slave was better off
under slavery than freedom. One cannot read Henry Bibb's tale of Indian
captivity, attack by wolves, and desperate fording of rivers without developing a deep appreciation of his longing for "the blessings of Liberty."

But Stowe departed explicitly from her literary models in order to create her most controversial character, Tom, the pious, loyal slave who refuses to run away. In Cincinnati, Josiah Henson had a chance to run away,
but he honored his master's trust; later, however, he regretted this decision and determined to escape, which he did. As for Henry Bibb, who ob-

served the effort of his master to get more money for him by making it appear that he "was so pious and honest" that he "would not run away for ill treatment," Bibb commented tersely, "a gross mistake, for I never had religion enough to keep me from running away from slavery in my life." Stowe shaped the character of Tom to her own purposes.[10]

The character of Tom can be set in contrast to that of Nat Turner, the slave who in 1831 led a revolt in Southampton, Virginia. Reading signs in the heavens and inspired by the Old Testament, Turner led his co-conspirators to the murder of fifty-seven white people. Although slave revolts were relatively rare, the specter of slaves turning against the masters whose houses they so intimately inhabited was, in the decades after Nat Turner's rebellion, never fully suppressed in the consciousness of the masters. As James Hammond wrote:

> If the slave is not allowed to read his bible, the sin rests upon abolitionists; for they stand prepared to furnish him with a key to it, which would make it, not a book of hope, and love, and peace, but of despair, hatred and blood; which would convert the reader, not into a Christian, but a demon. . . . Allow our slaves to read your writings, stimulating them to cut our throats! Can you believe us to be such unspeakable fools?[11]

Uncle Tom's fervent prayers for his masters and his passive resistance are in stark contrast to the model most fearsome to whites. It could be argued that Stowe shaped her character to appeal to the consciousness of her white audience. Yet, in her next antislavery novel, *Dred* (1856), she not only models her hero on the son of Denmark Vesey, the historical figure who was hanged in South Carolina for fomenting a slave rebellion, she appends to her novel "The Confessions of Nat Turner." It seems just as possible that in her creation of Uncle Tom, the martyr, she was drawn by the mythic demands of the narrative of nationalism.

In 1849—the year before she conceived of writing *Uncle Tom's Cabin*—Stowe helped her brother Charles write a fictionalized biography of Christ. *Uncle Tom's Cabin* is in part Stowe's retelling of Christ's story through the character of Tom. In choosing to make Tom a Christ figure, Stowe was also writing in the tradition of the historical novel, where religion is harnessed to nationalistic ends and heroes are freely given godlike characteristics. The extravagant claims made for Sir William Wallace ("[t]he Heaven-dedicated Wallace . . . the saint and the hero; the being of another world!") in Jane Porter's *The Scottish Chiefs* is a case in point. The death of the godlike Wallace fuels "the bloody final triumph of Bruce at Bannockburn. The Wallace coffin is literally carried onto that field, a saintly relic, where it effects wonders."[12] The death of Uncle Tom was the first part of the book Stowe wrote; she knew that her national narrative required a martyr.

Until Scott's "manly intervention" into the genre of the historical novel, it was in the hands of women. One of these women, Sydney Owenson, wrote a book that, like Stowe's, created an industry. Owenson's *The Wild Irish Girl: A National Tale* (1806), featuring a heroine named Glorvina, generated "a craze—surely one of the first of its now familiar kind—for Glorvina bodkins, mantles, harps and other Girl paraphernalia. Gaelic accessories and a Wild Irish Look helped create the disposable identity of the moment, a commodified romantic femininity with a Celtic Twilight flavour. . . ." This commercialism is related to the production of national stereotypes. Commenting on this in Owenson's *Wild Irish Girl*, Ian Dennis observes, "[n]ationalism understandably squirms at the resultant 'stage Irishmen' . . . but perhaps in varying ways, and for the benefit always of both a local and an overseas public, all national identities are stage personae, all nations performances." This suggests that the "truth" of *Uncle Tom's Cabin* or any novel engaged with the manufacturing of a national narrative is going to be shaped by the production of larger-than-life heroes and stereotypes.[13]

Yet, Stowe had to balance the mythic with the realistic demands of her story. Tom's greatest trial comes under Simon Legree. Legree, noticing Tom's Methodist hymnbook, tells him, " 'Well, I'll soon have *that* out of you. I have none o' yer bawling, praying, singing niggers on my place; . . . *I'm* your church now!' " Stowe describes Tom's response: "Something within the silent black man answered *No!* and, as if repeated by an invisible voice, came the words of an old prophetic scroll, as Eva had often read them to him,—'Fear not! For I have redeemed thee. I have called thee by my name. Thou art MINE!' " (p. 325). Stowe immediately moves from the prophetic to the seemingly mundane:

But Simon Legree heard no voice. That voice is one he never shall hear. He only glared for a moment on the down-cast face of Tom, and walked off. He took Tom's trunk, which contained a very neat and abundant wardrobe, to the forecastle, where it was soon surrounded by various hands of the boat. With much laughing, at the expense of niggers who tried to be gentlemen, the articles very readily were sold to one and another, and the empty trunk finally put up at auction. It was a good joke, they all thought, especially to see how Tom looked after his things, as they were going this way and that; and then the auction of the trunk, that was funnier than all, and occasioned abundant witticisms. (P. 25)

Tom's garments are divided and given away just as Christ's were before his crucifixion, but so embedded is this parallel in a realistic, sociologically accurate description that it is not obtrusive. Instead, Stowe directs our attention to the class resentment of the white hands who make jokes about "niggers who tried to be gentlemen." In his manners and dress, Tom is more of a gentleman than the white boat hands who envy his neat and abundant clothing. Stowe shows slavery to be a kind of robbery in which a racial caste system undercuts the democratic ideology of the United States. Like two halves of a Gothic arch, the realistic texture of her novel and its religio/national theme are mutually supportive.

Impelled by the contradiction of slavery in a democratic country, *Uncle Tom's Cabin* reaches something of an impasse when it comes to the issue of national identity. In the novels of Scott and his precursors, national identity is often a matter of genetic solidarity. In Porter's *The Scottish Chiefs*, when Wallace unifies Scotland, "a stranger is recognized as a brother because his captors saw not the dark hair of the Englishman; it was the yellow hair of Scotland that mingled with the blood on his forehead."[14] National identity in *Uncle Tom's Cabin* seems to be founded not on race but on the idea of liberty. Yet, in the tradition of the nineteenth-century historical novel, Stowe emphasizes racial differences, as in her opening remarks:

The scenes of this story, as its title indicates, lie among a race hitherto ignored by the associations of polite and refined society, an exotic race, whose ancestors, born beneath a tropic sun, brought with them, and perpetuated to their descendants, a character so essentially unlike the hard and dominant Anglo-Saxon race, as for many years to have won from it only misunderstanding and contempt. (P. 81)

Her narrative both insists on racial differences and demonstrates, in scene after scene in the commercial transactions in human flesh, that these differences are immaterial to our common humanity. But in her tying up of the plot, her black characters are either dead or in another country. Her decision to send George Harris and his family to Liberia was taken as an endorsement of the conservative wing of the abolition movement, the colonizationists, who advocated sending the slaves back to Africa. This provoked the following comment in a black newspaper: "Uncle Tom must be killed, George Harris exiled! Heaven for dead Negroes! Liberia for living mulattoes. Neither can live on the American continent. Death or banishment is our doom, say the Slaveocrats, the Colonizationists, and, save the mark—Mrs. Stowe!!"[15] Stowe later regretted her decision to exile her characters, but it was consistent with George Harris's speech: "My country! . . . what country have I, or any one like me, born of slave mothers? What laws are there for us? We don't make them,—we don't consent to them,—we have nothing to do with them; all they do for us is to crush us, and keep us down" (pp. 160–61). Having created a heroic character whose longing for liberty identified him with the ideals that brought the United States into being, Stowe was confounded. The next move was up to her readers. In her "Concluding Remarks," she once again sounded the trumpet of divine judgment: "Not by combining together, to protect injustice and cruelty, and making a common capital of sin, is the Union to be saved—but by repentance, justice and mercy; for, not surer is the eternal law by which the millstone sinks in the ocean, than that stronger law, by which injustice and cruelty shall bring on nations the wrath of Almighty God!" (p. 405). She did not imagine the Civil War, but she did bring her readers up to the brink of Armageddon.

Notes

1. Joan D. Hedrick, ed., *The Oxford Harriet Beecher Stowe Reader* (New York: Oxford University Press, 1999), 145. Subsequent references to this edition will be given parenthetically in the text.

2. As quoted in Thomas F. Gossett, *"Uncle Tom's Cabin" and American Culture* (Dallas, TX: Southern Methodist University Press, 1985), 167.

3. Albert E. Stone, *The Return of Nat Turner: History, Literature, and Cultural Politics in Sixties America* (Athens: University of Georgia Press, 1992), 16–17.

4. Gossett, 185.

5. Ellen Moers, *Harriet Beecher Stowe and American Literature* (Hartford, CT: The Stowe-Day Foundation, 1978), 7–8.

6. E. Bruce Kirkham, *The Building of "Uncle Tom's Cabin"* (Knoxville: University of Tennessee Press, 1977), 125.

7. James Henry Hammond to an English Abolitionist, January 28, 1845, in Drew Gilpin Faust, *The Ideology of Slavery: Proslavery Thought in the Antebellum South*, 1830–1860 (Baton Rouge, LA: 1981), 192.

8. Harriet Beecher Stowe to Gamaliel Bailey, March 9, 1851, in Hedrick, *Reader,* 66.

9. Alice C. Crozier, *The Novels of Harriet Beecher Stowe* (New York: Oxford University Press, 1969), 57, 56.

10. Material in this and the previous two paragraphs has been adapted from Joan D. Hedrick, *Harriet Beecher Stowe: A Life* (New York: Oxford University Press), 211–213.

11. Hammond to an English Abolitionist, 186.

12. Ian Dennis, *Nationalism and Desire in Early Historical Fiction* (New York: St. Martin's Press, 1997), 26, 28.

13. Dennis, *Nationalism and Desire*, 17–18, 49, 61.

14. Dennis, *Nationalism and Desire*, 29.

15. As quoted in Richard Yarborough, "Strategies of Black Characterization in *Uncle Tom's Cabin* and the Early Afro-American Novel," in Eric Sundquist, ed., *New Essays on "Uncle Tom's Cabin"* (Cambridge: Cambridge University Press, 1986), 69.

Bodies and Souls:
The Haitian Revolution and
Madison Smartt Bell's
All Souls' Rising

Michel-Rolph Trouillot

The revolution that shook the French colony of Saint-Domingue and eventuated in the birth of independent Haiti provides more than a setting to Madison Smartt Bell's eighth novel, *All Souls' Rising* (1995), a work nominated for the PEN/Faulkner Award and a National Book Award Finalist. The novel moves with the historical record, weaving facts and fiction, its pace punctuated by the chronology of the revolution itself. Bell's control of that calendar, of the twists and rebounds on the Haitians' road to final victory, is impressive. His "Chronology of Historical Events," a nineteen-page appendix to the novel, is better than most such summaries available in English.

Readers unfamiliar with Haitian history will find that chronology useful—and may want to read it first—inasmuch as Bell's interiorization of the details of that sequence drives the fictional narrative. History here is as much part of the plot as are the individual stories of the protagonists, fictional or real. That is no small feat. Indeed, from a historical viewpoint, Madison Smartt Bell's accomplishments take their full significance against the background of the monumental silence that his novel helps to break. Let me hint at the depth of that silence and at the magnitude of the events it surrounds.

✑

THE HAITIAN REVOLUTION created the first independent country of the Americas where freedom meant freedom for everyone. Like the French Revolution, it abolished an inequitable social system. Like the U.S. Revolution, it overthrew a colonial rule. It carried further than both the revolutionary spirit of the times in the Atlantic world. Yet because that feat was accomplished by black slaves, the majority of whom had been born in Africa, the Haitian Revolution remains largely ignored by world historiography.[1]

The facts are eloquent enough. The Seven Years' War and the independence of the United States had demonstrated to rulers and merchants in France and in England the enhanced value of their Caribbean colonies. Those were the days when Voltaire could quip that the "few acres of snow" of Canada were not worth the tiny sugar islands of Guadeloupe and Martinique.

Saint-Domingue was not tiny by Caribbean standards. The third largest territory of the Antilles, located on the western side of the island of Hispaniola (the eastern side was Spanish-controlled), it gained further importance in the 1770s when coffee production in the hillsides complemented the sugar exports from the plains. By the 1790s, Saint-Domingue held world production records for both sugar and coffee, becoming France's most valuable possession and the most profitable colony of the world. It was also, in the words of historian Eric Williams, "the worst hell on earth" for blacks.[2]

In 1791, that hell broke loose. The French Revolution was unfolding in Paris. From Louis XVI's call in 1787 convening the General Estates to his sequestration by the mob, the news from Paris had rendered restless white and mulatto landowners as well as lower-class whites in the colonies. Some in Saint-Domingue, especially the whites who owned the largest plantations, regarded these events with fear; others—including prominent leaders of the light-skinned *gens de couleur*, some of whom also owned slaves but had no political rights—tried to take advantage of them. In August 1791, in the midst of this agitation, the slaves of the sugar plantations in the north launched an insurrection that mushroomed into a colony-wide uprising. Three years later, the rebel slaves had a clear revolutionary goal and strategy: freedom for all and military control of the colony to consolidate that freedom.

The man most responsible for formulating that strategy and achieving this goal was a Creole black, Toussaint Louverture. From 1793 to 1801, Louverture provided coordination for the slave uprising and also directed its relations in a bewilderingly complex political situation within the colony and beyond its shores. Within Saint-Domingue, he helped the rebels exploit tensions among free mulattoes, who resented their exclusion from politics; lower-class whites, many of whom were sympathetic to the French revolutionaries but opposed political rights for mulattoes; and the white plantation owners, who sought at all costs to preserve slavery but were willing to form temporary alliances with mulattoes or radical whites to achieve their goals. Louverture also navigated the shifting shoals of French revolutionary politics and European military alliances. In 1794, when the French legislature abolished slavery, Louverture brought a majority of the armed slaves under the French flag. By 1797, having beaten the Spanish troops, repelled a British invasion, and outmaneuvered French local officials, Louverture became the most powerful figure on the island and commander in chief of the French army in Saint-Domingue. In 1799, he nullified the *gens de couleur* as a military force in opposition to his own troops. In 1801, he promulgated an independent constitution that recognized him as governor-for-life with absolute power.

Revolutionary France had reacted with growing amazement to this chain of events, sending to the island a succession of commissars whose impossible job was to keep into orbit the drifting satellite of a France that was itself careening out of control. Royalists in Paris tended to side with the white Caribbean plantation owners, a majority of whom favored the *ancien régime*. And the most extremist of the French revolutionaries, for all their rhetoric about the Rights of Man ("All men are created equal"), refused to support the blacks' claim to civil and political equality. On colonial issues, their revolutionary ardor rarely went beyond endorsing civil and political rights for the *gens de couleur*, many of whom had property—including slaves. Very few French revolutionaries questioned colonialism itself.

In 1802, Napoleon Bonaparte, whose own ascent in France paralleled that of Louverture in Saint-Domingue, sent his brother-in-law, Charles Leclerc, with a formidable army and an armada of twenty-two ships to regain control of the colony and restore slavery. Louverture was captured treacherously and exiled to France. However, pressed by a number of slaves—notably some African-born leaders—who had continuously rejected all compromise with the French, Louverture's lieutenants picked up the fight, soon joined by some of the most prominent mulatto leaders. Under the leadership of Jean-Jacques Dessalines, a Louverture follower of the early days, the rebels defeated a French army already weakened by yellow fever. On January 1, 1804, they proclaimed the independence of the island, which they called Haiti—one of its earlier Native American names.

The cost was heavy on all sides, the consequences extraordinary. French, African, British, Spanish, Polish, and Creole fighters of all shades died in Saint-Domingue by the thousands during more than twelve years of armed struggle. Britain alone lost sixty thousand men in a protracted Caribbean campaign of which Saint-Domingue was the most coveted prize. France lost the majority of the forty thousand soldiers who took part in the Saint-Domingue campaign, more than it did at Waterloo. That defeat impelled Napoleon to renounce the dream of a French empire on the North American mainland and persuaded him to sell all of the Louisiana Territory to the United States. The Haitian Revolution also precipitated a huge migration from Haiti to Louisiana itself and lesser flows of whites and nonwhites to towns such as Philadelphia, Charleston, and Baltimore. It created the first modern state led by blacks. It inspired slaves all over the Americas, including in the South of the United States, where it loomed over the Denmark Vesey trial. It fueled the ardor of white abolitionists from London to Philadelphia. Indeed, many historians today agree that the events in Saint-Domingue were the turning point that signaled the end of Afro-American slavery.

With its numerous twists, military highlights, epic overtones, and global implications, the Haitian Revolution combines all the features that popular historians favor. Yet, it has attracted very few professional historians outside of Haiti itself. For the first half of the twentieth century, even professional historians would have been hard-pressed to name a single title written by a non-Haitian that gave the revolution the treatment it deserves—with the spectacular exception of C. L. R. James's *Black Ja-cobins*, first published in 1938. Carolyn Fick, David Geggus, and Juilis Scott III are among the very few specialists now writing in English about Saint-Domingue/Haiti during the revolutionary period.[3]

There is no intent of conspiracy behind that two-century-long silence, no explicit political agenda. The historians who neglect the Haitian Revolution span the entire political spectrum, much as did the French delegates to the National Assembly for whom a slave revolution was unthinkable even as it happened. More than explicit design, behind that silence are shared assumptions about the nature of humankind, its internal hierarchies, and the distribution of attributes and possibilities across racial lines. There is also the fate of Haiti itself, ostracized for most of the nineteenth century and in decline for most of the twentieth. There is the worldwide silence on slavery and racism in academic discourse, broken only in the United States in the 1960s and 1970s. There are, finally, the procedures of the historical guild, the internal selection process that renders some topics unworthy of serious study, however inspiring they may be.

<p>

THE LITERARY IMAGINATION negotiates distance—social, spatial, and temporal—quite differently than academic scholarship. Uninspiring as it was to historians, the Haitian Revolution attracted a very small number of world-famous writers. Thus, at Louverture's capture, William Wordsworth dedicated a poem to him, assuring that the Haitian would not be forgotten. Victor Hugo made the revolution the setting of his first novel, *Bug Jargal*, in which some readers saw fictional segments of Louverture's life. French poet and politician Alphonse de Lamartine wrote a play, *Toussaint Louverture*, a minor work to be sure, but one which aroused virulent responses from French conservatives when it opened in Paris in 1850.[4]

This small list of big names spills over in the twentieth century with a noted shift from Europe to the Americas. Saint-Domingue/Haiti provides part setting, part background to William Faulkner's *Absalom, Absalom*, with obvious chronological distortions. Two plays from Martinique stand out: Aimé Césaire, *La Tragédie du Roi Christophe*, and Edouard Glissant's *Monsieur Toussaint*. So does Cuban writer Alejo Carpentier's spectacular novel, *El Reino de este mundo* (*The Kingdom of This World*), which frames the revolution through the experiences of a former slave. The life and times of a real slave, Boukman, provide the model for *Babouk*, a novel published in New York in the 1930s by the prolific and then quite popular Guy Endore.

With *All Souls' Rising*, Madison Smartt Bell joins this small and prestigious elite with an extraordinary gusto, a narrative breadth, a richness in documentation, and a detailed interlace of fact and fiction that carry the novel proper over five hundred pages. Three characters stand out, whose personal trials and thoughts help organize the narrative and its viewpoints: Dr. Hébert, a Frenchman, Louverture himself, and the slave Riau. Hébert and Riau are fictional.

Antoine Hébert is a Frenchman with enlightened ideals who has come to Saint-Domingue looking for his lost sister. Hébert has a tendency to be caught by events over which he has little control. He is shocked by the daily workings of plantation slavery, its inherent atrocity, and the social and emotional degradation that it causes, but he is no less surprised at the growing appeal of the uprising. He falls in love with Nanon, a mulatto woman, and follows Toussaint as a prisoner but tries to maintain throughout the distant yet engaged look of a naturalist. His interest is humankind, but the particular specimens under observation test his faith in human nature.

Observers such as Hébert existed, reluctant witnesses to the inherent hypocrisy of a project of Enlightenment financed by the sweat and blood of the very people it disparaged. François-Justin Girod de Chantrans traveled through Saint-Domingue, taking copious notes on the virtues of fats and oils extracted from lizards as possible cures for venereal diseases. His French contemporaries thought that work much more important than the observations on the daily routine of plantations, slave life, colonial customs, diet, and speech patterns he first published in 1785 as *Voyage d'un suisse dans différentes colonies d'Amérique*. Twenty-four years later, Michel-Etienne Descourtilz, an astute doctor who like Bell's Hébert was once a prisoner of the slave revolutionaries, similarly produced an account of Saint-Domingue from the viewpoint of an enlightened natural-

ist. Yet, as modern historians have noted in reviewing Girod and Descourtilz, and as Hébert's puzzlement at times demonstrates in *All Souls'
Rising,* the universalism of these enlightened observers cannot detach itself—nor should we expect it—from the North Atlantic historical trajectory that makes it possible. For Hébert as for Descourtilz, once the
revolution strikes, there is no place outside of history from which to look
at history.

Steeped in that history, pushing it from within, is Toussaint Louverture, the second major character. We first meet him in the prologue, in a
fleeting moment when he is fetched from the cabin where he is imprisoned in the ship that carries him to France. That introduction is telling.
Although Louverture's figure is central to the novel, Toussaint the individual remains below deck, never fully to come to life. Perhaps the real
man, who by most accounts was bigger than life, is not amenable to the
realist novel as a genre—his complexities too subtle, his ambiguities in-
ferred rather than revealed by the historical record against which he pro-
tected both his private life and thoughts steadfastly. An apocryphal story,
reworked in the novel, has Louverture separately requesting the same letter from two secretaries and having a third evaluating both, in turn, before producing a third draft. Fictitious as it may be, that anecdote reveals
a man of many layers. Historians have discovered not too long ago that he
was a free man at the time of the uprising, but they still argue about his
role in the early events of 1791.

Bell chooses to make Louverture one of the early insurrectionists,
commissioned by white planters, including his master, to launch a limited
revolt so as to provide justification for a reaction against political reform.
This royalist conspiracy theory, versions of which do not involve Louverture, was first proposed by French colonists who blamed each other,
rather than the slave system itself, for the insurrections. While republicans accused royalist planters and the military governor of the colony, a
delegation of planters testifying to the French Assembly in November
1791 blamed republicans, Parisian allies of the *gens de couleur* (notably the
Société des Amis des Noirs), and *the gens de couleur* themselves. Replying
to this attack, French deputy Jean-Pierre Brissot, a member of the Société, and mulatto leader Julien Raymond, amplified the royalist theory,
which became officialized during the trial of the old governor Philibert-

François de Blanchelande. Blanchelande was executed for treason during the Terror, even though he observed, quite rightly, that the prosecution had no proof to back its claims. Indeed, the extensive inquiries led by deputies Tarbé and Garran for the Assembly itself do not contain a single document proving a conspiracy by royalists or others. In fact, the Garran report repeatedly sheds serious doubts on the hypothesis.[5] What it best reveals, already suggested by the planters' testimonies, is that at the very news of the uprising the colonists looked for its origins outside of the slave quarters and for its cause outside of slavery itself.

To be sure, the possibility of influences and contacts outside of the slaves' quarters remains. There are silences in the record, unexplained movements, and hints of linkages. Some historians, past and present, insist upon the suggested linkages. Some Haitians, in turn, find the suggestions politically motivated. Bell himself does not use the royalist theory to sanitize slavery as others have done; *All Souls' Rising* exposes the system as a man-made horror, a point to which I shall return. Yet, within the terms of the novel, tying Louverture to the early days of the rebellion as the leader of a white-conceived plot makes Toussaint the individual even harder to dramatize. Here is a man whose sympathy for France and European cultural markers is well documented but who never compromised on the unconditional freedom for all slaves after the 1794 Camp Turel declaration that revealed his political acumen to France. We know of his adherence to Christianity, but we also know of his knowledge of local medicinal practices, some of which were associated with the emerging vodoun religion. There are chunks of his personality that have never been reconciled in the record. The documentation available presents mostly the faces that he himself chose to offer, and mostly after 1794. There is little on what he did before 1792 and almost nothing on what he said and did, then or after, that is not marked by his strategic sense of the public eye. Having him tied to the royalists in the novel makes him more cunning, more visible, but also more impenetrable.

Fictionalizing Louverture has always been risky, as all those who took the leap before Bell discovered. Yet, in inventing the figure of Riau, the African-born slave who ran away from the Bréda plantation at the age of fourteen, Madison Smartt Bell takes the biggest gamble of *All Souls' Rising*. How does one reconstitute the subjectivity of a maroon slave in eighteenth-century Saint-Domingue, not as a prototype, but as a unique human being? Behold the silencing of the Haitian Revolution by professional historians. Behold the paucity of the record on what slaves did and thought outside of the work gangs. Behold our near total ignorance of what the world looked like to an escaped slave in the eighteenth century anywhere in the Americas in spite of the painstaking research of rare scholars like Jean Fouchard and Richard Price or the later stories of the like of Solomon Northrop and Esteban Montejo.

Bell finds a most clever tool to face the self-imposed challenge. Riau is an early practitioner of a religion that has not yet solidified. The gods can "ride" him just as they do now current practitioners of vodoun, the native religion of Haiti. The language of possession rarely leaves Riau, even when the slave is not fully ridden by his favorite spirits—like Ogun, the African-derived god of war and fire. In the span of a paragraph, Riau often speaks of himself in the third person, switches unexpectedly to the first, and reverts to the third without ever stopping the flow of consciousness—as some Haitians do, and not necessarily in a state of trance. Thus, when Louverture tries to groom Riau for a leadership position by having Dr. Hébert read him Epictetus, a Greek philosopher of freedom born in slavery, Riau reacts accordingly.

> I, Riau, hated all this. Riau wanted Ogun in his head again instead of all the shadowy thinking words. I wanted my mait'tete [the spirit master of my head] to come again. Each week all of us would dance and feed the loa with Biassou serving, or some smaller hungan [vodoun priest]. Riau would be there dancing with the rest, hearing the drums the others heard, but Ogun did not want to come in my head because it was too crowded with the words Toussaint was putting there, and there were new words growing too that Riau was trying to learn to make an answer. (P. 290)

Riau's concept of freedom owes much more to his excursions in the mountains and to his relationship with the horse he took from a French officer than to Greek philosophy.

> I watched the trees shifting on the mountains behind the river, and I thought how Riau might ride away alone, not coming back. . . . I pulled the

sorrel up again and sat him quietly, leaning a little to stroke his neck. It was foolish to think that it was mine. He was not owned by Jeannot either, or Toussaint, or even the officer I had killed to get him. He was just a sorrel horse, like I was just Riau. Bayon de Libertat had fooled himself to think that he had owned Riau, one time. (P. 291)

Through a mixture of registers, Riau constantly measures his engagement and his distance vis-à-vis his surroundings. His speech sounds awkward at times, infantile perhaps, but the oddities of his expression reveal an inner self confused yet determined. I have paid some attention both to the personalities of some of the early leaders (such as Boukman and Biassou) and to the African-born slaves who staffed the middle ranks of Louverture's army and whose relentless zeal forced the Creole leadership to reopen the hostilities after Louverture's capture. The little we know of them does not reveal the univocal subjectivities that North Atlantic autobiographies impose as a necessary human attribute. I often find Riau convincing—exactly because of his confusion, exactly because Bell builds a bridge between the reader and Riau's tortured soul. Riau carries a watch, taken from a French opponent, but never winds it. "I did not like to hear it chopping up the time with no one looking at it. . . . Let the white men chop up time" (p. 294). Once, however, Riau comes home at night. His son Caco (whose name prefigures rural armies of independent Haiti, including those who fought the U.S. invasion of 1915) is crying. Riau winds up the watch for Caco to hear. "But to Caco, the watch sound was like the crickets in the jungle or water running from the spring into a pool. He did not make much difference between these things, only he liked the watch because it shone" (pp. 294–95). One wishes for more passages like this. Here, the knowledge of the record leaves room for the novelist's imagination and for the skill of the writer to develop out of what is known a sense of what might have been. Riau the ventriloquist, child-father-slave-revolutionary, is a monstrosity; but that may be Bell's best point: slavery creates monsters.

Indeed, at no time does Bell make slavery palatable. On the very contrary, the novel is bloody, violent to the extreme, not easy reading for the faint. *All Souls' Rising* is about bodies: bodies skinned, maimed, tortured, raped, and penetrated in ways that rupture the very souls they once hosted. The book is dedicated to the Haitian spirits, "*Les Morts et les Mys-tères*," and to "all souls bound in living bodies." This bondage is quite real and slavery exemplifies it at its worst: no soul can resist such violent entrapment by the physical world.

Violence permeates the book; some readers may find that it reduces the revolution to a bloodbath. Haitians in particular may wonder if the gory details do not obscure the epic. Yet Bell makes sure that the reader registers that the blood had been spilling long before the slaves took arms. *All Souls' Rising* stands as testimony that European civilization created a horror in setting up slavery in the Americas and that the slaves of Saint-Domingue reacted to this horror only with a violence equal to that imposed on them.

For at its most horrifying, *All Souls' Rising* stays close to the historical body count, to the catalogue of injuries inflicted both before and during the revolution. We can find evidence in the official record for almost every one of the monstrous acts committed in the book. In fact, Bell takes that record too often at face value. Hence, the scene where the rebel slaves parade with a white baby at the end of a spike is most certainly an invention. It entered the record with the testimony of planters from Saint-Domingue to the National Assembly. Although the planters claimed to have firsthand accounts of the event, this particular story was most likely a last-minute embellishment, inspired by the recent riots in France itself, during which the crowd around Versailles did carry the dead body of a noble child at the end of a spike. White violence at home was the model for alleged black violence in the colony. Similarly, although murders of white planters at the hands of their mulatto sons may have occurred, the few detailed stories we have come again from uncorroborated testimonies by conservative planters anxious to vilify the mulattoes. Surely, one cannot fault Bell for having repeated the record. The historiographical appraisal of the revolution is in its infancy, in part because of the general silencing of the main event itself.[6] Yet, except for the ambiguous figure of Nanon, Bell reminds us of Faulkner with his dearth of positive mixed-race characters.

More important, however, the huge accumulation of single scenes of torture, rape, or dismemberment ironically obscures the systemic violence that Bell seems keen on revealing. The miserable state of the slaves was not only due to mischievous treatment and torture by vicious planters or overseers—which occurred often enough. Rather, plantation slavery, as an economic enterprise fully entrenched in the capitalist world economy, required a peculiar cost accounting. On the one hand, slaves had to be treated as if they were disposable, regardless of the human cost to them. On the other hand, the plantation had to extract from them as much labor as possible. Slaves had to live long enough for their labor to generate profit that substantially exceeded the cost of their purchase and maintenance. Thus, perversely, the welfare of each slave—including health and longevity—became part of the cost accounting, with the ceiling cost of that welfare set by the general price of labor in relation to profit.

In Saint-Domingue, as everywhere, hard labor drove the death rate among slaves and in sugarcane higher than any other crop. An old Caribbean saying goes: "Sugar is made with blood." Saint-Domingue's value rested upon sugar and the blood of slaves—not only the blood spilled at the hand of the most vicious masters, but especially the blood sucked every day by the production machine. As Africans and their descendants died in the sugar fields, Saint-Domingue/Haiti imported more slaves in the last quarter of the eighteenth century than all of the United States did in three centuries.

Historian Eric Williams long insisted on the connection between capitalism and slavery. Yet popular imagination has overly focused on individual acts of cruelty and on the unevenness of interpersonal relations across races, especially in the United States, where ongoing racism is attributed too hastily—and quite conveniently—to an unmitigated "legacy of slavery." In part in reaction to that emphasis, some of the best historians of slavery are insisting on its ultimate rationale: profit. In the very first line of their anthology, *Cultivation and Culture: Labor and the Shaping of Slave Life in the Americas*, Ira Berlin and Philip Morgan thought necessary to remind us: "Slaves worked. When, where and especially how they worked determined, in a large measure, the course of their lives. So central was labor in the slaves' experience that it has often been taken for granted."[7] Further, and amazingly, plantation labor went on in Saint-Domingue, albeit reduced at times, throughout and after the revolution.

Bell is aware of the cost accounting inherent in slavery as expressed in passing by the colonist Maltrot. Likewise, Riau wonders in passing also about the ongoing plantation work in supposedly freed territory. But the routine of daily life is an incessant topic, since it is through that routine that the men and women of Saint-Domingue—both before and during the revolution and regardless of hues and origins—developed the individual attributes that made them conform and yet resist to past and present stereotypes. In the preface that quickly sketches Saint-Domingue's social life, Bell draws the racial and class divides of the colony, insisting, for example, on the sixty-four shades of color that allegedly divided the mulattoes. To be sure, such rigid classifications existed. Yet, in the routine of daily life, in Saint-Domingue as everywhere in the Americas, there were individuals born within one color (or racial) category who died in another one. There were petty criminals of lower-class origins who became noblemen. There were slaves who became slave-owners. There were disagreements about the extent and relevance of these categories themselves. While not modifying the rigidity of the principles of race and class, those individual transformations and the exchanges on which they were premised created individuals who were, at one time or another, angry, satisfied, expectant, or disappointed both at the rigidity of these lines and at the capacity to cross them. Yet, it is through those petty individual moods, decisions, and the transformations that occurred between the jaws of a system claiming and reinforcing impermeable boundaries that the Haitian Revolution made its way and gained its epic proportions. The most amazing aspect of the revolution is that it was unthinkable and yet occurred. Its epic dimension is inherent in that contradiction.

Bell fully finds the voice most appropriate to that dimension in an astonishing four-page "Envoi" near the end of the book. Gone here is the novelist as narrator of history. The pen moves with Sonthonax, with Toussaint, with Galbaud and Bonaparte, in a literary hallucination that recalls some of the best Haitian contemporary writers. To do this, Bell has to assume our knowledge of the history. That he can do so only for four pages—and only at the end of the book—points to a difficulty of the historical novel as a genre and the need, with which I started, to measure the achievements of *All Souls' Rising* against the background of the general silencing of the Haitian Revolution. How does one write a historical novel minutely based on real events about which your readers are expected to know nothing? Against that silence of the history books, Madison Smartt Bell has produced a piercing scream.

Notes

1. Yves Bénot, *La Révolution Française et la fin des colonies* (Paris: La Découverte, 1989); Michel-Rolph Trouillot, "Historiography of Haiti," *UNESCO General History of the Caribbean*, vol. 5 (Paris: UNESCO Publishing, 1999); Michel-Rolph Trouillot, *Silencing the Past: Power and the Production of History* (Boston: Beacon Press, 1995).

2. Eric Williams, *From Columbus to Castro: A History of the Caribbean, 1492–1969* (New York: Harper & Row, 1970), 245.

3. See C. L. R. James, *Black Jacobins* (New York: Vintage, 1938).

4. Léon-François Hoffman, Introduction to *Toussaint Louverture by Alphonse de Lamartine* (Exeter: University of Exeter Press, 1998).

5. J. Ph. Garran, *Rapport sur les troubles de Saint-Domingue, fait au nom de la Commission des Colonies, des Comités de Salut Public, de Legislation et de Marine* (Paris: Imprimerie Nationale, Pluviose An VI [1798]), 193–210. Other important primary sources include Ph. Blanchelande, *Précis de Blanchelande sur son accusation* (Paris: Imprimerie de N.-H. Nyon, 1793), and Charles Tarbe et al., *Rapport . . . In Pièces imprimées par ordre de l'Assemblée Nationale. Colonies Première et seconde partie* [sic] (Paris: Imprimerie Nationale, 1792).

6. Bénot, 1989; Trouillot, 1995.

7. Ira Berlin and Philip Morgan, eds., *Cultivation and Culture: Labor and the Shaping of Slave Life in the Americas* (Charlottesville: University of Virginia Press, 1993), 1.

ঔ

Engaging the Past

Madison Smartt Bell

Michel-Rolph Trouillot sent me a note in the spring of 1995, expressing an interest in *All Souls' Rising*. It turned out that he also had a book coming out in the same season. We agreed to exchange galleys and meet in the fall. Over the summer, I read the proofs of *Silencing the Past* with admiration and trepidation that grew at an equal rate. The book itself was a work of genius in terms of its ideas and their application, and it was clear that the author knew a hell of a lot more about the Haitian Revolution than I probably ever would.

Moreover, he was a Haitian and I was not. The truth was that Trouillot was the first Haitian intellectual I had ever met. I had written *All Souls' Rising* in a sort of vacuum, sealed by books. I had consulted no professional historians, Haitian or otherwise. Though I had planned to do research on-site in Haiti before advancing the novel very far, the 1991 coup d'état and ensuing embargo derailed my travel plans. Because I am stubborn, I decided to stay home and write the book anyway, solely on the basis of print research; I had not once been to Haiti at that time.

Then there was the whole problem of intellectual identity politics, which dictate that you're not supposed to write about any groups of people of which you are not yourself a member. I'd built my whole career as a novelist on breaking this stupid rule. However, in a climate in which it was verboten for a white American to write from the point of view of a black American, the idea of a white southerner adopting the point of view of (to pick the most extreme example) an African-born fugitive slave in eighteenth-century Saint-Domingue seemed provocative, to say the least. I was nervous when I went to meet Trouillot for the second time.

When I mentioned my anxiety about the "cultural expropriation" problem, Trouillot laughed long and loud. His laughter cleared the air marvelously. When he had caught his breath, he explained to me that Haitian scholars and thinkers looked upon that aspect of contemporary American intellectual life as a near unique aberration. They thought it peculiar, and a little sad, and they certainly wanted no part of it.

This disclosure brought me huge relief. As a writer, perhaps even as a human being, I had long done my best to act on my belief that one ought make an effort to imagine the lives of others, no matter how different they may be from one's own. Without this effort of imagination, mutual understanding has no ground on which to develop. In the late 1980s and early 1990s, though, this posture of mine had become a rather lonely one. Also, to extend the principle two hundred years into the past of a country I had never visited seemed a bit of a stretch even for me.

The generosity of Trouillot's reception of my work proved typical for the Haitian intellectual stratum as I encountered it later on. Not universal: I received, for example, a letter written in foot-high letters of flame, denouncing *All Souls' Rising* for having desecrated Haitian history, Haitian religion, and Haitian women. Also I must take into account the probability that Haitians who detest the work are less likely to get in touch with me than those who like it. By and large, though, the book's reception among Haitians has been unexpectedly hospitable. I found that when I made my first visit to Haiti in the spring of 1995, I could successfully use the book as a calling card. There was enough work in it of sufficient quality to establish some basic credibility for me. The entrée thus afforded has been especially valuable, since *All Souls' Rising* is only the first volume of a trilogy about the Haitian Revolution. For the composition of the second and third volumes, I have advantages I didn't have when writing the first, including the knowledge and opinion of Trouillot himself and a number of other Haitian scholars to whom that first novel introduced me. This ongoing exchange of information and ideas has significantly altered and corrected my course, although I have resisted the temptation (for example) to ask someone like Trouillot to read and analyze the manuscript of the forthcoming second volume, *Master of the Crossroads*. As in *All Souls' Rising*, the mistakes and blunders will be all my own.

My research for *All Souls' Rising* was informed by novelist's instinct rather than by any instruction in proper historical method. I tended to prefer sources closest to the period in question. Such sources were indeed the best for capturing the flavor and ambiance of life at the time, but I failed to realize (until after the publication of *All Souls' Rising*) that they also sometimes contained misreadings and errors of their own. I don't think I fully realized until reading Trouillot's essay that my system of preferences was a good way to get myself influenced by contemporary propaganda.

The idea that the first insurrections of 1791 originated with a royalist plot is a given in many early sources (though not, as Trouillot points out, in the ur-source, Garran de Coulon). Later sources had rejected it, I believed, for political reasons—the royalist plot theory tended to take responsibility and credit for the revolution away from the black revolutionaries. I never saw the question quite that way. The royalist plot scenario appealed to me for its novelistic irony. The insouciance of the colonists on the brink of the revolution was so extraordinary that it

seemed possible that they might have believed they could start and stop a
large-scale slave insurrection, controlling it throughout for their own political ends. If Toussaint was involved from the beginning, the irony becomes truly delicious.

Though I now think it more likely that it never happened, it would
have been consistent with Toussaint's overall style of operation to have
subtly encouraged the white slave-masters to invest in their own eradication. Why not, if they were willing? Toussaint Louverture, with few exceptions, preferred guile to force, though he was expert in combining the
two. And throughout the Revolution he was careful to maintain at least a
toehold in the white camp as well as the black. Like the Vodou spirit
Legba, Toussaint stationed himself at borders, crossroads, and gateways,
so as to control the traffic between them as much as he could.

The royalist conspiracy theory, with or without any actual validity,
made a handy propaganda tool during the revolutionary period. Even
Léger Felicité Sonthonax deployed it in an effort to discredit Toussaint
when he found himself on trial (a second time!) for his failure to restore
Saint-Domingue to Parisian authority. Likewise, the iconic image of
the infant impaled on a spear has its apparent usefulness in progaganda.
The Cossacks are supposed to have impaled infants on sabers during
Russian pogroms against the Jews. Whether or not anything of this kind
actually happened during the Haitian Revolution, I can't prove. I have a
vivid memory of reading an early account of this atrocity first being inflicted by whites conducting a pogrom against the mulattoes of the Western Department. If this account were true, we'd know where the rebel
slaves got the idea, if indeed they did take up the practice . . . but try as I
may, I cannot relocate that early account now, and maybe it is only a trick
my mind has played on me. The image is still a persistent one, recurring
in a reminiscence of a Duvalierist purge of Jérémie which I recently read
in an e-mail news group: "Some of the people who executed the killings
went afterwards to brag that they killed the infant baby by piercing it with
a bayonet and that 'li tordie tankou ve' (he squirmed like a worm)." With
the help of my character Riau, I came to understand the standard of the
impaled infant as an image of genocidal intent, which not only existed
during the Haitian Revolution (on the part of all three races) but became,
I believe, its fundamental subject.

I cling to certain other doubtful scraps of the record because of their peculiar beauty. For example, Moreau de Saint-Méry's sixty-four-shade compartmentalization of the gradations of Afro-European skin tone . . . the three-volume work of which it is part was completed by the exiled colonist in Philadelphia after the Revolution—perhaps under the excessive influence of Benjamin Franklin, as Trouillot has argued elsewhere. In any case, it certainly partakes of the general eighteenth-century fondness for minute categorization. But its very significance strikes me as meaningful even if it was never fully in force; thus I persist in reproducing it as an appendix to *Master of the Crossroads*.

My biggest blunder to date was to complete *All Souls' Rising* without realizing that Toussaint Louverture was a free man at the time of the revolution. I managed to make this mistake even though I had read more recent sources which asserted his freedom. I concluded (in my vacuum) that those sources were in error and that they must have misinterpreted the principle of *liberté de savane*, according to which a slave with managerial responsibilities (such as Toussaint was at one point) might have complete liberty on his owner's property, and perhaps a passport for travel elsewhere. But no, Toussaint was free and even owned some slaves himself, well before 1791. He himself did his best to suppress this interesting fact, for his power base was the mass of slaves freed by the revolution (not the tiny group of 100-percent black freedmen that existed beforehand). The best I can say is that Toussaint's subterfuge about his prerevolutionary status worked very well on me. I had been successfully propagandized by someone who was, after all, a master of the craft. . . .

When I was finally convinced of this mistake, I was horrified. Trouillot told me it didn't really matter. One of the arguments of *Silencing the Past* is that the overall image created by an historical narrative has more importance and plays a greater role in advancing the truth than the individual facts supposed to underlie it. Challenging as this hypothesis may be as a principle of historiography, it is certainly a very forgiving attitude for the historian to adopt toward the novelist.

Written history, recorded history, places the past at a greater distance than oral traditions do, or so it seemed to me when I first began traveling in Haiti in 1995. It was as if the Revolution of 1791 had happened just a short while back—a Haitian friend told me that his grandfather had been an officer in that conflict. I don't offer this anecdote as an example of primitive naïveté. It suggests a different attitude toward the past, which holds the whole course of human history in close proximity to the present.

The popular religion, Vodou, reinforces this attitude with great power. The religion holds to the African belief that the spirits of the dead do not depart to some faraway afterworld, but remain nearby, invisible but present. The living have a duty to offer the ancestor spirits food and drink, and in return the spirits may and often do manifest themselves in the corporeal world, to give advice and guidance and sometimes material help. A member of the Haitian majority which believes in this way walks in the constant company of numerous invisible companions who left their bodies years or centuries ago. A side effect of this situation is that the events of history are sucked forward and collapsed into an eternal present, where everything that ever happened continues to go on, right now, with an explosive simultaneity. Again, I see nothing "primitive" in this way of being; rather it seems to fulfill the promise of the revelatory angel: There shall be no more time.

The role of the Vodouisant is to incarnate the spirits of the past; the practitioner clears a space in his or her own head where the spirit can install itself. This extremely radical spiritual exercise demands regular and complete abdication of the ego. In such episodes of spirit possession, the personal ego departs altogether and frequently recalls nothing about the period of its absence, once the spirit has left and the ego returns to the body.

These transformations are what account for Riau's oscillation along a spectrum between subject and object and between first- and third-person narration. I had to struggle to preserve this facet of the novel in the published version, for my editor argued (reasonably enough) that the technique made difficulties and confusion for the reader. But I saw no other way to represent a mind so different from "our own"—i.e., a mode of consciousness unlike what most people in the United States take for granted as the norm. This different mind, the mind of the past, is the thing which is so difficult for the novelist to recapture, no matter what period, place, or people are involved . . . though in Haiti that mind still persists in the present, since history is ever-present, too. Or at least it seemed to me when I began going to Haiti regularly that my portrayal of Riau was reasonably accurate, even though it was based, at the time that I wrote it, solely on anthropological sources, with no direct experience to balance them. Since then, I have improved that ratio considerably, though I am uncomfortably aware of researchers' inclination to find whatever they're looking for—whether it's really there or not.

I don't see Riau as monstrous; it's a failure of representation if he appears so. His mentality is certainly antithetical to the modern model in which personal consciousness is firmly and permanently installed in the front of the brain and awarded control of everything. Hence the tyranny of the ego, which so many prisoners of this modern model would dearly like to escape. For Riau, the door is open, swinging in the wind. The altered state which he often visits is also the goal of hypnosis, of meditation, of a great many religious practices; it is what the early Christian saints were seeking when they went into the desert.

In the novel, Dr. Antoine Hébert represents the more modern mode of consciousness (and for this reason I am relieved that Trouillot does not find him to be anachronistic). Since his mind-set is a lot closer to my own, he was of course a much easier character to write than Riau. Moreover, he serves as the pilot fish for both the reader and the writer: the stranger who arrives in the strange land knowing nothing and needing to learn it all. In this project, Riau is the doctor's guide and preceptor. Over the course of the three novels planned, these two fictional characters emerge as dual protagonists. Their ways of thinking and being are very different, but neither is superior to the other; rather they represent certain extremes of human possibility. Riau proves capable of assimilating himself a long way toward the European, while the doctor shows a capacity to assimilate himself considerably toward what is emerging as the Haitian.

As for the historical protagonist, Trouillot is right to say that he is a shadowy figure in *All Souls' Rising*. There are several reasons for that situation. One is a matter of overall structure: my intention was and is to have each novel of the trilogy resolve its narrative on the basis of the actions of the fictional characters, while the three novels joined together in a larger story present Toussaint Louverture as the main protagonist, over the arc of his whole career. It's also true that during the initial period of the revolution covered by *All Souls' Rising*, not much is known for certain about what Toussaint was up to. The first card he played faceup on the table was the Proclamation of Camp Turel.

When I first happened upon Toussaint's career as a novelistic subject, part of the appeal was that rather less was definitely known about him than about most other historical figures of similar importance. Concerning Napoleon Bonaparte, for example, the record is exhaustive, and thus, for the novelist, exhausted. In the case of Toussaint, a certain paucity of biographical detail seemed an advantage, allowing the writer room to maneuver—to fictionalize a character who would not be false to the facts. That most of the existing readings of Toussaint's personality contradict each other in very broad terms also struck me as liberating.

In the writing, however, I found myself extremely unwilling to invent actions or speeches for Toussaint that I could not document in some way, or at least reason to be probable. My admiration for the historical man made me very reluctant to take any risk of falsifying him. The result was a degree of aesthetic failure. In this first volume, I wished Toussaint to remain mysterious but not quite so vague and remote as he actually appears. In Vodouisant terms, one might say that the spirit was called but did not come. Or, to judge my own effort somewhat more charitably, one might say that the spirit was present but very, very far away.

Since then, my experience in Haiti has influenced my approach to the whole question. Composing these novels has become much less a matter of making an object expressive of my artistic ego, etc., and much more a matter of preparing a receptacle suitable for another spirit to inhabit. It may sound a little eccentric, but bear in mind that according to the popular Haitian view of both religion and history, this project is not only quite practical but actually happens every day.

In more mundane terms, I can say that in gaining more firsthand experience of Haiti and Haitians, I have come to understand a little better what Toussaint's personality might have been, and what were the conditions that made it possible. Toussaint stood at a crossroads of enormous historical importance—on the island where Europeans met and destroyed for the first time the native people of the Western Hemisphere, where Las Casas, in hope of sparing the Taino people, first thought of replacing them with slaves brought out of Africa. Toussaint placed himself in the gateway between European culture and the African culture of Saint-Domingue, which had inherited something from the Taino people, too. It was for this reason among several others that he chose Louverture—the Opening—as his nom de guerre. He thus had set himself the task of straddling a cultural gulf.

As for the apparent contradictions in Toussaint's personality: He is most often depicted as a devout (or Tartuffian) Catholic, with the assumption that therefore he shunned Vodou. This assumption fails to take into account the fact that in Haiti, Catholicism and Vodou do not exclude but rather embrace one another (or, at any rate, the latter embraces the former). Similarly, Toussaint is usually portrayed either as a ruthless, Machiavellian monster or a temporizing, mediating hero, saint, and martyr. The historical record shows that he met both of these descriptions very completely at different times. The normative response to this apparent contradiction is that one of these extremes must have represented the real and essential Toussaint, while the other was a hypocritical mask and disguise. But the Haitian way of being doesn't require such an absolute choice. A human being who is not obliged to maintain an integrated self-conscious ego is free to inhabit one personality today and another tomorrow. I have come to believe that Toussaint Louverture was a master of this maneuver: that he could, when he chose to, take possession of a wholly European mode of perception and response, and at other times inhabit a mind almost purely African. Indeed, he claimed a freedom of passage between many very different worlds.

Trouillot's *Silencing the Past* is (to oversimplify) a study of why some historical events are remembered and others forgotten. The Haitian Revolution, of course, furnishes a magnificent case study. I was in my twenties, at work on my second published novel, before I ever heard of it, and I think my case is similar to that of most white people in the United States, though the story is significantly more familiar to the black community. I thought that I had discovered an immensely powerful secret—an opportunity to tell an important story that had never been told in fictional form. (Although I had read Faulkner's *Absalom, Absalom* and *Band of Angels*, a minor Robert Penn Warren novel which includes some scenes of the Haitian Revolution, I was blithely unaware of *The Kingdom of This World*, *Bug Jargal*, and *Babouk* until my own project was well under way.) This sense of pioneering on unexplored territory was hugely refreshing at first. However, I was soon forced to recognize that the expository problems were rather severe. For a while I toyed with the idea of weak specification—creating an abstract setting for the novel that would resemble eighteenth-century Saint-Domingue to about the same extent that the world of J. M. Coetzee's *Michael K* resembles twentieth-century South Africa before the end of apartheid. But finally I decided to try for the most realistic and historically accurate rendition of which I might be capable. It was at this point that the project metastasized from one novel into three.

"How does one write a historical novel minutely based on real events about which your readers are expected to know nothing?" If I had put Trouillot's excellent question to myself beforehand, I might not have had the fortitude to begin. The compensation for the difficulty is that one does, finally, get to tell one's readers something new.

One gets to tell them something important to the here and now. As a southerner raised on southern renascence literature, I was trained from an early age to recognize the bearing of history on the present. It now seems to me that the history of the Haitian Revolution bears on the present situation of the United States with a very considerable weight. I take into account the possibility that this idea is a distorted result of my ten-years'-and-counting concentration on this narrative and its actors. Nevertheless, I believe that in ignoring the Haitian Revolution, we in the United States lose an important part of the meaning of our own history.

Trouillot is not the only commentator to observe, with some justice, that the portrayal of the mixed-blood population in *All Souls' Rising* is unbalanced. (I myself see the colored woman Nanon as a wholly positive figure, but because she was a prostitute, most Haitian readers don't.) However, not all readers are displeased at the imbalance. Some months ago, I gave a lecture before a mostly Haitian audience. During the ensuing discussion, an imposing woman told me with great force that what she most admired about *All Soul's Rising* was the way in which it demonstrated how the mulattoes were heartless, inhuman, cruel, vicious, and malicious to the core! What struck me about this declaration, aside from its vigor, is that the lady herself was a person of mixed bloodlines—to judge from her complexion. As Trouillot observes, among Haitians there can be individuals born in one racial category who die in another.

The great humanitarian achievement of the Haitian Revolution was the work not of Toussaint Louverture (a figure far more amiable and palatable to whites than most of the other revolutionaries) but of Jean-Jacques Dessalines, whose Imperial Constitution of 1805 set forth that all citizens of Haiti would henceforth be defined as "black," while all non-Haitians would be defined as "white"—regardless of their pigmentation in either case. In the subsequent evolution of Haitian Kreyol, the word *neg* has come to mean simply "person," while *blan* means "foreigner." With that, the very concept of race has been, if not abolished, at least altered beyond recognition. A sort of racism does persist in Haiti, but it is unrecognizably dissimilar to what we still endure in the United States. In Haiti today, distinctions of race have been mostly unmasked as distinctions of class. A person is not racially categorized by skin tone alone; one's education, employment, family and social connections, and economic situation must all be considered before such an assignment can be made.

In this way, Haitian society has gone much further toward solving the problem of racism, derived from the history of colonialism en masse, than has the society of the United States. Proof of our own failure is brought before our eyes with terrible regularity: Rodney King, the LA riots, O. J. Simpson, Amadou Diallo. . . . The root of the problem is a good two hundred years in the past, enlaced with the three revolutions that concluded the eighteenth century.

The American Declaration of Independence claimed the rights of life, liberty, and pursuit of happiness for everyone! . . . who happened to be white. The French Revolution proclaimed *Liberté, Égalité, Fraternité* as natural rights for everyone! . . . who happened to be white. Third in the chronological sequence, the Haitian Revolution was the only one of the three to extend this ideology of natural human rights to all human beings.

Through what Trouillot defines as the silencing of the Haitian Revolution, its significance has been not lost but camouflaged. The failure of the American and French Revolutions to extend their ideology to all people created fault lines in the societies that resulted from them, fault lines that still promise and produce earthquakes today. The inhabitants of a tiny island now famous for being the most impoverished nation in the Western Hemisphere are also the only people in the Western Hemisphere to have answered the great revolutionary question correctly and with complete commitment. What that means—strangely enough—is that we must embrace the Haitian Revolution before we can fulfill our own.

William Styron's *The Confessions of Nat Turner:* A Meditation on Evil, Redemption, and History

Eugene D. Genovese

Aristotle taught that art captures historical truth as no history can. In the black experience of slavery, William Styron found a universal meaning—a truth, which he conveyed in *The Confessions of Nat Turner*. There is no profit to be gained by rehashing the endless assertions that he falsified history. Properly, he took liberties with the historical details. Improperly, he made unsustainable claims for a range of research and a precision no novelist need aspire to. In consequence, he provided ammunition for those who, with unerring instinct for the capillaries, confuse history with fiction or, worse, demand that both serve political and ideological agendas.

The most disturbing attacks, however, came from black intellectuals with an instinct for the jugular and a commitment to revolutionary politics. In 1967, when Styron published *The Confessions of Nat Turner*, self-styled revolutionaries were embracing Frantz Fanon's thesis that oppressed peoples could only liberate themselves psychologically as well as politically through murderous violence. While not averse to nitpicking, Styron's black critics cast a sharp eye on such central historical questions as the effects of social injustice and oppression and the nature not only of revolutionary resistance but also of the character and personality of dedicated revolutionaries. They invoked Marx, Lenin, Mao, and Ho, but primarily they invoked Fanon, most notably his *Wretched of the Earth* and *Black Skin, White Masks*. Fanon brought special credentials. A black psychiatrist born and raised in Martinique, he moved in Left Bank circles with Jean-Paul Sartre and others, and showed extraordinary courage in the service of the Algerian Liberation Front's blood-soaked rising against French colonialism. Embittered by his experiences in Martinique, Algeria, and even Paris, he concluded that colonial peoples, a category that ostensibly included American blacks, could only become visible, establish their dignity, effect their political liberation, and restore their psychic health through direct, personal violence against their oppressors.

Blacks had special claims on Fanon's teachings, but they were not alone in attacking the politics they attributed to the novel. In a fit of self-righteousness, many whites in the Academy and in literary circles joined the rejection of Styron's Nat Turner. For one thing, they regarded the historical Nat Turner as a black John Brown—the John Brown who, since Emerson and the abolitionists, has acquired the status of a saint. That John Brown was probably criminally insane has counted for little. That his breathtakingly eloquent final speech reeked with flagrant mendacity and hypocrisy has mattered not at all. Like Nat Turner, he was on the right side: truth and morals depend upon the "situation" at hand and have no philosophical much less theological foundation. Oppressed peoples have the right to employ "any means necessary." No wonder, then, that the aspirant revolutionaries, to say nothing of poseurs, hate Styron's portrayal of Nat Turner as a man driven by religious fanaticism to seek liberation through the shedding of blood even of innocents, but also as a man conscious of sin and in search of redemption.

Styron's Nat Turner does not resemble the prototypical revolutionary that ideologues require, for a sense of sin and a quest for redemption temper his hatred. Styron ennobles the historical Nat Turner by giving him qualities he may have possessed but the empirical record does not reveal: rational motivation, concrete objectives, a definite strategy, and tactics that required "timing and coordination"—qualities the most diligent historians have found no evidence of. In truth, those who read the record could not be faulted for concluding that Nat Turner, unlike Gabriel Prosser and Denmark Vesey, was a hate-driven madman who had no idea of where he was leading his men or what they would do when they got there. Styron even gratuitously makes him a descendant of the "Coromantees," known to slaveholders as an especially fierce warrior people in Africa who led slave revolts in the Caribbean. We know nothing of Nat Turner's ancestry, but, curiously, none of Styron's detractors has complained about this particular literary liberty.

In contrast, the aptly named Will, Nat Turner's most problematic lieutenant, appears in *The Confessions of Nat Turner* as a homicidal maniac, who thirsts not only for white blood, but also for "some *meat.*" Maniac or no, Will has contempt for *soi-disant* revolutionaries who think too much. He sneers at the hesitant-to-kill "preacher man," deriding him as "some fancy talker." Fascinated and repelled, Nat Turner knows he cannot do without Will, although he fears "his manner, his unfocused hatred and madness." He hopes against hope: "if I could channel his brutal fury . . ." The Will pictured here could, in fact, have been the Nat Turner of the historical record. By splitting revolutionary personality into these two discrete parts—the ruthlessly sane and the cold-bloodedly insane—Styron was able to represent the two warring souls of the historical Nat Turner: the one a single-minded, murderous fanatic whose moral sense and very humanity have been crushed by years of brutal treatment; the other an admirable man who, notwithstanding the destruction he wreaks, retains his humanity.

Hunger for vengeance consumes Will, whose blind recklessness threatens tactical mistakes that could undo everything. Nat tries to think politically. He foreshadows the dictum of the great West Indian revolutionary C. L. R. James, who admired Dessalines but condemned his slaughter of politically harmless French planters in postrevolutionary Haiti: "It was an act of revenge, and revenge has no place in politics." Yet, in the end, how much do Will and Nat differ politically? Will kills happily to slake his thirst for blood. Nat acquiesces in the killing of the same people and refuses to repent of the spilled blood. Revolutions, Mao pronounced, are not tea parties or the painting of pretty pictures. Revolutions are either thorough or doomed.

Alas, in creating a recognizable human being with conflicted but rational motives and a plan of action, Styron did a vast disservice to the cause of revolutionary myth, for he deprived Nat Turner of the one-dimensional single-mindedness that revolutionaries must display if they expect to prevail. In compensation, Styron offered Nat Turner's extraordinary ruminations on the nature of black hatred of whites, especially his own. Part III ("Study War") opens: "An exquisitely sharpened hatred for the white man is of course an emotion not difficult for Negroes to harbor." It is one thing to hate and wish to kill people who torment you indirectly or from afar and whom you can reduce to abstractions. It is another to hate and wish to kill people whose lives enmesh with your own; who are not all that bad and may even be pretty decent; who, despite condescension and worse, have shown you kindness. Nat Turner kills Margaret Whitehead not only because he must maintain his authority against the challenge posed by the immeasurably more ruthless Will, but also because of his proclaimed "desire and hatred" for her; because she tempts him with the unattainable; because she epitomizes those who kill the spirit with patronizing kindness. Will's challenge resurfaced during the 1960s when Ron Karenga, a militant black leader, demanded to know whether tough-talking black revolutionaries had what it takes: "When it's 'take that white girl's head too,' we'll really see how tough you are." Nat Turner ponders the conditions under which hatred threatens to become limitlessness—the "desolation," the "wrenching loneliness." His thirst for justice cannot readily keep from turning into a thirst for vengeance, which his God forbids ("Vengeance is mine, saith the Lord").

The charge that Styron distorts the black experience in slavery cannot be sustained, but a parallel charge has better prospects. *The Confessions of Nat Turner* explicates a judgment Styron has explicitly rendered elsewhere that the southern churches and legal system betrayed their professed ideals when they supported slavery. He unfairly characterizes the slaveholders and common white folk of Virginia as ignoramuses who invoked selected biblical texts to rationalize their greed and cruelty. Nowhere does he touch upon the powerful scriptural defense of slavery manifested in the work of the South's formidable array of honest and learned theologians and spread abroad by capable town and country preachers. Nowhere does he expose the feeble reasoning and biblical scholarship of the abolitionists who declared slavery sinful largely by the simple device of assuming everything they had to prove. Neither Jesus nor His apostles ever condemned slavery as sinful, as they did fornication, adultery, blasphemy, and much else. Jesus drove the money changers from the Temple; He did not drive slaveholders from His presence. It never occurs to Styron that the common folk he denigrates accepted slavery in no small part because their preachers made out a much better scriptural case than the abolitionists did. For good measure, he leaves the impression that most whites were illiterate, although he surely knows that the Old South had one of the highest literacy rates in the world.

There is not one noble, admirable white person to be found in the novel. Instead, we find a declining ruling class that no longer believes in much of anything, while it trumpets its racial superiority and flatters itself that it treats its slaves better than other ruling classes treat their laborers. Through this charade, it clings desperately to the human property that sustains its shaky hold on the sweetness of life. Yet, in the following years of partial economic recovery Virginians—Thomas Roderick Dew, Nathaniel Beverly Tucker, George Fitzhugh, George Frederick Holmes, and the reverends Robert Dabney, Thornton Stringfellow, William A. Smith, and George Armstrong—produced some of the most compelling defenses of slavery ever written. Beyond Virginia, where in *The Confessions of Nat Turner* do we find the slightest hint the intelligentsia of the Old South readily matched the best the North had to offer? Where are we told that its defense of slavery constituted only one part of the most powerful critique of transatlantic bourgeois culture that America has yet produced?

Styron—a clever chap, full of craft, connivery, and wily stealth—might reply that such criticism from outraged white folks is all well and good but colossally irrelevant. He might, that is, acknowledge his picture of the Old South as skewed, but insist that a more rounded picture would not undermine the essential truth of the story he chose to tell. Regrettably, he would be right. But so what? William Styron has exposed himself as a treacherous scalawag who has lived in Connecticut too long and has succumbed to Yankee bigotry and poisonous propaganda. He has nonetheless lucked out. The southern faction of the Vast Rightwing Conspiracy has failed to bring out the long-expected volume, *William Styron's Slaveholders: Ten Chivalric Southrons Respond.* I thought to edit such a volume myself but desisted when a potential contributor muttered that the penalty for hate crimes is running high these days.

Styron chose to tell the central truth about slavery—the truth that transcends all other truths. George Core, one of his most perceptive and sympathetic critics, has observed, "The very tensions within Nat—the discrepancy between what he believes and what he is forced to do—are representative of his society." In seeking the representation of southern slave society, Styron draws heavily on the work of Stanley Elkins, who depicted slavery in the United States as immeasurably worse than slavery in Latin America and elsewhere and argued that it infantilized its victims. Since Elkins has come under a barrage of criticism, much of it vicious and stupid but some of it valid, Styron stands accused of historical distortion. But who could fairly read Styron's Nat Turner and his comrades as infantilized or as remotely the creatures their masters programmed them to be? The enduring strength of Elkins's case, which Styron sees with a clear eye, lies in its delineation of the demonic logic of slavery. The weakness lies in its sly and preposterous suggestion that the slaveholding South qualified as a totalitarian society and in its failure to consider the countervailing forces that rendered the master's ideal slave incapable of general realization. The empirical evidence arrayed in the impressive scholarship of the 1970s—after Styron wrote his novel—supports Hegel's great set piece in *The Phenomenology of Mind*, which destroys the notion of absolute lordship and absolute bondage. Styron probably read Hegel, and although he did not have access to the scholarship of the next decade, he foreshadowed its central theme. Slavery, he suggests, came as close as any social system possibly could to dehumanizing its victims—therein lay its ultimate crime—but, although countless slaves succumbed, many did not and perhaps none totally. Styron's Nat Turner stands as testimony to the power of the human spirit, which at the very edge of ultimate degradation asserts itself at all cost.

That power itself exhibits painful inner tension. Styron's Nat Turner struggles with doubts about himself and his mission and, even more irritating to his black critics, he castigates his "shit-eating people," comparing them to "flies, God's mindless outcasts." Yet those words do not overmatch the fierce denunciation of black acquiescence in slavery that David Walker poured into the famous and widely circulated insurrectionary pamphlet he wrote shortly before the Southampton insurrection. It was, as I recall, Wladislaw Gomulka, the Polish Communist leader who, while risking his life to defy Stalin, said that he hated his generation of Poles and meant to create a new and radically different man. For better or worse, that is how genuine revolutionaries speak. And what they say almost invariably begins with a blistering assault on the very people for whose liberation they stand ready to die. How else are they supposed to rouse their people to self-criticism—to an understanding that there are things in life worth dying for, that they must be willing to sacrifice everything for the struggle? It was those very "shit-eating people" to whom Styron's Nat Turner appealed: "My brothers! Stop yo' laughin and listen to me." How did they respond? "My language was theirs. I spoke it as if a second tongue. My rage had captured them utterly." In this respect, Styron's juxtaposition of outbursts does limn a prototypical revolutionary.

These are some of the historical truths that an artist sought to bring into bold relief, and, necessarily, they emerge as transhistorical statements about the human condition. (The intellectuals of the Old South were fond of echoing Dionysius of Halicarnassus, who described history as "philosophy teaching by example.") Yet perhaps the most infuriating because the dumbest attacks on Styron have come from white literary critics who charge that he wrote a religious tract disguised as a novel and compounded the offense by confusing the religious questions it raised. Gravely, they added that since Styron had transhistorical concerns, he did not have to make his protagonist a black slave at all. Styron, a better student of theology and history than his eminent critics, knew better. Although he has focused on evil throughout his life's work, he has also confronted the possibility of absolute evil, which properly led him not merely to slavery but to the further abomination of racial slavery. Here his experiences in growing up in a segregated Virginia that tried to render blacks invisible proved decisive for the controlled passion he brought to a compounded injustice. The passion embedded in Styron's art led him to the heart of historical truth.

Historians shudder and labor mightily to obscure the thought, but historical truth, which postmodernists deny exists, raises theological questions and bares theological assumptions. Antonio Gramsci, the foremost Marxist theorist of the twentieth century and leader of the Italian Communist Party before Mussolini imprisoned him, announced famously, "The philosophy of everyman is contained in his politics." He might have

added, although as a Marxist he could not, "And his politics bares his theology, even or especially when he does not know he has a theology."
Among contemporary men of letters, few if any have focused on the nature of evil and, therefore, of justice, as consistently and thoughtfully as
Styron has. At the heart of his life's work lies a brooding confrontation
with the penchant for evil in everyman and with the possibilities for redemption. Thus Styron has described his novel as "a sort of religious
parable and a story of exculpation." But if that were all, only his superior
artistic talent would distinguish him from many other writers, especially
those who espouse a frankly Christian standpoint. Styron goes further
and, while resisting Manichean temptations, he explores the possibilities
for absolute evil embodied in concrete persons. In so doing, he displays
endless fascination with human responsibility for evil in a world created
and presided over by the omnipotent, omniscient, perfectly good God of
the Bible. No matter that Styron speaks as an agnostic. Everything he has
written leads back to that conundrum, which has plagued Christian theology from its beginnings.

In reply to an interviewer, Styron remarked, "Total domination of
human beings by others up to the point of extermination seems to me to
come as close as one can to the notion of absolute evil." He recognizes
that men may approach absolute evil, but he shies away from the thought
that an individual may embody it. His hesitation flows relentlessly from
his agnosticism, for an embodiment of absolute evil conjures up the
Devil—a believable figure only to those who believe in God. Indeed, as
Dostoyevsky, whom Styron much admires, saw, the Devil's most brilliant
and successful ploy has been to convince intellectuals that he does not
exist. The Devil in whom Styron cannot quite believe nonetheless keeps
reappearing, especially in his novels but also in his essays and interviews.

Thus Styron, a dedicated opponent of capital punishment, relishes as
"delicious pleasure" the execution of Hitler and his henchmen. Sensibly
recognizing the need to make exceptions to the sternest of rules, he dis-
tinguishes the "sane and evil" Nazis from "the crazy and evil" Nathan of
Sophie's Choice. Although he seems undecided about the Will of *The Confessions of Nat Turner*, the logic of his argument puts Will in the category
of Nathan, or at least a good deal closer to Nathan than to the Nazis. Styron, like Harriet Beecher Stowe before him, invokes biting irony in his

portrayal of Christian masters who abhorred the very thought of selling a slave but who, driven toward bankruptcy, swallowed their qualms and attended to business. He renders a severe judgment on the southern slaveholders but avoids the puerile identification of slaveholders with Nazis. However justifiable the severity of the judgment and salutary the refusal to equate slaveholders with Nazis, the implicit ambiguity creates problems of its own.

Styron presents Nat Turner as a prophet and "an avenging Old Testament angel." Simultaneously he presents him as ultimately in submission to Jesus' call for forgiveness and redemption. The agnostic Styron here moves from a questionable separation of the Old from the New Testament—a piece of theological juggling liberal theologians love to indulge in—to an orthodox affirmation of Jesus' assurance that He has come to fulfill, not overthrow, the Law. For if the God of the Old Testament is a God of Wrath and "a jealous God," He is also the first person of a triune God that includes a Jesus whose nature is inseparable from that of the Father. Recall that Jesus, the God of love, displayed that very wrath and asserted His own "jealous" nature when He drove the money changers from the Temple and, more tellingly, consigned those who blaspheme against the Holy Ghost to everlasting damnation. Father and Son alike declare wrath and redemption inseparable from justice, as well as from confession and atonement.

What does—should—Nat Turner repent of? His turn to violence? How else were slaves to secure their freedom in a society in which they lacked all political rights, even access to the right of petition? Did he sin by raising the standard of insurrection when no other standard was available? To be sure, he wavers. When Will kills the kindly, old Miss Sarah, he half-aloud thinks, "Ah my God! Hast Thou truly called me to this?" Still, he resists the suggestion of T.R. Gray, the white lawyer who is taking down his confession, that he repent for having led his people into a slaughter, for even the gravest political miscalculation hardly qualifies as a sin. He also resists Gray's suggestion that he repent for the butchering of defenseless white women and children. Styron does not presume to judge as evil, much less sinful, such acts of righteous wrath. Jesus taught submission to the powers that be, but He also taught resistance to that which contravened the laws of God. The apostle James declared, "The wrath of man worketh not the righteousness of God," but he did not assert that all acts of human wrath contravene the Law. Christian theologians have since stressed that resistance should stop short of violent challenge to constituted secular authority; if that means acceptance of fearful punishment in this world, so be it. Better to die a martyr than to sin by taking the sword. Yet most of these same theologians recognize the right of self-defense and therefore acquiesce in just war. Nowhere does Styron question that Nat Turner was waging a just war of self-preservation. Indeed, his insistence that slavery threatens to deprive its victims of their very personhood carries with it an acceptance, however apprehensive, of slave rebellion as just war. And he well knows that just revolutionary wars must be thorough.

In one of the more powerful scenes in the novel, Nat has a vision of a combat between a white and black angel. The white angel strikes the black with a sword that breaks without doing its intended damage. The black angel resumes the struggle with his shield as an offensive weapon. He vanquishes the white angel, casting him down, and he rides across the sky in triumph, crying, "The Lamb shall overcome them." That scene recalls one in Torquato Tasso's *Gerusalem liberato* (*Jerusalem Delivered*), which Styron doubtless knows and, presumably, has intentionally inverted. Styron may also know that the better-educated citizens of the Old South read, admired, and discussed it. Robert Bolling of Virginia and Richard Henry Wilde of Georgia qualified as Tasso scholars, and southern literary journals ranked Tasso among the great figures of world literature. Tasso's admirers included such leaders of southern opinion as Isaac Harby, Hugh Legaró, and Richard Furman, as well as such intellectually impressive ladies as Augusta Jane Evans, Catherine Edmonston, and Mary Moragne. In particular, Mary Chesnut's social circle discussed *Jerusalem Delivered*, which posed the moral problem of the limits of Christian charity in the duel. Do you kill an opponent whose sword has been broken? Christian charity rejects so mean a victory, and Tasso has the Christian Tancredi do everything possible to spare his pagan adversary. But the dauntless Argante scorns the offer of mercy and charges. Tancredi must kill him, for when your adversary is a fanatic who lives outside the code, even the most devout Christian gentleman has no honorable choice. The slaveholding planters, proclaiming themselves "The Chivalry," took special pride in being men ready to stand against all odds; men ready to die for their "southern way of life"; men who would keep on coming; men you could not intimidate, cajole, or bribe; men you must either submit to or kill.

And yet, Styron's Nat Turner does repent, and he emerges as a man uneasy about the violence he unleashed. He fails miserably in his efforts to kill defenseless whites, and Will has to finish them off. He nonetheless does kill Margaret Whitehead in part—but only in part—to ward off Will's challenge to his authority as a revolutionary leader. He has personal reasons for killing her and, notwithstanding the justice of his cause, the knowledge that he has sinned haunts him. For long stretches he cannot pray: "All I could feel was despair, despair so sickening that I thought it might drive me mad, except that it somehow lay deeper than madness." Notwithstanding the visions from God that urge him on, only when he finally seeks redemption through the forgiveness of the one person he has killed can he once again pray to his God. Did he in fact sin by killing her?

If so, what happens to the justification of just war? No, he sinned by killing her in a frenzy of vengeance accompanied by a political necessity that arose from his own weakness. His sin lay not in the act of waging revolutionary war, not even in the most gruesome excesses that accompanied it, but in the mean, unmanly, unworthy motives that drove him to kill in a rage of vengeful personal hatred. The extent to which God judges an act as sinful per se remains moot, but there is nothing moot about the sinfulness of a motive that contravenes His expressed Word.

Wisely, Styron neither offers Nat Turner as a Christ nor trucks with the blasphemy attributed to Nat Turner in T. R. Gray's famous interview, "Was Not Christ Crucified"? Rather, Styron interposes the words of Revelation: "Surely I come quickly," and leaves the reader to ponder the meaning of the words he does not quote: "And my reward is with me, to give every man according as his work shall be." Thus Styron probes the meaning of Christ in the black experience of slavery, as, simultaneously, he exposes the deepest horror in the suffering of the slaves. The bodily torments Jesus suffered, although ghastly, were hardly the worst anyone has ever suffered. But His humiliation, abasement, and momentary sense

of abandonment by His Father encapsulated the worst anyone might suffer. No greater torment has ever been expressed than that captured in the
words from the Son of Man on the Cross: "My God, my God, why has
thou forsaken me?" The slaves, humiliated not only as slaves but also as
black people, grasped with unique insight the depth of His sacrifice because every day of their lives they tasted the anguish of His momentary
sense of total abandonment, overcoming their despair through faith in
His promise of deliverance. And that searing historical truth the artistic
imagination of William Styron has illuminated as no historian could hope
to do.

♂♀

More Confessions

William Styron

W hen I was still in my twenties, more than fifteen years before sitting down to begin *The Confessions of Nat Turner*, I wrote to my father: "I hope that when I'm through with Nat Turner (and God, I know
it's going to be a long hard job) he will not be either a Great Leader of the
Masses—as a stupid communist writer might make him out—or a perfectly Satanic demagogue, as the surface historical facts present him, but
a living human being of great power and great potential who somewhere,
in his struggle for freedom and for immortality, lost his way." I was surprised to discover, upon reading this recently unearthed letter, that even
as far back as my fledgling years as a writer I was confronted by the difficulty of dealing with a protagonist revealed by the record to be, as Genovese says, a "hate-driven madman who had no idea of where he was
leading his men or what they would do when they got there." In fiction, it
has always been a daunting task to make psychopaths credible, much less
agreeable—and nearly impossible to make them heroic—so even then I
knew that my Nat Turner had to be given rational dimensions, differing

radically from those of the figure whose crazed visions dominate the original "Confessions."

In addition to my desire to create an admirable though necessarily flawed hero who struck a blow for liberty, I also wanted to show the nature of the system that held him and his people in bondage. "I had hoped," I wrote after the book was published, "that whatever light my work might shed on the dungeon of American slavery, and its abyssal night of the body and spirit, might also cast light on our modern condition, and be understood by black people, as well as white, as part of a plausible interpretation of the agony that has bound the present to the past."

That this was largely wishful thinking on my part—at least insofar as the novel's effect on black people was concerned—was demonstrated by the appearance in 1968, less than a year after the book's publication, of a volume of essays by ten black writers attacking everything I had done and impugning the motives and integrity of all I had set out to do. Like every writer, I was not unacquainted with bad notices, but this collection was something else. It was an amazing experience to read essay after essay, enraged and often hysteric in voice, that savaged me for being "psychologically sick," "morally senile," and for possessing a "vile racist imagination." While the personal insult was offensive, the relentlessly hectoring tone of the book did allow me, finally, to regard its message less with the pained resentment I first felt than with a kind of resigned contempt. The writing was, with few exceptions, so shoddy and pedestrian, and the essayists' logic and command of history were so addled, that the volume was hard to take seriously. Could any but the most credulous readers believe that *The Confessions of Nat Turner* had no virtues whatever? But that was the impression left by these essays, which did not even concede that I might have shed a small beam of light on the dark tragedy of American slavery.

The work of the ten black writers had the effect of imposing an informal boycott on the novel. Diehard antagonists of the novel, including some of the surviving essayists, have remained a faithful band of detractors after all these years and take regular potshots at the book in the media; as recently as 1999 in a *New Yorker* article, one of the black critics, Mike Thelwell, called the work "an ignorant monstrosity."

It remains an article of belief in at least part of the black community that *Confessions* is a "racist" work. It was termed in fact racist by another of the original critics, Alvin F. Poussaint, a Harvard psychiatrist, who reiterated this view not long ago on television. Interestingly enough, however, there has occurred a marked shift of opinion among many prominent black intellectuals, including a number of Dr. Poussaint's Harvard colleagues, who have publicly stated their regard for the novel. This well-known scholar and writer, Henry Louis Gates, Jr., commented about the ten black writers: "Censorship is to art as lynching is to justice, and it's just as disgusting when blacks do it as whites."

In his present meditation Genovese has returned to some of the major themes in the novel which provided fuel for the black critics' rage and which he was able so effectively to analyze and defend. As I implied in the letter to my father, a demented ogre beset by bloody visions who leads a drunken band of followers on a massacre of unarmed farm folk, largely women and children, hardly qualifies to be classed with a Spartacus or a Toussaint L'Ouverture. But the idea of such a noble and greathearted paradigm appeared over and over in the writings of the black critics, who insisted on a totally imaginary idealization of their hero rather than accept the reality of "a single-minded murderous fanatic" (in Genovese's words) who was—as the record shows unequivocally—"cold-bloodedly insane." Genovese's perception of a dichotomy—that I gave Nat's chief henchman, Will, the lineaments of crazed savagery, while endowing Nat with humanity—seems quite on the mark; this splitting of Nat's personality was a process I was only barely aware of during the writing of the novel, but it was plainly essential in order to give him tragic stature.

In a *Paris Review* interview, Toni Morrison conceded that I had the right as an artist to deal with Nat Turner as a subject, but she took me to task for creating a revolutionary hero who has bitter scorn for those whom he would incite to join his mission—that is, his fellow slaves. Morrison must never have read David Walker's stirring *Appeal*, and almost certainly none of the black critics had, but in fact I had taken the essence of Walker's withering expressions of contempt for the inertia and submission of black people and used it as a model for Nat Turner's own various denunciations. Genovese, in recognizing and emphasizing this, once again affirms his own admirable refusal to accept sentimental preconceptions of human behavior as a way to get at historical truths. He knows better than almost anyone that the study of history is not intended to make us feel good.

No aspect of *The Confessions of Nat Turner* caused more fury among the critics than the relationship of the protagonist with a young white girl, Margaret Whitehead, who was the only person among the sixty-odd victims that Nat (after several clumsy tries at dispatching his quarries) managed to kill. That her murder actually occurred was firmly on the record and I would have shirked my duty as a novelist had I not addressed myself to imagining the nature of Nat's motive and of his relationship with her. The essayists, *en bloc* and livid, claimed that the bond established between Nat and the nubile Margaret once again reinforced the stereotype of black men's perennial desire for the flesh of white women. (That Richard Wright virtually duplicated this connection in *Native Son* is a compelling irony.) It is true that in the novel Nat feels lust for the young woman and that on one occasion he entertains the idea of raping her; it is also a truth, ignored by the black critics, that his ultimate feeling toward her could be dignified by the word "love." Genovese has rightly divined, however, that the essayists utterly misread the nature of Nat's and Margaret's affinity; although unwittingly Margaret becomes the villain and the aggressor, "tempting him," as Genovese writes, "with the unattainable, because she epitomizes those who kill the spirit with patronizing kindness." She also epitomizes, in her innocence, an essential cruelty of American slavery: the reduction of black men, almost literally, to the status of animals.

A memory still lingers of my reading, in the summer of 1968, the book of essays, absorbing its rage over my alleged falseness about the sex issue, and then turning to read several times a crucial scene in the novel. In this scene, Nat, busily working at his carpentry in his owner's house, is interrupted by Margaret, who bursts into the bedroom, prattling away, and routinely changes her clothes directly in front of him. Undressing down to her long pantalettes, happily chatting, she engages in a nineteenth-century version of a teenage striptease, totally oblivious of the feeling she might be arousing in the young black man, crouched, heart pounding, whom she is treating in her customary way as a lovable and intelligent dog. This performance by Margaret, which stirs lust but also misery and hatred in Nat's heart, should have made clear to any receptive reader where the blame lay, if there could be blame in a society governed (in Genovese's words) by the "demonic logic of slavery." But I think it was then that I suspected that even so carefully crafted a scene as this would never change the minds of those bent upon making *The Confessions of Nat Turner* a symbol of the white man's distorted view of the black experience under slavery, and I was right.

Genovese's reflections on the religious aspects of the novel are provocative and fascinating, although he may give me more credit for spiritual insights than I deserve. As for the *mea culpa*s I need to express, I must readily say that I would have changed certain elements of the novel given a second chance. Certainly it was too facile of me, as Genovese points out, to claim in an author's note that I had examined all pertinent documents about the event, and, while I'm not sure that an exhaustive study of the records and papers of the period would have caused me substantially to alter the narrative, I should not have staked out more authority than I possessed. More serious are his animadversions about my treatment of the white people of that period, a treatment which was unwarrantably harsh and heedlessly unflattering, as anyone who reads Genovese's own magisterial *Roll, Jordan, Roll* will quickly realize. I wish that this work had been published before I wrote *Nat Turner.* One of the more absurd contentions that weave their way through the black essayists' volume is that I re-created a cartoon version of the slave-owner class, portraying the masters and mistresses as paragons of virtue and decency. This is another false charge, but one which, paradoxically, I might have employed in a modified form to give persuasiveness in my text to an important theme which Genovese properly finds insufficiently explored.

Elsewhere, I have quoted Georg Lukacs, the great Hungarian literary critic, who wrote that "historical novels which have no resonance in the present are bound to prove of only 'antiquarian' interest." Certainly this is a truth borne out by *The Confessions of Nat Turner,* which has had such resonance in the present that the novel and the controversy surrounding it have generated at least five books and hundreds of articles, with more appearing regularly even today. Save for the mistakes I've just acknowledged, and the careless use of some ancestral names, which has pained a few members of the white community in Southampton County, Virginia, where the event occurred, there is little in the novel I would correct or change. All works of literature are flawed, and their authors should have the humility to acknowledge it; but the passion and the honesty that originally animated the work bestow upon it an ultimate integrity, and I have never wavered from my belief that *Nat Turner* remains "a plausible interpretation of the agony that has bound the present to the past."

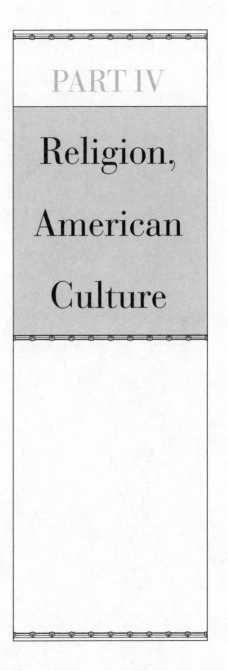

PART IV

Religion,

American

Culture

Hawthorne's Cultural Demons: History, Popular Culture, and *The Scarlet Letter*

David S. Reynolds

Hawthorne's *The Scarlet Letter* (1850) has long been regarded as one of America's classic historical novels. Puritan history, which Perry Miller identified as the author's "flood subject," exercised what Michael Colacurcio has called "a tyranny [over Hawthorne] that bent the mind and baffled choice," making him seem devoted primarily to writing the so-called "historical romance of New England." Charles Ryskamp argues that because Hawthorne "demanded authentic details of colonial history," he ransacked nonfiction texts like Caleb H. Snow's *History of Boston* for the novel's setting and subsidiary characters.

In the discussion of historical context, what has been largely disregarded is the degree to which Hawthorne determinedly reshaped the Puritan past in order to satisfy the tastes of his own contemporary readership in nineteenth-century America. The relationship between *The Scarlet Letter* and Puritan history is analogous to that between the R-rated 1995 movie version of the novel and the novel itself. Just as the director Roland Joffe catered to moviegoers by sensationalizing Hawthorne's narrative—adding such tawdry bits as Dimmesdale (Gary Oldman) skinny-dipping, Hester Prynne (Demi Moore) exposing her pregnant belly, and a slave girl (invented by Joffe) "pleasuring herself" while witnessing a love scene—so Hawthorne sensationalized Puritanism by introducing fictional elements he knew were attractive to novel readers in the 1840s.

Contrary to popular belief, Hawthorne in *The Scarlet Letter* was not particularly original in his choice of characters or themes. A reason the novel became one of his most popular works was that the antebellum public felt comfortable with a fictional exposé of hidden corruption involving a hypocritical preacher, a fallen woman, an illegitimate child, and a vindictive relative. By the late 1840s such depraved characters were stock figures in American fiction. For example, Sylvester Judd's *Margaret* (1845) included a subplot involving an abandoned woman, Rose Elphiston, who is forced to live alone with "a significant red letter" sewed on her clothes and whose haughty, skeptical nature anticipates Hester Prynne's. In the same novel, a little girl gives spirited retorts to her prying catechism teachers, much like Hawthorne's little Pearl.

Secret sexual escapades among preachers were such common topics in sensational fiction that one hostile reviewer, Arthur Cleveland Coxe, declared that Hawthorne's tale of the "nauseous amour of a Puritan pastor" was a book "made for the market" like many popular seamy works, "because," Coxe explained, "a running undertide of filth has become as requisite to a romance, as death in the fifth act of a tragedy." The antebellum public had a special interest in sensational sex scandals involving clergymen. Stories of so-called reverend rakes ensured a good sale for newspapers and crime pamphlets, while the more traditional virtuous preacher was considered too dull to sell copy. David Reese noted in *Humbugs of New York* (1838) that "tales of lust, and blood, and murder" dominated the American press, tales particularly popular "when they are represented as transpiring under the cloak of religion, and the criminals occupying and disgracing the holy office of the ministry." Among the most widely reported scandals were that of Ephraim K. Avery, a Methodist preacher who in 1833 was charged with seducing a convert in his charge; the ongoing drama of John N. Maffitt, a successful itinerant regularly reported as having illicit sexual affairs; and, most shocking of all, the 1845 trial of Benjamin T. Onderdonk, the Episcopalian bishop of New York, who was defrocked for philandering with several of his female parishioners. In the late 1840s reports of ministerial depravity filled George Wilkes's *National*

Police Gazette, which featured articles with lively headlines like "The Reverend Seducer," "Another Reverend Rascal," and "Incest by a Clergyman on Three Daughters."

Hawthorne's Arthur Dimmesdale, then, had many forerunners in popular newspapers. He had even more in popular novels, in which the reverend rake was typically portrayed as a manipulative clergyman with an overactive sex drive. By the 1840s, the reverend rake had become so common a figure in popular fiction that Hawthorne could not overlook it in his search for a main male character for *The Scarlet Letter*. Almost every sensational novel of the decade contains at least one scene in which a seducer uses religion as in instrument of seduction. The pamphlet novelist George Thompson generalized in *The Countess* (1849): "Within the pale of every church, hypocrisy, secret and damning hypocrisy, is a predominating quality." As a result, he concluded, "every church wants a purging, a complete cleaning out" (p. 262). In particular, he wrote, "the so-called reverend pastors of churches have been found to be on far too familiar terms with the young lambs of their flock." Like other sensationalists, Thompson concocted striking scenes of reverend lechery, such as one in *City Crimes* (1849) in which a young girl peeps through a keyhole to see her mother having sex with a clergyman, who later tries to seduce the girl herself. Thompson's portraits of reverend profligacy were outdone by George Lippard, who in his best-selling *The Quaker City* (1845) portrayed the lustful Reverend F.A.T. Pyne, an unbridled debauchee who nightly enjoys women, wine, and opium at a secret den of iniquity.

Dimmesdale is not the only character in *The Scarlet Letter* with predecessors in antebellum culture. Another is Hester Prynne, who can be viewed as a composite of female heroines in popular fiction. Hawthorne, a close reader of popular newspapers, may have seen in the *Salem Gazette* for January 29, 1833, a story called "The Magdalene," which recounts a squalid life of sin followed by her penitence (much like Hester Prynne's) while living in an isolated cottage and doing charity work for a nearby village. But Hester is not only the sympathetically portrayed fallen woman. She is also the struggling working woman who plies her needle as a seamstress; the feminist criminal bound in an "iron link of mutual crime" with a relatively feeble man; and the sensual woman who, in Hawthorne's words, has "a rich, voluptuous, Oriental characteristic" and who whispers to her lover, "What we did had a consecration of its own." She is the feminist exemplar who broods privately over women's wrongs and dreams of a revolution in relations between the sexes. All these iconoclastic female character types had been widely disseminated in subversive popular literature of the day. Hawthorne's innovation was to combine these rebellious traits in a heroine who also exhibits more conventional qualities as well. Like the heroines of the "scribbling women" Hawthorne aspersed (and half-envied for their popularity), Hester elicits from others "the reverence due to an angel," and one of the meanings associated with her letter is "Angel." Along with her angelic quality goes a practical ability to help others as a charity worker and an adviser.

In fashioning his main characters, therefore, Hawthorne borrowed extensively from popular culture. But he not only adopted popular character types; he determinedly transformed them, and his chief transforming agent was Puritanism. As much as he disliked the severity of the Puritans, he admired their moral seriousness, which he believed had been lost over time. Several times in the novel he pauses to indict what he sees as the crassness of nineteenth-century sensationalism. He underscores the soberness of Puritan punishment of sin by writing that "a penalty, which, in our days, would infer a degree of mocking infamy and ridicule, might then be invested with almost as stern a dignity as the punishment of death itself." He writes that the Puritans "had none of the heartlessness of another social state, which would find only a theme for jest in an exhibition like the present." He stresses that the Puritans valued "stability and dignity of character a great deal more" than contemporary Americans, and they possessed "the quality of reverence, which, in their descendants, if it survive at all, exists in smaller proportion, and with vastly diminished force."

Throughout the novel, Hawthorne treats earnestly topics that in popular sensational literature had become matters of mechanical prurience and shallow irreverence. True, he makes use of stock situations—a clergyman adulterously involved with a young woman; angry revenge against the lovers by the woman's cuckolded husband; gleeful reveling in sin by devilish side characters; and references to "mysterious" pseudosciences like alchemy and mesmerism. But because he allows such sensational images to resonate within a Puritan culture described with sympathy and seriousness, they never become gratuitous or perverse. Were Arthur Dimmesdale merely a reverend rake, he would be like the coarse, lip-smacking ministers of popular fiction. Because he is both a reverend rake and a devout Puritan Calvinist, he is sincerely tormented and explosively ironic. He tells Hester, "Were I an atheist,—a man devoid of con-science,—a wretch with coarse and brutal instincts,—I might have found peace, long ere now." He possesses both the profound convictions of the soul-searching Puritan and the lawless passions of the reverend rake. Hester, likewise, is a powerfully mixed character who is at once the rebel-lious modern woman and the self-lacerating Puritan. Because she brings Puritan soberness to her sin, she is inwardly tormented in a way that no popular heroine is.

Even the demonic Roger Chillingworth, an amalgam of the vindictive cuckold and evil pseudoscientist, has a retributive function absent from similar devil figures in popular fiction. His sadistic revenge leads finally to Dimmesdale's public confession of sin. As for little Pearl, she remains the anarchic, uncontrolled child (like the lawless children in pulp novels) as long as her parents remain within the amoral value system of nineteenth-century sensationalism: that is, as long as Dimmesdale remains a hyp-ocrite cloaking his sin while Hester brandishes her sin without truly confronting it. Pearl becomes a moral, respectable person only when her parents honestly expose their sin—when Hawthorne leaves the realm of nineteenth-century sensationalism and recaptures the retributive world of Puritan Calvinism.

As important as the resonance gained from Puritanism is the control gained through structure and symbol. Whereas popular novelists like George Lippard and George Thompson burst linear plot patterns with their fervid irrationalism, Hawthorne arranges popular sensational im-ages with almost mathematical care. The three gallows scenes, the seven-year time gap between the opening and middle sections, the studied alternation between public and private scenes, the balanced phrasing of the sentences: all of these stylistic elements have almost moral meaning for a writer who hated the disorganization of modern sensational texts. The relationships between the main characters are characterized by a profound interconnectedness that ranges from neurotic symbiosis to sadistic vampirism. Within the structure of the novel, none of the characters can exist without the others. Allegory and history also serve as important controlling devices. Although no single allegorical meaning can be assigned to the scarlet letter or other symbols, the very capacity of the letter and other allegorical elements to radiate meaning, the very suggestiveness of these elements, is an assertion of value when contrasted with the flat, directionless quality of sensational texts. The careful apportionment of nineteenth-century sensational images in a fully developed seventeenth-century New England setting is Hawthorne's highest achievement.

Simultaneously enlivening Puritanism and enriching sensationalism, Hawthorne created a resonant myth that itself has become a cornerstone of American cultural history.

The Great Gatsby?
Yes, a Historical Novel

John Lukacs

According to F. Scott Fitzgerald's principal exegete, Matthew J. Bruccoli, "*The Great Gatsby* has become an international source for American social history and is read as a record of American life at an actual time and place." (It is at least possible that such an international appreciation of *The Great Gatsby* may have been due to the movie rather than to the novel.) In any event, this international association of *The Great Gatsby* with the social life of rich Americans is relatively recent. (*The Great Gatsby* was not a publishing success when it first appeared, in 1925; its qualities were discovered or rediscovered only after World War II. I recently read a fairly serious book about society and social life in Sicily of the 1980s, peppered with adjectives about "Gatsbian" or "Gatsby-like" parties, meaning less parties that were "American" but parties that were excessively sumptuous. *Sic transit gloria Gatsbyi*).

It is probably due to the peculiar American, and democratic, structure of history that certain novels tell us more about a certain time and about certain people than even the best of histories. When I taught American history, particularly in my 1890 to 1945 undergraduate course, I put *The Great Gatsby* on my reading list, I think at the expense of requiring my students to read about the politics of the 1920s or otherwise good biographies of, say, Harding or Coolidge or Hoover. I had put some novels on

my reading lists of other times, though not for the 1910s or 1930s. For
what had happened in the twenties was that the development and changes
in society, including the modes of everyday life in America, were both
more interesting and important (meaning: more consequential) than the
history of its politics and of its government. (In spite of the suffrage given
to women, there was, for the first time in many decades, a definite drop in
the percentage of voters after 1920.) So between the Progressive Age (including World War I) and the progressive decade of the New Deal, there
was this Jazz Age—the twenties, a phrase that is recognizable even now.
(As a matter of fact, "The Jazz Age" is a phrase that was coined and
thrown into circulation by F. Scott Fitzgerald himself, in 1920.)

It will not fade soon, or easily. Our associations of the Jazz Age are essentially the same as they were decades ago. In this respect, Bruccoli is
wrong. In the preface of "the authorized text," Bruccoli wrote, "*The Great
Gatsby* was published in 1925; therefore many of its details now seem as
remote as those in the world of Charles Dickens's fiction." Not so. Auto-
mobiles, short skirts, movies, gramophones, lots of liquor, adulteries, the
cult of celebrities, suburban life, airplanes, the increasing fusion of middle class with upper class and of working class with middle class were all
there in the 1920s as they are here now. (Only television and the computer and air-conditioning are—perhaps—missing.) After all, it may be
said that the twenties (and not only in America) were the *only* "modern"
decade. For what else were the sixties, with their miniskirts and cult of
youth and sexual freedom, etc., but an exaggerated repetition of the
twenties? I am looking at the original jacket cover of the first edition of
The Great Gatsby. Its designer was a Spanish artist in Hollywood by the
name of Francis Cugat, who also worked for Douglas Fairbanks. Fitzgerald's publisher, Charles Scribner III, wrote that this cover "is the most
celebrated—and widely disseminated—jacket art in twentieth-century
American literature." Fitzgerald's editor, Maxwell Perkins, "believed that
the jacket was a masterpiece." I do not think that it was (or is) a masterpiece, but that is not the point. The point is that the midnight eroticism
of Daisy's eyes and luscious mouth hovering above a bright yellow explosion of electric glitter and sequins and background neons could easily
serve as a modern (or postmodern) jacket for a sexy book published in
A.D. 2000.

The protracted influence of, or respect for, *The Great Gatsby* alone suggests that *The Great Gatsby* is more than a period piece—except in the sense that all works of art are, to some extent, period pieces, including even such immortals as Mozart or Vermeer. Whether *The Great Gatsby* is immortal is arguable; what is not arguable is that it is representative of a period, not only because of its contents but also because of its style. And that there is nothing wrong with a period piece—and that there is also more to *The Great Gatsby* than a period piece—may appear from a comparison of *The Great Gatsby* with *An American Tragedy*, Theodore Dreiser's large novel, also published in 1925. The story of Clyde Griffiths, the tragedy, his aspirations, and his comeuppance could fit into the decades before or during or even after the twenties. This is not true of *The Great Gatsby*, which is suffused with the atmosphere and with some of the actual evidences and effects of the early 1920s—which is one, but only one, reason why it is such interesting and even informative and valuable reading. And now consider that *The Great Gatsby* (which was not Fitzgerald's original or preferred title) could be easily entitled "An American Tragedy." As with all fine creations of art and letters, *The Great Gatsby*—its meaning and its style—also transcends its period (which *An American Tragedy*, at first sight more of a historical novel than *The Great Gatsby*, does not).

The protagonist Gatsby, a successful and attractive man of dubious origins, is in love with Daisy Buchanan, a young woman of the American upper classes. His social ambitions are not simple. Yes, he wants to impress people, but even more important is his romantic quest for Daisy—which suddenly ends in tragedy (because of an accident involving Daisy, though not because of her wish to end their affair); Gatsby is killed (again, by an erratic coincidence); and no one, virtually no one, comes to his funeral. (In *An American Tragedy*, Griffiths kills his plain girl because of his social ambitions: he is about to be involved with a richer, more glittering girl. He is a villain, from beginning to end.) In the eyes of Nick Carraway, the narrator, Gatsby, with all of his faults, is not only not worse but better than the horde of rich people who had profited from his hospitality (and business), including Daisy. That *is* an American Tragedy—perhaps even more than that: *The* American Tragedy—the hollowness (rather than the failure) of social aspirations.

There are few such sad funerals in the history of literature: perhaps Emma Bovary's is one. And Jay Gatsby is a male American Emma Bovary at least in one sense—even as, unlike Emma Bovary, he dies suddenly when he is still healthy and rich. He is a romantic. Bruccoli is wrong when he writes that Gatsby "does not understand how money works in society. He innocently expects that he can buy anything—especially Daisy. She is for sale: but he doesn't have the right currency." No: Gatsby does not want to buy Daisy with money. Money is very important, but he wants to win her through love. He is innocent—in the way he idealizes Daisy, who, in the end, is hardly worth it—but that, too, is not the main point of the novel. He still has some of his midwestern innocence. His easterners have none. It is the people of West Egg and East Egg of Long Island, and their guests and visitors and spongers and hangers-on, mostly from New York, who are worthless—whether they have money or not. The tragedy that F. Scott Fitzgerald describes is not really that of American materialism; it is that of a—peculiar—American idealism. It is a gem, a historical cameo not of American thinking but of American feeling; not of calculations but of aspirations.

And that was an idealism that F. Scott Fitzgerald himself had imbibed and shared. Describing the automobile ride into New York from Long Island: "The city seen from the Queensboro Bridge is always the city seen for the first time, in its wild promise of all the mystery and beauty of the world." That was how a few people, including intelligent foreigners, saw New York in the 1920s; or how sensitive immigrants saw it within the city. It was F. Scott Fitzgerald, not Woody Allen, who comprehended the kind of Manhattan oddly resonant in George Gershwin's melancholy chords. But then that is, too, why the last famous lines of *The Great Gatsby* are so often misunderstood or at least imperfectly understood. Yes, Gatsby was drawn to the green light at Daisy's dock, now so close. And Daisy did come, easily, from across the water. Besides that green light—which has become a veritable literary-cultural cliché, employed by critics over and over again—there is on that last page that other, so often cited, famous Fitzgeraldian passage of the narrator, alone after Gatsby's death and looking across: "[I] became aware of the old island here that flowered once for Dutch sailors' eyes—a fresh, green breast of the new world." Well, there is something wrong here: for what the narrator sees is not the view of "the fresh, green breast of the new world" from the Atlantic but the brummagem Connecticut shore across from Long Island Sound, which is not what the Dutch sailors had first glimpsed. Yet it is F. Scott Fitzgerald's historical romanticism which suffuses *The Great Gatsby*, and not only on that famous last page: a soft, almost subterranean music that makes it transcend a period piece—something that is expressed, too, in another famous Fitzgeraldian phrase, that of America being the willingness of the heart. It is the willingness of Gatsby's heart, not his aspiration for more and more money, that characterizes him, while it is the unwillingness of the heart that characterizes most of the book's minor characters, perhaps especially Tom Buchanan, Daisy's muscular and brutal husband, a veritable villain who is somewhat overdrawn: a heartless, rather than mindless American, a rich Yalie.

There exists a rather thoughtful book, *Another Part of the Twenties* (1973), by the historian Paul A. Carter: "My father was attending an Eastern men's liberal arts college when *This Side of Paradise*, F. Scott Fitzgerald's archetypal novel by, for and about the college student, was first published. . . . Although an avid reader all his life, my father never read it. When he was in college he could not have afforded a raccoon coat, but years later in the bottom of the Depression he bought one in a secondhand store. My mother went to a coeducational church-related college in the Midwest. Snapshots and a portrait of her from the twenties show a strikingly attractive, high-spirited woman, but she was hardly a flapper as that term is ordinarily employed. Her idea of fun was a church social, and for vacations she and my father inexpensively went camping." From further queries and research, Carter "got the impression that my parents in their day were not alone in having missed a good deal of what we ordinarily characterize as 'The Roaring Twenties' . . ." "In fact . . . gazing away from Manhattan's Great White Way any night during the decade following 1920, one could have seen wide, dark stretches of the continent where the roar of the Twenties was muted indeed; where life was lived in a rhythm in which there was not the faintest echo of jazz." This is very true: but, then, this was (and still is) a big country. And *The Great Gatsby* is still a near-perfect period piece—and more: a description of a small segment

of American society but also something beyond that: a concern with the
insubstantial essence of what so many Americans thought (and still think)
reality is.

There are—and this is a minor point in this essay—many interesting
details (and phrases) that tell us something about Fitzgerald's people and
places and times, in retrospect. Here are some of them: a mistress is called
"a sweetie"; another, that already in the early 1920s, Celebrity was beginning to replace, or at least merge into, what was still called Society
(though Fitzgerald's term was somewhat different: "celebrated people").
Another, perhaps interesting, detail: James Gatz changes his name to Jay
Gatsby, for the sake of elegance; a few decades later it is arguable that
"James" may be at least as classy as, if not even classier than, "Jay." And
sometimes Fitzgerald's ambition of social perceptions carries his prose
too far: "my second glass of corky but rather impressive claret." About
some of the partying girls: "I have forgotten their names—Jaqueline [sic],
I think, or else, Consuela or Gloria or Judy or June, and their last names
were either the melodious names of flowers and months or the sterner
ones of the great American capitalists whose cousins, if pressed, they
would confess themselves to be." And: " 'He's a bootlegger' said the
young ladies, moving somewhere between his cocktails and flowers. 'One
time he killed a man who had found out that he was a nephew to von Hin-
denburg and second cousin to the devil.' 'Reach me a rose, honey, and
pour me a last drop into that there crystal glass.' " This is too much. But
then there are near-immortal perceptions, or summary phrases: for example, how Americans move "with the formless grace of our nervous,
sporadic games." And the true mark of a fine writer, which is the splendid
choice of some of his verbs, rather than the easier choice of his adjectives:
in Gatsby's tragic swimming pool "there was a faint, barely perceptive
movement of the water, as the fresh flow from one end urged its way to-
wards the drain on the other." And then much (if not all) of the Jazz Age
(and the American Dream?) is summed up in this exquisite paragraph:

> For Daisy was young and her artificial world was redolent of orchids and
> pleasant, cheerful snobbery and orchestras which set the rhythm of the
> year, summing up the sadness and suggestiveness of life in new tunes. All
> the night the saxophones wailed the hopeless comment of the 'Beale Street

Blues' while a hundred pairs of golden and silver slippers shuffled the shining dust. At the grey tea hour there were always rooms that throbbed incessantly with this low sweet fever, while fresh faces drifted here and there like rose petals blown by the sad horns around the floor.

Theodore Dreiser was not capable of writing such sentences. Nor was Henry James or Hemingway. It is impressionistic, elegant, and romantic: a rare American combination. But then this is an essay not about literature but about history. Fitzgerald's lyricism is not only stylistically extraordinary but also historically telling. Yes: *"le style c'est l'homme"*; but *le style c'est aussi l'histoire.*

✑

EVERY NOVEL IS a historical novel.

About two hundred years ago, the modern novel and professional history arose at the same time. Their relationship has been seldom explored—especially the essential matter, which is that both of them were the results of a developing historical consciousness. This meant, and still means, the interest of writers and of their readers in recognizable people with whom they could, by and large, identify themselves in recognizable places, and in recognizable times. It is wrong to think that the novel is a prose form of the epic. The novel and the epic, as Ortega y Gasset wrote already in 1914, "are precisely poles apart. The epic . . . speaks to us about a world which was and which is no longer, of a mythical age whose antiquity is not a past in the same sense as any remote historical time. . . . The epic past is not *our* past. Our past is thinkable as having been the present once, but the epic past eludes identification with any possible present." In other words: an *ideal* past, not a remembered past—a mythical past, which had its American examples, too, such as Parson Weems's Washington.

About fifty years after the appearance of the modern novel arose the historical novel, first exemplified by Walter Scott, where history served as a new kind of background that was more than decorative: it interested a growing number of people who were avid to read about the Middle Ages or Scottish heroes of centuries past. His contemporary, Jane Austen, did not write historical novels. But consider her preface to *Northanger Abbey*, in 1816:

> This little work was finished in 1803, and intended for immediate publication. It was disposed of to a bookseller, it was even advertised, and why the business proceeded no further, the author has never been able to learn. . . . But with this, neither the author nor the public have any other concern than as some observation upon parts of the work which thirteen years have made comparatively obsolete. The public are entreated to bear in mind that thirteen years have passed since it was finished, many more since it was begun, and that during that period, places, manners, books and opinions have undergone considerable changes.

It may be unnecessary to press the point: Jane Austen's concern was decidedly, evidently historical. Now consider what Thomas Hardy wrote eighty years later:

> Conscientious fiction alone it is which can excite a reflecting and abiding interest in the minds of thoughtful readers of mature age, who are weary of puerile inventions and famishing for accuracy; who consider that in representations of the world, the passions ought to be proportioned as in the world itself.

Another one hundred years later, it is my conviction that conscientious history has come to replace the desideratum which Hardy states as conscientious fiction. It is history which can excite a reflecting and abiding interest in the minds of thoughtful readers of mature age, who are weary (and how weary we are!) of puerile inventions and famishing for truth.

I say "truth" because I shall venture to go further than Hardy. I claim to detect the gradual absorption of the novel by history, not at all in the form of the historical novel, but through something else. It is my conviction that The Historical Novel, as such, was a nineteenth-century genre; and that, in spite of its scattered practitioners even now, it is by and large outdated. Meanwhile, something else has been happening. This is the increasing historicity of most novels. I think that this gradual, and often unconscious, transition from the historical novel where history served as a, certainly very important, background, to the kind of novel where the historical matter is in the foreground, began about 130 years ago. In the United States, Cooper and Irving and Hawthorne still wrote mostly what were in essence historical novels; but a perhaps minor writer such as Howells already did something else—describing a contemporary American society and its mores: people and settings that were familiar to his readers. And during the last one hundred years, we have had many American novels that tell us as much about the history as about the society of their times, knowing of course that the two are inseparable. Fitzgerald and Dreiser and Willa Cather and Edith Wharton and Robert Penn Warren are but a few who represent this phenomenon (as are some minor contemporary novelists, such as Richard Yates in *Revolutionary Road*)—a phenomenon in which I am inclined to see the evolution of our historical consciousness.

Let me repeat, at the risk of undue repetition: every novel is a historical novel. But now a warning: the present, and all-too-evident, intrusion of history into fiction is an even newer phenomenon—surely connected with the present crisis, and the eventual transformation, of the novel. A manifestation of this is not only the so-called documentary or docudrama but the new hybrid thing that has the silly name of "faction." All kinds of writers have been trying this (Upton Sinclair, Dos Passos, Irwin Shaw, Capote, Styron, Barth, Doctorow, Mailer, Sontag, DeLillo, Vidal, Pynchon, in this country, many others abroad, including Solzhenitsyn in *1914*, his least valuable book). What is significant is that these novelists are, all, interested in history. They have reversed the historical novel, where history was the colorful background: for these twentieth-century writers history is the foreground, since that is what attracts them. Yes, that is a symptom of the continuing evolution of a historical consciousness. But most of these writers don't really know that, which is why their books are flawed: for they illegitimately mix up history and fiction. They include and twist and deform and attribute thoughts and words and acts to historical figures (Lincoln or Wilson or Roosevelt or Kennedy) who actually existed. This is illegitimate, and antihistorical—no matter that some academic historians say that it serves salutary purposes, since it introduces all kinds of people to history, after all. They are wrong. What they ought to recognize, rather, is the untrammeled spreading of a historical consciousness whereby it is indeed possible that in the future the novel may be entirely absorbed by history, feeding the famished appetites of readers for what really happened, for a past that was real, for how men and women really were, how they acted and spoke and thought *at a certain time*—a time that may include the near-present. But let us not speculate about this further.

So *The Great Gatsby* is a historical novel: surely different, but not less historical, than *The Scarlet Letter* or *War and Peace*. And because of, rather than despite, its superficialities—essentially the superficialities of its cast of people—not a whit less historical; indeed, perhaps even more so.

T. Coraghessan Boyle
and *World's End*

Michael Kammen

bibliophile's *New Yorker* cartoon appeared in 1988 in which an owlish-looking woman says to a salesperson in a bookshop, "I'm looking for a book by T. What's-His-Face Boyle." Therefore, a brief background sketch of that enigmatic novelist and short story writer might be an appropriate way to begin. *World's End* (1987) is arguably his best novel, and unquestionably the pivotal one in his career to date. Important aspects of it are autobiographical, moreover, in terms of time, place, persons he knew growing up in Peekskill, New York, and then the subsequent curiosity that he experienced about his native region in the lower Hudson River Valley.

Although he was named Thomas John Boyle at birth in December 1948, he changed his middle name to Coraghessan (pronounced "kuh-RAGG-issun") at the age of seventeen, a time when his personal identity seemed anything but clear to him. Like Walter Van Brunt, the principal protagonist of *World's End*, Tom Boyle hung out during the mid-1960s with bikers who boozed, used drugs, engaged in mischief, and generally lacked any sense of focus or direction. He subsequently described himself as having been a "pampered punk," yet enrolled as a music student at the State University of New York at Potsdam, where he began to write plays and short stories after taking on a whim a creative writing course. Boyle continued to produce short fiction following his graduation, but he also continued bingeing on drugs and alcohol even while working as a high school teacher. (During the past quarter-century, his lifestyle has been comparatively sedate.) When the *North American Review* published one of his stories, Boyle felt encouraged to apply to the University of Iowa Writers' Workshop. While there, he married Karen Kvashay in 1974, and three years later, he received his Ph.D. in English literature.[1]

He promptly joined the English Department at the University of Southern California, in Los Angeles, as an assistant professor. With a prolific output of stories and novels during the 1980s, he was promoted to professor of creative writing and accumulated a series of awards, including the St. Lawrence Prize in 1980; the Aga Khan Prize of *Paris* magazine in 1981; the Faulkner Award in American fiction from the PEN American Center in 1989; and another PEN Award in 1990 for his now classic short story, "If the River Was Whiskey."

Meanwhile, despite Boyle's literary recognition as one of America's most creative contemporary writers—commonly identified as working in the "comic-absurdist mode" of Washington Irving, Gabriel García Márquez, and John Barth—and perhaps as a counterweight to his stable family life in Montecito, California (an upscale community in the beautiful hills near Santa Barbara), Boyle continues to present the public appearance of a residual character from the 1960s counterculture. He is most likely to be seen wearing an old leather jacket, jeans, and red sneakers. In addition, as journalists invariably note, he also affects "an off-kilter earring, a frankly bohemian hairstyle, a beard he might have picked up at a grunge convention and a waistcoat probably left to him in Jerry Garcia's will."[2] All the while, however, Boyle lives in a 1909 Frank Lloyd Wright house, the first one built in California, and drives a bright red BMW. Although the delinquent juvenile has grown up, what he has not outgrown is the burning ambition to be the best creative writer in the United States. His drive to write captivating tales is matched by his desire to entertain, and consequently his readings become antic performances that render his audiences hilarious yet intrigued by the wildly improbable plots. He is a showman in person as well as in print.

World's End, Boyle's breakthrough book (it received widespread and highly favorable reviews, frequently accompanied by interviews), takes place primarily on the east side of the lower Hudson River Valley. If the geography is fairly compact in focus, however, the chronology is far-reaching, spanning a century following the 1630s, when Dutch landlords and tenant farm families clashed ceaselessly and from the tenants' perspective, hopelessly, but also covering with even greater intensity a full generation ranging from the later 1940s to the close of the turbulent 1960s.

How are the two time periods connected? At the simplest level, many of the mid-twentieth-century characters are direct or indirect descendants of the colonial settlers. At a more significant and symbolic level, important events in modern times are explicitly foreshadowed by very similar episodes in colonial days. Jeremias Van Brunt, the son of a tenant farmer raised at "Nysen's Roost" in the early seventeenth century, loses a foot to a vicious snapping turtle and wears a peg stump as an adult, just as Peter Stuyvesant did. Walter Van Brunt, the central figure in a story with a large cast of characters, loses *both* of his feet in sequential and bizarre collisions with a lethal historical marker during the 1960s. Both Van Brunts, colonial and contemporary, come from socially humble origins (as does Boyle), both seem to be sexually attractive and potent, and both men marry or have had their most important romantic relationships with women of somewhat higher social status than themselves.

Wouter Van Brunt, the oldest son of Jeremias and a third-generation tenant in precarious economic straits, like all the rest, is bitterly disappointed in his father, who switches from idealistic defiance of the authoritarian patroon to craven submission. Three centuries later Walter Van Brunt would be equally disappointed in his father, Truman Van Brunt, for abandoning his wife and son and for concealing the reasons why he betrayed friends as well as family in favor of supporting a conservative group of nativist patriots in 1949—people once again of higher social status in the community than himself. Although tensions involving social class are not the *most* crucial theme of this book, they are pervasive and appear to stem from Boyle's own background. His father was a janitor and a school bus driver in Peekskill. Both of his parents died of alcoholism when they were still in their fifties.

Parallels and patterns of repetition over time persist in diverse ways that are clearly deliberate, although their overall purpose as a configuration is not entirely clear. Even Piet Aukema, an evil dwarf who conspires with the brutal forces of reaction in the mid-twentieth century, has a diminutive seventeenth-century prototype who is also a source of misery-making mischief. In a 1986 interview, conducted before *World's End* was published, Boyle acknowledged the following about his work in progress: "It's about the sins of the father, correspondences, the synchronicity of history, betrayal, turncoat-ism, and back-stabbing."[3] Just what Boyle means by the "synchronicity of history" is somewhat blurry. He appears to be much more preoccupied with *diachronic* recurrences and relationships than with synchronic ones. But because Boyle is a meticulous wordsmith, I doubt whether he would use the word "synchronicity" casually or carelessly. Yet its purpose in that interview is elusive.

Boyle commands our interest in *World's End*, and in several other novels as well as short stories, because of his evident interest in history and in the meanings of history.[4] Establishing the exact nature of that interest and his evident ruminations on the past is not easy, though. For example, if certain historical events seem to prefigure subsequent ones, that configuration is engaging and can also be fun. (If readers knew in advance that prefiguration would be such a prominent motif, they might choose to keep a kind of scorecard.)

What Boyle never makes clear, however, are just what implications all of his prefigurations are supposed to have for our understanding of history. Christian theologians traditionally regarded developments in the Old Testament as prefiguring certain events in the New. But in a very secular novel, the point is less obvious. George Santayana is frequently quoted for observing that "those who cannot remember the past are condemned to repeat it." If that is one of Boyle's deliberate messages, he remains almost too subtle about it. One reviewer of *World's End* remarked in 1987 that "what ties the novel together is a sense of recurring patterns, seeing the same behavior acquire added meaning through repetition."[5] Well, perhaps, but then one wonders whether it worked that way for Walter Van Brunt, the anguished antihero in *World's End?* What, if anything, did he learn about the past when he lost his foot in a collision with a historical marker? (At the very least, perhaps, that a superficial encounter with history can be a perilous pursuit.) And did he discover anything more about the meaning of history when it happened a second time at the expense of his other foot?

There is a real risk of worrying these issues to death in dealing with a novel that seeks to entertain by means of comic inventiveness, situational peculiarities, and serendipitous coincidences. But in a recent interview Boyle raised a rhetorical question and provided his own answer. "How did we get here? That's the fascinating thing about history, and about writing historical novels. That's why history interests me. I don't know what's coming, but at least I can look back and see that something happened before."[6] That fairly general statement is about as explicit as Boyle gets regarding his reflections on history. Although he does not seem to be any species of determinist, there is a cumulative sense of fatalism in *World's End*—that with or without knowledge of history, events are almost foredestined to repetition.

A major irony casts a very long shadow throughout the considerable length of *World's End*. On one hand, the author almost seems to reify history as a monumental force with a mind of its own. Referring to Walter Van Brunt during the later 1960s, for example, Boyle writes that "the chill of history was descending yet again—Walter could feel it, familiar as a toothache, and he shivered inwardly" (p. 268). Later, referring to Walter's inability to unlock the crucial secrets of family and local history, Boyle describes Walter's poignant plight: "his wife was living with his best friend, he himself was crippled, unloved and doomed by the scourge of history" (p. 314). Wondering just what, then, is the major irony, the reader discovers that this book, so rich in carefully researched historical details, is really about the problem of pastlessness. Walter is not interested in the past, despite several symbolic close encounters with death precisely because he had ignored historical warnings. Eventually, however, he realizes that the key to understanding his very own identity is kept and concealed by his fathomless father, a man who had fled to Barrow, Alaska, the northernmost community in the entire United States, in order to seek redemption by writing local history, an account of rent wars and class conflict in the lower Hudson Valley.

When Walter finally finds his father, who is teaching history high above the Arctic Circle in a remote secondary school, Truman turns out

to be obsessed by history. In part that obsession is his penance for the betrayal of people who did not deserve his treachery. But history is also in
Truman's blood; he went to night school at CCNY to earn a B.A. in
American history, "his passion," and he had lived in Peterskill, New York
(aka Peekskill), a place where history is almost immemorial by customary
standards in most of the United States. It dips back deep into the seventeenth century. Thus, Boyle describes Walter's disappointment after sacrificing so much to find and confront Truman in order to learn the truth:
"His father was nothing, neither hero nor criminal, he was just a man,
weak, venal, confused, impaled on the past" (p. 407). Commenting on
Walter's confusion at this anticlimactic moment of disillusionment, Boyle
closes that paragraph with rhetorical questions: "Following in his father's
footsteps? History come home to roost?" (p. 407). The latter question
could virtually serve as an epigram for the entire book. Be sure to note the
ironic pun: how does a footless young man follow in his father's footsteps?
He cannot.

Throughout this absorbing novel, almost to the end, we are told that
Walter suffers from or braces for yet "another attack of history" (p. 436).
But the reification of history as some malevolent monster really *isn't*
Boyle's agenda. Rather, this book might almost be given a descriptive title
that paraphrases William James: for this book is really about the varieties
of historical experience. Walter and Truman Van Brunt are not the only
characters who endure problematic relationships with the past and with
historical knowledge. Depeyster Van Wart, twelfth heir to Van Wart
Manor and a local manufacturer, erstwhile friend of Truman and surro-
gate father to Walter after Truman disappears in 1949, is profoundly re-
actionary and infatuated with family and local history. Boyle tells us that
he "dwells in history," even to the point of eating small amounts of manorial dirt as an emblem of his devotion to the glorious Van Wart heritage.

The problem with Depeyster, who becomes increasingly despicable, is
that he dwells in history for all the wrong reasons: ancestor worship, social
pride, and insufferable self-aggrandizement. Even when his wife cuckolds
him and becomes pregnant by Jeremy Mohonk, last of the Kitchawank Indian tribe, Depeyster accepts his half-breed son as his heir (who will per-
petuate the line) and names him for his own father. The significant irony

here, of course is that Jeremy Mohonk is descended from a seventeenth-century liaison between Katrinchee Van Brunt and young Mohonk, son of Sachoes, sachem of the Kitchawank Indians. That, in turn, means that the infant born at the close of *World's End* in 1970 carries the genes of all three groups that have been historically at odds ever since the 1630s: the high-born Van Warts, the peasant-stock Van Brunts, and the embittered Kitchawanks they had dispossessed. This convergence turns out to be vastly more ironic than harmonic.

But we still have not exhausted the varieties of historical experience. Boyle serves up a virtual typology. Walter Van Brunt's best friend (until he neglects and abuses his wife, Jessica, who then moves in with the friend) is Tom Crane, a dropout from Cornell University during the mid-1960s, an ascetic "saint" who opposes the war in Vietnam and lives exclusively by ecological precepts. Boyle is mildly satirical about the Cranes, who represent yet another lineage, Yankee schoolmasters, because of their unrealistic nostalgia for earlier, simpler times. Not really knowing or understanding history, the Cranes don't seem to be aware that social relations had *always* been complex and cruel—and not just in the 1960s. In their own way, the Cranes, too, were Clio's innocents, ill informed by the Muse of History.

And what about the Kitchawanks? Were the Indians also innocent of history? No, unlike the naïve Cranes, and unlike Walter, who was simply ignorant of history, unlike Depeyster, who cherished a self-serving version of the past, and unlike the treasonous Truman, who eventually, in remote isolation from his geographic roots, tried to write a true history of Westchester, Putnam, and perhaps Rockland counties, some Kitchawank Indians falsified history for personal gain—or at least their officially designated remembrancer did, in yet another act of treason. As Boyle carefully explains, describing a bribery scam in the seventeenth century:

Wasamapah was the memory of the tribe. As each term of a treaty was struck, he would carefully select a polished fragment of clam, mussel or oyster shell from the pile spread out in the dirt before him, and string it on a piece of rawhide. Each article, each proviso, amendment and codicil had its own distinctive signifier. (P. 274)

Unfortunately, after he received a bribe of two thousand guilders from Stephanus Oloffe Rombout Van Wart (the patroon), Wasamapah "surreptitiously added three jagged bruise-colored shells to the treaty string, shells that extended the boundaries of the patroon's purchase till they encompassed every last verst, morgen and acre of the Kitchawanks' homeland" (p. 275). History here became an instrument of tribal betrayal, adding still another instance of abusing the past. Like Walter, the Kitchawanks got impaled by history, but for corrupt causes rather than reasons of lost identity and immature values.

As one reviewer phrased it in 1987, then, *World's End* is really a "meditation on the meaning of history. Or, precisely, on what it means to have a 'sense of history': The [various] episodes are reminders of the constant threat of crippling forgetfulness."[7] Although that is true, as a novelist who often chooses to work with historical material, Boyle has other objectives that we must keep in mind because they help us to appreciate what poetic license is all about and why historical fiction can be richly informative, insightful, even inspirational without replicating the historian's vocation and obviating some of the constraints of that craft.

It is instructive here to trace Boyle's responses to two interviews that took place six years apart. The first one occurred in 1987, when the *New York Times Book Review* showcased *World's End* as the feature review on page one, a young writer's dream come true. In a conversation that accompanied the review, Boyle acknowledged that he had changed the name of Pete Seeger's environmental sloop *Clearwater* (on which Boyle crewed for a week in 1984) to *Arcadia* and made other related changes in order to create a sense of "hyper-reality" and remind readers that the book is a work of fiction rather than "replicated history." "I wanted to re-invent history," Boyle explained, "to use it as a point of departure for a meditation on what my life has been, where I came from, what my antecedents and the antecedents of the region I grew up in were."[8]

In 1993, when *The Road to Wellville* appeared, a novel about the Kellogg brothers and food fads that emerged at Battle Creek, Michigan, early in the twentieth century, the *Washington Post* included extracts from an interview in a feature story. Here is Boyle's response to being asked whether the novelist can be too historically accurate: "I think you can," he replied, "and get bogged down with facts that people would be better off getting through history books. I'm interested in history as a setting for working out my feelings about contemporary society, and for making entertainment and seducing the reader into having the same fascination for the period as I do."[9]

Given those explicit admonitions and acknowledgments, we need to ask about their implications for *World's End*. How did Boyle's credo as a novelist affect his appropriation and use of history? The most apt illustration may be found in his treatment of the notorious anti-Communist hysteria that led to bloody riots at Peekskill during the late summer of 1949. There had, in fact, been a kind of utopian colony, located close to Peekskill, of Jewish socialists, Communists, and anarchists from the New York City area. Although the group was ideologically diverse and internally fractious—problems that Boyle prudently ignores—its members presented a united front to the "outside world." That fateful summer, when Red Scare hysteria ran very high in the United States, the radical community, called the Kitchawank Colony Association in the book (latter-day "Reds" supplanting the despised red natives of yesteryear?), invited Paul Robeson to visit and give a concert that would attract thousands of Left-oriented sympathizers to the bucolic countryside for a weekend of festivity and ideological fellowship.

When local veterans and superpatriots learned of this suspiciously subversive event, they determined to prevent it at all costs, using rocks, bottles, clubs, and brute force to keep the buses from reaching the concert site, smashing car windows, and severely beating many of the "colonists" who had volunteered to provide a security force for the pro-Soviet Robeson. The New York State police, meanwhile, who had been alerted to the need for protection by local law enforcement officials, refused to honor the constitutional right of peaceable assembly. The troopers came and simply observed the obscene fray, legitimized by Governor Thomas E. Dewey's total lack of sympathy for the socialist colonists. No one was ever held responsible or punished for this vicious outburst of right wing hatred and violence.

Peekskill was not "saved for democracy," and instead became a notoriously unsafe place for Americans with progressive ideals. Most important of all, perhaps, especially from Boyle's perspective, the ugly episode became barely a blip in the annals of nativist hysteria in the United States.

Until recently, a reader could find few accounts of what prompted the mob's rage and what actually happened during the week of August 27 to September 4, 1949. A detailed biography of Paul Robeson does devote a solid chapter to the sordid fracas, and several television programs aired film coverage during Black History Month in 1999, showing extensive scenes of the out-of-control mob. This nasty explosion of American paranoia turns out to be remarkably well documented.[10]

As it happens, moreover, Boyle is not the first modern American writer to incorporate the Peekskill riot into a major historical novel. E. L. Doctorow did so in *The Book of Daniel* in 1971 (pp. 54–66), an imaginative gloss concerning the controversial treason case of Julius and Ethel Rosenberg early in the 1950s. That book, like Boyle's, explores intergenerational themes; and it shifts back and forth between 1949–1954 and the later 1960s. Although Doctorow's "Rosenberg" character happens to be present at the Peekskill riot, his role there is inconsequential compared with Truman's, and the causes and character of the riot are much less fully developed than they are in *World's End*. There is, however, an intensely dramatic moment at the end of Doctorow's work when Daniel, the son of "Rosenberg," confronts the daughter of "Mindish," the man who betrayed the Rosenbergs almost thirty years earlier, and says: "No, Linda. You've turned your back on history," because she refuses to explain *why* her father committed the fatal act of betrayal (p. 299).

As a novelist, Boyle is not especially concerned about context—at least, not in the sense of E. P. Thompson's famous dictum that "history is the discipline of context." Boyle does not give very much detail about the Kitchawank Colony Association, nor does he situate the episode against the background of HUAC hearings and the nationwide anti-Communist hysteria of the late 1940s. Instead he personalizes the intensity of mob ferocity by viewing it through the eyes of Lola and Hesh Solovay, Walter Van Brunt's adoptive parents: "the rabid women thumbing their noses, eyes popping with hate; the boy who'd leaned forward to spit on the windshield; a man she recognized from the butcher shop in Peterskill who'd bared his teeth like a dog, cupped his genitals in both hands and then clasped the crook of his arm in the universal gesture of defiance and contempt. . . . These were her ghosts, her attack of history" (p. 224).

What matters to Boyle is the traumatic experience of living through history, rather than passively reading its carefully contextualized narrative. And what also matters in *World's End*, which makes it such a distinctive work of fiction, is the insistent pattern of prefiguration. Thus we learn on page 326 that the Peterskill riots of 1949 took place less than half a mile from the site of an ugly confrontation in 1679 between tenant farmer Jeremias Van Brunt and Jongheer Stephanus Van Wart, second lord of the manor.

Jeremias Van Brunt has an egalitarian, antiauthoritarian temperament, like Tom Crane (the Cornell dropout) three centuries later. Yet the figures with progressive values are not winners in this tale. They are fortunate to be survivors, in fact. But Boyle is not interested in the traditional teeter-totter of winners and losers in American fiction. Or else his vision of the uses of power and the problem of survival when odds are uneven is a dark but realistic one. What makes this novel both timeless as well as a tale for our own time is its persistent emphasis (in the seventeenth century as well as the twentieth) upon the complexity of generational relationships. Married couples split up with dismaying consequences (Truman Van Brunt abandons Christina, and their son Walter betrays and loses his Jessica). Children are repeatedly deprived of one or both parents; yet there is often compensation when one sibling becomes fiercely protective of another.

Boyle is obviously intrigued by acts of betrayal as a historical theme. We know that early in the 1970s, during a summer break from the Iowa Writers' Workshop, he visited a friend at a location not far from his boyhood haunts. "Each morning I would take a little dirt path and walk down to the Hudson River," he told a journalist, "which was maybe half a mile away. One day I noticed a historical marker there—I'd been by it a thousand times—and I stopped to read it. In fact, that was the trail that Benedict Arnold had taken to escape to the British."[11]

Boyle's fascination with the potential meaning of local history attendant upon that "discovery" has all sorts of specific implications for *World's End*. Truman Van Brunt had married into the Kitchawank Colony, joined the Communist Party, and became a spy. But Depeyster Van Wart, assisted by the evil homunculus Piet, covertly converted him to the conservative side in 1949, with the consequence that Truman betrays his idealistic, radical community, his wife and son. He becomes a Whittaker

Chambers, who is never mentioned in the novel even though he became a controversial figure of betrayal in 1948 because of his testimony before HUAC against Alger Hiss. Those charges led to Hiss's two trials in 1949–1950 and his conviction for perjury as an ex-Communist who had belonged to a spy ring. Here is still more "shadow history," even though Boyle is too subtle to hit us over the head with it. Instead, he successfully re-creates the anxieties and bitter ideological conflicts of 1949–1950—locally and dramatically.

That daily little walk down to the Hudson also explains the book's title. A "fleet" of World War II ships is anchored there in a maritime graveyard called World's End. The site does not play a significant role in the narrative until the penultimate chapter, "World's End," when Walter sets the thirteen-ton environmental vessel called *Arcadia* adrift from her moorings at Garrison, New York, and it is then carried by the flood tide "dead on for Gees Point and the black haunted immemorial depths of World's End" (p. 445). The *Arcadia*'s collision with historic ships caused damage to the schooner roughly comparable to Walter's loss when he collided with the historical marker. Yet another act of betrayal, and yet another instance of ignoring remnants of the past at one's peril. The *Arcadia* could be repaired, just as Walter's prosthesis had provided him with mobility. But having committed betrayal with damaging consequences, the self-destructive, drunken Walter then dies of hypothermia when he loses consciousness in the snow. Unable to escape wanton disregard for history, he becomes a hapless victim of alcohol abuse and the elements. The pattern of repetition persists to the bitter end. Walter's trajectory moves from fateful to fatal.

Over and over, he endured "collisions with history," and eventually Boyle warns us that his alter ego in the novel was "doomed by the scourge of history" (p. 314). (Actually, the aspect of young Tom Boyle who lacked a clear sense of identity and a sure sense of values during the 1960s characterizes Walter, but the aspect of Boyle in his mid-thirties who became intrigued with the importance of local history also shapes Truman when he flees to Barrow, Alaska, a changed man, to write a book titled *Manorial Revolt: The Crane/Mohonk Conspiracy*.) Hence, *World's End* is a kaleidoscopic saga of history neglected, betrayed, and yet earnestly pursued.

World's End commands our credibility as a historical novel, in part, because the author so evidently immersed himself in selected aspects of Dutch and English colonial developments. There certainly are hundreds of "touches" of authenticity involving language, geography, social, and economic relations. Any serious student will see and hear echoes of books by Irving Mark, *Agrarian Conflicts in Colonial New York, 1711–1775* (1940); Dixon Ryan Fox, *Yankees and Yorkers* (1940); Patricia U. Bonomi, *A Factious People: Politics and Society in Colonial New York* (1971); and perhaps my own *Colonial New York—A History* (1975). Boyle obviously does sufficient background work in order to steep his historical fiction in situations, discourse, and relationships that resonate with authenticity.

But his impulses as an entertainer, quite literally as a showman, propel him to go beyond re-creating the past just for the sake of doing so—even with an overlay of provocative questions and messages. In 1993, when he published *The Road to Wellville*, Boyle told an interviewer that he had returned to the historical genre that worked so successfully in *World's End* because "it gives me a setting to exercise my imagination." Boyle likes to compare his way of mixing historical fact with fiction to that of creative jazz musicians who borrow or adapt from classic compositions. "John Coltrane would take the tune from some famous song and state it, then go off on his own improvisation and come back and state it again. That's what I try to do."[12]

I am convinced that Boyle's emphasis upon "stating it again" can help us appreciate the purpose of all that prefiguration, mentioned earlier, in which seventeenth-century characters and episodes anticipate those in the twentieth century. Boyle thereby presents us with a challenge to the conventional way of thinking about history as a process of change over time. Although he would not deny or reject the centrality of physical, social, and environmental changes, so many of the situations narrated in *World's End* are really timeless because they offer recurrence and repetition rooted in human nature, but also in the unequal distribution of power and resources in society. If Boyle ultimately leaves us, on balance, with more questions than answers, and more meditations than affirmations, one might very well say: so does the past.[13]

World's End invokes a wild sequence of "collisions with history," presumably to awaken (perhaps even astonish) the reader with the relevance of the past. Rudderless Walter Van Brunt receives several devastating "attacks of history," and winds up much the worse for wear as a result. I, too, have undergone numerous attacks of history over the past forty years, but it has invariably been an experience of enrichment. Perhaps the difference is this. On the back of my car the blue bumper sticker reads: "I brake for historical markers."

Notes

(Unless otherwise indicated, the page references are to T. Coreghessan Boyle, *World's End*, New York: Viking, 1987).

1. *Contemporary Authors: New Revision Series* 44 (Detroit: Gale Research, 1994), 36–40.

2. Tom Lappin in *The Scotsman*, November 10, 1995, p. 16.

3. Quoted in Paul Ciotti, "T. Coraghessan Boyle Is a Former Juvenile Delinquent Turned USC Professor Whose Books Have Been Getting Rave Reviews. As He Will Be the First To Tell You," *Los Angeles Times Magazine*, August 3, 1986, p. 16.

4. See *Water Music* (New York: Little, Brown, 1981), *The Road to Wellville* (New York: Viking, 1993), *Riven Rock* (New York: Viking, 1998), and *The Collected Stories of T. Coraghessan Boyle* (New York: Viking, 1998), esp. "Ike and Nina," "John Barleycorn Lives," "Stones in My Passway, Hellhound on My Trail," "The Overcoat II," "Beat," and "A Bird in Hand."

5. David Plott, "The Tangles of History: T. Coraghessan Boyle Has Written a Rich, Intricate Novel That Celebrates the Idea of Having a Past," *St. Petersburg Times*, November 8, 1987, p. 6D.

6. David L. Ulin, "Guided by the Belief That Fiction Can Illuminate the Past, Novelist T. C. Boyle Mines Montecito Lore in His New Book," *Los Angeles Times*, February 26, 1998, part E, p. 1.

7. Plott, "The Tangles of History."

8. *New York Times Book Review*, September 27, 1987, pp. 1, 53.

9. Peter Gilstrap, "Novelist with a Twist: T. Coraghessan Boyle Has Talent, Big Goals and a Way of Standing Out," *Washington Post*, July 5, 1993, p. C 1.

10. See Martin Bauml Duberman, *Paul Robeson* (New York: Alfred A. Knopf, 1988), 364–74; Howard Fast, "Remembering Peekskill, USA, 1949," *Pennsylvania History* 66 (Winter 1999):65–70; Joseph Walwik, "Paul Robeson, Peekskill, and the Red Menace," Ibid., 71–81. Film footage of the Robeson concert and mob violence aired on PBS, February 22, 1999.

11. *New York Times Book Review*, September 27, 1987, p. 53.

12. Quoted in Steve Garbarino, "The Cult of the Flake," *Newsday*, June 27, 1993, p. 36.

13. See Margaret Atwood, "In Search of *Alias Grace:* On Writing Canadian Historical Fiction," *American Historical Review* 103 (December 1998), 1503–16, esp. 1515.

⅋

History on Two Wheels

T. C. Boyle

I am indebted to Professor Kammen for his thoughtful and comprehensive analysis of *World's End*, and I would like to comment on some of the points he raises, but I must be cagey here. I do believe that it is neither the novelist's business nor right to explicate his own fictions—oh, what trouble we could get ourselves into if only we tried—and while many novelists do have a decidedly analytical bent (DeLillo and Unsworth come to mind), the reader must never forget that we are artists and that our primary gift is intuitive. That said, I do feel that Professor Kammen is right on the money when he says that *World's End* is "really about the problem of pastlessness." Absolutely. One reviewer who tickled my heart said that the book was a kind of imagined autobiography, and so it is.

World's End is dedicated *In memory of my own lost father*, and *The Road to Wellville* is dedicated to my late mother, Rosemary Post. My father was lost to me early, before he could impart his sense of the past to me, before we could achieve that rapprochement men can achieve with their fathers once they leave their teens, and my mother grew up without a father. Her father was reputedly of Dutch descent—a mysterious figure by the name of Post. (Ed Post, Joe Post, Peter Post, C. W.— who knows?) Rather than dig up my actual antecedents, I caught the fever of history, pursuing one of any number of possible pasts for myself, and in the process writing a biography of my place, my own ancestral earth. The book, like all good novels, is a kind of dream. As I have said in reference to my first novel, *Water Music*, it is a fugue, a variation on themes. Further to the point, I quote from the Apologia at the front of that book: "I have been deliberately anachronistic, I have invented language and terminology, I have strayed from and expanded upon my original sources. Where historical fact proved a barrier to the exigencies of invention, I have, with full knowledge and clear conscience, reshaped it to fit my purposes."

Professor Kammen's observation that I am not interested in Santayana's dictum is also a perceptive one. In *World's End*, I am exploring a kind of genetic determinism, wondering if what one receives from one's parents isn't merely physical but behavioral as well. Is there free will? Recent discoveries in mapping the human genome have gone a long way toward negating the notion—we are the product of our genes in every possible way. Behavior—behavior beyond tendencies toward alcoholism or madness or bliss, for instance—can perhaps be passed down from generation to generation. That is, if your father was an apostate, if your father was a betrayer, a thief, a murderer, then so are you, at least *in potentio*. If this is the case, then what does a knowledge of history avail you? Nothing. You are doomed to repeat history whether you know history or not. We lack faith. Indifferent, or perhaps even malevolent, forces act on us. It is no accident that Walter was stunted by existentialism.

There is another aspect at work here, too, and that is the influence of fiction on history. Washington Irving is a principal inspiration for the book, as significant in informing it as the papers in the Peekskill Room at the Field Library or the texts Professor Kammen cites. Irving's mock history of Dutch New York gave me many of the bastardized Dutch expressions used to comic effect in *World's End*, and his touchstone story, "The Legend of Sleepy Hollow," provided the types for two of the book's principal lineages. On the one hand, we have the dreamy, sleepy Cranes; on the other, the muscular, physical, daredevil descendants of Brom "Bones" Van Brunt. This is fun. This is great fun. We have my invented history relying upon conventional accounts, as well as the characters from another invented history. Wheels within wheels.

And yet I should emphasize that each book is different in its aims— each of my own four collisions with history has a distinct take on its material, and my hope is that in writing, in pursuing my career as a novelist, I will continue to chase the meaning I need to build in my own life. I feel like a proselytizer (the story of Stanley McCormick and Katherine Dex-

ter, very true to the facts of history as I've received them, makes an astonishing tale in *Riven Rock:* Come, friends, and wallow in it), but an explorer,
too. Like Mungo Park, I am seeking the indefinable and the unknowable,
tramping off over vistas of the past, digging through texts, musty or not,
and sifting the earth for bones, precious bones.

Albany the Wondrous:
William Kennedy's History
in Quinn's Book

Mark C. Carnes

D aniel Quinn begins his book with an account of a single, fateful day in late December, 1849. He describes how, as an adolescent, he watched Magdalena Colon, a voluptuous actress who attempted a crossing of the ice-clogged Hudson. She was accompanied by Maud, her thirteen-year-old niece. A crowd gathered on a pier to watch. Magdalena's skiff pushed off, darting between the floes, but soon was crushed and sank. Quinn's master, a boatman named John the Brawn, set out to salvage Magdalena's trunk. While fishing it from the water, he hooked Magdalena's dead body and plunked it into his boat; and Quinn reached into the water and grabbed the shivering Maud.

The spectacle drew more people to the pier and it collapsed, plunging hundreds into the river. Then came a "rush of ice like none in Albany had ever seen (p. 10), and the ice piled up to form a dam. The pressure from the river caused the dam to explode—"a Vesuvius of crystal"—and a torrent swept through Albany. The floodwater inundated the plaster works, reacted with the lime, ignited a conflagration, and set the waterfront ablaze. Soon the entire city went up in flames: "fire rising out of flood—the gods gone mad" (p. 11), Quinn explains.

More madness was in the air. Later Quinn and Maud watched as John the Brawn pulled down his pants and brought the dead Magdalena emphatically back to life; the youngsters saved an escaped slave named Joshua, who had been entombed by accident; and they stared as the corpse of a Revolutionary hero, exhumed from a crypt, exploded in a puff of dust. Transfixed by the apocalyptic spectacles wrought that day, the youngsters kissed, and could never be separated. Out of death came life—and love.

But first came the remainder of *Quinn's Book*, a chronicle of kidnappings and heroic escapes; of pitched battles between Irish immigrants and nativists, factory overseers and workers; of séances and abolitionist ferment; of civil war and draft riots; and of much, much more. "I was in the midst of a whirlwind panorama of violence and mystery, of tragedy and divine frenzy that mocked every effort at coherence" (p. 108), Quinn reports, and his summary is as good as any.

The opening pages of *Quinn's Book* display Kennedy's prodigious historical research. His descriptions of the city's midcentury waterfront, economic infrastructure, social relations, architecture, house furnishings, clothing, and the like are informed by many hours in the Albany archives. His thumbnail sketches of his characters' antecedents, moreover, provide a collective biography that neatly summarizes several centuries of Albany history. As for the wild events of that fateful day, they did take place. In an interview, Kennedy assured readers that "the fire, the insane crossing of the river there in the middle of that ice floe, the bridging of the river with that iceberg and the explosion of that iceberg, the breaking up of the ice. Those are real historical moments that I just discovered and probably embellished to a degree that makes it more dramatic. People falling into the river from the bridge, those things happened. The pier being washed away by the ice, those things happened."[1]

But they did not all happen on the same day, or in quite the way Quinn relates. Although a calamitous flood did inundate Albany during a snow-storm in late December of 1849, destroying hundreds of buildings and leaving thousands homeless, the great Albany fire occurred the previous year on a stifling summer day. Kennedy acknowledges that he has perhaps "amalgamated" historical events "and made them happen on top of one another in ways that history had not seen fit to do, or Mother Nature had not seen fit to do, but I'm not being false to possibility."[2]

Kennedy employs a similarly agglomerative approach to his principal characters. Magdalena, for example, is partly a composite of several real persons, most obviously the actresses Lola Montez and Adah Isaacs Mencken. Montez was born in Ireland in 1818, took to the theater as a "Spanish" actress of limited parts (and these chiefly physical), endeared herself to King Ludwig I of Bavaria and subsequently to countless American male theatergoers who savored her Spider Dance, an erotic variation on the tarantella. Kennedy borrows these details and overall characterization and gives them to his Magdalena. Then Kennedy adds to Magdalena information from the life of actress Adah Isaacs Mencken, who in 1859 fell in love with a prizefighter; Magdalena similarly falls in love with John the Brawn, who becomes a prizefighter.

Maud, the triumph of the book, is derived from several historical actresses and spiritualists. In the 1860s, Mencken became a sensation when she appeared, on horseback and seemingly nude in flesh-colored tights, as Byron's Tartar hero Mazeppa. Mencken's greatest success as Mazeppa occurred during a three-week run in Albany, when she broke all attendance records. Kennedy assigns these and subsequent biographical details to Maud, who abandons the theater and commences communicating with spirits. These respond to her queries with rhythmic raps and thumps, and now her art loosely follows the life of the real actress-turned-mesmerist Anna Cora Mowatt (1819–1870) and also two sister-spiritualists, Katherine and Margaretta Fox, who became famous for their spirit-rapping séances (later proven to be hoaxes) in the Albany area. The wondrous Maud is doubtless composed of still other historical materials. For example, Quinn once describes her as a "sojourning spiritualist," which may be an allusion to upstate New Yorker Sojourner Truth, the African-American religious visionary who became a spiritualist.

The compression of events and characters is a staple of fictionalized history—plays and films as well as novels. The device enables writers to increase the points of view without adding more characters than can be developed effectively. So while the merging of characters and events entails a falsification of the past, it also allows for a deeper and more complex rendering. A cartoon may be "accurate" in that it includes no errors, but it may be far less real—and certainly less realistic—than several accurate photographs whose images have been superimposed. So, too, a complex fiction may be more realistic than a sparse if errorless narrative.

Kennedy prefers complexity. He conceives of the past as an elaborate mosaic, whose bits and pieces have been unearthed from the recesses of the Albany archives. By digging deeply, he has found hundreds of arresting details, strange facts, and unusual stories. Kennedy's art consists of rinsing and polishing them so they gleam, and then arranging them in a manner of his own devising. The result of these labors, as the biographical basis of his characters attests, is indisputably composed *of* history. But can the overall effect—the brilliant, almost artificial colors, the swirling, surreal images, the weird and sharp-edged characters—in any sense be regarded *as* history?

❧

KENNEDY'S STORIES, LIKE the sinking of Magdalena's skiff and the great Albany fire, are unusual; often they relate to sex, violence, death, madness, or other manifestations of life at its extremes. But these anecdotes are not ahistorical. I encountered hundreds of such stories while researching another small mid-nineteenth-century American city. Then, as a college history major, I had been eager to enlist in the ranks of the "new social historians." These scholars proposed to bring to light the lives of those missing from conventional historical accounts. I was then unaware, as were many of the scholars themselves, that the "new social history" in fact dated from the publication of James Harvey Robinson's *The New History* in 1912 and that it culminated in the thirteen-volume *History of American Life* series edited by Arthur M. Schlesinger, Sr., and Dixon Ryan Fox during the 1920s and 1930s. These volumes provided a descriptive chronology of American social history: the evolution of houses and fashion, of sports and recreation, of health, medicine, education, and work.

Insofar as the "new social historians" of the 1960s and 1970s were cognizant of such work, it was dismissed as impressionistic and unscientific. These new scholars instead amassed information culled from census schedules, church and government records, and credit reports and company histories. These data were coded, keypunched, and subjected to computer analysis. The results, festooned with regression formulas and tables aplenty, appeared modern and scientific. This history resembled science—social science, truly—and for a time nearly everyone applauded.

One consequence of this approach was that while mining their thick veins of data, the social historians often became interested in the communities in which they were prospecting. To gain perspective, they read the local newspapers, which sometimes provided useful information and context; sometimes the scholars also became seduced by the content of the newspapers themselves. This was less true of the local newspapers prior to the 1840s, which were subsidized by state political parties and chiefly reported on political matters. But by the late 1840s and 1850s, as villages and towns were becoming cities, mass-circulation newspapers emerged in response to a growing demand for local news. The newspapers soon discovered that the most popular stories were about people residing on the edges of normality. Many social historians found themselves ensnared by these old accounts of murders and suicides, of humorous mistakes and horrible accidents, of weird coincidences and unexplainable happenings.

But such materials had no real place in the New Social History II. Social sciences intent on devising models with universal applicability had little room for anecdotal materials that focused on the peculiar behavior of individuals, the particularities of place, or the manifestly irrational. The monographs of the "new social historians" therefore focused on topics of scholarly interest: geographical and social mobility; locational factors in economic growth; party formation and voting behavior; community structure and cohesion; religious and ethnic subdivisions, and the like. The human *stories* that enlivened dinner conversations rarely found a place in their scholarly analyses.

An important exception was Michael Lesy's *Wisconsin Death Trip* (1973), which juxtaposed photographs of people in late-nineteenth-century Black River Falls, Wisconsin, with newspaper excerpts on suicide, insanity, illness, accidents, and myriad adventures and misadventures. The book was haunting and even unsettling. By focusing on what was missing from the monographs of the "new social history," Lesy's book raised an important question: How could social historians presume to describe the lives of those who had been neglected by traditional history if individual people were largely missing from the monographs? The social historians' lumping of hundreds or thousands of workers or urban

poor or women into vast data sets had submerged their individual lives—
their stories—into a murky, statistical mean.

This gnawed at the psyche of many social historians, as did the fact that
so few of their books attracted much general attention. Their specialized
monographs, in fact, were seldom read even by social historians whose
fields were far removed from the subject in question. The new social history, devoid of individual people and stories, often wasn't very interesting. And uninteresting social history seemed a contradiction in terms. By
the 1980s many historians were assigning novels to provide the rich social
context missing from scholarly texts; and some historians were rediscov-
ering the appeal of narrative—of stories!

ぷ

AT ABOUT THIS time, too, William Kennedy, fresh from the success of
Ironweed (1983), winner of the Pulitzer Prize, and further buoyed by a
MacArthur "genius" grant, resolved to make sense of the thousands of
stories he had been accumulating for over a decade. Kennedy's approach
was analogous to Lesy's: his novel would be composed of thousands of
bits and pieces of the historical record. While Lesy had merely selected
and juxtaposed affecting accounts and photographs, Kennedy resolved to
find a means of investing such materials with meaning. His task was substantially that of an historian. But where historians organize materials in
topical fashion—politics, community structure, education, economic infrastructure—Kennedy arranged his raw materials with the help of a variety of literary devices.[3]

One of these was mythology. In the opening paragraph of "his" book,
for example, Quinn explains that Magdalena crossed the Hudson in order
to reach "Troy, a community of iron, where later that evening she was
scheduled to enact, yet again, her role as the lascivious Lais, that fabled
prostitute who spurned Demosthenes' gold and yielded without fee to
Diogenes, the virtuous, impecunious tubdweller" (p. 5). This early, di-
gressive mention of ancient Athens is amplified by the reference to Troy,
an allusion, perhaps, to the ancient Ionian city famous for its metal technology. And the sinking of Magdalena's boat and the Albany fire perhaps

allude to the culminating events of the Trojan War: the burning of Troy and the sinking of the Greek fleet. Quinn's explanation of the weird events of the day is Homeric: the apocalypse was all a "divine frenzy," the work of "gods gone wild."

Nineteenth-century Albany as ancient Athens! A motley chorus of actresses, prostitutes, and poseurs as Greek goddesses! Kennedy's simile is preposterous, his tone ironic. But if Kennedy drags the gods a bit down from Olympus, he also lifts the folks of Albany above the sleepy shores of the Hudson. His ironic ambivalence is captured in the title of his collection of historical essays entitled *O Albany!*, a volume dedicated "to people who used to think they hated the place where they grew up, and then took a second look."[4]

By suggesting that what transpired that day in Albany somehow echoed the goings-on of ancient Greece, Kennedy also hints at a relation between Daniel Quinn, an Irish immigrant, and Leopold Bloom, the antihero of James Joyce's *Ulysses*, whose wanderings through Dublin echoed those of Odysseus through the Aegean. Daniel Quinn is not a latter-day Odysseus; and Quinn's Albany is no more Dublin than it was Athens. Kennedy is waving literary flags to remind the reader that his Albany is worth all the fuss.

Kennedy's interest in mythology is also doubtless related to his enthusiasm for Jungian archetypes. Kennedy has acknowledged a debt to Joseph Campbell, the foremost popularizer of Jungian psychoanalytical precepts. And the opening episodes of *Quinn's book* take on a powerful Jungian theme: the archetypal notions of regeneration through death, of ubiquitous tricksters, etc. John the Brawn, an expression of the elemental shadow as a "Palaemonic figure bereft of sanity," an "overmastering Priapus," anticipates the primordial Iron John of Robert Bly's devising (Bly's book, to be sure, appears two year's *after* Quinn's).

But if Kennedy is mindful of mythology, James Joyce, and Jung, his most obvious literary referent was the one most familiar to American readers in the mid-nineteenth century: Charles Dickens. Quinn, who relates his story himself, resembles nothing so much as Dickens's most famous first-person narrator, Pip, of *Great Expectations*. Like Pip, Quinn is an orphan and an innocent in a world of gothic secrets. What triggers both novels is the protagonist's first kiss, which blossoms into a consuming love: Pip's, for the quixotic Estella, and Quinn's, for the enigmatic Maud. The young men's pursuit of their elusive and inconstant lovers is the chief complication of both novels.

There are additional parallels. Pip assists Magwitch, an escaped convict who becomes Pip's benefactor. Quinn likewise assists fugitives: first a runaway slave, and then Dirck Staats, who had been kidnapped and tortured by the members of a nativist secret society. Dirck rewards Quinn with a substantial bequest.

What is Quinn's purpose in using Dickens's blueprint for his novel? Perhaps Kennedy means to suggest that Quinn was himself so taken with Dickens's recent novel that Quinn could not resist borrowing elements of its plot (Quinn begins "his book" in 1864; *Great Expectations* was published in 1861). My own hunch is that Quinn and Maud function *in Kennedy's mind* to provide an ironic, perhaps even "American," contrast to Pip and Estella. For if the virginal and misanthropic Miss Havisham wreaked vengeance upon all males by ensuring their sexual frustration, Maud's patron, Magdalena, is a woman of a very different stripe: a "sexual philanthropist," as Quinn generously labels her. The inversion is neatly symbolized by the fact that while Pip and Estella first "play" in Miss Havisham's parlor, where that woman's untouched, moldering wedding feast symbolizes deathly sterility, Quinn and Maud first kiss in the "Dood Camer"—the death room—where the dead Magdalena has been laid out, and where she soon comes to life by getting laid. Unlike the England of Queen Victoria (and of Dickens), Quinn's world is abloom with sexuality.

There's more literary prestidigitation. *Quinn's Book* chronicles prescient foreshadowings, telekinetic happenings, and miraculous events. In the early episode, Maud warns Quinn not to look into the frozen eyes of the (seemingly) dead Magdalena, lest he catch a glimpse of his fate. Quinn of course takes a glance and perceives a weird and unsettling scene; and it so happens that that scene is replayed at the end of the book. But like most of the book's wondrous premonitions (Quinn provides a full complement of spiritualists, spirit rappers, mesmerists, electromagnetists, phrenologists, freaks, voodoo traditions, and the like), this one is partly wrong. Even the miraculous is unpredictable.

Scenes such as these have caused critics to place Kennedy among the school of magical surrealism in the manner of Gabriel García Márquez.

But Kennedy makes use of strangeness in a different way, and he expresses skepticism toward the miraculous. When Quinn proposes to write articles on Maud's spirit-rapping, an editor tells him to "hold down that spirit nonsense. People want real stuff, not all that folderol about spooks" (p. 147).

Quinn describes the world about him as a "moving mosaic," but the simile is too drab. Quinn's idea of history more nearly resembles an enormous and quivering hologram, where real events and people have been superimposed, overlayered and finally morphed into composites. Then, as if the reader were viewing it bug-eyed through an ophthalmologist's steel goggles, Kennedy snaps down one literary lens after another—mythological, Jungian, Joycean, Dickensian. As the eye strains to discern the overarching patterns (are there any?), Kennedy flicks on the strobe light, which bathes this wonder in magical surrealism.

♪

THIS IS TO acknowledge that *Quinn's Book* is a novel. It lays claim to our attention as a work of literature, not of history. But Kennedy is himself ambivalent on this score. "I've never thought of myself as an historian," Kennedy told an interviewer, but he confessed that he was becoming "more and more of one in spite of myself." He even mentioned that he repeatedly dreamt that he was in Albany, circa 1880, conducting interviews, abetted by a huge tape recorder that he lugged around in the back of a wagon.[5] Kennedy's novelist/historian schizophrenia is reflected in the title. *Quinn's Book* is Kennedy's novel; it is also Daniel Quinn's work of history.

And like any thoughtful historian, young Quinn struggles to make sense of the world. His first lesson is that things are not as they appear. The dead come back to life. Maud loves him, and yet leaves him without a word. Bad people, bent on mysterious evil, lurk in the shadows. Thus, Quinn decides to become a newspaper reporter: someone who looks hard at the swirling chaos of the world, discerns its solid, discrete facts, and fixes them on paper. Quinn's tasks resemble those of the historian, for he is "compelled to fuse disparate elements of this life, however improbable the joining, this done in a quest to impose meaning on things whose very existence I could not always verify" (p. 130).

Quinn's reportorial instincts are stimulated by Maud's longing to see everything. When John the Brawn commences his amatory exertions with the dead Magdalena, Quinn interposes himself to spare Maud sight of the "brazen necrophile." But Maud shoves him aside. "Get out of my way, you ninny, I've never seen anyone do this before" (p. 29). When a corpse is accidentally disinterred, Maud again pushes forward. "I would like to see what he looks like" (p. 42). That Maud's powers of perception should eventually penetrate the spiritual realm comes as little surprise. Quinn's summation is both lyrical and matter-of-fact: "Her left eye sees through brick and mortar/Her eyes are golden beauty/Her eyes are hard as Satan's heel" (pp. 156–57).

Vision is a quirky business. If Maud sees the world (and beyond) especially well, other characters suffer from ailments of the eye; the Dutch patroons were wall-eyed, or cross-eyed, seemingly blind to the moral implications of their dispossession of the Indians, and blind as well to the inevitable dispossession of their heirs by the new swarms of English settlers. Similarly, a nativist bigot, whose blind hatred leads to murder, loses his eye during a brawl with an Irish mob. Quinn's talisman is a bronze disk, an ancient family relic, perhaps dating from the Vikings, imprinted with a "trompe-l'oeil" design that changes, depending on the viewer's perspective: "Now it was a screaming mouth with vicious eyes, now a comic puppy with bulbous nose and tiny mouth. Depending on where the light hit the eyes they were glassy, or sad, or hypnotic" (p. 73). Seeing the world clearly will not be easy.

Quinn seeks guidance from a newspaper editor who succeeds in opening Quinn's "eyes to the world in ways not accessible to the being I used to be" (p. 102). Equipped with better vision, Quinn seeks to acquire a better perspective on the "moving mosaic" that is the human experience. He detaches himself emotionally from society and its conventions, its genteel sensibilities, its romantic notions. Quinn and Maud, separated for much of the book, come together again toward the end. In the intervening years, he has been observing and reporting on the mayhem of the Civil War. "Daniel, I feared you were dead," Maud notes. Quinn's response shows his sharper, more skeptical faculties: "I seem to have survived," he replies, "but it may be an illusion" (p. 198). Later that evening, while addressing an Army Relief Bazaar whose genteel audience expects patriotic blather, Quinn instead reports the facts, stark and unsettling. His audience is appalled; some are sickened.

If historian Quinn must learn to see better, he must also learn to find a language appropriate to his task. Words, like perception, can deceive. After Quinn decides to become a reporter, and acquires the requisite implements, someone observes, "Now you are a writer." "I think I will have to write something first," Quinn replies. He seeks a job with a newspaper as a "paragraphist." "You'd best learn to set those paragraphs in type if you want to earn a living, boy," the editor responds. "Words are flimsy things. Type is solid and real" (p. 146). Though flimsy, elusive, and unreal, words demonstrably possess power. A writer who threatens to expose a secret society has his tongue cut out (p. 77).

By the end of the book, Quinn's own words—hard, objective, direct—accord with his new realistic way of looking at the world. His speech to the Army Relief Bazaar unsettles the audience not merely because of its grim content, but also because of Quinn's stark use of words: "A pile of dead people, that's the reality I'm talking about. The bigger the pile, the bigger the reality" (p. 222). Quinn has learned to see the world dispassionately, objectively, even coldly, with a keen eye for the telling detail; and he has learned to use words with similar economy and precision.

But Kennedy does not seem to be satisfied with his creation, and in the final pages of his book, Quinn doubts the solidity of historical fact, the objectivity of detached perspective, the explanatory value of the historian's language and narrative. He senses there is something more, and imagines that his mysterious bronze disk, perhaps of Viking provenance, may provide some clue. He wonders at its strange, shifty eyes, and concludes that

> what was wrong with my life and work was that I was so busy accumulating and organizing facts and experience that I had failed to perceive that only in the contemplation of mystery was revelation possible; only in confronting the incomprehensible and arcane could there be any synthesis . . . I had become a creature of rote and method at a time when only intuitions

culled from an anarchic faith in unlikely gods could offer me an answer. How could I ever come to know anything if I didn't know what I didn't know? (Pp. 265–266)

Then Quinn confesses that his book was predicated on a lie: he began it as a laudatory obituary of Magdalena, who at the time was not dead; in this instance, she did not even *appear* to be dead. This foundational deceit invited others. Quinn (or is it Kennedy?) admits to "taking the facts not from her cuttings but from my imagination, where, like a jungle flower, she had long since taken root" (p. 280).

Quinn's "realism" is thus a sham; throughout his book, realism is further subverted by weirdness. Though Maud expresses doubts about the "reality" of the spirits, they *do* respond to her; mesmerists, phrenologists, soothsayers, and Mexican dwarfs predict the future, sometimes accurately; characters skip back and forth across the chronological divide, thereby undermining the distinction between present and future, and past and present: the dead sometimes come back to life; and sometimes those who are alive are not. ("Now I'm dead," reports a victim of the cholera epidemic, an illogical statement that on the moment of being uttered becomes true [p. 198].)

ঔ১৯

KENNEDY'S COMPLEX AND surreal story seems to have floated far above the terra firma of historical fact. But during the past dozen years, social and cultural historians have sunk a variety of new analytical shafts into the social and cultural landscape of mid-nineteenth-century America. They have discovered that beneath the familiar narratives—of the advance of scientific knowledge and secular values; of the proliferating web of political and economic institutions; of the ordered familiarity of Victorian sensibilities—there lay a molten substratum of unusual religious and utopian excitations, of a widespread literature of the subversive and the bizarre; of crackpot notions in medicine, psychology, and sexuality.

In *Beneath the American Renaissance* (1988), for example, David S. Reynolds concluded that the familiar literary figures of the mid-nineteenth century—Hawthorne, Whitman, Emerson—had another "subversive" and "perverse" side; and that the less famous (but often more popular) writers were preoccupied with the "bizarre and sensational aspects" of American culture, ranging from erotic and pornographic stories to ghoulish tales of the supernatural to wildly surreal comic books and frontier tales. Of the ribald and fantastic Davy Crockett almanacs, for example, Reynolds observes that the phenomenon was "at once totally American and totally bizarre" (pp. 171, 452).

Many scholars of American religion have discarded their ecclesiastical garb, and in so doing have freely explored an exotic antebellum world of occult, alchemical, and magical pursuits as well as unorthodox sexual and religious beliefs, ranging from a host of millennial sects—the Millerites, the Kingdom of Mathias, the Cochranites, and the Mormons[6]—to all manner of utopian communes. Though the utopian impulse had deeper roots in the American past, the mid-nineteenth century was *the* era of utopian communes, ranging from the Shakers, who endeavored to rid the world of sin by eliminating intercourse, to the Oneidans, who promoted community by institutionalizing promiscuity.

The appeal of the extraordinary was shared by stolid, middle-class men. In *Secret Ritual and Manhood in Victorian America* (1989), I proposed that the men who by day modernized the nation's corporate and political institutions spent most of their evenings performing initiatory rituals of purportedly ancient or primitive peoples as Freemasons, Odd Fellows, and members of hundreds of fraternal organizations. In *No Place for Grace* (1991), T. Jackson Lears similarly found that many of the nation's intellectuals, weary of the "modern world" of the late nineteenth century, were similarly drawn to the deeper experiences and cultures of exotic peoples and premodern cultures. Victorian America was not the ordered, rational, self-controlled world many have supposed.

☙

DID NINETEENTH-CENTURY AMERICANS truly *believe* in phrenology and spiritualism and mesmerism and the immanence of the miraculous? Did they imagine that their humdrum activities were tinged with literary meaning or cosmic portent? Did they inhabit an imaginative world suffused with sexuality, weirdness, and the bizarre?

The best "historical" answer to these questions is a resolute no—and yes. Most Americans were, like Quinn, pragmatists, realists, materialists. Yet these same people, like Quinn, seemed to crave something more and searched hard to find it. Tocqueville had perceived this long before the recent spate of monographs by social and cultural historians. In the 1830s, he observed that while the "prevailing passion" of Americans was making money, they were also uniquely drawn, as if in reaction, to "a fanatical and almost wild enthusiasm." "I should not be surprised," Tocqueville speculated, "if mysticism did not soon make some advance" amongst such people.[7]

Kennedy's insight is remarkable in that he happened upon it several years in advance of the historians. He was guided, plainly, by the newspaper accounts of unusual stories; historians had long been aware of these sources, but could not make sense of them. Kennedy set Quinn upon a quest to find, in the clear light of reason, the hard facts about lives that flitted in and out of the shadows of irrationality; like the historians, Quinn lacked the language to make sense of that which could not be properly apprehended by the senses. And that is why Kennedy stepped in to help out.

The weird, surreal, extraordinary world of *Quinn's Book* is, if literally inconceivable, not historically unrealistic. Indeed, it is all the more realistic for encompassing the unreality that was an important aspect of how nineteenth-century Americans perceived their world. Kennedy and Quinn, novelist and historian, have together reconciled, at times uncomfortably and always complexly, the basic contradictions of what intellectual historians have unthinkingly termed "the American mind." Quinn put it this way:

> The message emerging from my febrile imagination during these tumultuous days was a single word: "linkage"; and from the moment I was able to read that word I became a man compelled to fuse disperate elements of this life, however improbable the joining, this done in a quest to impose meaning on things whose very existence I could not always verify. (P. 130)

"Let them be," one of Kennedy's characters says elsewhere. "History needs elbow room tonight."

If the purpose of the historian's craft is somehow to replicate an elusive if not illusory reality, then historians cannot simply dig up and classify the hard facts of the past; they must, like Kennedy, clean them off, polish them up, and set them forth in their glorious or terrible array, because that was how people lived them.

Notes

(Unless otherwise indicated, all page references are to William Kennedy, *Quinn's Book*, New York: Viking, 1988).

1. Cited in Edward C. Reilly, "On an Averill Park Afternoon with William Kennedy," *William Kennedy* (Boston: Twayne, 1991), 47.

2. Ibid.

3. This assertion and the ones that follow leave me uneasy. As an historian I weigh evidence and attempt to figure out what it *means*. But in this essay I propose to *explain* a cultural artifact when the person who created it is well placed to demolish my conceit. Of course, a novelist may not understand why he writes what he does; and an autobiography is often less reliable than a biography. Rarely, however, does a novelist respond directly to a reviewer, and rarely is a biographer directly confronted by his own subject. It is somehow fitting and fair and suitably cautionary that my failings be so baldly displayed.

4. William Kennedy, *O Albany! Improbable City of Political Wizards, Fearless Ethnics, Spectacular Aristocrats, Splendid Nobodies, and Underrated Scoundrels* (New York: Penguin, 1983).

5. *Conversations with William Kennedy*, Neila C. Seshachari, ed. (Jackson: University Press of Mississippi, 1997), xv.

6. The religious ferment of the Second Great Awakening has long been a source of interest to scholars. The seminal work was Witney R. Cross, *The Burned-over District: The Social and Intellectual History of Enthusiastic Religion in Western New York, 1800–1850* (Ithaca, NY: Cornell University Press, 1950). But this book, and those that succeeded it, regarded the proliferation of antebellum religious sects as an expression of economic change and social dislocation. The ideational content of the beliefs themselves was mostly ignored. The reexamination of the unorthodox ideas and their origins was chiefly the work of a cohort of scholars writing in the late 1980s and afterward. See, for example, Ronald L. Numbers and Jonathan M. Butler, eds., *The Disappointed: Millerism and Millenarianism in the Nineteenth Century* (Bloomington: Indiana University Press, 1987); Paul E. Johnson and Sean Wilentz, *The Kingdom of Matthias* (New York: Oxford University Press, 1994); and especially John L. Brooke, *The Refiner's Fire: The Making of Mormon Cosmology, 1644–1844* (Cambridge: Cambridge University Press, 1994).

7. Tocqueville, Alexis de, *Democracy in America* (New York: Schocken, 1974), 159–60.

c)℗

Quinn's Book:
Looking for the Buried Myth

William Kennedy

The purist attitude of Robert Penn Warren bugged me for years. In a conversation I had with him in 1973, he said he did no research for Willie Stark, the Huey Long figure in his classic novel, *All the King's Men*, "not a damn minute of it, didn't even read a newspaper." And in his *Paris Review* interview, he said, "Researching for a book in the sense of trying to find a book to write" was an "obscenity. . . . You can't research to get a book. You stumble on it, or hope to. Maybe you will, if you live right."

I was intimidated. I could have lived right all the way into senescence and not come up with the raw material for *Quinn's Book* without some research. I knew enough of my city's very old, and venerable, and raucous history to know it was a cornucopia for a novelist. But what was on my mind was delving into my own prehistory, and one idea kept prodding me: the buried myth of Quinn's life, and his enduring belief in something that did not exist. This, in part, was the history I could never know, the matrix of a life that could have been my own, but was lived almost a century before I was born. In college, I wanted to have been alive and writing in the 1920s. As I grew older, I yearned for the turn of the century. By the 1960s I had crossed back into the nineteenth century and thought of telling the whole of Albany's very old history, through characters real and imagined, in a single novel. This was an absurd plan and I soon knew it. In the early 1980s I leaped backward into this coveted prehistory and tried to write it through two stories with a single life line, Quinn the pubescent moving through adolescence and into manhood, but traveling back and forth between the nineteenth and twentieth centuries as he does so, always the same Quinn: acquiring money or wisdom or love in one century, spending it in the next. But the twin lives seemed wrong. The twentieth-century Quinn not only intruded, he bored me silly.

I settled on Daniel Quinn as born in 1835, and gave him entry to the world stage in 1849, and I did this because I had found language that was neither parody nor slavish echo of nineteenth-century literary language as I knew it, and this seemed to personify the mature journalist Quinn reinventing his mid-century youth on the page. The opening of the novel set the baroque style of his memoir:

> I, Daniel Quinn, neither the first nor the last of a line of such Quinns, set eyes on Maud the wondrous on a late December day in 1849 on the banks of the river of aristocrats and paupers, just as the great courtesan, Magdalena Colon, also known as La Ultima, a woman whose presence turned men into spittling, masturbating pigs, boarded a skiff to carry her across the icy water . . .

Near his book's end Quinn explains his method:

> Mine was clearly a life fulfilled by language. . . . By devising a set of images that did not rot on me over night, I might confront what was worth confronting, with no expectation of solving the mysteries, but content merely to stare at them until they became as beautiful and valuable as Magdalena had always been, and as Maud now was.
>
> It was in this elated frame of mind that I picked up a pen and set down a handful of words that I hoped would begin the recovery not only of what had been lost but also of what I did not know had been lost, yet surely must have been. I was persuading myself that if I used the words well, the harmony that lurked beneath all contraries and cacophonies must be revealed. This was an act of faith, not reason . . . [I] would, with the courage false or real that comes with an acute onset of hubris, create a world before which I could kneel with awe and reverence as I waited to be carried off into flights of tragic laughter.

Quinn lived and wrote his book in the age of virulent nativism, slavery, and the invasion of America by immigrant Irish masses. That age saw the beginning of modern theater (just starting to get lusty) and modern journalism (roving correspondents, like Quinn, first appeared in the Civil War), the powerful canals, the foundries, the wild capitalism of the railroads, and the labor movements that came in the wake of all that. It was the era of secret societies and political conspiracies (slavers ready to take over Mexico, Fenians trying to conquer Canada), a time of widespread spiritualism, cholera epidemics, and untamed rivers, of race wars and ethnic wars; and when Irish newcomers weren't fighting their common enemies, they factionalized and fought each other.

My father was born at the end of some of this, in the late 1880s, and some of my grandparents came into it during the peak years. I knew only my maternal grandmother but she rarely spoke of her early days, and I wasn't smart enough to be inquisitive. But I grew into inquisitiveness, discovered where my ancestors came from in Ireland, where they lived in Albany and Troy, what they worked at, whom they procreated and voted for, and how they died. It was meager, but compelling, and demanded elaboration.

The house where one branch of the family lived was a trove of history: the papers of a great-uncle who was sheriff, ward leader, bon vivant, and colleague of governors; the books and papers of another great-uncle, a "graduate" civil engineer with the New York Central, as he was known in the family; the witty jottings of my grandfather, an engineer who drove steam engines, including a record run with the Empire State Express; the memorabilia of my great-uncle who became a big-league baseball player; plus family letters from Ireland, and the accumulated ephemera of a family over two generations. When I came to see the house the rooms were empty, the furniture sold to a dealer, everything else thrown out days before and carted away by a trashman. All that remained, overlooked by the annihilators, were some torn photographs I found on the back porch, frozen in a bucket of ice. The small find was thrilling: photos plus some news clippings, of my uncle Eddie (Coop) McDonald, the big leaguer who had played with Boston and Chicago, and later played and managed in the Southern League, where the photos had been taken. He was a beloved figure in the family, and in Albany, where he coached youth baseball in retirement; and I borrowed a bit of his career to create Francis Phelan, protagonist of my novel *Ironweed*.

The destruction of the trove was a tragic and incalculable loss only to the writer I was becoming. Everybody else was glad to be rid of dead and useless history. In time I talked to almost everyone who survived in the family and came to know much about all branches. Later still, as my novels were published, people came to me with more stories of my relatives, and their own, and I began to shape a context in which to evaluate those lives. A casual remark from an aunt would suddenly flourish in the imagination like tropical foliage, and I would see living forms moving amid the sharp outlines of the lost world.

Entering it was the motive for *Quinn's Book*, and for the novels that followed: *Very Old Bones*, *The Flaming Corsage*, and now the new novel, *Roscoe*. They all exist in two centuries, and their characters continue to inhabit the world I created out of shards of history, a hubristic imagination like Quinn's, and, invaluably, newspapers. When I was writing one of my early novels, I dreamed I was traveling in a horse-drawn wagon in the rural nineteenth century with an enormous tape recorder. The absence of electricity was irrelevant. The recorder was a prod for accurately preserving the long-dead voices and the stories they told. It was an instrument of my oversized desire for authentication.

My office overflows with books of history, but what brings me closest to taping the very old dead are the newspapers of the past, with their Mardi Gras of vanished life: an ad for the Oriental nervine compound, Hasheesh Candy, being introduced to America in 1864: "Will rejoice the hearts"; the woman who sued her husband who never stopped talking, even in sleep; the man who beat his wife with crockery because she wouldn't sing with him; the man who murdered his wife with a knife and fork; the undertaker who advertised his professional talents with the embalmed corpse of a dog; the snowstorm that froze two thousand scavenging crows to a butcher's boneyard; the horrific Delavan Hotel fire, when eighteen died because doors were nailed shut, there were no fire escapes, and squabbling among politicians over profits from proposed water rights had left firemen with an antique system that provided insufficient water to fight any serious fire. The Delavan discovery found its way into *The Flaming Corsage*.

I stumbled on a newspaper story about the notorious Lola Montez crossing the raging Hudson River by small boat at Albany in the midst of the breakup of river ice, a publicity stunt for her next lascivious performance across the river in Troy. One of her trunks went off the boat and into the water, but Lola made it across. I liked her audacity and decided to reinvent her as part of Magdalena Colon, dancer, courtesan, and aunt of Quinn's young love, Maud Fallon. I also decided to drown her, and did, but by the time the scene ended, she was so vital to me that I put her into chapter two with the river-rat boatman, John (The Brawn) McGee, who rescued her corpse from the icy waters. And later, while she lay dead on a catafalque in the Staats mansion, John-the-shameless-necrophile raised her skirt, violated her, and resurrected our Magdalena through the friction of joy. Improbable? Are there no moribund resurrected by such friction?

Reaffirming the grim nature of an icy death for Magdalena was not what I wanted to write. I wanted for Quinn the surprise of the unknown, a story that was perhaps an elaborate and beautiful lie but which in time might be beautifully true. The resurrection seemed right since it leaped up at me from some arcane corner of the imagination, demanding to be taken seriously.

Mark C. Carnes, in his essay, writes that *Quinn's Book* is bathed in "magical surrealism." He also says that in spite of this, it is "not historically unrealistic," and I am very grateful to him for this affirmation of my intent on this and other matters. I have always had a fascination for surrealism as practiced by a few: Magritte and Buñuel and, especially, before the term existed, Goya, whose work I just saw again and at length in Spain, soon after touring the personal museum of another surrealist, Salvador Dalí. Juxtaposed to Goya, Dalí seems like Dr. Seuss; the one grounded in realistic images that have a relentlessly profound, often shocking, effect on us, even when they are most mysterious, such as the black paintings; the other, the Dalís, however brimming with talent and comic invention, awash in preposterous triviality.

Nothing in *Quinn's Book* is impossible, not even the dusty soldier, whose story was told to me by a contemporary couple who, when moving the remains of relatives from one cemetery to another, marveled—as a coffin was opened—at the sight of the perfectly intact face and body of the long-buried corpse, but then saw it explode and collapse into itself with a puff of dust a few seconds after exposure to the air. As to Magdalena's resurrection: a year or so after I wrote that scene a news story appeared about a drowned boy who lay at the bottom of an icy pond for forty-five minutes, and was then brought back to life at a hospital.

Likewise, the rapping spirits of the novel were genuine bemusements—polterzeitgeists?—of an age in which spiritualism took hold of the nation. Even sturdy realists like Horace Greeley, who witnessed the rappings and publicized them in his newspaper, giving impetus to the movement, and the diarist George Templeton Strong, who wrote of it over the years, were baffled witnesses to the cogent but inexplicable noises and table-moving by the spirits. Strong, a most intelligent skeptic, assumed it was probably humbug, but possibly some "magnetic or electric or mesmeric agency." As his mystification continued three years later, he wrote: "These stories are a phenomenon, true or false. For if it be all a delusion, as I suspect, they establish the fact of mortal fallibility even on subjects within the range of sense, and tend more or less to illustrate the value of our 'rational' judgment, on various subjects. If true, they point to the existence of something in physical science that upsets many of our received notions."

Further on Professor Carnes: he cites Dickens as my "most obvious literary referent," but I would say that it was not that obvious to me. What I read of Dickens so very long ago may well have embedded itself in my imagination and is still up there directing traffic. If I can certify the Dickens influence as distantly unconscious, I'll yield the point. I plead wholly guilty, however, to trafficking in the mythic dimension, to which Professor Carnes also points. The task, as I know it, is first to authenticate the time and place into which I am carried by an intuition that takes me by the throat and then becomes a compulsion; and at the outset I suppose I behave as responsibly as any historian looking for the truth. But the novelist needs an authenticating witness to the historical instant being uncovered, and so characters appear who live through the instant, but who lack all perspective on their own ongoing lives. What's more, they are creatures moved by genetic and legendary and mythic forces, by the collective will of their age as well as by their own wishes and imaginative dreaming, without which they would have no soul. And what respectable historian would be caught trying to authenticate anybody's soul? Defining the whatness of the witnesses' history as it is propelled by their mythic drives and dreams is clearly the responsibility of someone other than the historian. I propose the novelist for the task.

My aim in *Quinn's Book* was for Quinn to inhabit the present tense of his life—adventure as it was happening—amid these wonders, horrors, frauds, and mysteries of his age, as I've lived through my own. Everything he encounters has an analogue that resonates somewhere in my world; and I saw to it that Quinn was actually the grandfather of Daniel Quinn, the ten-year-old in *Billy Phelan's Greatest Game* and *Ironweed*. As children in *Quinn's Book*, Quinn and his true love, Maud, see their innocence destroyed, becoming powerless witnesses to death by ice and fire, to resurrection through rape, and betrayal through stolen love and enforced separation. They thereafter live in conflict with their loss and the compulsion to rediscover. They become radical figures as a way of restoring meaning lost when innocence died; and yet they refuse to believe it is gone forever, so important was it. Maud is a mystic, but very hard-edged about it. Quinn quests for the unknown because nothing known seems to solve his need.

I wanted to believe that in putting Quinn through his days and years I would resurrect history that had belonged to me before memory. Certain choices made me conclude I was on target. I had created a rascal, John (The Brawn) McGee, the river boatman who is Quinn's master, and whom I made a roustabout who becomes a bare-knuckle fighter and finds work breaking heads for politicians on Election Day. Even to the name John, these facts fit a real historical figure I stumbled on when I was partway through the novel. This was John Morrissey, a boatman and bare-knuckle fighter from Troy who worked for politicians, and was rewarded by the pols with gambling houses (nineteen in New York City), through which he became a millionaire and the intimate friend of wealthy horse breeders. Eventually he opened a gambling casino in Saratoga and became the behind-the-scenes founder, with his horsy friends, of the Saratoga racetrack. This was such a fortuitous invasion of my novel by not only relevant but coincident *actual* history, that I fused my John McGee with John Morrissey and carried the hybrid character into the future with the rest of my gang: Magdalena, Maud, and Quinn.

That fusion now seems simply an obvious choice, but it was more than that. I thought the discovery extraordinary, as significant as those photos and clippings frozen in that bucket of ice—both of them gifts from the past, both the source of some new generative power. I had long since understood the trustworthiness of the unconscious. Whenever a blockade loomed in my writing I didn't do battle with it, I slept on it. Invariably I awoke to find a way around or through it. I also discovered how prolonged dwelling on found objects, or isolated images, could bring on a near-mystical awareness of the past, an intuitive memory, perhaps, a retrospective prescience. What else was my invention of John the Brawn in the precise image of John Morrissey, before I knew Morrissey existed?

Through this odd intuition Quinn and I both had, I felt I was creating an authentic world that I had never seen but could seriously believe in, even though I knew it did not exist.

"You do not need to leave your room," wrote Kafka. "Remain sitting at your table and listen. Do not even listen, simply wait. Do not even wait, be quite still and solitary. The world will freely offer itself to you to be unmasked, it has no choice. It will roll in ecstasy at your feet."

That is the historical gaze that yields what never was, but can be. History doesn't change, but we do, and our new perceptions of it become the exhilarating illumination of mystery, the compelling architecture of the unknown, the portrait of the buried myth, the novel.

White Men in Africa:
On Barbara Kingsolver's
The Poisonwood Bible

Diane Kunz

> When a white man in Africa by accident looks into the eyes of a native and sees the human being (which it is his chief preoccupation to avoid), his sense of guilt, which he denies, fumes up in resentment and he bring down the whip.
>
> —*Doris Lessing,* The Grass Is Singing

C laire Timberlake, America's first ambassador to the Congo, faced unprecedented challenges in 1960, the year the Congo received its independence from Belgium. On a day so difficult that he believed he might be seeing the Congo's "death throes as a modern nation," Timberlake ended a cable to the State Department with these words: "The situation is ugly and imperative. The historians will assess the blame and the merit. . . ."[1] He was right. But historians are not alone in this task. Novelists also take stock of the past. Indeed, one of the most accessible accounts of American involvement in the Congo, later Zaire, now once again the Congo, comes in the form of an enthralling novel, *The Poisonwood Bible*, by Barbara Kingsolver.

Kingsolver gives us the Price family. The father, Nathan, is an unbending Protestant minister, racked by guilt at having evaded a brutal Japanese POW camp while the rest of his army company did not. He decides that his mission is to minister to the Africans in the Belgian Congo in 1959. That the missionary board is pulling out of the country and discourages his vocation is irrelevant. For Nathan hopes that by bringing the word of Jesus and by his own suffering and that of his wife and four daughters, he will find redemption.

The story is told in turn by wife Orleanna and by her four daughters, Ruth May, Adah, Leah, and Rachel, who range in age from five to sixteen. While the girls' accounts are apparently contemporaneous, Orleanna's voice is retrospective. The girls experience Africa; Orleanna, oddly detached if not quite dispassionate, reflects on the experience, rather like an historian. Kingsolver, a writer of lyrical prose, does not precisely render these varied voices. Rather her approach is to enrich, explain, and reveal the past through the approximation of contemporaneous voices. In style, *The Poisonwood Bible* bears comparison to *The Glass Menagerie* by Tennessee Williams. Tom, the narrator of the play, explains that "I am the opposite of a stage magician. He gives you illusion that has the appearance of truth. I give you truth in the pleasant disguise of illusion." Adah Price feels the same way: "Illusions mistaken for truth are the pavement under our feet."

The Price family lands in the remote village of Kilanga unequipped to deal with either the day-to-day struggles of life in the bush or with the unrealistic goals that they have each in their own fashion embraced. They inherit the home, servant, and profane parrot which belonged to a mysterious predecessor named Brother Fowles. Equally shadowy is their only white neighbor, private pilot Eeban Axelroot. Gradually, it becomes clear that these two men represent the polar opposites of American intervention in the Congo. Fowles is the idealist. Rather than disdain African ways, he embraces them. He marries an African woman and compromises with the indigenous religion, always attempting to meld his belief in Jesus Christ with the needs and desires of the Congolese. Axelroot personifies the evil side of American policy. His flying taxi service serves as both a convenient cover and a facilitating device for his two businesses: smuggling and spying for the CIA.

The reactions of the Price family to their new environment fall on various points of the spectrum separating the choices made by Fowles and Axelroot. Nathan dogmatically intends to impose his view of Christianity on the natives to save them, if necessary, from themselves. Kingsolver's title, *The Poisonwood Bible*, illuminates the result. Poisonwood is an African tree that causes terrible pain and suffering to anyone foolish enough to touch it. The Kikongo word for poisonwood, *Bangala*, pronounced differently, means something that is precious and dear (p. 276). Because Nathan's Christianity is so dear to him, he cannot give an inch. So his "fixed passion" is *batiza*, baptism in the Congo River, even after he learns that the villagers are terrified of its waters because a crocodile claimed the life of a girl unlucky enough to be within snatching distance.

Ironically, Leah, who is the most sympathetic to African aspirations, helps trigger the climactic crisis of the novel. A talented markswoman, although still a teenager, she insists on violating village norms and participating in a traditional hunt designed to assuage the famine that is stalking Kilanga. In her own way, she is as guilty of American hubris as Nathan. Together, their actions poison village life, upset the local order, and ultimately cause the death of Ruth May, the youngest daughter. The price the Prices have paid is indeed high.

The personal tragedy of the Price family is intertwined with the destruction of civil order in the Congo. Forced to flee Kilanga, the Prices take separate roads (literally and figuratively) as they attempt to find salvation. Both Nathan and Orleanna become hermits—Nathan in the African bush, Orleanna on Sanderling Island, Georgia. Adah becomes a doctor and devotes herself to researching African viruses such as Ebola and AIDS, which now threaten Western nations. Rachel inherits a hotel in the former French Congo from her last husband and stays there, exploiting the kind of economic opportunities that persist no matter what regime is in power. Leah marries Anatole, the African schoolteacher she met in Kilanga. Like Brother Fowles, she goes native, bearing children, supporting her husband's socialist policies and succoring him, in and out of jail.

Kingsolver is eager to educate the reader about the political events which form the backdrop to her story. Orleanna, Leah, and Anatole are the narrators of what to Kingsolver is a simple morality play: Africa was a premodern Garden of Eden. The fall came not from corruption within but because of European sin without. When it comes to the depredations of King Leopard II, Kingsolver is not far off—no one could disagree with the deliberately downplayed comment of the narrow-minded missionary wife Mrs. Underdown: "King Leopold was a bad egg. I'll admit that" (p. 183). But until 1908 Leopold, not the Belgian government, owned the Congo. Desperate to match the more prominent European monarchies in wealth if not in power, Leopold took advantage of the worldwide thirst for rubber to extract millions of Belgian francs from his fiefdom. His overseers were ordered to produce without scruple. The result was officially sanctioned slavery and torture.

The gruesome manner in which Leopold exploited his spoils and squirreled away the profits in various secret European bank accounts brought about the first European human rights movement directed at aiding black Africans. Thanks largely to the dedicated efforts of two British men, shipping clerk E. D. Morel and civil servant Roger Casement, the barbarities of life in the Belgian Congo became a matter of international concern and the raison d'être of the first African-centered NGO, the Congo Reform Association. These lobbying efforts proved successful: in 1908, the Belgian government nationalized the Congo, after first paying Leopold a king's ransom.

As late as 1958, Belgium proclaimed its intent to hold on to the Congo (eighty times larger than the mother country) until the end of the twentieth century. Riots in the capital, Leopoldville, in December 1959, however, convinced Belgian leaders to try a radical tack. They announced that the Congo would receive its independence on June 30, 1960. The Brussels government gambled that because Belgian policy against higher education for indigenous citizens had left Africans unprepared for self-government, Belgium would be able to run the country through Congolese puppets after independence.

Leah is present at the ceremony where the Belgian king Badouin hands over the official reins of power to native leaders. Like the crowd of Africans, she is swayed by the rhetoric of Patrice Lumumba, the first prime minister of the Congo: what he said came "to me in bursts of understanding, as if Patrice Lumumba were speaking in tongues and my ears had been blessed by the same stroke of grace" (p. 184). Lumumba was indisputably charismatic, a likely leader for a new nation.

To this point, the United States had had little contact with the Belgian Congo. Of course, most schoolchildren had learned about the noble explorer Dr. Livingstone and the reporter for the *New York Herald* Henry

Morton Stanley, who had found him in the Congo after mounting the largest African expedition yet. The literati were familiar, too, with Joseph Conrad's *Heart of Darkness*. And, in 1959, Americans went to the movies to see Audrey Hepburn star in *The Nun's Story*. Hepburn plays Sister Luke, a Belgian missionary who arrives in the Congo, where the mother superior extols missionary education. Pointing to a group of Africans rolling bandages, she tells Hepburn: "Only one generation ago their fathers were savages in the forest and now we cannot run the hospital without them."

The American government similarly assumed that the Africans required guidance. As Vice President Richard Nixon expounded at a National Security Council meeting in January 1960, "It was difficult to realize the problems facing Africa without visiting the Continent. Some of the peoples of Africa have been out of the trees for only about fifty years."[2] While the United States had been content to leave Africa to the management of its Europeans allies, rapid decolonization after World War II made the continent an American problem. Kingsolver's novel takes place at the height of the Cold War. It was, as Americans now struggle to remember, a zero-sum world, where those who were not supportive of the policies of the United States were presumed to be allies of the Soviet Union. With Europe divided by the Iron Curtain that ran across the two Germanys, and sufficiently fortified that neither side dared risk aggression there, the action shifted to other continents. Asia had been the battlefield during the 1950s, first in Korea, then in Indochina. By 1960, another continent seemed up for grabs.

Belgian policy clearly contributed to the chaos that descended over the Congo that summer. The issue was the secession of the province of Katanga from the Congo. Katanga, located in the south of the nation, possessed some of the richest mineral deposits in the world, mostly controlled by Belgian interests. Although an African, Moise Tshombe, assumed leadership of the Katanga secessionist movement, he relied on Belgian soldiers to protect his breakaway state. And Belgian soldiers took over the airport in Leopoldville, the national capital, after Congolese army soldiers rioted against their Belgian officers and attacked whites still resident in the Congo.

According to Kingsolver's pro-African nationalist Anatole, Lumumba asked the United Nations to bring an army to restore unity to the Congo. But American policymakers were also enthusiastic about the United Nations solution which Secretary General Dag Hammarskjöld proved willing to oversee. In July, the Security Council authorized the secretary general to provide military assistance until "national security forces could fully meet their tasks." In the meantime, Lumumba arrived in the United States for official talks with the secretary of state. The correct treatment accorded Lumumba as the prime minister of an independent nation infuriated Belgian officials, who saw American politeness as an affront to their country, a staunch NATO ally.

There it was again, the Cold War. Lumumba played this card as well. Anatole insists that Lumumba is simply bluffing when he turns to the Soviet Union for assistance, but in fact Lumumba welcomed the aid offered by Premier Nikita Khrushchev, including planes and military advisers. The prime minister rationalized his relationship with the Soviet Union as the only way to deal with the Katanga secessionist movement, which threatened to rip his country apart. Lumumba also maintained that he would have willingly accepted American aid or assistance from any other country that would help him quash the Katanga rebellion, evict United Nations peacekeepers, and unify his splintering coalition.

But the United States could not back Lumumba without offending Belgium and other NATO partners with large substantial colonial interests, particularly France and Portugal. Moreover, American officials were wary of the unstable, unreliable, and overwhelmed Lumumba and justifiably horrified by the massacre caused by Lumumba's soldiers in Kasai (another breakaway region). Moreover, they recognized and feared his charismatic talents, especially if they were to be backed by Soviet power and prestige. Adah overhears Axelroot talking on his shortwave radio and learns that President Dwight Eisenhower himself ordered Lumumba's death. As indeed he did. That Lumumba might allow the Soviets control of a key African nation outweighed the fact that he was the legally elected prime minister of the Congo. As Senate hearings later revealed (well summarized in Kingsolver's novel by Orleanna), American attempts against Lumumba personally included sending a CIA doctor (code-named "Joe from Paris") to Leopoldville with a poison that could be secreted in Lumumba's food or toothpaste. Nothing that Kingsolver's CIA stooge Eeban Axelroot intimates to his common-law wife Rachel, the oldest of the Price sisters, compares with the reality of the CIA's machinations against Lumumba in the name of Cold War victory.

Even better, the Americans had found their own candidate for Congolese power. He was Colonel Joseph Mobuto, a former sergeant major in the Belgian-officered Congolese army, the Force Publique, who by 1960 was serving as Lumumba's military attaché. While Ambassador Timberlake for one initially questioned whether Mobuto had "the stamina, moral courage and political savvy necessary" for his complex new role as an American puppet,[3] he did have two very clear advantages: he was anti-Communist and he appeared pliable.

Mobuto launched his first takeover attempt in September 1960. He promptly removed Lumumba from office and established himself as a major player in the Congo, before ceding ostensible authority to civilian officials. But it was too late for Lumumba. At the beginning of December, the Congolese army, now renamed the Armée Nationale Congolaise, arrested him. Lumumba escaped briefly but was recaptured and, in January 1961, African soldiers loyal to Tshombe murdered him in Katanga. Lumumba's death ended Khrushchev's Congo gamble but his name lived on in Moscow; Patrice Lumumba University became the educational base for Africans invited to the Soviet Union for higher education.

The Congo's travails continued. While Tshombe acknowledged defeat of his separatist campaign struggle in 1963 and rejoined the national government, the following year a bloody leftist rebellion broke out throughout the country. With whites under siege, Tshombe called for Belgian mercenaries and the United States intervened as well, sending American planes to ferry six hundred Belgian soldiers into Stanleyville, after the rebels had taken sixteen hundred foreign hostages. The ensuing conflict claimed the lives of eighty hostages as well as thousands of Congolese. Mobuto proved to be the big winner. He used the conflict to stamp out what democracy remained in the Congo and claim absolute power over the country. With his staunch pro-Western stance, Mobuto became a favored African ruler in Washington, especially during the Nixon-Kissinger years. Washington officials understood that Mobuto's Africanization drive (renaming himself, renaming his cities, and renaming his country) was symbolic and blithely ignored it.

As he continued his increasingly despotic rule, Mobuto proved to be a canny survivor. His mores were those of Kingsolver's Rachel Price. He found his allies where he could; a close business associate was Maurice Templesman, diamond merchant and intimate companion of Jacqueline Kennedy. Her first husband, President John F. Kennedy, had credited Mobuto with saving the Congo for Western interests, telling him, "General, if it hadn't been for you, the whole thing would have collapsed and the Communists would have taken over."[4] Templesman's chief local contact was Lawrence Devlin, the CIA station chief in the Congo in the early sixties and a clear model for Eeban Axelroot.

Mobuto's self-aggrandizement knew no limits. Kingsolver ably demonstrates this in her account of the 1974 prizefight between Muhammed Ali and George Foreman that Mobuto staged in his capital. As she points out, Mobuto spent millions of dollars on the "rumble in the jungle," at a time when the local standard of living was steadily declining. Indeed, in its infrastructure, education, nutrition, and annual per capita income, today the Congo ranks far below where it stood before independence. Mobuto grew increasingly indifferent to anything except increasing his multi-billion-dollar foreign bank accounts.

By the time of his death in 1997, Mobuto's regime had disintegrated into nothingness, much like the Kilanga Kingsolver describes after the visitation of the African ants that devour everything in their path. Unfortunately, the Congolese government that replaced Mobuto proved as incapable of unifying the country as did Lumumba's coalition forty years earlier.

Other circles have come round. Hammarskjöld viewed 1960 as the year of Africa, but subsequent events have proven this optimism to be unfounded. The vicious fighting in the Congo ended any triumphalism that Africa's rapid decolonization might otherwise have engendered. Recently, United Nations delegates have dedicated the first year after the millennium celebrations to Africa. And once more the Congo is riven by war. The end of the Cold War allowed the great powers largely to disengage from the continent. Unfortunately, their absence has brought not peace but even more brutal conflicts. Instead of the United States and the Soviet Union using the Congo as a battlefield, now seven African nations fight within its mineral-rich and contested borders in what Secretary of State Madeleine Albright has labeled "Africa's World War."

How do we assess responsibility for the tragedy that befell the Congo? Kingsolver placed it squarely on Washington's shoulders. Certainly, the United States bears significant responsibility for the path taken by the Congo since independence. But the American role is not the end of the story. How to conduct a moral foreign policy in an immoral world has always been a particularly difficult question for Americans, no more so than at the beginning of the Cold War. Other countries may have prided themselves on a foreign policy based on sheer self-interest. The United States, in contrast, has always preached the gospel of democracy. The all-encompassing nature of the Cold War, together with the proliferation of atomic weaponry, which robbed the United States of its former impregnable borders, placed American leaders in a quandary. Granted their fealty to the traditional American ideals of democracy and self-determination, what principles should guide America's foreign policy in a now-threatening world?

The interventionist, chattering class consensus came to be expressed best by diplomat George Kennan and theologian Reinhold Niebuhr. Kennan, a Soviet expert who had also served in Germany before and during World War II, penned the Cold Warriors' realist manifesto. In his anonymously authored article, published in *Foreign Affairs* in July 1947, Kennan laid down the creed of containment: "The Soviet pressure against the free institutions of the western world is something that can be contained by the adroit and virulent application of counter-force at a series of constantly shifting geographical and political points, corresponding to the shifts and maneuver of Soviet policy. . . ." In other words, for every Soviet push, the United States must always vigilantly respond to Soviet actions, wherever they may take place.

But what if American counteractions were less than honorable? Not to worry. Niebuhr, a prominent Protestant theologian, had the answer to that. *Moral Man and Immoral Society* became the sacred text for the good soldiers of the Cold War who believed that we could "not afford any more

compromises. We will have to stand at every point in our far flung lines."
What may be morally unacceptable on an individual basis was permissible under the new conditions that the Cold War had spawned.

Ten-plus years after the Cold War's end, it is both easier and more difficult to understand the temper of those times. Befuddled students watching the Russian army repeatedly stumble ask their professors, "Were we ever really afraid of the Soviet Union?" Yes, we were. The quick takeover by the Soviet Union of virtually all of Eastern Europe, as well as the Soviet development of the atomic bomb a mere four years after Hiroshima, created a climate of fear unprecedented in American history. At home, it translated into the lamentable Red Scare which left the careers of thousands of premature anti-Fascists in tatters. Abroad, it meant the creation of a more aggressive and expansive foreign policy. It also elevated "the ends justify the means" into the eleventh commandment of American foreign policy. As Barry Goldwater, the 1964 Republican candidate for president, put it, "Extremism in the defense of liberty is no vice. And let me remind you that moderation in the pursuit of justice is no virtue."

But democracies find it very difficult to countenance casualties. And the United States in the twentieth century has been particularly resistant to accepting battlefield deaths as a necessary part of warfare. This reluctance grew geometrically as the battlefield shifted away from terrain familiar to white Americans to Asia and Africa. Enter the Central Intelligence Agency. Founded in 1947, not coincidentally the year of Kennan's article, the CIA seemed the perfect weapon for this everywhere, anywhere conflict. Even better, its bag of dirty tricks promised a zero-cost victory. Knock a leader out here, foment one coup there, and another triumph is ours.

Eisenhower had blessed the Iranian coup in 1953, run by the CIA and British intelligence officers, which returned the shah to power. One year later, the CIA was back in action—this time helping to depose the democratically elected socialist leader of Guatemala. How natural it seemed to send agents to the Congo. Washington saw it very simply: Lumumba was either a stooge that Soviet agents would manipulate or he was a Communist. Either explanation justified American intervention.

As America was drawn deeper into the Vietnam morass, it became fashionable to dismiss the views held by Cold Warriors. Historians, as well as novelists, increasingly blamed the United States for the Cold War. Chinese dictator Mao Tse-tung had long been a cult figure on campuses. Now members in good standing of the chattering classes rehabilitated Joseph Stalin as well. He lost his position as the head of an evil empire and regained the kindly Uncle Joe reputation he had enjoyed among American literati in the glorious days of World War II's Grand Alliance.

But the end of the Cold War exposed the falsity of this worldview. For the first time, historians could see the other side's archival records as well as interview actual participants on the Communist side of the divide. This newly available information relegated the benign view of Soviet conduct to the dustheap of history. It is clear that Stalin and his ilk sought to dominate the world by fair or foul means. The great liberal victims of the Cold War such as Alger Hiss turned out to be guilty as charged. Communist agents actively subverted liberal institutions in the United States and elsewhere. American officials had worried that Lumumba would be easy prey for such an assault. It had been fashionable to discredit their views, as Orleanna scoffingly does: "Imagine if he could have heard those words—dangerous to the safety of the world! from a roomful of white men. . . ." Now we can see how credible their fears were.

Equally clearly we can understand that for Africa, Communist domination would have been at least as great a disaster as what eventually befell the continent. The rosy view of the Chinese Cultural Revolution has faded, as has Western faith in the genuineness of the German Democratic Republic. It turned out that Communist rule was every bit as bad as the worst nightmare an American right-winger could have conjured up. When those who had actually lived under Communist domination could choose their government, their actions exploded any Communist claim to legitimacy. They rejected Communist totalitarianism while embracing with enthusiasm the American capitalist lifestyle that Leah and Anatole spurned after several visits to Georgia. While these revelations do not exculpate the United States from responsibility for its actions during the Cold War, they place them into proper context. What we now know also goes far to vindicate the American belief that Cold War justified U.S. intervention far from home. And this knowledge supplies the missing links between the political events that Kingsolver recounts.

Reality is nothing if not messy. Novelists who use historical settings as the linchpin of their fiction have a great advantage over those of us who labor in the thicket of archives and footnotes. They can hew toward an Aristotelian unity, where characters behave as they should, where cause leads to effect, and where tragedy brings catharsis. The resulting strong narrative line is what gives novels like *War and Peace* and *Gone With the Wind*, as well as *The Poisonwood Bible*, their power. Pity the poor historian. As long as she or he hews to Von Ranke's injunction to tell it like it really was, history books, like the facts they recount, will be full of the same jagged edges that defied diplomats who attempted to find neat solutions to the geopolitical problems of their time.

With the end of the Cold War, Americans have lost their automatic connection to events abroad. While formerly everything mattered, it now seems that in a period where the United States is the only superpower and a universal role model as well, nothing abroad need trouble us. Kingsolver views this evolution as a beneficial development for Africa. Yet Orleanna, early in the novel, justifiably contemptuous, quotes Kennan's observation that he felt "not the faintest moral responsibility for Africa." But Kingsolver and Kennan have the same goal: an America that does not interfere in the affairs of that continent. Kingsolver clearly approves of Leah and Anatole's chosen path. Having rejected the materialism of America, they settle in an Angolan utopian community where they do their best to re-create the premodern world that Anatole believes was Africa before the depredations of Europeans of various nationalities brought disaster to his native land.

Be careful of what you wish. It was this hands-off attitude that led the Clinton administration to deny the patently genocidal murders in Rwanda in 1994 and to ignore the Rwandan infiltration of the Congo three years later. The Congo suffered dreadfully from American intervention in the 1960s; American indifference may yet prove to be even more damaging. And to us as well. Today, as vicious civil wars batter Africa, Kingsolver's apparent faith that Africa's problems would be solved if the continent were left alone seems touchingly naïve. Indeed, in one of the ironies that historians and novelists both enjoy, Mobuto in his decline resembled no one so much as King Leopold II—the mirror-image conclusion of *Animal Farm* brought to life. Only outside intervention rid the

Congo of both these men; to prevent a third such tyrant, outside intervention may well be necessary again.

Notes

1. *Foreign Relations of the United States, 1958–1960,* vol. 14, *Africa* (Washington, DC: United States Government Printing Office, 1990) 320.

2. *FRUS,* 75.

3. *FRUS,* 511.

4. I have relied on Madeleine G. Kalb's fine work, *The Congo Cables: The Cold War in Africa—From Eisenhower to Kennedy* (New York: Macmillan, 1982), for my account of American relations with the Congo.

PART V

War

A War Like All Wars

Tom Wicker

*C*old Mountain* is properly called a "Civil War novel" but it contains no battle scenes, save in hazy recollection by Inman, the protagonist. Even though set in a time of struggle and division, it suggests no political ideology, unless it's the decision by Inman, a wounded and recovering Confederate veteran, to go home to Cold Mountain, in western North Carolina, rather than back to the fighting. Inman identifies the initial appeal of war, and his subsequent repudiation of it, in language common to soldiers at all times.

> Inman now guessed it was boredom with the repetition of the daily rounds that had made [men] take up weapons. The endless arc of the sun, wheel of seasons. War took a man out of that circle of regular life and made a season of its own . . . [b]ut sooner or later you got awful tired and just plain sick of watching people killing one another for every kind of reason at all, using whatever implements fall to hand.

Inman devotes little attention to the political context of the Civil War, and when any passage seems to favor one side or the other of the national ordeal, Charles Frazier quickly balances the ticket. Thus, when an old woman takes Inman in and nurses his festering wounds with folk medicine (on which Frazier seems expert; she uses laudanum made of home-cooked poppies, a salve of "bitter herbs and roots," and "a great soggy bolus . . . like a chaw of tobacco" that sticks in Inman's throat and tastes of "old socks"), she asks whether "all that fighting for the big man's nigger" was "worth it." For that matter, she pointedly adds, did Inman even own any slaves?

"No," he replies. "Not hardly anybody I knew did." The war, he continues, is not really about slavery.

> [A]nyone thinking the Federals are willing to die to set loose slaves has got an overly merciful view of mankind.

He sees opposing soldiers as men, not political advocates:

> the downtrodden mill workers of the Federal army, men so ignorant it took many lessons to convince them to load their cartridges ball foremost. These were the foes, so numberless that not even their own government put much value to them. They just ran them at you for years on end, and there seemed no shortage. You could kill them down until you grew heartsick and they would still keep ranking up to march southward.

Cold Mountain is therefore less a novel of the Civil War than of war—any war in any time—and what it does to men and society. Inman's decision to leave the official war of his time makes him technically a deserter, but actually he is more like the man who declares he has "made a separate peace," in the World War I story by Ernest Hemingway,[1] who also was writing more about war itself than about any particular war.

The theme of soldiers declaring a "separate peace" is familiar, not only in literature but in history. The horrible slaughter on the Western Front in World War I was not concluded, for example, by any identifiable Allied "victory"—such as the Union's at Gettysburg, or Napoleon's at Marengo—or by a government capitulation in Berlin that left its army at the front no alternative but to cease fighting. Rather, it was the sudden and still rather inexplicable mass desertion and capture of German troops beginning in August 1918 that finally led to the war's end. By some indices, the Central Powers actually were winning that war, yet in its last phase, nearly 400,000 Germans surrendered or were captured by British, French, and American forces. That made it impossible for Germany to continue the war—just as, earlier, the mass surrender and capture of Russians on the Eastern Front had led to the massive German triumph.[2]

More relevant to *Cold Mountain*, at Appomattox Courthouse on April 9, 1865, when Robert E. Lee surrendered the army from which Inman had separated himself, it numbered only 28,000 men. Nearly 14,000 more had been captured in that final campaign and 3,800 had deserted (against 6,266 killed and wounded). Exactly how many of those "captured" or deserting actually were declaring their own separate peace is not known, but their total was more than half of Lee's remaining army.[3]

Inman, a reader deduces, walks off from a Confederate hospital to return to Cold Mountain out of personal revulsion at the death and destruction of war. Literature is replete with such stories—not only by Hemingway, but by Erich Maria Remarque in *All Quiet on the Western Front*, Tim O'Brien in *Going After Cacciato*, even Tolstoy in *War and Peace*. The theme seems inherent in the basic truth uttered by William T. Sherman that "war is hell."

Why men fight, therefore—even when the likelihood of death is overwhelming—is a conundrum: patriotism, personal honor, the desire for glory, the pursuit of a cause, coercion, the lack of an easy alternative? All, no doubt, in some proportion. It is equally a mystery why many of the same men, sometimes in herdlike numbers, give up, walk away, surrender, lay down their arms. To neither question can a single, logical answer be given—just as those surrendering Germans in 1918, who had been for four years such exceptional and nearly victorious fighters, cannot be precisely explained. Can it be that a sort of warrior spirit causes men to lust for superiority in battle—only to cause them also to submit to superiority once they see, or at least believe, where superiority must lie?

Frazier does not dwell on these eternal mysteries but invests Inman's particular story with personal and historical detail—including an obscure but quite real aspect of the Civil War period: the savage, often lawless efforts of official and unofficial bands of men—sometimes brutal killers—to control the southern home front, in particular to round up deserters and draft dodgers, ostensibly but not always to send them to the fighting front.

Frazier's scenes of this particularly vicious war within a war, though shocking, are not fanciful. Union sentiment had always been strong in mountainous western North Carolina, where slaves were few; nevertheless, after the state's secession, numerous young men of the region, like Frazier's Inman, volunteered to fight for the Confederacy. Those early enlistments as well as later conscription laws stripped the region of able-bodied and law-abiding men and left it vulnerable to depredation by outlaws, deserters, skulkers, draft resisters, and "outliers" of all kinds.

As the war persisted, moreover, battle fatigue, homesickness, broken promises of furloughs and promotions, service in "foreign" regiments (from other southern states) and under disliked officers, the mounting sense that it was "a rich man's war but a poor man's fight"—all caused a monumental and never-solved problem of desertion from the Confederate armies. From the Army of Northern Virginia especially, mountain ridges made good natural highways along which deserters could flee into western North Carolina; in that then-wild region of hills, valleys, forests, caves, few roads, less law enforcement, and persisting union sympathies, hiding was easy. So was open preying on the locals, of whatever political disposition, and on each other.

Three Confederate laws also embittered the people of the mountains: conscription of white men, at first those between the ages of eighteen and thirty-five, later even older white males ("Our pore class of men are all gonn to the ware to fight to save our country," wrote a Madison County, North Carolina, man, "and the rich man negroes . . . are all at home"); tax-in-kind legislation compelling farmers to send a tenth of their produce to the authorities at Richmond; and the establishment of committees empowered to impress livestock, slaves, provisions, and wagons for Confederate army use, at prices set by the committees.

In these conditions of unrest in remote western North Carolina, armed and lawless bands of thugs and desperadoes—"buffaloes," as they sometimes were called—often were numbered in the hundreds and sometimes took actual control of certain counties and towns. As one complaint to the Confederate secretary of war put it, "malicious bands of marauders . . . now openly parade themselves . . . west of the Blue

Ridge." Few men or women dared to travel alone, or to leave their houses and farms.

Even some of the Confederate forces detailed to maintain order took advantage of an essentially lawless situation. In one engagement in contiguous east Tennessee, Indians fighting as part of a Confederate unit scalped some of the federal wounded and dead. And as one Tar Heel complained to North Carolina's governor Zeb Vance, Confederate forces were "doing no good going from house to house, disturbing the people all they can killing dogs and chickens and stealing eggs." Vance got himself reelected in 1864 with the slogan "Fight the Yankees and Fuss with the Confederacy."

In January 1863, a band of Union sympathizers from Shelton Laurel, North Carolina, descended on Marshall, the seat of Madison County, to reclaim salt they thought was being withheld from them owing to their Unionist views. After this violent raid on private stores, Vance appealed for help from Confederate general Henry Heth, later of Gettysburg fame, then commanding the Tennessee–North Carolina mountain area from headquarters in Knoxville. Heth dispatched a force that reported killing, on January 20, twelve "tories" and capturing twenty others. Later, however, Governor Vance and others learned that part of Heth's troops, commanded by Lt. Col. J. A. Keith, had captured thirteen other "tories"—mostly old men and boys—shot them in cold blood near Shelton Laurel, and left the bodies unburied. Vance ordered a formal investigation of this atrocity, with the result that Keith was forced to resign from the Confederate army—on grounds of incompetence! He claimed, but Heth denied, that Heth had ordered that no prisoners should be taken.[4]

Similarly murderous events and the frequent depredations of uncontrolled thugs and killers—not always clearly identified with either side of the war still raging in Virginia and the West—figure largely in *Cold Mountain.* Captured by one such "home guard" gang, Inman is strung by the wrists with other prisoners and marched "like tailed colts" back the way he had come, presumably to be returned to the army. One night, provoked by a captive who calls them "a pack of shit," the outlaw guardsmen shoot all the prisoners; but the ball that strikes Inman had already passed through another captive and wounds him only slightly. All the supposed dead, including Inman, then are buried in shallow graves. Inman remains alive, however, though covered with dirt, until

> feral hogs descended from the woods, drawn by the tang in the air. They plowed at the ground with their snouts and dug out arms and feet and heads, and soon Inman found himself uprooted, staring eye to eye, forlorn and hostile and baffled, into the long face of a great tushed boar. Yaah, Inman said. The boar shied off a few feet . . . his little eyes blinking. Inman prized his length out of the ground. To rise and bloom again, that became his wish.

As Inman resumes his dogged journey across his southern world— North Carolina in the last stages of the war—"to rise and bloom again" becomes more than his personal wish. All about him is a landscape and a people left for dead but struggling to survive—in a situation unknown to most Americans but traumatic in the southern heritage, and far from the usual tales of pitched battles and yellow-sashed cavalry. Inman's westward trek involves escapes from various "buffaloes," being shot at by vigilantes, threatened by some travelers, befriended by others, ferried across rising rivers—all of which, together with the near-mythological nature of the journey and Charles Frazier's frequent references to myth, perhaps validates the belief by some reviewers that this deeply American novel is rooted in the *Odyssey*.

Frazier tells Inman's story in chapters alternating with an account of the difficult back-home life of Ada Monroe, the educated minister's daughter Inman idealizes and to whom he thinks he still may be engaged (though he doubts she can any longer love or accept a man who in the war "had grown so used to seeing death, walking among the dead, sleeping among them . . . that . . . he feared . . . he would never make a civilian again"). In one letter, he has asked Ada not to look at a picture he had sent her, fearing his knowledge of death had registered on his face. As for Ada, she has not seen Inman for four years and has had only a few impersonal letters. She has no idea he is on the way back to Cold Mountain, or where he might be. She thinks the small picture he's worried about never looked much like the man who went off to war anyway. Her struggle, paralleling Inman's effort to return to the near-mythical Cold Mountain, is to survive on a mountain farm in a backwoods world infested by those ominous out-law bands, with only a city woman's irrelevant knowledge and the help of her friend Ruby, a skilled farmhand and woodswoman.

Cold Mountain is by genre a historical novel, but what fiction isn't? History is yesterday as well as the last century; even those fantasies set in the future depend for minimum believability to some extent on historical experience—or counterexperience. As history, however, *Cold Mountain* steers well clear of familiar blue-and-gray, brother-versus-brother clichés. Instead, Frazier's concerns are with a world nearing the end of a calamitous war, with a society in devastation, and with people who seem mostly to want the battle to be over so that their men can come back and rebuilding can begin.

In privileged America, with its oceans and distances, only the South has experienced the defeat and destruction of a losing war. But it's not the South as such, but the collapse of a society—perhaps any society—which is a central theme of Cold Mountain. This is no sociological tract, however. Frazier does not dwell on this theme to the detriment of Inman and Ada, who are as human and real and as vividly drawn as, say, Scarlett and Rhett—and more affectionately observed—in that universally known but very different Civil War saga.

At one point in their ultimate reunion, Inman sees Ada–digging with her hands for "goldenseal" to use in a poultice, and thinks that the scene could have occurred "any place in time at all. So few markers to show any particular epoch." Indeed, Inman and Ada would be recognizable in any setting. Yet they also are part of, and shaped by, the particular world of Cold Mountain—a timeless rather than a historic world.

It is a world observed with acute social instinct and a piercing eye for detail. Coming upon a woman alone in "a lonesome little one-room cabin of squared-off timbers" above which "thin brown smoke rose from the mud-and-stick chimney and then whipped away on the wind," Inman offers to pay for something to eat. "I'm hard up," the woman replies, ". . . but not that far gone that I have to take money for what little I can offer. There's a pone of corn bread and some beans is all."

Her husband has been killed in the war and she outfits Inman in the dead man's clean clothes. That night, when she has gone to bed, "taken the plait out of her hair and it spread thick across her shoulders," the scene seems set for a conventional sex romp. But Sarah, the woman, says from the bed, "If I was to ask you to come over here and lay in bed with me but not do a thing else, could you do it? Could you?"

Inman thinks only a moment before replying that he could.

"I believed you could or I'd never have asked . . . ," Sarah says, and goes on to talk about her dead husband and their happiness together. She has "required of Inman only that he bear witness to her tale."

There is more human reality and eroticism in that sexless scene than in any number of lurid bodice rippers. Inman, in fact, may be unrealistic as a soldier only in that he thinks more of home than of sex; even his thoughts of Ada are seldom physical and "what he knew he wanted most was to disburden himself of solitude"—just as the woman in the cabin had wished, and what love mostly is.

Cold Mountain is rich in such human insights; admirers of modern technological "advances," in particular, might reflect on Ruby's belief that

> Everything added meant something lost and about as often as not the thing lost was preferable to the thing gained, so that over time we'd be lucky if we just broke even. Any thought otherwise was empty pride.

The novel, however, is even richer in what ought to distinguish any good "historical" novel—a deep sense of how things were, how life was lived. If a function of art, as Joseph Conrad observed, is to make a reader or a viewer see and feel the thing or the event depicted, Charles Frazier has given us as good an idea of nineteenth-century life as we could hope for. In the last year of the war, for instance, Ruby and Ada find that

> . . . on their first trip together into town, they had . . . to give fifteen dollars for a pound of soda, five dollars for a paper of triple-ought needles, and ten for a quire of writing paper. Had they been able to afford it, a bolt of cloth would have cost fifty dollars. . . . But even if they had it, shopkeepers really didn't want money since the value of it would likely drop before they could get shut of it . . . Ada and Ruby hoed and pulled weeds among the rows of young cabbages and turnips, collards and onions, the kind of coarse food they would mostly live on for the winter. Some weeks earlier they had

prepared the garden carefully, plowing and sweetening the dirt with fireplace ashes and manure from the barn and then harrowing the cloddy ground, Ruby driving the horse while Ada rode the drag to add weight. The harrow was a crude device, knocked together . . . from a fork in an oak trunk. Holes had been augered through the green wood of the two spreading ends of the trunk and fitted with long pikes of cored black locust. As the oak dried it had tightened hard around the sharpened locust and needed no further attachment. During the work, Ada had sat at the fork, braced with hands and feet as the harrow jounced across the ground, breaking up clumps of plowed dirt and combing it smooth with the tines of locust.

Frazier uses a far-off war as a double-edged metaphor—first, for an old life upon which Inman and Ada, in their separate ways, necessarily have turned their backs, and from which the South that Inman traverses has been delivered in ruin and retribution. An epigraph suggests a second edge of the metaphor—for a far more persistent clash than one of mankind's frequent conflicts: "that dreadful but quiet war of organic beings, going on in the peaceful woods & smiling fields" (Darwin).[5]

Frazier's preoccupation with nature, in fact, is pervasive, encompassing that "quiet war" as the way of things, rather then focusing upon the selection of species. In *Cold Mountain*, when the big fish eat the little fish, man is most often the predator, and it is his unnatural feasts that are detailed, while the flora and fauna attend only to their necessary business. Inman and particularly Ruby, and ultimately even the urban-bred Ada, seem to know every growing thing—tree, shrub and weed, fish and fowl—what it can be used for, where it's to be found, what its presence and status may signify about weather and seasons. Animals are so much a part of Inman's awareness, for instance, that he has vowed to kill nothing that he cannot eat; when he is forced to shoot a bear, he feels the act was "in the order of sin."

Nature is described with precision, as if on film. Two peregrine hawks, "bursting out of the fog . . . flew into the shifting wind, their wings making short choppy strokes for purchase against the difficult air." Ada and Ruby see, "near a hole in the river where people were sometimes dipped in baptism, a cloud of martins erupt[ing] out of a maple tree nearing the peak of its color." Against a sky resembling "hammered pewter," the martins "flew in one body, still in the shape of the round maple they had filled."

Often, such limpid observations have relevance to the life of men. Inman, scooping water from a creek, sees

> . . . A salamander, wildly spotted in colors and patterns unique to that one creek . . . [H]e held it cupped in his hand . . . and the way its mouth curved around its head shaped a smile of such serenity as to cause Inman envy and distress. Living hid under a creek rock would be about the only way to achieve such countenance.

Ada, discovering a thistle, thinks that "since every tiny place in the world seemed to make a home for some creature," she'll see if there were "thistle dwellers" even in the dried blossom. She strips it to find only "one fierce little crablike thing" that "waved a minute pair of pincers before it in a way intended to be menacing."

As in any good fiction, characters and events do not move in a vacuum. We feel almost as if we're walking with Inman, learning to plow with Ada, swapping apples for beef with Ruby, moving through their war-marked world. As Inman nears home country, for instance, he stands on a high promontory and watches as "shadows slid down the slopes of the nearest line of ridges, falling into the valley." Winter is coming on and

> . . . rags of cloud hung in the valley . . . but in all that vista there was not a rooftop or plume of smoke or cleared field to mark a place where man had settled . . . [C]rest and scarp and crag, stacked and grey, to the long horizon.

Inman views the scene with "growing joy . . . in his heart" for he has "recognized the line of every far ridge and valley." One far mountain stands "apart from the sky only as the stroke of a poorly inked pen, a line thin and quick and gestural . . . plain and unmistakable. It was to Cold Mountain he looked."

A certain near-grandiloquence occasionally marks Frazier's writing, almost as if he were trying to reproduce what has come down to us of old-fashioned speech. Inman "fared forth" one morning; "I'd not keep a 'flogging rooster,' " Ruby says of a bird that has attacked Ada. She strips its head off and observes: "He'll be stringy so we'd best stew him awhile." A traveler encountering Inman remarks that he's "a pilgrim like yourself. Though maybe I speak too soon, for all who wander are not pilgrims."

The plot of *Cold Mountain* has an unhappy (but not tragic) ending. Upon concluding the story, however, I was profoundly satisfied that things had turned out as they should have, as in boundless experience things do. *Cold Mountain* reassures us that life goes on despite all sorts of "unhappy" events and endings, and yields its joys not alone in ephemeral moments of gratification but continually, in natural compensations—sunsets, a child's discoveries, a task completed, crops in season—that have only to be realized.

Notes

1. "A Very Short Story" from *In Our Time* (New York: Scribner, 1930).

2. For a fuller discussion of these remarkable events, see Niall Ferguson, *The Pity of War* (New York: Basic Books, 1999).

3. Mark M. Boatner III, ed., *The Civil War Dictionary* (New York: David McKay, 1959), 22.

4. For this account of Civil War turmoil in the Blue Ridge Mountains, I am indebted to *The Civil War in North Carolina*, by John G. Barrett (Chapel Hill: University of North Carolina Press, 1963).

5. Another epigraph, this one from Han-shan, declares "there's no through trail" to Cold Mountain.

ঔ৷ৎ

Some Remarks on History and Fiction

Charles Frazier

Many aspiring novelists, I suppose, hang the portraits of writer-heroes above their worktables for encouragement or example or perhaps for some vaguely iconic reason. On my wall now, and during the years I worked on *Cold Mountain*, I have facing me neither tweed-jacketed William Faulkner nor fellow Ashevillian Thomas Wolfe. Instead, I have a photograph of Henry James. It is a late photograph. The Master. His head is Olmec in its mass and rotundity and utter indifference. He looks out from under raptor eyelids with equal measures of suspicion and contempt. "So you propose to be a writer?" he seems poised to say. The tone, I imagine, would be withering. Below that unwelcoming face, I have affixed two Jamesian pronouncements, copied out on three-by-five cards. One reads, "The historical novel is, for me condemned . . . to a fatal cheapness." The other is, "The sense of the past *is* our sense." How—no matter which target, in the end, one more nearly hits—to shoot toward the latter and away from the former is a question any writer working with historical material must consider, for at the heart of the matter is the difference between *The Scarlet Pimpernel* and *The Scarlet Letter*.

Not long ago, I met a reader who told me her husband was convinced that at some point in *Cold Mountain*, I began making things up. Her husband wondered when that was. I said I knew exactly at what point I began making things up. It was on page one. That exchange keeps coming back to me, largely because its assumptions raise any number of questions—not unrelated to James's statements—about how historical fiction works and, indeed, what its goals as a genre should be. Where, for example, should we place the balance point between the history and the fiction? (I'm supposing, perhaps unfairly, that the husband would position it to leave a great weighty length of history and only a bare nub of fiction, just enough to keep the plot rolling along.) Might we wish to limit historical fiction to a retelling—or repackaging—of so-called actual past events? To what extent are we writers free to introduce well-known historical figures into our work and have them carry on conversations and commit acts we cannot verify? Are we free to lash them with emotions they never actually felt?

When faced with such questions of genre and definition, I'm inclined to agree with Raymond Chandler, a writer who mostly—but not always—slipped the confines of the form in which he chose to work. He said, "There are no vital and significant forms of art; there is only art, and precious little of that." It's a good line, and nearly convincing, marred only a little by the underlying defensiveness of a fine writer bristling at being sorted unwillingly into an ill-fit pigeonhole. Any writer from the South or West—the regions—knows the feeling.

At any rate, Chandler's position is both liberating and exacting, a good place to start, and one that would surely set one's aim at least in the general direction of James's latter observation. In regard to such matters, I learned early on in writing *Cold Mountain* that it worked best for me to let the fiction drive and the history ride. Doing it the other way took me places I did not want to go. Partly, that decision was imposed by the particular shard of history I had to work with. I never knew more than a handful of facts about the historical Inman—my great-great-grandfather's brother. Expressed as simple declarative sentences, they could be scrawled on the back of an envelope. Among the first is that he was wounded badly in the final spasms of the War Between the States, when the fighting had bogged down in the muddy trenches outside Petersburg. The last fact is that he was killed a half-year later in a gunfight with Confederate Home Guard under the brow of Cold Mountain in the southern Appalachians.

I had nothing else. He left no artifacts and no writing. His grave is unmarked. Save for a few impersonal entries in his military record and a few orally transmitted bits of family history, he has been wiped from the slate of the world's memory, as we all will be one day.

Those few stark facts, though, were like a very preliminary outline; they formed a gesture toward narrative, but not much more. Early on in the writing, I used to wish for much more. Perhaps Inman's journal, a battered leather-bound relic filled with detailed day-by-day accounts of actions, thoughts, feelings. Rich descriptions of a varied array of closely observed acquaintances. Catalogs of the passing weather and the forms of landscape he most closely attended. But no such record existed, and by the midpoint of the book, I had grown quite content with my meager clutch of facts and with the freedom they gave me to make up a character, beginning with only his desertion to provide firm knowledge of what he feared and what he desired—to put the war behind him and go home to the mountains.

Like Tom Wicker, I suspect that the high desertion rates in the Confederate army have a number of causes, and I would like to add one to his list, at least in regard to the mountain regiments. Many of those men volunteered for limited terms of military service in the heat of war fever in 1861, and many of them considered themselves to be something like independent contractors. Of their various strengths as warriors, military discipline was not a notable feature. One of their commanders is reported to have said that the mountain men were the best soldiers he had ever seen in a fight and the worst in camp. Many of them apparently felt that they had signed on to kill Federals; what they did in between was nobody's business but their own. During slow times, they were prone to go off hunting for days without leave. For such men—in a time when our current notions of nationalism were decades from forming—the individual decision to quit fighting, to declare a separate peace, must surely have been made with fairly different judgments in regard to the abstractions of patriotism, loyalty, honor, etc.

As for the war itself, I have not since childhood romanticized the Confederacy and the "Lost Cause," an impossible proposition once you acknowledge that while it may be true that many—perhaps most—Confederate foot soldiers did not think they were fighting to preserve slavery, it is equally true that no matter how you parse it, to a large extent they were. And it provides no particular mitigation to point out that no great majority of Federal soldiers thought they were fighting and dying to bring about slavery's end. To be beaten is bad enough, but to know you've been fighting for a bad cause and beaten by a sorry enemy is bitter indeed. Nevertheless, as a child, when my friends and I played war games, it was always the War Between the States from the southern perspective that we reenacted and not just because we could buy gray-felt forage caps and plumed cavalry hats at any souvenir shop. We all wanted to be Rebels, not blue-jacketed, mill-worker draftees, and therefore we had nothing but imagination to fight. Even today's grown-up reenactment groups generally find it hard to round up enough people willing to be Federals to make a convincing battle. Apparently rebellion and loss still have their own romance, and for some it remains hard to accept fully the Confederate foot soldier's hard-won and tersely stated realization that they were in "a rich man's war but a poor man's fight."

While working on *Cold Mountain*, I found myself growing less and less interested in the war itself, despite the long and dramatic shadows its primary actors and events cast forward in time. On library research days, my favorite part of writing, I had little trouble resisting the urge to read much about the near-mythic personalities of the war—Lee, Jackson, Forrest, Stuart. I may have been a little afraid they would come sweeping in and overrun my position, but mostly I was much more drawn to other matters. The fictive world I was making was marked by change and threat and beauty, and I wanted to get its concrete elements as right as I could, to make the detail of the imagined past as rich and convincing as possible so that I might be able to see how my characters could learn to live with the loss and breakage. I wanted to know what that world's processes—human and nonhuman—were, how things looked and how they worked. Subsistence farming, vernacular architecture, herbal medicines, and the mysterious ways of wild turkeys, for example. And what were the names of things once common and useful but now almost gone: tools, kitchen implements, various equipage? Snath, spurtle, hame. Lost harsh words, but perhaps as representative of that culture as bytes and bits and RAM are of ours.

The world of nineteenth-century America intersects ours at only a few points that we can now experience directly. Walking a few miles of remnant dirt road that once linked two now-vanished villages or sitting awhile in a small tract of virgin Appalachian forest often proved more useful than a stack of Mathew Brady photographs in shaping my sense of the past, at least the particular slice of the past that held my interest. Sketching the floor plan of a two-centuries-old house could help give shape to an entire chapter. The old music—the fiddle tunes and ballads and hymns, either in the form of early recordings or of old men and women playing and singing the ancient tunes live—always astonished me with its power to sum up a lost culture with all its mournfulness and exuberance and fatalism.

An Essay by (Historian) Thomas Fleming on *Time and Tide*

(Novelist) Thomas Fleming

*T*ime and Tide, published in 1987, was Thomas Fleming's fifteenth novel. In some ways, it can be regarded as a successor to Fleming's best-known novel, *The Officers' Wives*, which sold two million copies worldwide. Both novels were well received by the critics and spent a number of weeks on the best-seller lists. Both books employ fiction to discuss serious historical issues. *The Officers' Wives* explores the American military's response to undeclared wars in Korea and Vietnam and a growing civilian hostility toward their profession. *Time and Tide* explores the unpreparedness of the American navy, in ships, strategy, and tactics, for combat against the Japanese in the Pacific in World War II.

I write about *Time and Tide* rather than the novelist's better-selling book because it is, in my opinion, a more profound work of fiction—and because it explores a part of American history that is relatively unknown to average readers. The triumphalism that pervades recent American writing about World War II has all but obscured the precarious and agonizing contingencies of the first eighteen months of that tremendous conflict. This was especially true in the Pacific, where a combination of racial condescension toward the Japanese and President Roosevelt's decision to commit most of America's men and weaponry to the war against

Germany left the sailors and soldiers of the Pacific theater badly outgunned and frequently outfought.

The central event in *Time and Tide* is the battle of Savo Island. Most
Americans have forgotten this disastrous encounter, which took place off
Guadalcanal on August 8–9, 1942. Savo is a small steep-sided volcanic
dot at the entrance to the sound between Guadalcanal and nearby Florida
Island. While American sailors frantically unloaded the transports of
Task Group X-Ray, which had landed sixteen thousand marines on
Guadalcanal two days before, two groups of warships plodded back and
forth on the south and north sides of Savo, barring an enemy attack on
the beachhead.

On the south side were the heavy cruiser USS *Chicago* and the Australian heavy cruiser, HMAS *Canberra*. On the north side were three
American heavy cruisers, USS *Quincy*, *Astoria*, and *Vincennes*. Five destroyers were on picket duty in the open sea beyond the cruisers' patrol
patterns. Thick clouds shrouded the stars. The night was as black as the
inside of a witch's hat. Thunder rumbled in the distance and rain from a
passing squall pattered on the dark water. Lookouts stared blearily into
the inky gloom. The crews of all the ships had been at general quarters almost continuously for two full days. The topside deck apes and fire con-
trolmen were baked and blistered by the brutal tropical sun. In the fire
rooms and engine rooms, the black gangs were drained by temperatures
as high as 140 degrees.

No one expected the Japanese to let the Americans keep Guadalcanal
without a fight. Already enemy torpedo planes and dive-bombers had
damaged two destroyers and set the transport George F. Elliott afire. It
was burning in the distance as the Allied warships plodded through the
night. But no one considered the possibility of an attack by surface ships.
The nearest Japanese warships were in New Britain's Rabaul Harbor, six
hundred miles away. A surface force big enough to do serious damage
would presumably be spotted by patrolling planes long before it reached
Savo. The captains of the Allied ships decided to let their weary men get
some sleep. They went to Condition Two—only half the crews would remain on watch.

At 1:13 A.M. parachute flares came wobbling down from the starless
sky. Aboard the destroyer *Patterson*, a lookout cried, "Ships ahead!" The

officer of the deck shouted into the TBS (talk between ships) radio. "Warning, warning! Strange ships entering the harbor!" His words were a waste of breath. The descending flares silhouetted the HMAS *Canberra* and the USS *Chicago*.

A moment later, two torpedoes smashed the *Canberra*'s bow. Simultaneously, a rain of 8- and 4.7-inch shells raked the fourteen-year-old cruiser from the bow to the stern, catching the crew as they raced to general quarters. The captain, asleep in his sea cabin, stumbled to the bridge just in time to be killed by a direct hit from a full salvo. In less than two minutes, *Canberra* was smashed into a burning hulk.

Aboard the *Chicago*, a different story unfolded. A torpedo tore a thirteen-foot gash in her bow and a shell struck the foremast, wounding twenty-five men topside. But damage control crews quickly contained the flooding in the bow and the ship's captain ordered the 5-inch guns to fire star shells to illuminate the enemy. Not a single shell in the first two salvos ignited. Like many other weapons in the navy's peacetime armory, notably torpedoes, neglect had turned the shells into duds. Meanwhile, the elusive enemy—seven cruisers and a destroyer—were rounding Savo to attack the northern force. Although the *Chicago*'s captain was the OTC (officer in tactical command), he did not radio a warning to the other ships. Instead, firing an occasional star shell, he continued to steam west, away from the transports he was supposed to be protecting and the northern cruisers who badly needed his assistance. It was one of the strangest performances in the history of the U.S. Navy.

On the other side of Savo, the attacking Japanese split into two columns and snapped on their searchlights. In the blinding glare lay the *Astoria*, *Vincennes*, and *Quincy*, puzzling over the gunfire on the other side of Savo. They were so totally surprised, the captain of the *Vincennes* ordered his radio room to tell them to "turn those searchlights off us—we are friendly." The captain of the *Quincy* turned on his running lights to demonstrate his amity.

Seconds later, a rain of shells battered all three ships. In a few minutes, the *Astoria* was dead in the water. A torpedo plowed into the *Quincy*'s number-four fire room, tearing the ship's guts out. A salvo killed everyone on the bridge. No less than three torpedoes slammed into the *Vin-*

cennes. An appalling fifty-six direct hits knocked out every gun on the ship. Fifteen minutes later, she sank.

By the time the *Chicago* came about and reached the vicinity of Savo an hour later, the enemy was long gone. The *Quincy* and the *Canberra* swiftly joined the *Vincennes* in the four-hundred-fathom depths of what would soon be nicknamed Ironbottom Sound. The *Astoria* sank the following day. Over a thousand American sailors were dead and another seven hundred were wounded. The panicky admiral in command, Richmond Kelly Turner, gathered the surviving ships and retreated one thousand miles to New Caledonia, leaving the marines on Guadalcanal to fend for themselves.

What intrigued novelist Fleming was the incomprehensible behavior of the USS *Chicago* in this humiliating debacle. He was no doubt further intrigued when he learned that her captain was relieved and a few months later he killed himself with a bullet in the head. In place of the *Chicago*, Fleming invents an imaginary heavy cruiser, the USS *Jefferson City*, and begins the story after the episode at Savo Island, a memory that haunts the entire crew, from the captain to the lowliest deck ape.

The story is told by a former member of the crew, Frank Flanagan, who, we learn in the introduction, has become an historian. Readers may conclude Fleming is subtly advertising his schizoid talents here—telling us that the historian, when he undertakes a novel, is no longer the objective observer, emotionally detached from his sources. On the contrary, he is existentially engaged by memory, loss, regret, even by love. Fleming's schizoid tendencies evidently predate the present essay.

The novel functions somewhat as a detective story. After Savo, the captain of the *Jefferson City*, arrogant, aristocratic Winfield Scott Schley Kemble, scion of an old navy family, is replaced by his Annapolis roommate, a quiet, unassuming Kansan named Arthur McKay. Fleming has obviously been influenced by one of Arthur Schlesinger's better obiter dicta—the American military tend to divide between cavaliers like Douglas MacArthur and roundheads like Dwight Eisenhower. (Fleming has an unsparing characterization of the World War I MacArthur in his 1992 novel, *Over There*, under an all but transparent name: Douglas Fairchild.) McKay has orders from Cominch (commander in chief of the U.S. fleet)

Ernest King to dig up dirt that will enable the navy to make Kemble the scapegoat for Savo.

Cominch King's saturnine shadow pervades much of *Time and Tide*. He was not a nice man and he knew it, supplying historians with a revealing obiter dictum of his own: "When a war starts, they send for the sons of bitches." A humane man, McKay resists King's ruthlessness, refusing to act as prosecutor-cum-judge of his close friend Kemble. When the repaired *Jefferson City* rejoins the struggle for Guadalcanal, a mix of psychological and military crises enables Fleming to explore a number of interesting historical issues that revolve around King. Was the admiral right or wrong to attempt to take the offensive in 1942 without the ships and men to make victory a reasonable certainty? Was King acting out of a sound strategic sense or out of a determination to make the Pacific the navy's war—thereby guaranteeing the admirals a bigger share of the budget? Was he a patriot or a navy politician? Looming above these questions is a more basic one: What was President Franklin D. Roosevelt thinking when he cut off Japan's oil imports from the United States, provoking them to start a war that the Americans were grossly unprepared to fight?

Also in this interesting historical mix is another large factor that is seldom mentioned: the Americans' condescending attitude toward the Japanese, whom they saw as an inferior race with bad eyesight and little or no ability to act or think independently. In a 1939 article, Fletcher Pratt, the highly respected military commentator, dismissed Japanese warships as top-heavy and poorly built. Pratt also declared that the Japanese "can neither make good airplanes nor fly them well." He claimed that Japanese stupidity made them good infantry because group obedience was a virtue in ground battles. But alone in a plane a Japanese pilot was hopeless—and the planes were no good in the first place. Within six months of Pratt's pronouncements, the Japanese fielded the world's most advanced fighter plane, the Zero, against the Chinese. Its existence went unnoticed by the smug American and British military.

On December 4, 1941, Secretary of the Navy Frank Knox told a group of top Washington bureaucrats that the United States would be at war with the Japanese within the week. (The Americans had broken Tokyo's diplomatic code and knew there was an attack forthcoming somewhere.

They never dreamt the target would be Pearl Harbor.) The bureaucrats goggled and asked agitated questions. Knox serenely dismissed their concern. It would only take six months at the outside to demolish the Japanese, he assured them. Then the United States would go to work on the Germans.

In *Time and Tide*, Arthur McKay has spent many years in the Far East and does not share this racist prejudice. At one point, he writes to his wife, Rita: "We're fighting brave men out here. Some of the best damn sailors and fliers who ever put to sea." McKay also understands why the Japanese are at war. He tells of finding a Tokyo-issued book on the body of a dead Japanese pilot, *Read This and the War is Won*. It described how in China, Malaya, Indo-China, and other parts of the Far East, a few thousand white men were squeezing profits out of five hundred million Asians. "I agree with every word of it!" McKay writes.

McKay also takes exception to Admiral William "Bull" Halsey's directive: "Kill Japs, kill Japs and keep on killing Japs." McKay doubts that strategy was ever war-gamed at the Naval War College. The captain's stance has ample support in John W. Dower's extraordinary book, *War Without Mercy*, about the appalling racism that permeated America's war with Japan. Tokyo, it should be noted, replied by virulently demonizing the white race.

When Arthur McKay is onstage, *Time and Tide* sometimes sounds like an antiwar tract—an interesting notion to find in the context of our supposedly Good War. One suspects Fleming has imbibed not a little of Benjamin Franklin's attitude (he has written a biography of Ben) as summarized in that pithy line the good doctor wrote to an English friend: "There never was a good war or a bad peace."

Besides McKay, there is a gallery of portraits drawn from the *Jefferson City*'s crew, many of whom develop other pertinent historical themes. One of the most interesting characters is a veritable man of war, barrel-shaped boatswain's mate first class Ernest Homewood, with twenty-eight years of hash marks (symbols of reenlistments) on his sleeve. Around his neck is his badge of office, the ancient bo'sun's pipe that his predecessors had been shrilling in sailors' ears for centuries.

Homewood would have been equally undaunted facing Moby-Dick aboard Ahab's *Pequod* or Spanish men-of-war aboard Sir Francis Drake's

Golden Hind. He would have given either captain the same compulsive devotion he offers Arthur McKay—and he would have treated the men under his immediate command with the same ferocious combination of bravado and paternalism. Homewood and his breed are the warriors who make the *Jefferson City* a warship. He turns reluctant civilians like Frank Flanagan into fighting sailors whether they like it or not.

At his direction finder in the exposed superstructure of the *Jefferson City*, Fire Controlman Flanagan gradually becomes a grim-eyed killer, training his forty-millimeter guns on oncoming Japanese planes—including, as the war progresses, the dreaded kamikazes. *Time and Tide* is a graphic demonstration of what historian David M. Kennedy has aptly dubbed "the war of the machines"—the inner secret of America's triumph in World War II. Flanagan grows more and more confident in his country's technological superiority as the number of planes and ships around him multiplies exponentially and new weapons such as the proximity fuse enable him and his shipmates to wreak ever-increasing havoc on the enemy. The *Jefferson City* becomes the flagship of Admiral Raymond Spruance's immense Fifth Fleet, an entity that engulfs the horizon in all directions.

Fleming manages to explore another interesting historical theme, even though most of the novel takes place in the far reaches of the vast Pacific: the women in the sailors' lives. He tackles this tricky subject boldly in his introduction: *At the risk of his reputation, the historian talks of women sharing, surviving the voyage of the USS Jefferson City. It is simply the truth, although only a handful of them ever walked her decks.*

Through Arthur McKay's brusque wife, Rita, daughter of an admiral, we gain eye-opening glimpses of internecine World War II navy politics and the lifestyle of the prewar navy on the China Station. Rita's sister, Lucy, is married to Win Kemble. She is the ethereal opposite of her earthy, aggressive sibling. After Win Kemble kills himself like his historical model, the captain of the *Chicago*, a grief-stricken McKay offers his love to Lucy. To his astonishmentt, Lucy tells him at Savo Island Win deliberately sailed the *Jefferson City* away from the enemy because he was overwhelmed by disgust with the premature war that Roosevelt had provoked with Japan and the brainless way the navy was fighting it. Lucy also reveals her long-concealed hatred of the navy, rooted in the way her admiral father humiliated her mother with his perpetual womanizing.

The stunned McKay decides Win was wrong. He had violated the obligation to put his ship in harm's way, the U.S. Navy's oldest, proudest tradition, first voiced by John Paul Jones aboard *Bonhomme Richard*. McKay decides he respects this tradition, in spite of his spasms of antagonism to the navy's ways. The captain stumbles back to the *Jefferson City* and realizes that the ship has become the only meaningful thing in his life. He vows to give her the best leadership that is in him.

Here Fleming advances another historically significant concept—one that obviously interests him a great deal—the struggle that intelligent military men undergo to sustain their admiration, even their love, for the service to which they have given their lives. In *The Officers' Wives*, it becomes a major issue in the career of Adam Thayer, a West Point intellectual who sets himself up as the U.S. Army's foremost critic. He ends his career a bitter, wasted man. His nonintellectual wife, Honor, sees what has gone wrong. "Adam, you've lost your way," she tells him. He has failed to love the army while she, paradoxically, has managed this difficult challenge.

Arthur McKay is a more complex and nuanced character than Adam Thayer. During a storm at sea, he gets into a conversation with Montgomery West, a movie actor turned officer, who has had a difficult time adjusting to the *Jefferson City*. McKay talks about the importance of luck in a sailor's view of the cosmos. When West says he doesn't believe in rituals or charms, McKay opines that it's just a sailor's way of admitting no man can control something as huge and menacing as the ocean. He compares it to reciting the navy hymn. West confesses he doesn't know the words and McKay recites them in a quiet, casual voice.

> *Eternal father, strong to save*
> *Whose arm doth bind the restless wave*
> *Who bids't the mighty ocean deep*
> *Its own appointed limits keep*
> *O hear us when we cry to thee*
> *For those in peril on the sea.*

West realizes he is in the presence of something authentic. McKay took the words seriously, if not literally, as part of a tradition to which they all belonged. "That makes me almost glad I joined the Navy," West says.

"Every so often I feel the same way, almost glad," McKay replies.

In his oblique, wary style, the captain also gets involved in another important aspect of the wartime shipboard experience: religious faith. The theme is sounded in the opening chapter, when historian/novelist Flanagan remarks that every sailor believes—or at least hopes—that his ship is a dot in the eye of God. "That is a comforting thought," Flanagan/Fleming writes, "even if the nature of that God is in doubt in every honest sailor's mind."

Boats Homewood fills Flanagan's lapsed Catholic soul with the ancient superstitions of the sea. In the boatswain's cosmos, perpetual war rages between good spirits and evil spirits, with the captain the mediating figure. If his "joss" (a metaphor drawn from incense burnt in Chinese temples) is good, the ship will survive storms, shells, and torpedoes.

The *Jefferson City*'s chaplain, Emerson Bushnell, is a nondenominational pacifist with no real religious convictions. He is also more than a little hostile to the military, often criticizing the navy's "authoritarian" ways. McKay startles him by maintaining that it looks as if the navy's system is based on fear. But it is really based on faith. Homewood verifies this statement repeatedly, but Bushnell, the elitist intellectual personified, is barely aware of his existence.

Later, McKay asks Bushnell if he knew what Win Kemble did at Savo. Bushnell admits he knew—and agreed with Win's "position" on the war. Furiously, McKay says, "He came to you, the only priest around, in search of forgiveness. Instead you discussed politics with him! Jesus Christ, Chaplain, when are you going to start doing your job?"

What interests the historian in these explosions of doubt and belief aboard the *Jefferson City* is the utter absence of ideology. Not once does any officer or sailor so much as mention the Four Freedoms, the Atlantic Charter, the Century of the Common Man, or any of the other slogans with which American politicians tried to ennoble the war. This absence of political purpose is one of the many surprises uncovered by recent research into the supposedly Good War. In a 1998 article in the *Journal of*

American History 85(1) (June 1998), Benjamin L. Alpers noted a study by the Office of War Information which found one out of three servicemen had never even heard of the Four Freedoms and only one out of ten could name all four.

All right, you say: the saga of the *Jefferson City* is the stuff of history. But is it the real thing? Even when we find out everything that Captain Arthur McKay eventually learns about the *Jefferson City* at Savo Island, we don't get the whole story of the battle. From an historian's point of view, that is one of the larger flaws of historical novels. They create the illusion of delivering history to the reader, but they inevitably fall wide of the mark.

Unquestionably, a complete historical account of Savo is a very different kind of thing. Perhaps because it was such a calamitous defeat, not until 1997 did a thorough treatment of the battle appear—*The Shame of Savo*, by Commodore Bruce Loxton of the Royal Australian Navy. Loxton had been a midshipman aboard one of the ships sunk, HMAS *Canberra*.

Loxton tells a tangled tale of confusion and panic among American captains in combat for the first time against a Japanese foe who had brought night-fighting techniques to a state of deadly effectiveness. In his account, HMAS *Canberra* is accidentally torpedoed by an American destroyer, the captains of other ships refuse to fire without orders that never arrive, the commanding admirals, ashore on Guadalcanal, have ignored warnings from Australian patrol planes about the oncoming Japanese cruisers and left their ships without a battle plan or, for that matter, a commander.

Loxton declines to speculate about what happened aboard the USS *Chicago*. He notes that there is a paucity of information from the crew and the captain's statements in defense of his actions make no sense. He wryly concludes her behavior was "extraordinary." *Chicago* is not the centerpiece of the book. By far the greater part of Loxton's narrative concerns the Australian patrol planes, the Allies divided command structure, and what was happening on the other ships, in particular *HMAS Canberra*. He also devotes many pages to the weaponry, tactics, and command decisions aboard the attacking Japanese warships.

An historian could make similar complaints about the *Jefferson City*'s story when she joins the outgunned American fleet in the desperate series of sea battles that were fought during the six-month struggle for Guadalcanal. We see these horrendous night encounters through the eyes of Captain McKay and other officers and enlisted men in the *Jefferson City*'s crew—not exactly objective observers. The big picture eludes all of them, including McKay, who is so depressed by the second-rate American admirals and their atrocious strategy and tactics, he takes to drink in his cabin.

The historian may also choose to make ominous noises during the latter part of the book, when the *Jefferson City* assumes the identities of several other cruisers. Off the Aleutians, she becomes the USS *Salt Lake City*, a key player in the little-known battle of the Kamandorski Islands, where Captain McKay demonstrates an uncanny ability to outguess Japanese gunners as they "walk" dozens of murderous salvos across the icy, fog-shrouded ocean.

Returning to California for repairs, the *Jefferson City* is ordered to San Francisco to pick up a top-secret cargo. It is the atomic bomb, being shipped to Tinian for its fateful rendezvous with Hiroshima. Now the cruiser is becoming the USS *Indianapolis*. McKay confesses doubts about the bomb to Admiral Raymond Spruance, who comments acerbically against using it. The admiral and the captain have similar low-keyed roundhead personalities. They also share a detestation for Cominch Ernest King—and a dislike of Franklin D. Roosevelt's vengeful policy of unconditional surrender.

Here *Time and Tide* sails into even more controversial waters. One historian-reviewer pointed out there was nothing in the written record to support Spruance's opposition to the bomb. Novelist Fleming may have something to say in response to this charge in the companion essay of this exploration of his split literary personality.

A week after delivering the bomb, the *Jefferson City* meets the *Indianapolis*'s fate. She is torpedoed, en route to the Philippines. Captain McKay, trapped in his stateroom, his back broken by the blast, orders the survivors to abandon ship. As he dies, he has a vision of Win Kemble, urging him to choose the eternal loneliness of the naysayer. McKay refuses, glimpsing a meaning in his own and his ship's agony that connects to the terrible weapon she has carried to Tinian.

For a nightmarish four days, the *Jefferson City*'s survivors await rescue in their waterlogged life jackets. Many die painful deaths. Some act selfishly. Most demonstrate the sense of brotherhood Captain McKay has struggled to foster among them. Chaplain Bushnell finds faith and gives his life jacket to a sailor without one. Boats Homewood swims from raft to raft, assuring everyone that his beloved navy will not abandon them. Ultimately, even his awesome physical strength falters.

The navy finally rescues the survivors and Admiral Spruance visits the hospital in Guam to apologize for the failure to get them swift help. From him, they learn the war is over, thanks to the atomic bomb, dropped in spite of his and Captain McKay's forebodings. In this mournful epiphany, both the sailors and the man who commanded the tremendous Fifth Fleet implicitly confess their mutual awareness that God presides over history for His own mysterious purposes. Again, the historian notes the utter absence of the politicians' pale ideology of antimilitarism and antifascism. *Time and Tide*'s voyage pursues larger concerns.

In its later pages, *Time and Tide* carries an ever-larger freight of historical reality. The historian is tempted to admit that while a dozen characters and a single ship may not sum up the entire Pacific War, they can deliver a hefty slice of it. After all, no single book can grasp the war's stupendous entirety. Historians are still reporting discoveries about the attack on Pearl Harbor and the decision to drop the atomic bomb. While *Time and Tide* cannot claim to deliver new factual information of this sort, it unquestionably enhances our understanding of an epic experience in American history.

ЛР

(Novelist) Thomas Fleming Responds

Historians are driven by curiosity and a desire to find a pattern in the unnerving randomness of history. Novelists are driven by visions. Almost all my novels have originated in a flash of imagination so overpowering I was sometimes left immobilized for several minutes.

Historians have flashes, too—of insight, of theory. But they usually come from immersing themselves in a subject. My book *1776: Year of Illusions* organized itself around that title after three years of struggling to construct a narrative of the year of America's birth.

Novels are much more mysterious. The central vision of *Time and Tide*, the suppurating conflicted friendship between democratic Arthur McKay and aristocratic Winfield Scott Schley Kemble, leaped into my head while I was reading Samuel Eliot Morison's account of the battle of Savo Island. I had been in the U.S. Navy at the close of World War II, serving as a fire controlman aboard the light cruiser USS *Topeka*. For twenty-five years, I had made sporadic attempts to write a novel about the navy with no success. It always petered out after a few dozen pages.

Suddenly T&T was *there*—McKay relieving Kemble, their very different sister-wives, the faithless chaplain, Bushnell, "Boats" Homewood with his ancient superstitions and his worship of the navy, the actor Montgomery West discovering the difference between the real navy and Hollywood's version. Above all, the *Jefferson City*, a paradigm of America's search for that perpetually elusive ideal, brotherhood. The only thing I didn't know at first was the ship's name—which I chose after I went through a list of heavy cruisers in the Pacific war, many named after state capitals. Jefferson City was not among them.

A reviewer in the *Chicago Sun-Times* caught the book's symbolic overtones and compared it to *Moby-Dick*. Other reviewers seemed more impressed by the novel's realism. One exclaimed that before it was over, the reader became part of the crew, experiencing their fear, their rage, their desperation. Here, as in many of my other novels, my historian's appetite for research has enabled me to pour in a wealth of details.

I have occasionally wondered whether my realism conflicts with my deeper novelistic purposes. This may have been the case in *Time and Tide*. The reality of shipboard life in wartime is so strange, so often horrendous, it may easily overwhelm other perceptions—and inadvertently lead to confusing fiction's realism with the very different facts of history.

Moby-Dick is a towering comparison which I would not have dared to make myself. But any American who writes about the sea has to have his head full of Melville, and I am no exception. He has been a strong influence in my writing life ever since college days. Not just *Moby-Dick*, but his poems (I have "The Eagle of the Blue" pasted on my study wall), his other novels, particularly *The Confidence Man*, with its searing vision of America on the make, and *Billy Budd*, his sad, desperate attempt to resolve the mundane and metaphysical contradictions that tormented him—and still harrow us.

I see now—it never occurred to me when I was writing the novel—that Captain McKay is my anti-Ahab. He flinches at the individual and systemic failures around him. But he somehow maintains his American faith in the essential goodness, rightness of the human enterprise, even unto the moment of final desolation, as the *Jefferson City* sinks.

McKay (and Kemble) are totally creatures of my historical imagination. With Homewood, memory played a part. He is the only real character I imported intact, down to his symbolic name, from my days aboard the USS *Topeka*. Many a night I and other sailors in F (for Firecontrol) Division used to hoist him into his rack after he returned from liberty, often escorted by a half-dozen cursing shore patrolmen who told the officer of the deck how he wrecked yet another bar or brothel. We listened to his drunken retelling of the story of his life, from the sharecropper's shack in Alabama to his wild youth in Shanghai and Hong Kong on the China Station. He was the living, breathing, brawling personification of the ultimate sailor. I loved the man. He made me glad I had joined the navy, Arthur McKay–style—almost.

(Unlike his fictional counterpart, the real "Homewood" survived the war and spent twelve peacetime months trying to talk me into going to Annapolis. I told him in my best Seaman I/C-proletarian style that if I ever went near that #%!&! nursery of the officer corps, I would try to blow it up. When I became editor of the ship's paper in the closing months of my naval career, Homewood despaired: "FLEMING!" he roared. "YOU'VE BECOME A GODDAMN YEOMAN!")

The Homewood of memory is similar but not the same as the man in *Time and Tide*. He has been altered—"expanded" is perhaps a better word—by becoming part of the imaginary world of the *Jefferson City*. These inevitable transmutations have led me to dislike the term "historical novel." I much prefer "novels of the historical imagination"—underscoring by implication that the novel is not competing with the history book. It has also led me, with the help of Cornell intellectual historian

Cushing Strout, to reject the idea that the novelist's imagination merely "makes things up." Strout's book, *The Veracious Imagination* (a term originally used by George Eliot), argues that the imagination is an intellectual tool, just as potent as the historian's analytic approach for discovering an important aspect of the historical experience—how history impacts on individuals—and how individuals respond to the crises of the mind and heart—the spiritual dimension of human experience—that history evokes.

Samuel Eliot Morison once remarked that the public, when it reads history at all, prefers it in the "painless" form of the historical novel. I thought wryly of that comment after I published *Time and Tide*. I received many reproachful letters from readers, crying out, "You let so many of them die!" Too many people think the novelist can decide how his story ends—which is almost as erroneous as presuming an historian can decide how his narrative of 1776 or the Battle of the Argonne ends.

At the same time, the novelist must remain true to an 1890s exhortation by William Francis Allen, the mentor of Frederick Jackson Turner, that the historical fiction writer should feed his imagination with the accurate scholarship of the historian. I have found this important, not only because realistic details are vital to achieving the reader's suspension of disbelief. In *Time and Tide* and other novels, research has often deepened my narrative.

From an interview with the former executive officer of the USS *Enterprise*, I learned that there were "wet ships" during World War II, where the captain tolerated liquor. (This was not the case aboard my own ship, the USS *Topeka*. Bringing liquor aboard was a court-martial offense.) This discovery added a crucial dimension to my characterizations of McKay and others aboard the *Jefferson City*. McKay drunk was able to say many things he could never have expressed while sober.

From interviewing veterans of the ships that fought off Guadalcanal, I got firsthand memories of those nightmarish night battles, including scathing comments on the awful tactics of the first series of American admirals. I added insights from Fletcher Pratt's superb narratives of these battles, which more than redeemed his early foolishness concerning Japanese fighting abilities.

From a diary of Ward Bronson, a lieutenant junior grade aboard the

USS *Chicago*, I picked up the rage of the navy's regulars at Roosevelt and the admirals who backed him in provoking Japan into war before the Americans had the ships and men to fight them on equal terms.

From research on Admiral Spruance, I discovered his postwar hostility to dropping the atomic bomb, making it plausible that he would comment to someone he trusted, such as Captain Arthur McKay, against its use on the eve of Hiroshima. The underlying hostility between the branches of the American military machine made this remark even more probable. The Navy had won the war and now the insufferable Army Air Force would steal credit for the final victory!

I can summon the great-grandfather of the historical novel (I guess we can't escape the term), James Fenimore Cooper, to support me on Admiral Spruance. Cooper maintained the novelist was permitted to "garnish a probable fact" while an historian should "record facts as they occurred" without fear or favor. At the same time, Cooper warned that the novelist should not "dwell on improbable truths." That latter point is important to Cushing Strout, too. He calls this tendency "the voracious imagination," in which the truth is devoured in a narrative that contradicts the known facts of historical events or the characters of the real participants. I took considerable pains to avoid this flaw in *Time and Tide*.

Above all, if the novelist's historical imagination is working at the top of its form, is the vision. Through Arthur McKay and his crew, I tried to give readers not the history of the navy's Pacific war but an exploration of the American soul in a time of terrific crisis. Though I drew on some of my historian's research techniques, my discoveries were transmuted by my (hopefully) veracious imagination.

In an epilogue, *Time and Tide* is finished, but my alter ego, historian Frank Flanagan, decides to wait a week, to see if further messages emerged from the mysterious depths in which books were born. Flanagan does not expect any for this book. Long before he reached the last page, it had become a living thing, more and more indifferent to its creator. He sums up the ultimate goal of the novelist's art in the last line. *Beyond memory, beyond the vagaries of time, the moon-tugged tides of circumstance, the* Jefferson City *voyaged toward eternity.*

Kicking the Denial
Syndrome: Tim O'Brien's
In the Lake of the Woods

H. Bruce Franklin

"They were only war casualties," he said. "It was a pity, but you can't always hit your target. Anyway, they died in the right cause."
>   —*Graham Greene*, The Quiet American, *1955*

We didn't know who we were till we got here. We thought we were something else.
>   —*Robert Stone*, Dog Soldiers, *1974*

In the colleges and high schools I sometimes visit, the mention of My Lai brings on null stares, a sort of puzzlement, disbelief mixed with utter ignorance. Evil has no place, it seems, in our national mythology. We erase it.
>   —*Tim O'Brien, "The Vietnam in Me," 1994*

Denial" has been, in every sense, the term necessary to fathom the depths of deception and delusion essential to America's war in Vietnam. Denial is therefore a central theme, maybe the main theme, in that astonishing body of literature produced by American veterans of that war. Denial is certainly at the heart of the works of Tim O'Brien, perhaps the greatest American fiction writer to come out of that war, especially in his 1994 novel *In the Lake of the Woods*, about a domestic tragedy in the life of an American politician who attempts to deny his participation in the most infamous Vietnam atrocity, the 1968 massacre of hundreds of women, old men, children, and babies in the village of My Lai.

When the men in the White House and Pentagon decided in 1945 to support France's attempt to recolonize Vietnam, they tried from the beginning to keep their actions secret. When they decided to send Americans to fight in Vietnam, they conspired at first to wage war covertly, later to conceal how the war was being conducted, and finally to expunge the memory of the entire affair or bury it under mounds of false images. Moreover, U.S. policy toward Vietnam was continually based on a total denial of Vietnamese history and culture. After mid-1954, that policy also depended on a denial of the Geneva Accords, the origin and character of Ngo Dinh Diem's dictatorship in Saigon, and the indigenous roots of the revolution against his regime.

One meaning of denial is *claiming* that something is not true or does not exist. For example, President John F. Kennedy denied any involvement in the 1963 coup he had personally approved against Ngo Dinh Diem. When Kennedy himself was assassinated three weeks after Diem was killed in this coup, one of the first acts of his successor, Lyndon Johnson, was secretly to authorize a plan (National Security Action Memorandum 273) for covert air, sea, and land attacks against North Vietnam as a prelude to a full-scale U.S. war. Part of the plan called for an assessment of whether the American people would believe the president and the Pentagon when they denied doing what they were doing. That section was entitled "Plausibility of Denial."[1]

Another meaning of denial is *believing* that something is not true or does not exist despite convincing evidence. This is a psychological condition, and it can become a chronic disease of an individual or even a culture. The various forms of denial of the Vietnam War and of the people, history, culture, and even the very nation of Vietnam have spread widely and deeply in American politics, psychology, and culture.

Throughout the decades that the United States was waging war in Vietnam, even during those years when the war had become an agonizing national crisis, no incoming president uttered the word "Vietnam" in his inaugural address.[2] The first presidential inaugural speech to mention the word "Vietnam" came in 1981, when Ronald Reagan included "a place called Vietnam" in a list of battlefields where Americans had fought in the twentieth century. Then at last in 1989, a newly elected president used the taboo word to tell the nation what to do about the Vietnam War: forget it.

It was George Bush who broke the silence with these words: "The final lesson of Vietnam is that no great nation can long afford to be sundered by a memory." The president's usage of the term reflected what had become standard in American speech. "Vietnam" was no longer a country or even "a place called Vietnam." It had become a war, an American war. Or maybe not even a war. It had become an American tragedy, an event that had divided and wounded America. The grotesque title of one widely adopted history textbook reveals far more than intended: *Vietnam: An American Ordeal.*[3]

President Bush's inaugural speech blamed "Vietnam" for the "divisiveness," the "hard looks" in Congress, the challenging of "each other's motives," and the fact that "our great parties have too often been far apart and untrusting of each other." "It has been this way since Vietnam," he lamented. Two years later, gloating over what seemed America's glorious defeat of Iraq, President Bush jubilantly proclaimed to a nation festooned in jingoist yellow ribbons, "By God, we've kicked the Vietnam syndrome once and for all!"[4]

The "Vietnam syndrome" phrase had been introduced into America's cultural vocabulary in a 1980 campaign speech by Ronald Reagan to the Veterans of Foreign Wars, the same speech in which he redefined the Vietnam War as "a noble cause."[5] For the war to be seen as a noble cause, its history had to be thoroughly rewritten and reimaged, a national cultural project assiduously performed throughout the presidencies of Reagan (1981–1989) and Bush (1989–1993). The actual history of U.S. warfare in Vietnam was buried under layer after layer of falsification, fabrication, illusion, and myth. A growing part of the vision was an artfully retouched image of the war that simply erases the Vietnamese from the picture altogether. The cultural march from demonization of the Vietnamese in the late 1970s to eradication in the 1990s was graphically displayed by Hollywood. Whereas the Academy Award for the Best Picture of 1978 went to *The Deer Hunter*, with its meticulously reversed images of victims and victimizers, the winner of the Academy Award for the Best

Picture of 1994 was *Forrest Gump*, which projects Vietnam as merely an uninhabited jungle that for inscrutable reasons shoots at American soldiers.

Tim O'Brien's novel *In the Lake of the Woods*, which appeared the same year as *Forrest Gump*, confronts all this denial. It challenges readers to swim through treacherous vortices churned by the confluence of the Vietnam War, the meaning of fiction, and the role of denial in the lives of individuals and the American nation. O'Brien provided a most useful navigational aid for this chilling journey in the form of a companion piece, a painfully revealing memoir entitled "The Vietnam in Me," published as the cover story of the October 2, 1994, *New York Times Magazine*, a month before the publication date of the novel.

As O'Brien explains in "The Vietnam in Me," he knew that America's war in Vietnam was wrong and so he participated in peace vigils, wrote "earnest editorials" against the war for his college newspaper, and rang doorbells for presidential peace candidate Eugene McCarthy in 1968. But he then marched off to fight in the very war he considered "probably evil."[6] So from his first book, the somewhat fictionalized autobiography *If I Die in a Combat Zone* (1973), right on through *In the Lake of the Woods*, denial—both personal and national—has been a central theme of O'Brien's writing.

The most revealing chapter in *If I Die in a Combat Zone*, entitled "Escape," exposes the core of his own denial. Recognizing that if he kills people in a war he knows to be immoral he will be jeopardizing his very "soul," he decides his only moral choice is to desert. But he discovers that he lacks the courage. He lets himself be sent off to Vietnam, he confesses, because "I was a coward."[7]

This confession—that cowardice kept him from making the moral choice of running away rather than becoming a killer—appears again and again in O'Brien's writings, sometimes elaborately sublimated, sometimes candidly blunt. It is central to his 1978 novel *Going After Cacciato*, winner of the 1979 National Book Award and often hailed as the great American Vietnam War novel, a book all about soldiers trying to run away from the war, in body and in mind. In the climax of an escapist fantasy, the protagonist announces to the world. "I am afraid of running away. . . . I fear what might be thought of me by those I love. . . . I fear the loss of my own reputation. . . . I fear being thought of as a coward. I fear that even more than cowardice itself."[8]

In *The Things They Carried*, O'Brien's award-winning 1990 collection of somewhat autobiographical Vietnam stories (labeled *A Work of Fiction*), the narrator—named Tim O'Brien—tells "one story I've never told before," the story of his life's crucial event, which takes place on the Rainy River between Minnesota and Canada. "For more than twenty years," he reveals, "I've had to live with . . . the shame" of the moment when, just yards from Canada, he didn't flee the draft because "I did not want people to think badly of me": "My conscience told me to run," but, he confesses, "I was ashamed of my conscience, ashamed to be doing the right thing." The final words of "On the Rainy River" are: "I was a coward. I went to the war."[9] In the *New York Times Magazine* memoir, he repeats, "I was a coward. I went to Vietnam" (p. 52). Therefore, each thing he did in Vietnam "was an act of the purest self-hatred and self-betrayal" (p. 53).

This awareness generates for O'Brien a tortured dialectic of concealment and exposure, which in turn spins the dazzlingly intricate webs of imagination and memory that constitute his fiction. Central to the conception of all his works labeled fiction is an almost intractable contradiction between what O'Brien calls "happening-truth" and "story-truth." As he puts it in *The Things They Carried*, although all stories—including accounts that purport to tell what actually happened—are "made up," "story-truth is truer sometimes than happening-truth" (p. 203).

Many critics have radically misinterpreted O'Brien's fictional webs, praising them as projections of the Vietnam War as unknowable or crazy or "unreal." O'Brien himself as early as 1984 attacked such interpretations for promoting the phony idea that "we're all innocent by reason of insanity; the war was crazy, and therefore we're innocent": "For me, Vietnam wasn't an unreal experience, it wasn't absurd. It was a cold-blooded, calculated war."[10]

The reality of that war, which can be denied but not escaped, underlies every page of *In the Lake of the Woods*. The main action takes place in late 1986, when that reality had been nearly buried under Ramboism and national amnesia. It is set near the mouth of the Rainy River—where O'Brien had located his own fateful choice—on the Minnesota edge of the Lake of the Woods, whose labyrinthine shoreline of twenty-five thousand miles extends deep into the Canadian wilderness. Vietnam veteran and would-be U.S. senator John Wade has just suffered a humiliating defeat in the primary because it was revealed that he had taken part in the 1968 My Lai massacre and then altered his service record to conceal his participation. He and his wife, Kathy, from whom he had also hidden his dreadful secret, have fled to a remote cabin, where they are futilely attempting to resurrect their relationship and their lives, built, as they now both know, on layers of concealment, illusion, and lies. On the seventh night, Kathy vanishes along with the only boat at the cabin. More than a month later, John borrows another small boat, ostensibly to search for her, heads into the remote recesses of the lake, and also disappears.

On one level, the book is a mystery story, with multiple solutions. What happened to Kathy Wade? Did she wander off and die accidentally? Did she deliberately flee, either alone or with a lover? Is she still lost in the wilderness? Did she and John conspire to disappear together and begin a new life? Or did John murder her? All of these are presented as "hypotheses," but the novel is not quite as indeterminate or unresolved as it may seem. Some of the hypotheses could not have happened, others may possibly have happened, and one evidently did happen. But how do fictional events "happen"? After all, don't they take place entirely in the imagination of author and reader? Don't fictional characters themselves exist only in the minds of people who create or translate the verbal symbols of which they are composed? O'Brien thrusts into this paradox and into the center of his fictional mystery the most terrifying facts of American personal and historical experience in Vietnam.

The purported author of *In the Lake of the Woods* is a Vietnam veteran whose own experience closely resembles that of Tim O'Brien. For this fictitious character, the book is not a novel at all but a profoundly disturbing investigation and exploration of a real-life mystery, the disappearance of a flesh-and-blood woman named Kathy Wade. The investigation takes him deeply into the life of John Wade, whose experience in Vietnam and afterward closely resembles his own. The trail leads him into the midst of the hideous massacre at My Lai, and thence to the significance of My Lai not just in the history of the Vietnam War but also in the history of the American nation back to its origin in continental genocide.

One fifth of the book consists of seven chapters entitled "Evidence," including 133 footnotes from this ostensible author. The first of these chapters consists of pure fiction: exhibits from fictional events and documents; statements from fictional characters, including interviews the "author" conducts with people who, like himself, exist only in the pages of this book. As the novel takes us deeper into its troubled waters, however, actual historical materials, including quotations from articles and books such as a Lyndon Johnson biography and Richard Nixon's *Six Crises*, begin to take over these "Evidence" chapters. And as the massacre at My Lai moves ever closer to the core of the novel, both the fictional and actual authors become real historians, reporting on their own research at the site of the atrocity and inserting passages of testimony from the trial of Lieutenant William Calley and other materials about the event, accurately footnoted to their sources: *Report of the Department of the Army Review of the Preliminary Investigation into the My Lai Incident*, Volume I, Department of the Army, 1970; Richard Hammer, *The Court-Martial of Lt. Calley* (New York: Coward, McCann & Geoghegan, 1971); Michael Bilton and Kevin Sim, *Four Hours in My Lai* (New York: Viking, 1992). Even here, however, O'Brien's prestidigitation mingles history and fiction; amid quotations from actual participants in the massacre are some from fictional participant Richard Thinbill, documented by citations to invented folders in the National Archives.[11] The fictitious author only gradually reveals his identity as a Vietnam veteran who (like O'Brien) fought in My Lai's province of Quang Ngai, has his own dreadful secrets about what he did there, and wrote this book to exorcise "the long decades of silence and lies and secrecy": "To give me back my vanished life."[12]

This fictional character who writes the book ends by suggesting that we readers can choose to believe whichever solution we wish to the mystery of what happened to Kathy Wade. Each possibility is dramatized in one of the eight chapters entitled "Hypothesis," where it is liberally sprinkled with "maybe" and "perhaps," emphasizing its fictive nature. Except for one, every hypothesis contains details that are inconsistent with the main narrative. For example, the first two hypotheses, that she drove off with a secret lover or simply got lost in the woods near the cabin, do not account for the fact that the boat is missing from the boathouse. The next hypothesis, that she was zooming across the lake at such high speed that she was hurled from the boat, is contradicted by the fact that the boat was powered by an old 1.6-horsepower outboard motor. And so on. The one hypothesis that does not contain contradictions is also the only one filled with details consistent with the main fictive narrative. And it is also the only one that makes the horrors of My Lai, and its denial, relevant to the horror and denial at the center of John Wade's life and relation to Kathy.

Indeed, every other hypothesis involves some form of escape from the hideous event that did happen, an event recalled in fragments that float to the surface in the chapters "What He Remembered," "How the Night Passed," and "What He Did Next," titles indicating the actuality that can be remembered—or denied. Although John apparently cannot remember whether or not he murdered his wife, enough details bubble up from the depths of his memory—not his imagination—to allow readers to reconstruct the gruesome scene. Unless, O'Brien suggests, readers would rather indulge in elaborate fantasies of denial.

On the night of Kathy's disappearance, John got out of bed in a murderous rage, poured a kettle of boiling water on each houseplant in the cabin, and then poured another kettle of boiling water on Kathy's face. Fragments of her screaming death agony, buried deep under strata of denial, later keep erupting from Wade's memory. He next concealed the crime by carefully weighting both her body and the boat and then burying them at the bottom of the lake. He thus reenacts once again the murder committed at My Lai and his attempts to expunge all records—and memory—of this act that was too awful to be possible.

My Lai, in Wade's mind, has become just a nightmare of "impossible events": "This could not have happened. Therefore it did not" (p. 109). The most grisly detail of Kathy's death, repeated several times in the novel, evokes the same response:

Puffs of steam rose from the sockets of her eyes.
Impossible, of course. (P. 84)

But My Lai did happen, as we know. Or do we? That is the most troubling question posed by the novel, which includes page after page of the actual testimony and other evidence of the massacre that was not an aberration but a sample of how the United States conducted its genocidal warfare against the people of Vietnam.[13] As Jonathan Schell revealed before the My Lai massacre, 70 percent of the villages of this entire region had already been annihilated by the fall of 1967; Schell also documented, from written materials and interviews, the fact that this was part of an official policy of terrorizing and massacring all civilians deemed sympathetic to the insurgents.[14] At My Lai, American soldiers did not just slaughter as many as five hundred unarmed people. They also sodomized young girls, raped women in front of their children, bayoneted children in front of their mothers, and used babies for target practice.[15] Does John Wade's frenzied murder of the houseplants seem "impossible"? Then, suggests O'Brien, so must Lieutenant Calley's actions: "He reloaded and shot the grass and a palm tree and then the earth again. 'Grease the place,' he said. 'Kill it' " (p. 103). This was, after all, the U.S. strategy for much of Vietnam, especially My Lai's province of Quang Ngai, as O'Brien, citing Schell and his own experience, reminds us in "The Vietnam in Me":

> In the years preceding the murders at My Lai, more than 70 percent of the villages in this province had been destroyed by air strikes, artillery fire, Zippo lighters, napalm, white phosphorus, bulldozers, gunships and other such means. . . . Back in 1969, the wreckage was all around us. . . . Wreckage was the rule. Brutality was S.O.P. Scalded children, pistol-whipped women, burning hootches, free-fire zones, body counts, indiscriminate bombing and harassment fire, villages in ash, M-60 machine guns hosing down dark green tree lines and any human life behind them. (P. 53)

In Vietnam, John Wade was so adept at making things disappear that he acquired the nickname Sorcerer. He had perfected his magic expertise as a young boy, who needed it to build means of denial about his own identity as the son of an alcoholic father who killed himself. Performing his magic tricks before a mirror, John had learned how to construct mirrors inside his own mind to deflect reality and to hide behind. Wade is a magician, a master of illusion. And so is O'Brien, who is such a wizard of narrative that he can make the most implausible fantasies seem believable. But this does not mean that in *In the Lake of the Woods* (any more than in *Going After Cacciato*), the products of imagination have the same ontological status as actual material events. Magic, O'Brien recognizes, is an art of illusion.

Of course, imaginary events are also *real*. Although Wade's murder of his wife, just like the fantasies of escape offered as alternatives to it, is a fiction that takes place only in a novel, each scenario, whether remembered or merely imagined, has the reality offered by fiction, what O'Brien calls "story-truth."

Inverting the conventions of the mystery novel, O'Brien opts to leave the mystery to be solved by the reader's imagination. We are free to choose any of the hypotheses, even one that contradicts the evidence, which itself is fictional. Of course that freedom is also something of a trap, because our choice may be more revealing than a Rorschach test.

Not everything, however, is fiction. There is another kind of reality— what he calls "happening-truth"—such as the 1968 events at My Lai and O'Brien's own experience around My Lai the following year. Because John Wade, Kathy, and the "actual" and "imagined" events of that night all exist entirely in words and in the imagination of O'Brien and his readers, the fictive murder may or may not have "actually" occurred. But there is literally a world of difference between this act of the imagination and what happened in Vietnam. In that actuality, as O'Brien tells us over and over again, he himself, like his fictive John Wade and the American nation he represents, committed acts so horrible that they continually evoke denial.

And then there is the actual political world of 1980s and 1990s America, in which Wade's fictional Senate campaign is firmly located. In that political world, it is not what Wade *did* in Vietnam that devastates his candidacy and thus destroys his life, but rather his concealment and falsification—that is, words, verbal constructs, *fictions*. As his cynical campaign manager points out, a different verbal construct could have turned Wade's participation in My Lai into a political advantage: "All you had to do was *say* something. Could've made it work for us. Whole different spiel." After all, he sardonically quips, "A village is a terrible thing to waste" (p. 202).

Indeed, "The Battle Hymn of Lt. Calley," a 1971 song celebrating the man who led the massacre, sold more than a million copies, and there are now men sitting in the U.S. Senate who killed many more Vietnamese civilians in fact than John Wade did in fiction. In O'Brien's 1994 novel, Kathy and John Wade vanish in late 1986. It was just over two years later in the actual world of American politics that President George Bush told us in his inaugural address how to make Vietnam vanish: "The final lesson of Vietnam is that no great nation can long afford to be sundered by a memory."

Although the stunningly original storytelling magic of *In the Lake of the Woods* makes it feel quite postmodernist in form, the novel's relation between history and fiction may actually be much more traditional than its seems. Dissenting from the fashionable notion that history is merely a verbal construct, O'Brien forces both his fictional characters and his readers to confront the inescapability of historical reality. Unlike the fate of Kathy Wade, there is no mystery or even significant debate about what did happen at My Lai. The only disagreement is about why. That question leads O'Brien deep into history and the most terrible mysteries of the human heart. For Tim O'Brien, the true story of My Lai, which is also the true story of the war, is the story at the center of *In the Lake of the Woods*, a story that fulfills his definition of "a true war story":

> There is no rectitude whatsoever. There is no virtue. As a first rule of thumb, therefore, you can tell a true war story by its absolute and uncompromising allegiance to obscenity and evil.[16]

(Unless otherwise indicated, all page references are to Tim O'Brien, *In the Lake of the Woods* (Boston: Houghton Mufflin, 1994).

Notes

1. *The Pentagon Papers: The Defense Department History of United States Decisionmaking in Vietnam*, Senator Gravel edition (Boston: Beacon Press, 1971), iii, 141.

2. Christian G. Appy, *Working-Class War: American Combat Soldiers and Vietnam* (Chapel Hill: University of North Carolina Press, 1993), 9.

3. This 1990 text written by George Donelson Moss and published by Prentice-Hall, a subsidiary of Viacom, had gone through three editions by 1998. Among the important studies that have explored how the war has been transformed into a trauma inflicted not by America on Vietnam but by Vietnam on America, see Susan Jeffords, *The Remasculinization of America: Gender and the Vietnam War* (Bloomington: Indiana University Press, 1989);

Fred Turner, *Echoes of Combat: The Vietnam War in American Memory* (New York: Anchor, 1996); Keith Beattie, *The Scar that Binds: American Culture and the Vietnam War* (New York: New York University Press, 1998).

4. "Kicking the 'Vietnam Syndrome,' " *Washington Post*, March 4, 1991.

5. Turner, *Echoes of Combat*, 63; Arnold R. Isaacs, *Vietnam Shadows: The War, Its Ghost, and Its Legacy* (Baltimore: Johns Hopkins University Press, 1997), 49.

6. Tim O'Brien, "The Vietnam in Me," *New York Times Magazine*, October 2, 1994, p. 52.

7. Tim O'Brien, *If I Die in a Combat Zone Box Me Up and Ship Me Home* (New York: Dell/Laurel, 1979), 66, 73; originally published by Delacorte Press/Seymour Lawrence, 1973.

8. *Going After Cacciato* (New York: Dell, 1979), 377. O'Brien revised this paperback from the original hardback published in 1978 by Delacorte Press/Seymour Lawrence.

9. *The Things They Carried* (New York: 1991), 43, 54, 63.

10. Eric James Schroeder, "Two Interviews: Talks with Tim O'Brien and Robert Stone," *Modern Fiction Studies* 30 (Spring 1984): 146. O'Brien personally reviewed and corrected the transcript of this interview.

11. Letter from Richard L. Boylan, Textual Reference Branch, National Archives at College Park, December 6, 1996 (furnished to me by Michael Aaron Rockland).

12. *In the Lake of the Woods* (New York: Penguin, 1995), 298. This paperback edition was revised by O'Brien from the original hardback published by Houghton Mifflin/Seymour Lawrence in 1994.

13. By 1968, tens of millions of Americans and hundreds of millions of people elsewhere on the planet were convinced that the U.S. war in Southeast Asia, with its massive use of chemical warfare, wholesale slaughter of the civilian population, intentional devastation of the countryside, and conscious destruction of food supplies, constituted genocide. Two widely read volumes documenting this view were: *In the Name of America: A Study Commissioned and Published by Clergy and Laymen Concerned about Vietnam, January 1968* (New York: Clergy and Laymen Concerned About Vietnam, 1968); John Duffett, ed., *Against the Crimes of Silence: Proceedings of the International War Crimes Tribunal, Stockholm-Copenhagen* (New York: Simon & Schuster, 1968), which included Jean-Paul Sartre's essential work, "On Genocide."

14. Jonathan Schell, *The Military Half: An Account of Destruction in Quang Ngai and Quang Tin* (New York: Knopf, 1968).

15. In addition to the sources cited in the novel, see Seymour Hersh, *My Lai 4: A Report on the Massacre and Its Aftermath* (New York: Random House, 1970), 45–75.

16. *The Things They Carried*, 76.

ℐℛ

The Whole Story

Tim O'Brien

Mr. Franklin's argument is convincing. I dispute almost none of it. Except perhaps this: *The Things They Carried* is not only "labeled" a work of fiction; it *is* a work of fiction, in the same sense and to exactly the same extent of, say, *The Sun Also Rises* or *Alice in Wonderland*.

I am embarrassed to say, however, that I have very little to say about *In the Lake of the Woods*. Almost everything I know about the book is *in* the book, and it seems fruitless—perhaps even destructive—to begin paraphrasing my own sentences. Those sentences were very, very hard to get even approximately right in the first place. Moreover, to extract the "meaning" from a work of fiction is like extracting hydrogen from a molecule of water. The atomic bonds are broken; fluidity goes; you end up with a fistful of gas. Literary analysis, even expertly done, has a similar effect. The rhythms of language, the sound of story, the exploratory babble of human speech, the contradictions of character, the ambiguities and uncertainties and unknowns of fact and motive, the power of imagination, the very prose upon which "meaning" drifts and bobs—all this seems to vanish in the great blinding clarity of abstraction.

I do not mean to be anti-intellectual about this. We can and must and certainly do talk about stories. Still, it seems to me that a good story appeals not only to the intellect, but also to the stomach and the scalp and the tear ducts and the heart and the nape of the neck and the back of the throat, the whole human being. One could argue, abstractly and convincingly, that war is hell. But a successful story brings the body into agreement with the mind. In the end, after discussing a book or poem or short story I have loved, I most often shrug and fall silent, partly out of frustration, partly out of shame, and then find myself muttering, "Anyhow. You've got to *read* it."

Mr. Franklin's excellent essay reminds me, finally, that the literature I admire most is not only rooted in history, not only about and of and within history, but *is* history. *War and Peace* is history. *Hansel and Gretel* is history. These books are no less real for having been imagined, just as the American war in Vietnam is no less real for having been remembered.

Are dreams unreal?

They are real dreams.

What we imagine, like what we remember, represents a good part of what we are and a good part of what we will become.

Contributors

Russell Banks is the author of fourteen works of fiction, including the novels *Continental Drift* (1985), *The Sweet Hereafter* (1991), *Rule of the Bone* (1995), *Cloudsplitter* (1998), and most recently *The Angel on the Roof: The Stories of Russell Banks* (2000). He is the Howard G. B. Clark University Professor in the Humanities, Emeritus, at Princeton, and resides in the Adirondacks of New York State.

Madison Smartt Bell is the author of nine novels, including *The Washington Square Ensemble* (1983), *Waiting for the End of the World* (1985), *Straight Cut* (1986), *The Year of Silence* (1987), *Doctor Sleep* (1991), *Save Me, Joe Louis* (1993) and *Soldier's Joy*, which received the Lillian Smith Award in 1989. His eighth novel, *All Souls' Rising* (1995), was a finalist for the 1995 National Book Award and the 1996 PEN/Faulkner Award. His ninth, *Ten Indians* (1997), was published by Pantheon. *Master of the Crossroads*, the second volume of a trilogy of novels about the Haitian Revolution, appeared in 2000. Since 1984 he has taught at Goucher College, where he is currently Writer in Residence, along with his wife, the poet Elizabeth Spires.

Paul Boyer is Merle Curti Professor of History at the University of Wisconsin–Madison, where he is also director of the Institute for Research in the Humanities. His books include *Salem Possessed: The Social Origins of Witchcraft* (with Stephen Nissenbaum, 1974), *Urban Masses and Moral Order in America, 1820–1920* (1978), *By the Bomb's Early Light: American Thought and Culture at the Dawn of the Atomic Age* (1985), and *When Time Shall Be No More: Prophecy Belief in Modern American Culture* (1992). He is editor-in-chief of the *Oxford Companion to*

United States History (2001) and the author or coauthor of several college and high-school level American history textbooks.

T. C. Boyle is the author of fourteen books of fiction, including most recently *A Friend of the Earth* (2000) and *After the Plague* (2001). Four of his eight novels make use of historical settings: *Water Music* (1981), *World's End* (1987), *The Road to Wellville* (1993), and *Riven Rock* (1998). He is the grateful recipient of a number of literary distinctions, including the PEN/Faulkner Award for *World's End*, the Prix Medicis Etranger for *The Tortilla Curtain* (1995), and the PEN/Malamud Award for his collected short fiction, *T. C. Boyle Stories* (1998). After receiving his M.F.A. and Ph.D. degrees from the University of Iowa, he joined the faculty of USC as a member of the English Department in 1978. Most nights, he sleeps in Santa Barbara.

David T. Courtwright is Distinguished Professor of History at the University of North Florida. He is the author of several books on American social history, most recently *Violent Land: Single Men and Social Disorder from the Frontier to the Inner City* (1996). He holds a B.A. in literature from the University of Kansas and a Ph.D. in history from Rice University.

Don DeLillo published his first short story when he was twenty-three. He has since written twelve novels and two stage plays. He has said that his books could not have been written in the world that existed before the assassination of President Kennedy. The aftereffects of that moment of violence, caught on film—the ambiguity and distrust, the technological twinning of camera and gun—have informed his work generally and contributed directly to *Libra* (1988), his novel about the assassination. His work has won many honors including the National Book Award, the Jerusalem Prize and the PEN-Faulkner Award for Fiction.

John Demos is the author most recently of *The Unredeemed Captive: A Family Story from Early America* (1993). This book, as well as his current teaching, reflect his strong interest in "narrative history" and the relationship between historical scholarship and fiction. His previous books include: *A Little Commonwealth: Family Life in Plymouth Colony* (1970) and *Entertaining Satan: Witchcraft and the Culture of Early New England* (1982). He is a professor of history at Yale.

John Mack Faragher is Arthur Unobskey Professor of American History and director of the Howard R. Lamar Center for the Study of Frontiers and Borders at Yale University. He is author of *Women and Men on the Overland Trail* (1979), *Sugar Creek, Life on the Illinois Prairie* (1986), *Daniel Boone: The Life and Legend of an American Pioneer* (1992), and *The American West: A New Interpretive History* (with Robert V. Hine, 2000), and is currently writing a history of the Anglo-American expulsion of the Acadians from Nova Scotia in 1755.

Thomas Fleming is a New Yorker whose twenty history books have been praised as often as his twenty novels. He has written biographies of Thomas Jefferson and Benjamin Franklin as well as narratives such as *1776: Year of Illusions* (1995) and *West Point: The Men and Times of the U.S. Military Academy*. In 1999 he published *Duel: Alexander, Hamilton, Aaron Burr and the Future of America*. His most recent historical novel, *The Wages of Fame*, is part of a series he is writing about an archetypal American family, the Stapletons. He is the only writer who has won main selections in both fiction and nonfiction in the long history of the Book-of-the-Month Club.

H. Bruce Franklin is the author of almost two hundred articles on culture and history and the author or editor of eighteen books, including the *The Vietnam War in American Stories, Songs, and Poems* (Boston: Bedford Books, 1996) and the forthcoming *Vietnam and Other American Fantasies* (Amherst: University of Massachusetts Press), from which parts of this essay are adapted. He is currently the John Cotton Dana Professor of English and American Studies at Rutgers University–Newark.

Charles Frazier grew up in the mountains of western North Carolina. He is the author of *Cold Mountain* (1997), which won the National Book Award, the Sue Kaufman Award of the American Academy of Arts and Letters, the Chicago Tribune Heartland Award, the Lillian Smith Award, the Southern Book Critics Circle Award, and the American Booksellers Association ABBY Award. He and his wife and daughter have a farm in North Carolina where they raise and train horses.

Joanne B. Freeman is an expert on early national politics. Her publications include "Dueling as Politics: Reinterpreting the Burr-Hamilton Duel," *William and Mary Quarterly* (1996) and "Slander, Poison, Whispers, and Fame: Jefferson's 'Anas' and Political Gossip in the Early Republic," *Journal of the Early Republic* (1995). Forthcoming works include *Alexander Hamilton: Writings* (Library of America), and *Affairs of Honor: Political Combat in the Early Republic* (2001), a study of the logic and culture of national politics before political parties. She teaches history at Yale University.

Eugene D. Genovese has been president of The Historical Society from its inception in 1997 to 2000. He has specialized in the history of the Old South and modern slavery. His books include *Roll, Jordan, Roll: The World the Slaves Made* (1974), *From Rebellion to Revolution: Afro-American Slave Revolts in the Making of the Modern World* (1979), and, most recently, *A Consuming Fire: The Fall of the Confederacy in the Mind of the White Christian South* (1998).

Joan D. Hedrick is the Charles A. Dana Professor of History at Trinity College, Hartford, where she teaches courses on American cultural history and women's studies. Her *Harriet Beecher Stowe: A Life* (1994) won the 1995 Pulitzer Prize for biography. She is also the author of *Solitary Comrade: Jack London and his Work* (1982) and *The Oxford Harriet Beecher Stowe Reader* (1999).

Gary Jennings is best known as the author of blockbuster historical novels such as *Aztec* (1980), *The Journeyer* (1984), and *Raptor* (1992) and the intensive and sometimes dangerous research trips he made for them. He was born in 1928 in Buena Vista, California, served as a copywriter and an account executive in the advertising industry in New York City from 1947 to 1958 and as a newspaper reporter in California and Virginia from 1958 to 1961. He was in the U.S. Army infantry from 1952 to 1955, served as a correspondent in Korea, and was awarded the Bronze Star. Prior to his career as a novelist he published twenty-two short stories in the science fiction and fantasy genre. He died February 13, 1999.

Michael Kammen is the Newton C. Farr Professor of American History and Culture at Cornell University, past president of the Organization of American Historians, and a member of the American Academy of Arts and Sciences. He is the author of *American Culture, American Tastes: Social Change and the 20th Century* (1999). *Mystic Chords of Memory: The Transformation of Tradition in American Culture* (1991), *A Machine That Would Go of Itself: The Constitution in American Culture* (1986), and *People of Paradox: An Inquiry Concerning the Origins of American Civilization* (1972), awarded the Pulitzer Prize for History.

William Kennedy has published seven novels in his "Albany Cycle," treating life in Albany, N.Y., during the nineteenth and twentieth centuries. His novels are *Ink Truck* (1969); *Legs* (1975); *Billy Phelan's Greatest Game* (1978); *Ironweed* (1983), which won the Pulitzer Prize, the National Book Critics Circle Award, a PEN-Faulkner Award, and was chosen by the Modern Library as one of the one hundred best novels of the twentieth century; *Quinn's Book* (1988); *Very Old Bones* (1992); and *The Flaming Corsage* (1996). His work has been translated into two dozen languages. *Roscoe*, a novel about the Albany political machine between the World Wars, will be published in the fall of 2001 by Viking/Penguin.

Diane Kunz is the author, most recently, of *Butter and Guns: America's Cold War Economic Diplomacy* (1997). A former corporate lawyer, she received her M. Litt. from Oxford University, where she studied at St. Antony's College, and her Ph.D from Yale University. Her book, *The Economic Diplomacy of the Suez Crisis* (1991), was the co-winner of the Myrna Bernath Prize and the Robert Ferrell Prize given by the Society for Historians of American Foreign Relations. She teaches international relations at Columbia University.

John Lukacs is a retired professor of history. His twenty-one published books have dealt with a considerable variety of subjects. The most recent are *The Hitler of History* (1997), *A Thread of Years* (1998), and *Five Days in London* (1999).

Larry McMurtry, winner of the Pulitzer Prize for fiction, among other awards, is the author of more than twenty novels, two collections of essays, and more than thirty screenplays. He lives in Archer City, Texas.

James M. McPherson is George Henry Davis '86 Professor of American History at Princeton University. He has written numerous books, mostly on the Civil War era, including *Battle Cry of Freedom: The Civil War Era* (1988), which won the Pulitzer Prize in History, and *For Cause and Comrades: Why Men Fought in the Civil War* (1997), which won the Lincoln Prize. He is editor of *"To the Best of My Ability": The American Presidents* (2000) and is coeditor of a series entitled, "Pivotal Moments in American History," the first volume of which will be published in 2001.

Tim O'Brien is the author of six works of fiction, including *Going After Cacciato* (1978), *The Things They Carried* (1990), *In the Lake of the Woods* (1994), and most recently *Tomcat in Love* (1998). Beginning with his memoir *If I Die in a Combat Zone*, he has drawn extensively from his experience as an infantryman with the U.S. Army in Vietnam. His work has received many honors, including the National Book Award, France's Prix du Meilleur Livre Etranger, and the James Fenimore Cooper Prize from the Society of American Historians.

David S. Reynolds is Distinguished Professor of English and American Studies at Baruch College and the Graduate Center of the City University of New York. His books include *Walt Whitman's America: A Cultural Biography* (1995), *Beneath the American Renaissance: The Subversive Imagination in the Age of Emerson and Melville* (1989), and *Faith in Fiction: The Emergence of Religious Literature in America* (1981).

Jane Smiley is author of ten works of fiction, including *The Age of Grief* (1987), *The Greenlanders* (1988), *Ordinary Love and Goodwill* (1989), *Moo* (1995), *Horse Heaven* (2000), and *A Thousand Acres* (1991), for which she was awarded the Pulitzer Prize. She lives in northern California.

Michael E. Smith is an archaeologist who has directed excavations together with his wife, Cynthia Heath-Smith, at Aztec sites in the Mexican state of Morelos. His books include *The Aztecs* (1996), *Aztec Imperial Strategies* (1996), *Economies and Politics in the Aztec Realm* (with Mary G. Hodge, 1994) and *The Ancient Civilizations of Mesoamerica* (with Marilyn A. Masson, 1999). His hobbies include playing the piano, reading historical fiction, and taking walks in the woods with the dogs.

William Styron is author of *Lie Down in Darkness* (1951), *The Long March* (1952), *Set This House on Fire* (1960), *The Confessions of Nat Turner* (1967), *Sophie's Choice* (1979), *This Quiet Dust* (1982), *Darkness Visible* (1990), and *A Tidewater Morning*

(1993). He has been awarded the American Book Award, the Howells Medal, the Edward MacDowell Model, and the Pulitzer Prize.

Michel-Rolph Trouillot is Professor of Anthropology at the University of Chicago. He has taught at Duke and at Johns Hopkins. His interests include social theory, historical anthropology, plantation slavery in the Americas, and the emergence of Caribbean peasantries. His books include: *Ti dife boule sou Istoua Aviti*, a history of the Saint-Domingue/Haiti slave revolution in Haitian Creole; *Haiti: State against Nation: The Origins and Legacy of Duvalierism* (1990); and *Silencing the Past: Power and the Production of History* (1995). He is currently doing research on the wave of historical apologies that began in the last quarter of the twentieth century.

John Updike is the author of nineteen novels and a number of collections of short stories, poetry, and criticism. Born in Pennsylvania in 1932, he has lived in Massachusetts since 1957 as a freelance writer.

Gore Vidal is the author of twenty-two novels, five plays, many screenplays and short stories, more than two hundred essays, and a memoir. Two of his American chronicle novels, *Lincoln* (1984), and *1876* (1976), were the subject of cover stories in *Time* and *Newsweek*, respectively. In 1993, a collection of his criticism, *United States: Essays 1952–1992*, won the National Book Award. He received an award from the Cannes Film Festival for best screenplay for *The Best Man*. He divides his time between Ravello, Italy, and Los Angeles.

Elliott West is Distinguished Professor of History at the University of Arkansas. Two of his five books have received the Western Heritage Award as the best book on the history of the West and a third, *The Contested Plains: Indians, Goldseekers and the Rush to Colorado* (1998), received the Francis Parkman Prize, Ray Allen Billington Award, and the Caughey Western History Association Prize. He lives with his wife and two of his five children in Fayetteville, Arkansas.

Richard White is a Western historian and the Margaret Byrne Professor of American History at Stanford University. His most recent book is *Remembering Ahanagran: A History of Stories* (1998).

Tom Wicker is the author of seven novels, including *Unto This Hour* (1984), about the American civil war. A retired political columnist for the *New York Times*, he lives in Vermont with his wife, Pamela Hill, a former executive with ABC News and the Cable News Network.

About the Editor

Mark C. Carnes teaches history at Barnard College, Columbia University. In addition to serving as co–general editor of the *American National Biography* (24 volumes, 1999), he has edited the *Dictionary of American Biography, Past Imperfect: History According to the Movies; Meanings for Manhood;* and other volumes. His books include *Secret Ritual and Manhood in Victorian America, Mapping America's Past,* and *The American Nation* (10th edition, with John A. Garraty). He lives in Newburgh, New York, with his wife and daughter.